British Ships in the
Confederate Navy

British Ships in the Confederate Navy

Joseph McKenna

McFarland & Company, Inc., Publishers
Jefferson, North Carolina, and London

LIBRARY OF CONGRESS CATALOGUING-IN-PUBLICATION DATA

McKenna, Joseph.
British ships in the Confederate navy / by Joseph McKenna.
p. cm.
Includes bibliographical references and index.

ISBN 978-0-7864-4530-1
softcover : 50# alkaline paper ∞

1. Confederate States of America. Navy — History. 2. United States — History — Civil War, 1861–1865 — Participation, British. 3. United States — History — Civil War, 1861–1865 — Naval operations. 4. Confederate States of America — Foreign relations — Great Britain. 5. Great Britain — Foreign relations — Confederate States of America. I. Title.
E596.M458   2010   973.7'57 — dc22   2009046987

British Library cataloguing data are available

©2010 Joseph McKenna. All rights reserved

No part of this book may be reproduced or transmitted in any form or by any means, electronic or mechanical, including photocopying or recording, or by any information storage and retrieval system, without permission in writing from the publisher.

On the cover: CSS *Alabama* by J.W. Schmidt, 1961; *inset* James Dunwoody Bulloch, Confederate naval officer and agent

Manufactured in the United States of America

McFarland & Company, Inc., Publishers
Box 611, Jefferson, North Carolina 28640
www.mcfarlandpub.com

To the British seamen who fought in the Confederate States Navy

> The arrival of the crew caused no small stir. People were surprised to see the landing of a number of swarthy-complexioned, weather-beaten men, dressed in gray uniform, and wearing eccentric looking hats and caps. When it became known that they were the crew of the notorious cruiser, a large crowd of persons assembled, who stood watching the sailors as they were taking their baggage on shore. Some people were desirous of knowing their cause of leaving the vessel, and their intended movements, but the sailors were discreetly silent. They were for the most part, able bodied, determined looking fellows, and would no doubt, have proved themselves equal to the work they had in view. —"The Return of the *Shenandoah*," *Liverpool Mercury*, 9 November 1865

Table of Contents

Preface   1
Introduction   3

1. Bulloch   9
2. The *Florida*   20
3. Semmes   55
4. The "290"   77
5. The *Alabama*   90
6. The Castigation of Mr. Lancaster   145
7. The *Georgia* and the *Rappahannock*   152
8. The *Alexandra* and the *Pampero*   161
9. Laird's Rams and French Rams   165
10. The *Tallahassee* and the *Chickamauga*   175
11. The *Shenandoah*   185
12. Blockade-Runners   203
13. The Men and the Ships That Ran the Blockade   217
14. Tales of Old Men   250

Appendix: The Sinking of the Alabama   257
Chapter Notes   267
Bibliography   273
Index   275

Preface

History, they say, is written by the victors, and this is no more true than in the accounts of the American Civil War. The official version is the Northern version, showing the war from their perspective. It is not perhaps completely accurate. It certainly does not take into account the true reasons why the South sought to break away. Nor does it give equal credit to the bravery of her soldiers and sailors in the war that followed. They are referred to as traitors, rebels and pirates. What the South attempted was nothing more than what the founding fathers of the United States achieved a century earlier— severing the tie with an oppressive regime that denied it true democracy. Slavery, with all its attendant evils, was never the true reason for the war. The South was locked into a democratic system where it was outnumbered by its Northern counterparts; it was denied democracy. As an agricultural society the South looked abroad, and in particular to Great Britain and France, to provide the arms that it needed to pursue its war of independence.

So if history is written by the victors, we must look elsewhere for anything approaching an unbiased account of the war. The *Illustrated London News*, a popular British magazine of the time, covered the war with correspondents operating on both sides of the lines. As accounts go, theirs was perhaps the most balanced version of the war, beautifully illustrated with engravings. Amidst the illustrations of battles and war heroes from both sides, I found an illustration of the Confederate ship *Alabama*. What struck me as interesting was the fact that the ship had been built in Liverpool. This was curious, as Britain was supposedly neutral. Was this a bias? I read Warren Armstrong's *Cruise of a Corsair*, published in 1963. It was a rather fanciful account of the voyage of the *Alabama*, with words being put into the mouths of the subjects. Replacing the book in the stack of the library where I worked for over thirty years, Birmingham Reference Library in England, I discovered the source for Armstrong's factional account. Its title was *My Adventures Afloat*. Lacking a vibrant wartime title, this sounded like some old duffer's holiday experiences. Taking the book from the shelf, and just skimming through the pages, it proved to be anything but. It was a book written with passion — even hatred, in places. It was an account of a great adventure, but ultimately an account of the war from the losing side. The book was published by an English company, Richard Bentley of London, in 1869. It was a first edition. There was no indication that it had ever been published in America. Delving into the biography of its author, Raphael Semmes, I discovered why. He was a dyed-in-the-wool Confederate, an unreconstructed Rebel. There was no way that an American publisher at that time would have looked at it, let alone considered it for publication. Here was an account of the *Alabama*'s construction, and the evasion of Britain's strict neutrality laws in that construction — bending the rules but never breaking them. There was an account of the raising of a British crew for the ship, which required again careful sidestepping, this time of the law of Foreign Enlistment.

Semmes' accounts of his adventures on the high seas—the destruction of America's merchant marine—threw up lots of names of coconspirators and others. The man who had made it all possible was James Dunwoody Bulloch. An entry in the library catalogue revealed that he was the author of a book titled *The Secret Service of the Confederate States.* On the face of it a book relating to the Southern states but in reality a book with a truncated title, missing were the words "in England." Here it was, a fully documented account of Britain's unofficial participation in America's war. And there were more names: Maffitt, Morris, Read and Whittle. Looking these names up in British and American catalogues of books and magazines in print revealed accounts of their exploits; many were published in Southern magazines and newspapers. As such, many of them written long after the war had finished were not of interest and were thereby overlooked. The "official" account of the war had already been written. The title of the multivolumed *Official Records of the Union and Confederate Navies in the War of the Rebellion* seemed to sum it all up. The title even refused to accept that it was a civil war fought between two nations. Though the title had a bias, the contents of these volumes, published between 1894 and 1922, was a revelation. It was, as its title suggested, a record of both sides; but more importantly it was unbiased. It was a straightforward account, written without editorial comment. Within the volumes relating to the blockade of the Southern ports were accounts of blockade-runners. The worst offenders turned out to be British sailors, but not just ordinary sailors. Included in the lists proved to be some of the bravest ex-officers of the Royal Navy, including a holder of the Victoria Cross, Britain's highest award for gallantry. For them it was a great adventure, and an adventure that proved lucrative.

Finally, on the top shelf of one of the presses that contained Birmingham Library's books relating to the American Civil War, there were the different editions of the Alabama Claims, including an apparently unread French edition. In an international judgment, decided in Switzerland, the United States was awarded $15 million in compensation from Britain. There were claims and counterclaims, with evidence provided from many sources. One of the more interesting accounts was the evidence presented by the U.S. Consul in Liverpool, Thomas Haines Dudley, a very vigilant man indeed. He lists the comings and goings of the Confederates and their supporters in the minutiae of detail that brings history to life. Additional information from the British perspective was found in the Government's Parliamentary Reports, which led to further research in the Public Record Office at Kew, in London.

Often overlooked, and never completely trusted without further verification, are the sites to be found on the Internet. These are useful, but often frustrating where a source is not given. Can you trust them, that's the question? There is so much, because the American Civil War holds a fascination worldwide. In England there is even a Civil War reenactment society, which stages events in the summer months. Some sites I learned to trust, and I have acknowledged these sites where used, as sources in the chapter notes.

This then is my account of the Confederate States naval struggle in the American Civil War and the part played by British companies and British people.

Introduction

George Yeoman died at the age of 79 at his home at 4, Chapel Lane, Dover, England, on 8 April 1924. He was one of the last British sailors to have served in the Confederate Navy during the American Civil War. He served aboard CSS *Alabama*, itself a British ship, launched at Laird & Sons shipyard, Birkenhead, on 15 May 1862. James Dunwoody Bulloch, who commissioned the building of the *Alabama*, died at 76, Canning Street, Liverpool, on 7 January 1901. He was buried at Toxteth Park Cemetery. On his headstone is the inscription "An American by birth, an Englishman by choice." This chapter of the American Civil War was fought well away from that native land. It was played out in England, and upon the oceans of the world. Six months after the end of the war, the last rebel flag was lowered, not in the United States, but on English shores. Due to Britain's policy of neutrality, the part played by British soldiers and sailors has largely gone ignored. The emphasis of this work is to show, through the activities of the commercial raiders and blockade-runners, the active support given to the Southern cause by these men. One cannot say that they volunteered to serve through patriotism. The reasons were varied, financial gain not the least. Many were in the Naval Reserve, former Royal Navy men who had served during the late Crimean War. They were experienced sailors, battle-hardened, and not content to finish their days aboard some rust-bucket in coastal waters around Britain. They sought adventure, and in the service of the Confederate Navy they found it. Inasmuch as it can be, this is their story, viewed from a British perspective.

The election of Abraham Lincoln as president of the United States of America was the catalyst, rather than the cause, of the Civil War. One of his major policies was the abolition of slavery, a "peculiar institution" closely linked to the agricultural southern states. The war was more than just an issue over slavery though. There were cultural differences between North and South. A further factor in the breakaway of the southern states was their feeling of exploitation by the rapidly industrializing northern states. The North's protectionist policy to boost its growing economy saw the imposition of high tariffs on the importation of cheaper foreign goods from Europe, and in particular, Britain. This enabled the northern manufacturers to sell their goods, such as machinery and agricultural tools, at inflated prices, to the nonindustrial states in the South. In essence there already existed two states within the union, an industrial north and an agricultural south. As the northern states held the majority in Congress the southern states felt a resentment in that they were powerless under the present system to redress the balance. Jefferson Davis, soon to become president of the Confederate States, summed it up in Congress:

> What do you propose, gentlemen of the Free-soil party? Do you propose to better the condition of the slave? Not at all ... you say that you are opposed to the expansion of slavery ... is the slave to be benefited by it? Not at all. It is not humanity that influences you ... it is that you may have

an opportunity of cheating us that you want to limit slave territory ... it is that you may have a majority in the Congress of the United States and convert the Government into an engine of Northern aggrandizement.... [Y]ou want by an unjust system of legislation to promote the industry of the United States at the expense of the people of the South.

The system needed to be changed if Southern grievances were to be redressed. The Constitution of the United States guaranteed that each state in the union could act "in its sovereign and independent character." That is, each state was an independent contracting party which had the right to govern itself. In other words they were free to secede from the existing union if they so wished and form a new coalition with other states. So it began. The secession started in January 1861 with South Carolina. The states of Mississippi, Florida, Alabama, Georgia and Louisiana soon followed. Delegates from these states met at Montgomery, Alabama, on 9 February 1861, and formed a provisional government, with Jefferson Davis as president. Arkansas, Texas, and North Carolina then joined the Confederacy. Tennessee, Maryland, Missouri, Kentucky and Virginia, acting in concert to secure a peaceful separation, opened negotiations with the Federal government in Washington with a view to joining the Confederate States of America. Unionists within Maryland, Kentucky and Missouri seized control of their states by force and the leading secessionists were arrested. Federal forts within the secessionist states, including Fort Sumter in South Carolina, were then blockaded by hastily raised Confederate militias in order to prevent similar actions from taking place within their states.

Lincoln took office on 4 March 1861. In his inaugural speech he appealed directly to the secessionist states: "In your hands, my dissatisfied countrymen, and not in mine is the momentous issue of civil war. The government will not assail you. You can have no conflict, without being yourselves the aggressors.... We are not enemies but friends. We must not be enemies...." Lincoln assured the breakaway states that he would negotiate with them, but pressure in the North to do something forced him to act. He informed the governor of South Carolina of his intention to reprovision Fort Sumter. The response was swift. The Confederate militia called upon the fort to surrender. A deadline was issued, and passed. At 4.30 A.M. on 12 April 1861, Confederate gunners opened fire on Fort Sumter. The Civil War had begun.

On 19 April 1861, in a bid to bring the "insurrection" to a swift and successful end, Lincoln issued a Proclamation of Blockade Against Southern Ports. It read: "Whereas an insurrection against the Government of the United States has broken out in the States of South Carolina, Georgia, Alabama, Florida, Mississippi, Louisiana and Texas ... I, Abraham Lincoln, President of the United States ... have further deemed it advisable to set on foot a blockade of the ports within the States aforesaid, in pursuance of the laws of the United States, and the law of Nations, in such case provided."

Blockading the ports prevented the export of cotton and tobacco, thus economically damaging the Confederacy, cutting it off from its markets in Europe. If the Confederacy suffered, so too did the mill workers of England. Nearly 400,000 Lancashire workers were thrown out of work because of the Federal blockade. Yet despite these hardships the cotton workers gave their full support to Abraham Lincoln's policy of eradicating slavery. Mindful of their suffering, Lincoln wrote in response: "I know and deeply deplore the sufferings which working people of Manchester and in all Europe are called to endure in this crisis. It has been often and studiously represented that the attempt to overthrow this Government which was built on the foundation of human rights, and to substitute for it one which should rest exclusively on the basis of slavery, was likely to obtain the favor of Europe."

When European ships attempted to enter the blockaded ports they were seized and condemned by the United States prize courts. Lord Lyons, the British Minister in Washington asked for clarification. Justice Grier of the Supreme Court adjudicated on the subject: "To legitimize the capture of a neutral vessel or property on the high seas, a war must exist de facto, and the neutral must have knowledge or notice of the intention of one of the parties belligerent to use this mode of coercion against a port, city, or territory in possession of the other.... The proclamation of the blockade is itself official and conclusive evidence to the court that a state of war existed which demanded and authorized a recourse to such a measure under the circumstances peculiar to the case. The correspondence of Lord Lyons with the Secretary of State admits the fact and concludes the question."

By the very careless wording of his proclamation — using the word "blockade" rather than "closure"— Lincoln, according to Justice Grier's findings, acknowledged that there was a war, and the Confederate states had "belligerent" rights. As such the European powers acknowledged that this was not some irresponsible insurrection, as the American administration inferred, but a war, and the Confederacy was a de facto state. It was a curious thing that the United States administration never came to terms with the European powers recognizing the Confederacy as a belligerent state, and looked upon their recognition as a bias towards the Confederacy. In reality the powers had accepted the status quo as created by the United States itself. On 13 May 1861 Queen Victoria proclaimed British neutrality, treating both sides as belligerents. On 10 June Napoleon III declared French neutrality. The other European powers followed suit, as did Brazil and the other South American republics. U.S. secretary of state William Henry Seward responded with bluster and threats, warning the British and French governments of the dire consequences of recognizing the government of Jefferson Davis. In the face of this perceived threat the British government took elementary precautions to defend Canada, the obvious target for American aggression. In addition, contingency plans were also made by the Royal Navy to sink the blockading force off the Confederate coast should the United States declare war.

This edge to relations with the United States, caused by the Federal government's attempt to bully Britain and France, brought Britain, in particular, close to war with the United States on more than one occasion. Public opinion in Britain, not necessarily in favor of the Confederacy, moved temporarily away from the Federal government. It is true that there was some sympathy in Britain by some sectors of the public for the Confederate cause, those sympathizers seeing it as a struggle for freedom against an aggressor. In the eyes of some of the British public, their struggle was equated with the struggle of the Italian states or the German states in their efforts to throw off the Austrian yoke. This support for the Confederacy was not indicative of support for slavery though, but more a reflection of the lack of importance attached to the slavery question. To the upper middle classes of Britain, the people of the South were looked upon as kith and kin. In Parliament, the Right Hon. Edward Horsman, Conservative member for Stroud, addressed the House:

> In the South there is no shackling of the Press, no suppression of the Law, no abridgement of the liberty of the citizen, but all classes have rallied as one man under Jefferson Davis who, by the dignity and moderation of his counsels, by the high bearing of his armies, the will and the dar-

ing of his navy, few though its ships may be, and the devotion of all concerned in his fighting forces and no less among the civilian population of the South, has given an elevation to the Southern cause which has won for it slowly and incredulously the irresistible, the universal and generous sympathies of the people of all Europe.

But when we turn to the North, what contrast is there exhibited! Their military failures, great as they have been, sink into mere insignificance compared with the moral downfall they have displayed. Their war has been and is a war against freedom and civilization, and, as for the emancipation of the colored people, what judgment can we in this Christian assembly put on it except to denounce it as one of the most atrocious crimes against the accepted laws of civilization and humanity that the world has ever witnessed?

This once-free Republic has been metamorphosed into a military tyranny. The President is a more irresponsible despot that the Czar of Russia! Liberty of person, of movement, of speech, of writing and worship and thought are all annulled; the Press is coerced and gagged, the state prisons are filled with untried and unconvicted political offenders! I tell you gentlemen, the South must not be defeated and, if necessary, we must intervene to force a settlement which would recognize the full independence of the Secession States.

The Prime Minister, William Gladstone, as well as his Foreign Secretary, Lord Russell, were both in favor of intervention, but the majority in the House were opposed to it. So throughout its strained relations, the British government continued to maintain its policy of strict neutrality, with perhaps even a slight bias towards the United States. Benjamin Moran, assistant secretary to the United States minister in London, Charles Adams, noted in his journal for 3 June 1861:

At Mr. Adams' request I went to the Commons this evening to hear Mr. Forster ask the Gov't what determination they had come to with respect to allowing the Privateers of the so called Confederate States of the U.S. to bring their prizes into British ports. The question was cheered, & L[or]d J[ohn] R[ussell] replied that the Gov't had decided not to permit the vessels of war or privateers of either the U.S. or the so-called Confederate States to bring their prizes into the ports of Great Britain or her Dependencies, & read a dispatch to that effect wch had been sent to the Colonial Governors last Saturday. He also stated that the Gov't had been in communication with that of France on the subject, and had learned that the Emperor would enforce the French law of 1681, by wch privateers & their prizes could not remain in a French port longer than 24 hours. This was cheered. Mr. Forster considered it finished privateering; but I pointed out to him that it placed the true and the spurious Gov't on the same footing. This he allowed, but said we must not be nice about such a little matters, as G[reat] B[ritain] had done all they could to aid us.

The Trent Incident: By his rash actions in seizing the two Confederate commissioners from a Royal Mail ship, Captain Wilkes (top) brought Britain and the United States to the brink of war. (*Illustrated London News*, 14 December 1861)

Despite this good will, Anglo-American relations were further strained by American irresponsibility in the Trent Affair. On 8 November 1861 two Confederate diplomats, James M. Mason, minister to Britain, and John Slidell, minister to France, were forcibly removed from aboard R.M.S. *Trent,* a British mail steamer, by Captain Charles Wilkes of the USS *Jacinto*. When news of the affair arrived in London on 27 November, it was seen as a flagrant violation of maritime law and an insult to the British flag. Such an act had been the cause of the Anglo-American war of 1812, when the roles had been reversed. There was anger in Britain and talk of war. The government issued an ultimatum demanding an apology and the release of the Confederate diplomats. Prince Albert intervened to soften the British government's original letter, but the threat remained that unless the Federal government complied with Britain's demands within seven days, Britain would declare war. France, who likewise was subject to American bullying, was quick to announce her willingness to support Britain in a war against the United States.

While she awaited a reply, Britain sent further troops to Canada, and mobilized the Royal Navy. The Confederate government, its armies waging a success-

Experienced in the United States Diplomatic Corp, Dudley Mann was appointed Confederate commissioner to Great Britain. (*Illustrated London News*)

ful war against the Union army, eagerly awaited the decision of the European nations. They knew that if the Europeans entered the war then the Confederacy was assured. The dilemma facing the Federal government, after Lincoln stamped his authority on his cabinet with his decision of "one war at a time," was how to comply with Britain's demands without losing face at home. Secretary of State Seward wrote to the British ambassador, Lord Lyons, what has generally been agreed was a brilliantly drafted reply, agreeing to release the diplomats into British custody, but adding, for home consumption, the sarcastic response that he was pleased to see that Britain had finally adopted the American view of neutral rights over which the two nations had fought in 1812. The "apology" was accepted, and the crisis was averted. Confidence between the two nations was restored — after a fashion.

Right up until the defeat of Lee at Gettysburg, there was still a feeling in America that if the Confederate States' armies could succeed in defeating the Union armies in one or two more major battles, Europe would acknowledge the Confederate States as a de jure nation. In reality however, following Lincoln's Emancipation Proclamation on 22 September 1862, to have intervened in support of the Confederacy would have been totally unacceptable to the British public, for it would have suggested that Britain supported slavery, and this of course she did not.

Into these continual Anglo-American tensions stepped a number of very unique and distinct characters, who if they had fought on the winning side would now be known as American heroes. These men, later vilified by their Northern countrymen, include James Dunwoody Bulloch, Confederate States Navy commissioner, Commander John N. Maffitt, Lt. Charles Manigault Morris, Lt. Charles W. Read, Commander Raphael Semmes and Captain William C. Whittle. We should not forget the crews that sailed with them. So many were British, their names unknown.

1

Bulloch

James Dunwoody Bulloch is one of the great unsung heroes of the American Civil War. His was the shadowy world of the secret agent. A Confederate naval commander serving in England, he brought the United States merchant fleet to its knees. No American ship was safe from his raiders. The ships he commissioned from British yards developed an almost mystical quality as they harried the enemy and evaded their pursuers. The United States government put the overall cost of losses caused by his ships at $15,500,000. Like Robert E. Lee, Bulloch was never forgiven for what he did — humiliating the United States. Like Lee, a general pardon was also withheld. Bulloch became persona non grata in his own country and lived out the rest of his life as an exile in England. As the years passed he was urged by family and friends to record this chapter in the history of the Civil War. The result of this was *The Secret Service of the Confederate States in Europe*, published in 1884. His is not a history dictated by his own ego; he was a very modest man. He gave credit to all those who were involved in this secret war. His praise for others is unstinting. The man himself we have to search to find. He was modest, he was honest, and he was possessed of an integrity not given to many. Bulloch was a keen businessman, discreet in his dealings; even twenty years after the war, he was most circumspect, fearing that an unguarded comment might give offense. He bore personal disappointments well, recognizing and accepting his part in the greater good as envisaged by his superiors. His greatest desire was to fight the war as a captain aboard his own ship, but this was denied to him. Disappointed in this, he did the job that was assigned to him and in a way that few, if any, could have equaled.

James Dunwoody Bulloch was born near Savannah, Georgia, on 25 June 1823, the son of Major James Stephens Bulloch and Hester Amarinthia Bulloch, the daughter of Senator John Elliott. Upon the death of his mother, his father remarried and fathered four more children, including Irvine and Martha. Martha in 1853 married Theodore Roosevelt Sr. and became the mother of future president Theodore Roosevelt. In 1839, at the age of sixteen, James became a midshipman in the United States Navy. He served aboard the frigate *United States* and later onboard the sloop *Decatur,* on the Brazil station, first under the command of Henry W. Ogden and later under David Farragut. In 1842 he was transferred to the battleship *Delaware,* cruising in the Mediterranean. Two years later he began his studies at the naval school at Philadelphia, where he graduated second in his class. He returned to active service, seconded to the Pacific squadron, serving aboard the store-ship *Erie* at the time of the Mexican war. During 1849–1851 Bulloch was employed in the coastal survey. He succeeded Lt. D.D. Porter in command of the USS *Georgia,* a subsidized mail steamer to California, and thereafter commanded various vessels in the Gulf mail service in a scheme designed by the government to give its junior officers experience in steam navigation. On 19 November 1851, Bulloch married Elizabeth Euphemia Caskie, daughter of a prominent Richmond, Virginia, family. Tragically, she died barely three years later, and this proved to be a turning point in Bulloch's career. He resigned from the navy and found employment in the private mail service. Bulloch moved to New York, and in 1857 he remarried. His second wife was Harriett Cross Foster, a widow and the daughter of Brigadier General Osborne Cross of Maryland. The Bullochs had five children, James Jr., Jessie, Henry, Stuart and Martha.

At the outbreak of the Civil War, Bulloch was in command of the mail steamer *Bienville,* sailing between New York, Havana and New Orleans. When news of the assault on Fort Sumter broke, Bulloch was in New Orleans. He immediately offered his services to the Confederacy. Bulloch was approached by two members of the Board of War with a view to securing the *Bienville* for the naval service of the Confederacy and

Captain James D. Bulloch was commissioned by the Southern government to build and equip a Confederate navy.

was asked to name his price. Bulloch, a man of honor, informed them that the ship did not belong to him, and that he had no authority to sell the ship nor transfer her to the service of the Confederate States. Recognizing him to be a man of integrity, the secretary of state for the navy, Stephen Mallory, knew that he had found in Bulloch a man for a very special mission. The state governor, upon instruction, informed Bulloch that the offer of purchase was still open, but nothing would be done to prevent his departure. At 8 o'clock on the morning of 14 April, the *Bienville* slipped its moorings and proceeded downriver from New Orleans, bound for Havana, en route to New York. She berthed in New York on the evening of 22 April. The directors of the company came on board and informed Bulloch that the Federal government had chartered the *Bienville* to take troops to defend Washington, then under threat from the Confederate army. Bulloch declined to take charge of the venture and tendered his resignation, which was accepted without undue question as to his loyalty. Returning to his New York home, he found a letter awaiting him in response to his application for service in the Confederate navy. It was short and to the point:

> Department of Justice. C.S.A.
> Montgomery, Alabama.
>
> The Secretary of the Navy desires you to come to Montgomery without delay.
>
> Yours, etc.,
> (Signed) J.P. Benjamin.[1]

Bulloch returned south by a circuitous route to avoid suspicion, He traveled to Philadelphia, and from there to Cincinnati, where he boarded a steamer to Louisville, then caught a train to Nashville, Tennessee. From there a further train took him south through Chattanooga and Atlanta, finally arriving at Montgomery very late on the night of 7 May. The next morning Bulloch reported to the secretary of war, Judah P. Benjamin, who introduced him to the navy secretary, Stephen R. Mallory. Much to Bulloch's surprise, he was asked to go to Europe. His mission was to buy or build a Confederate navy.

The South had lacked the facilities to build and equip its own ships ever since the destruction of its only installation, the Norfolk Navy Yard in Virginia. On the night of 20 April 1861, Commodore McCauley, USN, the Federal commander, put the yard to the torch rather than let it fall into the hands of the Confederacy. The ships in the yard, the battleships *Pennsylvania*, and *Delaware*, the frigates *Raritan* and *Columbus*, and the corvettes *Plymouth* and *Germantown*, were also set on fire and scuttled. The screw-frigate *Merrimac* was also set alight, but the fire was extinguished after the Federal forces evacuated the yard. Even if the Confederate government had later been able to rebuild the yard, they still lacked the technical ability to build and equip ships of war. In addition they were faced with the problem of getting past the naval blockade. Thus, with their facilities destroyed, the Confederacy had no choice but to look abroad, and particularly to Britain, to provide its navy.

On 9 May Bulloch reported back to Mallory. The naval secretary gave him detailed instructions of the navy's requirements. He was to acquire six steam propeller-driven vessels and was allocated an initial $1,000,000. His instructions were to travel to Liverpool and make himself known to Charles K. Prioleau, a native of New Orleans but now a naturalized Englishman, at the offices of Fraser, Trenholm & Co., at 10, Rumford Place. These English-based cotton merchants were the secret bankers in Europe for the Confederate government. Bulloch left on his mission that very night. He traveled by train to Detroit, Michigan, crossed Lake Erie into Canada, and from there took the train to Montreal, where he boarded the Allan Line steamer *North American*. Bulloch arrived at Liverpool on the evening of 4 June 1861. Finding temporary accommodation, Bulloch introduced himself to Prioleau the next morning. Prioleau allocated him an office at Rumford Place, with an entrance at the rear that permitted him to come and go without being seen by Federal spies. Later Bulloch arranged for his wife, Harriett, to join him. They established a home at 12, and later 3, Wellington Street, Waterloo. Raphael Semmes, soon to become captain of the *Alabama*, recounted a happy visit to the family home:

> I took an affectionate leave of him. I had spent some days with him, at his quiet retreat, in the little village of Waterloo, near Liverpool, where I met his excellent wife, a charming Southern woman, with whom hospitality was a part of her religious faith. He was living in a very plain, simple style, though large sums of public money were passing through his hands, and he has had the honor to come out of the war poor.... I had not only had the pleasure of his society during a number of anxious days, but he had greatly assisted me, by his counsel and advice, given with that modesty and reserve which always mark true ability.[2]

In accordance with instructions, Bulloch traveled up to London to introduce himself to the Confederate commissioners, William L. Yancey and Dudley Mann. The commissioners as yet had not been officially recognized by the British government and were at pains not to jeopardize their position. Bulloch was advised to familiarize himself with the details of British neutrality, and the enforcing Foreign Enlistment Act, in order to avoid embarrassing violations which might bring discredit to the Confederacy. This act forbade either of the two belligerents to equip, furnish, fit out, or arm any vessel within the realm, for the purpose of making war upon the other. Nor could British citizens be recruited within the realm or its dependencies, to serve aboard a ship of a belligerent nation. Bulloch outlined the difficulty of his task:

> To build or even to buy ships suitable for either attack or defense, to get them out of English ports, and then to equip and arm them, were undertakings requiring the utmost secrecy and reserve, the success of every effort depending upon the fidelity and discretion of many subordinate agents, and the precise correspondence of many complicated arrangements. It was necessary, first, to build or buy a ship, and to disguise or omit the semblance of equipment for purposes of war; to obtain the guns from one maker, and often their carriages and gear from another; to get the shot and shells from a third, and the small arms and ammunition from at least two other parties.[3]

Stephen R. Mallory, naval secretary to the Confederate States of America.

He set about the under-taking with a will. Barely three days after his arrival, Bulloch approached the shipbuilding firm of William C. Miller & Sons of Toxteth, Liverpool. Miller had formerly served in Her Majesty's dockyards as a naval constructor, and thereby was more than equal to the task. Bulloch described the type of ship he required. It had to be capable of distant and continual cruising, fast, and capable of carrying ample supplies, a ship that was a combination of sail and steam, with an arrangement for lifting her screw to cut down on drag when she was under sail. A steamer alone would not do, as she could only proceed from one coaling station to another; and under maritime law regarding neutrality, she could only coal at the port of the same country once in three months. Also, it had to be a wooden ship, as most dock facilities then were not geared up to repairing iron-built ships. With these specifications in mind, Miller drew up scale drawings for a ship, based on the modification of one of the Royal Navy's gunboats. A slight increase in length produced a more graceful shape, its clear lines giving higher speed, its floor flattened for greater carrying capacity, its rigging increased for a greater expanse of canvas. Miller's designs were for a steam cruiser of some 700 tons, 191 feet in length, with a beam of 27 ft. 2 in. Her draft was 13 feet. In steam her average speed would be 9½ knots, and in sail 12 knots. She was ideal for Bulloch's purpose, and construction was begun in late June 1861. Miller's yard, it was agreed, would build the hull of the ship, its masts and rigging. As the firm were not engineers, Messrs. Fawcett, Preston & Co., also of Liverpool, were commissioned to design and build the engines. The ship was given the working name of *Oreto*; a rumor was put about that she was an Italian ship, officially the property of John Henry Thomas, the local agent for an Italian firm based in Palermo in Sicily. One month later, on 27 July 1861, Bulloch approached Messrs. Laird & Sons of Birkenhead about the construction of a second ship. For convenience of recognition the ship was designated number 290, it being the 290th ship to be built by them.

Bulloch now received additional orders from Mallory. The Confederate congress had authorized their Treasury Department to buy, or have built, steamships suitable for blockade-running. Bulloch was put in charge of the venture, and he was ordered to liaise with Major Caleb Huse, the army's purchasing agent in Europe. Huse was a graduate of West Point Military Academy, and had served as an artillery officer before resigning his commission when the Southern states seceded. He had been sent to Europe some time before Bulloch, to acquire arms, ordnance, and other military accoutrements. Bulloch described him as a "man of ability, and of unusual energy, but his services were scarcely known beyond the office of his departmental chief. I have always felt that the safety of Richmond at the time of General McClellan's advance from Yorktown up the peninsula, in the spring of 1862, was largely due to the efforts of Mr. Charles K. Prioleau and Major Huse, because the former furnished the credits, and the latter bought and forwarded the rifles and field artillery without which the great battles of Seven Pines and the Chickahominy, could not have been successfully fought."[4]

It is typical of Bulloch that he does not mention his own part in the forthcoming affair. In order to ship Huse's arms, Bulloch not only purchased the *Fingal*, but he also ran the blockade in her. She was well suited to the task, an iron-hulled, schooner-rigged screw steamer, newly built by James and George Thompson at their Clyde Bank Iron Shipyard. She had briefly been in the service of Hutcheson's West Highland Service when Bulloch chartered her with an option to purchase. The ship was berthed at Greenock, and the arms were forwarded to her by rail and by the coastal steamer *Colletis* from London. They included the following:

On Account of the War Department
10,000 Enfield rifles	1,000,000 ball cartridges
2,000,000 percussion caps	3,000 cavalry sabers (with accoutrements)
Material for clothing	Medical stores.

On Account of the Navy Department
1,000 short rifles, with cutlass bayonets
1,000 rounds of ammunition per rifle
500 revolvers, with suitable ammunition
Two 4½ inch muzzle-loaded rifled guns with traversing carriages, all necessary gear, and 200 made-up cartridges, shot and shell per gun.
Two breech-loading 2½ inch steel-rifled guns for boats or field service, with 200 rounds of ammunition per gun.

400 barrels of coarse cannon powder.
A large quantity of made-up clothing for seamen.

For the State of Georgia	**For the State of Louisiana**
3,000 Enfield rifles	1,000 Enfield rifles

In addition to the arms, a number of high profile passengers also prepared to embark. These included Colonel Edward Anderson of the Confederate army, sent to England in July 1861, Messrs. Charles Foster and Moffat, two Charleston gentlemen detained in Europe at the beginning of the war, and Dr. Holland, who had served as a surgeon during the Mexican War. Traveling with Bulloch was his right-hand man, John Low. Born in Aberdeen in 1836, Low had been raised by relatives in Liverpool following the death of his parents. At the age of sixteen he joined the British Merchant Service, but in 1856, at the age of twenty, he emigrated to America and settled down in Savannah, Georgia, where he established his own merchant supply business. At the outbreak of the war Low enlisted as a private with the Georgia Hussars, but later, because of his nautical experience, he accepted an appointment as Acting Master in the Confederate Navy. Bulloch knew Low by repute, and when Bulloch was sent to England, he requested that Low join him. Low was a man whom Bulloch held in high esteem.

Bulloch meanwhile exercised his right to buy, and the *Fingal*, though sailing under British colors, became a Confederate ship. On the morning of 10 October the *Fingal* slipped her moorings, and without fuss, proceeded down the Firth of Clyde, to rendezvous with her passengers at Holyhead in Anglesey in North Wales. At about 3 o'clock on the morning of the fifteenth, with a storm blowing, the *Fingal* approached Holyhead. As she broached the breakwater she suddenly came upon an unlit brig lying at anchor. This brig was the Austrian registered *Siccardi* out of Trieste. The captain of the *Fingal* ordered the engines to reverse, but the ship did not respond quickly enough. Her metal stem struck the stern of the wooden ship, and within minutes the *Siccardi*, complete with her cargo of best Welsh coal, was sunk. As dawn broke Bulloch went down to the harbor. All that could be seen was the upper spars of the brig standing straight up out of the water. Fearing that they would be stopped by the customs officers, and detained, Bulloch ordered the passengers aboard, and the *Fingal* set sail. Before they sailed, Bulloch wrote a hasty letter to Messrs. Fraser, Trenholm & Co., informing them of what had happened and asking them to arbitrate with the owners of the Austrian ship, which was accordingly done, and the affair was satisfactorily settled.

Heavily laden, the *Fingal* could make only nine knots, an insufficient speed to outrun any Federal warship sent after her. This was of some concern to Bulloch, but a worse calamity was then revealed. The *Fingal* was intended for Bermuda, but it was discovered that she had insufficient water aboard. The captain had failed to check before they sailed. An alternative course had to be set for the Azores so the crew could replenish stocks. After several days sailing, the *Fingal* arrived safely at Praya, a bay on the northeast side of the island of Terceira. This was to prove a fortunate accident, for the bay was an ideal anchorage, and Bulloch made a mental note to use it in future for other Confederate ships taking on armaments. Provisioned with fresh water, fruit, vegetables, fresh meat and other sundries, the *Fingal* set sail once again, and arrived at St. George's, Bermuda, on 2 November. Riding at anchor was the Confederate States ship *Nashville*, under Captain R.B. Pegram. He supplied the *Fingal* with a Savannah pilot, John Makin. Further replenished with coal, the *Fingal* made ready to sail. Bulloch summoned the crew, who had only signed up for the voyage to Bermuda. He told them of his intention to run the blockade, and that he had no right to take them anywhere else without their consent. He asked them, "Will you go?" Overwhelmingly they agreed. Two men in particular came to Bulloch's attention at this time as men to be relied upon: the engineer, a Scotsman called McNair, and George Freemantle. Both of them were to return to England with Bulloch and sail aboard his second purchase, the CSS *Alabama*, formerly Laird's 290.

At Bermuda the *Fingal* was armed with two 4½ inch rifled guns in the forward gangway ports, and two steel boat guns on the quarterdeck. The British flag still flying, the *Fingal* set sail. McNair promised Bulloch that he would do his best to raise the speed to eleven knots, but because of the weight of the cargo he could keep it up for only a few hours. A course was set to bring them parallel to Wassaw Sound at noon on 11 November, with a view to making a dash and making land about 3:00 A.M. on the following day. As night approached, the dash at full speed began. At about 1:00 A.M. they approached the coast and observed a dark line to the west, which proved to be a mist over the marshes. Soon, driven by a strong land breeze, they were encompassed by the fog, which concealed them from the enemy blockaders. All lights were extinguished or covered as they continued on to Savannah, barely seventeen miles away now. John Makin the pilot, took the helm. Approaching the Confederate Fort Pulaski, the *Fingal* fired a gun to announce their presence and ran up the Confederate flag. Unfortunately, in the fog, the tide being on the ebb, they ran aground in the soft mud while trying to avoid two large wooden ships that had been deliberately sunk to prevent Federal warships from sailing up the channel to attack Savannah. Three river steamboats were sent to drag *Fingal* off the mud, and at 4:00 P.M. on the afternoon of 12 November 1861 the blockade-runner, amidst the cheers and waves of the onlookers, anchored at Savannah.

Bulloch telegraphed his arrival to the naval secretary, Stephen Mallory. The next day he received orders to proceed to Richmond, as soon as arrangements could be made for the unloading of the arms. As he traveled by rail to Richmond, accompanied by Colonel Anderson, Bulloch became aware of how unprepared the South had been for war. The troops were armed with a multitude of outdated and inappropriate guns, and their dress and accoutrements lacked uniformity. Nevertheless morale was high. There was a feeling that the war could be won.

At the outbreak of the war Confederate policy was to starve Europe of cotton, in the expectation that, blaming the Federal blockade, the European nations would intervene on the part of the South. This policy had failed, and the Confederacy stood alone. Cotton would have to finance the war. John Fraser & Co. of Charleston, the parent company of Fraser, Trenholm & Co. of Liverpool, were charged by the Confederate government with buying cotton for shipping to Europe. Bulloch's orders from Mallory were to fill the *Fingal* with cotton, run the blockade and sell the cargo in England to finance the purchase of more arms. Unfortunately events were overtaking them. Following the Union's victory at Port Royal, South Carolina, Flag Officer Samuel Du Pont, commanding officer of the South Atlantic Blockading Squadron, stationed a naval force off Savannah. On 24 November Commander John Rodgers led a party of Union sailors and marines ashore at Tybee Island, which strategically controlled the mouth of the Savannah river. The only exit, and that not without peril, was through Wassaw Inlet. Bulloch wrote to Mallory:

Savannah, November 25, 1861.

SIR,—

I have the honor to report that the steamship Fingal has been discharged, and now lies in the Savannah river ready to receive freight. Paymaster Kelly has written to Columbus to have the necessary quantity of coal sent down at once, and expects it to be here tomorrow or next day. I cannot refrain from urging the necessity of getting the ship off without delay. Yesterday five of the enemy's gunboats stood cautiously in, and after throwing a number of shell upon and over Tybee Island, a force was landed without opposition.

This morning the Federal flag is flying from the lighthouse, and they will doubtless soon have a battery upon the point of the island. The only egress left for the Fingal is through Warsaw [sic] Inlet, and it can scarcely be supposed that the enemy will permit it to remain open many days. The small quantity of naval stores and cotton required for the Fingal could be got on board in a couple of days if they were brought here on the spot.

I am, etc.,

(Signed) James D. Bulloch.

Hon. S.R. Mallory,
Secretary of the Navy."[5]

Loading the *Fingal* was frustratingly slow. Trains were diverted. The movement of troops and arms was given priority over cotton. Days passed, November turned into December. It was not until 20 December that the *Fingal* was fully loaded. On the morning of Sunday, 24 December, the *Fingal* moved down to Wilmington Island, ready to run the blockade. News came from the Confederate battery at Skidaway Island that a Federal gunboat had approached up the channel, within half a mile of its guns, but had turned and moved back down. Bulloch sent his second officer, John Low, with an experienced pilot, in an eight man boat to investigate. Low discovered that two additional gunboats had joined the third and were anchored in the main passage through Rommerly Marsh. All communications between Savannah and the open sea had been effectively cut. The *Fingal* was trapped. Low reported back to Bulloch. On Christmas Day the three Federal ships were joined by further reinforcements, a large paddle steamer, and a screw steamer, pierced for eight guns. Among the blockading squadron Bulloch thought he recognized his old ship, the *Bienville*.

He accepted the inevitable, and wrote to Mallory that "If the Fingal is irretrievably locked up for the war, I presume you would desire me to get to England by some other means."[6] The answer was in the affirmative. The very capable John Low was promoted to Master in the Confederate Navy and ordered to return to Liverpool with Bulloch. Also assigned to the party were two midshipmen, E.C. Anderson and Eugene Maffitt. Clarence R. Yonge, an assistant in the paymaster's office at Savannah, traveled with them. He had been appointed acting paymaster to one of the two ships under construction in Liverpool. In late January, Bulloch and his companions traveled to Wilmington, North Carolina, and there on 5 February boarded the *Annie Childs,* formerly the *North Carolina,* a ship owned by Fraser, Trenholm & Co., to run the blockade. The *Annie Childs,* commanded by Captain Hammer, was laden with a cargo of cotton, rosin and tobacco. Clear of the blockade, the ship sailed with all haste to Fayal in the Azores, where despite the best efforts of the American consul to prevent it, they were able to recoal and continue their journey. On the afternoon of 8 March they arrived at Queenstown (now Cobh), and took the short train journey up to Cork. The following day the Confederate agents boarded a train for Dublin, and from there by ferry proceeded to Liverpool. Bulloch and his men arrived there on 10 March 1862. It was about this time that Bulloch enlarged his staff at Rumford Place with the addition of James Evans, former Master's Mate aboard the privateer *Savannah*. Evans, born in Wales around 1840, was taken to live in Ireland as a child; but in 1855 the family emigrated to America, and settled in Charleston, South Carolina. Before the outbreak of war Evans had been a harbor pilot.

Meanwhile, at the United States Legation in London, progress reports concerning the construction of the *Oreto* were received from the very able Thomas Haines Dudley, the American Consul in Liverpool. Dudley, a Quaker lawyer from New Jersey, had taken over from former consul Henry Wilding in November 1861. He acquired offices at 22, Water Street, just around the corner from the offices of Fraser, Trenholm & Co., and from there was able to keep a very close eye on the comings and goings at the unofficial Confederate embassy, even to the extent of employing a private detective, Matthew Maguire. Benjamin Moran, the assistant secretary at the legation, had noted the following in his private journal the previous month: "Wed. 12th February 1862: There is a great activity among the rebels again at Liverpool. The Herald, a Dublin side wheeled steamer, said to be very fast, is about to sail with a cargo of contraband of war, under the command of Coxeter, the master of the late Pirate "Jeff Davis," to run the blockade; and the screw steamer Bermuda is up again for another enterprise. It is hinted that a new steamer called the "Oreto" is also being fitted, but as a pirate. She is to carry a heavy armament. This Mr. Adams should bring to the notice of the Govt. here...."[7]

On 17 February, Dudley wrote to Adams:

Sir,

The gun-boat Oreto is still here at this port. She is making a trial trip in the river today. No armament as yet on board. She has put up a second smoke-stack since I wrote you. She therefore has two funnels, three masts, and is bark-rigged. I am now informed that she is to carry eight rifled cannon, and two long swivel-guns on pivots so arranged to rake both fore and aft. No pains or expense has been spared in her construction, and when fully armed she will be a formidable and dangerous craft. In strength and armament quite equal to the Tuscarora; so I should judge from what I learn.

Mr. Miller, who built the hull, says he was employed by Fawcett, Preston & Co., and that they own the vessel. I have obtained information from many different sources, all of which show that she is intended for the southern confederacy. I am satisfied this is the case. She is ready to take her arms on board . I cannot learn whether they are to be shipped here or at some other port. Of course she is intended as a privateer. When she sails, it will be to burn and destroy whatever she meets with bearing the American flag.

H.DUDLEY,
United States Consul[8]

United States minister to Great Britain Charles Francis Adams wrote to the British foreign secretary, Lord John Russell, of his concerns. Russell responded with the fiction created by Bulloch, that the ship was intended for the Kingdom of Italy. Adams dispatched Moran to the Italian embassy. Count Maffei, the secretary, assured him that the *Oreto* was not intended for them. Russell also made enquiries through the British ambassador at Turin. On 1 March 1862 he telegraphed back: "Ricasoli tells me that he has no knowledge whatever of the ship Oreto, but will cause inquiry to be made."[9] While the Ambassador made further enquiries, Russell also instigated enquiries, discovering that the *Oreto* was registered as ship 44,200, at the port of Liverpool, in the name of "John Henry Thomas, of Liverpool, in the county of Lancaster, merchant." This was the name bandied about in the rumors. He was apparently the sole owner. In his declaration in the Registry, Thomas made the following statement:

James Alexander Duguid, whose certificate of competency for service is No. 4073 is the master of the said ship. I am entitled to be registered as owner of sixty-four shares of the said ship. To the best of my knowledge and belief no person or body of persons other than such persons or bodies of persons as are by the merchant-shipping act, 1854, qualified to be owners of British ships is entitled, as owner, to any interest whatever, either legal or beneficial, in the said ship. And I make this solemn declaration conscientiously, believing the same to be true.

(Signed) JOHN H. THOMAS.[10]

There was a degree of ambiguity in the declaration, but it was not the duty of the registrar to question or ascertain the accuracy of the declaration of the owner. The "managing owners" were Fraser, Trenholm & Co. Three days later the *Oreto* was cleared for Palermo and Jamaica. So on the face of it, Thomas (who was born in Palermo) was owner, and the ship was destined for Palermo in Italy. The clearance signified that the final official act had been carried out, and the ship was free to sail.

By the time of Bulloch's return, on 10 March, the *Oreto*, originally to have been known as the CSS *Manassas,* had already undergone a sea trial. She was now provisioned and prepared for her great adventure. Bulloch pointed out, however, in his narrative that "not a single article contraband of war was on board the ship — not a weapon, not an appliance for mounting a gun. In this condition I was advised that according to the Municipal Law of Great Britain, she was a perfectly lawful article of traffic."[11] That this was so was confirmed in an enquiry in August 1862 by the Commissioners of Customs. The pilot, Edward Morgan, who took the *Oreto* out of the Mersey, testified:

I am one of the surveyors of customs at this port; pursuant to instructions I received from the collector on the 21st of February in the present year and at subsequent dates, I visited the steamer Oreto at various times, when she was being fitted out in the dock, close to the yard of Messers. Miller & Sons, the builders of the vessel. I continued this inspection from time to time until she left the dock, and I am certain that when she left the river she had no warlike stores of any kind whatever on board.

After she went into the river she was constantly watched by the boarding officers, who were directed to report to me whenever any goods were taken on board, but, in reply to my frequent inquiries, they stated nothing was put in the ship but coals.

EDWARD MORGAN, Surveyor.[12]

At the United States Legation in London, under secretary Benjamin Moran noted in his journal: "Tues. 11th March 1862: The Gov't have permitted the Oreto to sail & a twin ship to the Bermuda called the Bahama, is now ready at Hartlepool, with a cargo of munitions of war, to run the blockade."[13] The following week however on the 17th, he recorded that the ship had returned to Liverpool, following her sea trial, and is suspected of a design to take her guns on somewhere near that port.

The *Bahama,* as Moran rightly reported, was at West Hartlepool Docks, loading armaments and ammunition sent up from London. Her mission, though, was not to run the blockade, as Moran speculated, but to arm the *Oreto* somewhere off Nassau. By the end of the month, the *Bahama,* commanded by Fraser, Trenholm & Co.'s senior captain, Eugene Tessier, sailed to Hamburg to receive four 7-inch rifled guns. By May, she was on the high seas once more.

Bad luck now overtook Bulloch. It was intended, by orders dispatched by the secretary of the navy, that Captain Robert B. Pegram of the CSS *Nashville,* then in England, would allocate officers and men to the *Oreto*, with Pegram himself taking command. Before the orders arrived, however, Pegram had sailed.[14]

Bulloch was aware that pressure was mounting on the British government to take some action regarding the *Oreto*. There was also the strong possibility that a Federal warship might well be on its way to intercept her. He had to act quickly, and get her away as soon as possible. Captain James Alexander Duguid, in temporary command of the *Oreto*, had already begun to take on men. An engineer and crew of fifty-two British sailors were eventually hired, under articles for a voyage from Liverpool to Palermo (thus maintaining the allusion that she was destined for Italy), and there, if required, to a port or ports in the Mediterranean Sea, or the West Indies.

Desperate to prevent her sailing, Thomas Dudley, the U.S. consul, was still collecting intelligence. On 22 March 1862 he wrote to Adams:

> Sir,
>
> The Oreto is still in the river. A flat-boat has taken part of her armament to her. A part of the crew of the steamer Annie Childs, which came into this port loaded with cotton, have just left my office. They tell me that Captain Bullock [sic] is to command the Oreto, and that four other officers for this vessel came over with them in the Childs. The names of these three are Young, Low, and Maffitt or Moffitt; the fourth was called Eddy; the two first are lieutenants, and the two last-named, midshipmen. They further state that these officers during the voyage wore naval uniforms; that they came on the Childs at a place called Smithville, some twenty miles down the river from Wilmington; that it was talked about and understood by all on board that their object in coming was to take command of this vessel, which was being built in England for the southern confederacy. They further state that it was understood in Wilmington, before they left, that several war vessels were being built in England for the South. As they were coming up the river in the Childs, as they passed the Oreto she dipped her flag to the Childs. I have had this from several sources, and the additional fact that the same evening after the arrival of this steamer a dinner was given in the Oreto to the officers who came over in the Childs. I understand she will make direct for Madeira and Nassau.
>
> I have, & c.,
>
> (Signed) THOMAS H. DUDLEY.[15]

That very day, 22 March, the *Oreto*, soon to be renamed the *Florida*, quietly slipped her moorings and set sail. Her crew, according to the Customs, comprised some fifty-two men, all British with the exception of three or four, and one of them being American. Bulloch had got away the first of the six steamships ordered by Mallory. It was with some disappointment that Bulloch watched her leave, for he had been promised command of the ship only to have his hopes dashed. Mallory had decided that Bulloch was of far more use to the Confederacy in his present position. Sailing in the *Oreto*, with a letter to the navy secretary and special orders for Captain John Newland Maffitt, then known to be in Nassau, was Bulloch's assistant, the very capable John Low.

2

The *Florida*

The British steamship *Oreto,* having sailed from Liverpool on 22 March, arrived at Nassau in the Bahamas on 28 April 1862, most of the journey under sail. She registered her arrival with the authorities, and this was duly noted in the Account Book of the Revenue Department:

Inwards

(No. 48)

In the British steamer Oreto, Duguid, master from Liverpool; 178 tons; 12 feet; 52 men. Ballast.

From Nassau on 1st May 1862, John Low wrote to Bulloch:

Sir,—

I have the honor to report to you the safe arrival at this port of the Confederate States steamer Florida, on the morning of the 28th of April, after a passage of thirty-seven days, which, in compliance with your instructions, has been made principally under canvas. We wished to be as economical as possible in regard to the consumption of fuel, but rather unfortunate in having light winds and frequent calms, more especially in the Trades. During the latter we thought it prudent to steam, thinking that if we made too long a passage the steamship Bahama would be here some time before us. The amount of coal, as you are aware, was one hundred and seventy-five tons, including Welsh and English. Our consumption of the former was eighteen tons per day, and of the latter twenty-four. We have now on board good two days' coal, so I trust you will find, after taking into consideration the weather, and our reasons for not making a long passage, that we have been as economical as possible, not only as regards fuel, but with everything on board.

I took particular notice of the vessel as regards her speed under steam and canvas, and am happy to report most favorably of her in all respects. Our average steaming is nine knots and a half; her sailing averages, with the wind abeam or quarterly, so that the fore and aft canvas will draw, twelve knots. The above is the average; I now give you what I have seen her do during the passage. Under steam, with smooth water, ten and a half knots, and under canvas alone, with quartering wind, so that we could carry main top-gallanting studding sail, thirteen and a half good.

As regards stability, I do not think there is a stronger vessel of her class afloat; when pitching, you could not see her work in the least, not so much as to crack the pitch in the waterway planks, where I believe a vessel pitching is as likely to show weakness as anywhere else.

I am etc.,

(Signed) John Low.

Commander J.D. Bulloch.[1]

As per his orders Low called at the offices of Messrs. Henry Adderley & Co. the Confederate States agents in Nassau, where he discovered that Captain J.N. Maffitt was at sea. In his ship, the *Nassau* (a former Trenholm ship), Maffitt was making yet another successful blockade run into Charleston. While he waited Maffitt's return, Adderley put Low in touch with Mr. Louis Heyleger, another Confederate agent, who advised that the *Oreto* be moved to New Anchorage, where the ship would be less conspicuous. On 30 April the wisdom of this move was evidenced by an attack upon a British owned and British flagged steamship, the *Stettin,* out of Falmouth. Just a short distance off the island, and in British territorial waters, she was fired upon twelve times by shot and shell by an unidentified U.S. gunboat. Being the faster vessel, though, the *Stettin* got into Nassau. The arrival of the *Oreto* had not gone unnoticed though. The American consul in Nassau, Captain Samuel Whiting, began to agitate for the seizure of the ship. Officers of the Royal Navy went aboard her for inspection, but all they could report was that while she was suited to the purpose of a war ship, she was not armed, nor were there war-like stores aboard. She was not breaching British neutrality.

On 4 May, Maffitt returned from a successful run, his ship's hold, and her deck now filled with

Captain J.N. Maffitt, C.S.N., commander of the *Florida*. U.S. Admiral David D. Porter wrote of him: "We do not suppose there ever was a case where a man under all the attending circumstances, displayed more energy, or more bravery." (*Century Magazine*)

cotton. In his journal, Maffitt wrote: "At 11 P.M. Mr Low, provisional master, C.S. Navy, came to my room in private and informed me that he had come over in the C.S. gunboat Oreto, and at the same time handed me a letter from Commander J.D. Bulloch, requesting I would at once assume command and send Mr. Low back."[2] In his letter Bulloch had written:

> I hope it may fall to your lot to command her, for I know of no officer whose tact and management could so well overcome the difficulties of equipping her, or who could make better use of her when in cruising order.
> It has been impossible to get the regular battery intended for her on board, but I have sent out four 7 inch rifled guns, with all necessary equipments in the steamship Bahama, bound to Nassau, and Mr. Low will give you all particulars as to her probable time of arrival, and will also hand you a list of everything on board the gun vessel....[3]

As Bulloch had wished, Maffitt was given command of the *Oreto*. His mission now complete, John Low returned to Liverpool, arriving back there in July 1862. From Nassau Maffitt wrote to the secretary of the navy requesting to be furnished with experienced lieutenants, a paymaster, engineers, an assistant surgeon and money. Secretary

Mallory sent him two junior officers, Master (Acting Lieutenant) Mr. O. Bradford, a man Maffitt described as having "little ability," and Midshipman Sinclair, who on his voyage to Nassau "saw the ocean for the first time." Things were not looking too promising.

Unbeknownst to Maffitt, Samuel Whiting, the U.S. consul in Nassau, had taken over where Dudley had left off. He wrote to the Governor of the island:

> UNITED STATES CONSULATE
> Nassau, New Providence, May 9, 1862
>
> Sir,
>
> I have the honor to communicate to your excellency several facts of importance, deeming it to be my duty so to do, as representative of the Government of the United States of America.
>
> The tug Fanny Lewis, which arrived here from Liverpool on the 6th instant, has on board, I am credibly informed by letters received from that port, a large quantity of powder for the rebel States of America, or for the so-called Confederate States.
>
> On the 28th ultimo the steamer Oreto also arrived off this port from Liverpool, and now lies at Cochrane's Anchorage, where it is believed, and so reported by many residents here, that she is being prepared and fitted out as a confederate privateer to prey on the commerce of the United States of America.
>
> I cannot but think that your excellency will consider it proper that some inquiry should be made to ascertain how far the vessels alluded to are preserving the strict neutrality so earnestly enjoined by Her Majesty's late proclamation, and I am confident that I pay but a deserved tribute to your excellency's high character when I express my firm belief that no illegal steps will be allowed to those who seek to subvert the Government which I have the honor to represent.
>
> I am, & c.,
>
> (Signed) SAML. WHITING,
> United States Consul.[4]

On 7 June the *Bahama* arrived at Nassau, with the *Oreto*'s armaments. They had been sent by train from Liverpool to Hartlepool, and there loaded aboard the *Bahama*. At Nassau they were unloaded and stored at the public warehouse. Also aboard the *Bahama* as passengers were Captain Raphael Semmes, Lt. John Kell and Surgeon Francis L. Galt, late of the Confederate warship *Sumter*. Soon after, the *Melita* arrived in Nassau, with more of the *Sumter*'s crew, including Lt. John Stribling and Lt. Beckett Howell. Seeing Maffitt's plight — a desperate lack of seasoned officers — Stribling requested Semmes to be allowed to serve aboard the *Oreto*. Semmes gave his consent. Further officers for the *Oreto* then began to arrive, including Maffitt's stepson, J. Laurens Read, Acting Master Floyd, Midshipman Bryan, Engineers Spidell, Scott, Quinn and J. Seely, Acting Marine Officer Wyman, Acting Paymaster Read, Clerk and Acting Master's Mate Lionel Vogel and a few deckhands.

In Washington, navy secretary Gideon Welles received the news of these arrivals with some alarm. He urged Consul Whiting to apply pressure on the British authorities to either seize or stop the *Oreto* from sailing. Whiting, as Maffitt later discovered, bribed a member of the *Oreto*'s crew, the boatswain, a man called Jones, to inform the authorities that she was a Confederate gunboat. Captain McKillop, of HMS *Bull Dog*, accordingly seized her as a lawful prize. The next day, however, upon the advice of Mr. Anderson, the Queen's Attorney, she was released. Her tour completed, the *Bull Dog* sailed on 9 June, to be replaced by HMS *Greyhound,* then commanded by Commander Hickley. Once again Whiting approached the authorities with the suspicion that the *Oreto* was attempting to raise another crew, in violation of the Foreign Enlistment Act. Hickley seized the ship for adjudication. Two days later, on 17 June, the Attorney General decided there was insufficient evidence to hold her and ordered her release. Livid at this, the American consul then appealed to the governor, and that very day she was rearrested. Proceedings against the *Oreto* and her captain were instituted before the admiralty court of the colony. Meanwhile United States naval secretary Gideon Welles sent orders to Commander Gansevoort of the USS *Adirondack*:

> Sir,
>
> The department has information that the fast-sailing steamer Oreto, now or recently at Nassau, New Providence, has been fitted for war purposes, and the intelligence received is of such a character as to leave little doubt that she is to be employed in hostile demonstrations towards this Government, its commerce, and its people.... Should the Oreto or any other armed vessel have left Nassau with the intention of hostile demonstrations ... you will proceed with the Adirondack in pursuit of her. Among the vessels that have been reported as having arms, munitions of war, etc., and as having sailed from Europe with the intention of violating the blockade or throwing their cargoes into the Southern States by transshipments, are the steamers, Julia, Usher, Bahama....
>
> The steamer R.R. Cuyler, Commander Francis Winslow, will touch at Nassau on the way to Key West, under instructions of a similar import to the foregoing.
>
> I am respectfully, your obedient servant,
> Gideon Welles
> (Secretary of the Navy).[5]

The USS *Adirondack* proceeded with all haste, and arrived at Nassau on 28 July. Gansevoort wrote to Welles that very day:

> Sir,
>
> I have the honor to report the arrival of this ship at this port. We left New York on the 17th, and after an eight days' passage arrived here on the 25th ... as to the Oreto, she is at present in charge of a prize crew from the Greyhound.... The vessel herself looks trim and man-of-war like. She has sixteen ports in which guns could be mounted; these ports are small though, and no heavy guns could be used in them. She is fitted, I am informed, in all respects as a vessel of war, and the purpose for which she is intended is known to everyone, high or low.[6]

The trial dragged on until 2 August, but the result was the same. Much was suspected, but nothing could be proven. The *Oreto* was freed. Very wisely Maffitt ordered the ship to sail as soon as possible. The following morning the Federal gunboat *Cuyler* arrived at Nassau to join the *Adirondack*. Maffitt recorded that "On the following day the Cuyler (Federal gunboat) came and ran all round us. The [HMS] Petrel, commanded by my friend Watson, immediately went out and ordered her in the harbor or to go without the marine limits. That night the Petrel gave me a hawser and we hung on by it, as we had not men enough to weigh our anchor. At 12 or a little after we dropped quietly down under the shadow of the land until off the west end of the island, when we steamed to the southward.[7] As she did so, the *Oreto* slipped past the USS *Adirondack*.[8] There was no sign of the *Cuyler*. The armaments aboard the *Bahama*, transferred to the public warehouse, had been transshipped to the schooner *Prince Alfred*, purchased the day before by Adderley & Co. At 1:00 A.M. that morning, 7 August, the *Oreto* rendezvoused with the *Prince Alfred* at Hog Island, just beyond the harbor at St. John's, and the *Oreto* took the *Prince Alfred* in tow. The two ships proceeded to Green Cay, a small island on the edge of the Great Bahama Bank, some sixty miles from Nassau. Here the armaments were transferred from the *Prince Alfred* to the *Oreto*. The work of transferring the armaments at sea was laborious, Maffitt recorded:

Now commenced one of the most physically exhausting jobs ever undertaken by naval officers. All hands undressed to the buff, and with the few men we had, commenced taking in one 6 and 7-guns, powder, circles, shell and shot, etc. An August sun in the tropics is no small matter to work in. On the 15th C. Worrell, wardroom steward died and we buried him on Green Cay. Several cases of fever appear among the crew. At first I thought it but ordinary cases, originating from hard work and exposure to the sun, but in twenty hours the unpalatable fact was impressed upon me that yellow fever was added to our annoyance. Having no physician on board, that duty devolved upon me, and nearly my whole time, day and night, was devoted to the sick. On the 16th August all the armaments and stores were on board; took the tender in tow and ran to Blossom Channel, in which we anchored at sunset.[9]

On the morning of 17 August the Confederate flag was hoisted for the first time and the ship was commissioned as the CSS *Florida*. The ship's log lists the officers:

J.N. Maffitt, commanding	C.W. Quinn, acting second
J.M. Stribling, lieutenant	assistant engineer
O. Bradford, acting lieutenant	G.D. Bryan, midshipman
R.S. Floyd, acting master	G.T. Sinclair, midshipman
J. Spidell, acting first assistant engineer	L. Vogel, captain's clerk
J.L. Read, acting assistant paymaster	A. Vesterling, paymaster's clerk

Many of the crew had been struck down by yellow fever, and with just thirteen men well enough to man the vessel, and with enemy warships searching for them, Maffitt decided to run the *Florida* through the Federal blockade in the Bahama channels and sail for the neutral port of Cardenas, in Cuba. In his journal Maffitt wrote the following: "August 18.— At 11:30 P.M. passed a Federal Cruiser. We were so close to the reef that he did not see us. At 1:20 A.M. on the 19th August entered the harbor of Cardenas; one fireman on watch perfectly exhausted and about four men. Anchored in 4 fathoms. At 9 got underway, and stood into the inner harbor; communicated with the authorities, and represented our helpless condition; received permission, per telegram, from the governor-general to remain as long as is necessary."[10]

From Cardenas Maffitt wrote to Bulloch, on 20 August 1862:

My Dear Bulloch,

I took on board at sea all my battery, but many things in the haste and confusion were forgotten, such as rammers, sponges, etc. Had but two firemen and eleven men; have run the gauntlet splendidly, my Coast Survey experience being of great service. Where I went the Federal ships dared not follow, and here I am, with prospects of filling up my crew and obtaining what is necessary. The "prize-crew" committed many acts of robbery, and left the vessel in a terrible plight.... I hope to give a good account of myself soon, if I get the men. I write in great haste. Have Lieutenant Stribling — good officer; acting master Bradford, acting-midshipmen Bryan, Floyd, Sinclair — young men of no nautical experience. No doctor, no paymaster....

Yours affectionately.
(Signed) J.N. MAFFITT.[11]

Here at Cardenas Maffitt now succumbed to yellow fever himself. With presence of mind, while he still could, he ordered Stribling to proceed to Havana, there to acquaint the Confederacy's agent, Major Charles J. Helm, of their perilous state and of the necessity of recruiting additional men to the crew. Despite Spain's professed neutrality, Helm was able to provide twelve men, and Stribling returned to Cardenas with them. Maffitt wrote in his journal: "August 22.— My duties as physician have prostrated me considerably; do not feel well. At 2 P.M. was taken with a slight chill, which I fancied originated from getting wet in a thunder squall. Took a foot bath and felt better for a time. At 4, while giving medicine to the sick, was seized with a heavy chill, pain in the back and loins, dimness of vision, and disposition to vomit. The painful conviction was forced upon me that I was boarded by this horrible tropical epidemic. I sent for Mr. Floyd and Mr. Wyman, and gave full instructions in regard to the duty of the vessel. Ordered a physician sent for, and the sick sent to hospital ... by this time was in the embrace of a fierce fever.... From this period until the 29th all was blank to me."

Maffitt and his men, suffering from yellow fever, were transferred to the Spanish hospital ashore. They were cared for by one Dr. Gilliard, surgeon aboard the Spanish gunboat *Guadalquivir,* lying at anchor nearby. Upon his recovery Maffitt discovered that many of his crew had died from the disease, and sadly this included his own 16 year old stepson, J. Laurens Read. Later, his strength regained, Maffitt had the good fortune to meet one Dr. Barrett of Georgia, a warm-hearted Irishman and physician at the hospital. To demonstrate his devotion to the South, Barrett offered his temporary services to the Confederacy as surgeon aboard the *Florida.*

Major Helm telegraphed Maffitt, following an interview with the captain-general of Cuba, requesting that he should bring the *Florida* to an anchorage at Havana. Why was not made clear, but it seems that the Spanish government was concerned about violation of its neutrality. In addition to the recruitment of sailors, rumors abounded concerning the Federal navy's intention of running into Cardenas and attacking the *Florida* in Spanish waters. For the moment they remained just off the coast in international waters. Maffitt buried his dead, then proceeded to get underway. The American consul, a man by the name of Shefeldt, dispatched a swift craft to inform the Federal blockaders that the *Florida* was preparing to sail. At 8:00 P.M., as darkness descended, the Spanish mail boat for Havana left port just before them. Mistaking it for the Confederate ship, the Federal squadron set off in pursuit, open firing with both shot and shell. The Spanish ship made all haste, unable to communicate with her pursuers who she was. Eventually she made the safety of Matanzas.

The *Florida* left a little later that same night, under the cover of darkness, and hugging the coast ran into Havana unmolested. Here the restrictions were so rigid that Maffitt found it impossible either to recruit more men or to refit the *Florida.* He resolved to run the blockade that very night and make for Mobile, along the Gulf of Mexico. At 9:30 on the night of 1 September, the *Florida* set sail from Cuba. Maffitt with a greatly reduced crew, his armament still not mounted, was only too aware of the grave danger he faced from Federal gunships. By two o'clock on the afternoon of the fourth, the *Florida* was standing off Fort Morgan, at the entrance to Mobile Bay. Between her and safety were three Federal warships. Clearly they could see the *Florida* as she approached. Maffitt had two choices, either to turn and run, and risk being pursued and sunk, or to charge straight through. He had nowhere to run, so he lowered the Stars and Bars and raised the British red ensign, hoping to buy time. Sailing on towards the blockading force, Maffitt still had the element of surprise on his side. He hoped to get well among them, then make a dash for Mobile. Commander Preble, senior officer of the blockade, positioned his ship, the *Oneida,* directly in the path of the oncoming ship. The other two Federal ships, *Winona* and the *Rachel Seaman,* moved into position in support. On she came, this British flagged ship; then within hailing distance, Preble ordered her to heave-to. There was no response from the *Florida.* On she continued to come. Maffitt takes up the story in his journal:

At 4.50 P.M. the cannonading commenced upon our helpless craft, for we could not return their shots for want of men and proper provision for our guns. The Oneida, Commander Preble, of 10 guns, made an effort to cut us off, but I sheered towards him, and feeling he would be run down he backed, giving me a momentary advantage. As I ranged ahead of him he poured out a whole broadside, that swept away hammocks and dome rigging. One gunboat opened on my port bow, the other on our port quarter, and the cannonading became rapid and precise. Having passed the Oneida, gave a starboard helm to bring the gunboats in line, and escaped, by this range, the fire of one of them, for this grouping around me bid fair to send the little Florida to the bottom. Hauled down the English flag, and as soon as the signal halyards could be removed, ran up the bars and stars. A shell entered the port quarter but fortunately neither that or the XI-inch shell exploded. Several expended Parrott shells struck the masts and fell on board. Our boats were much injured and all the standing rigging (except three shrouds) shot away; our hull well peppered. Finding that we did not distance the Federals rapidly, sent the men aloft to loose topsail and topgallant sails, and our sailors responded to the order with alacrity. As soon as they were seen on the yards, all the gunboats commenced firing 24-pound shrapnel; the standing rigging was shot away as our men came down front aloft; several were wounded, and the boats, masts, spars, and hulls were cut with thousands of the shrapnel. The sea was smooth, and our helpless condition gave the enemy confidence and security, which enabled them to coolly use us as a target. The sails availed us considerably, for a light S.E. wind had sprung up. I sent all below but the officers and two men at the wheel.

As we approached the bar an XI-inch shell entered on our port beam, about 9 inches above the water line, passing through coal bunker, grazing the boiler and entering among the men on the berth deck; by this shot 4 men were wounded and James Duncan's head taken off. Duncan was captain of the maintop and one of our best men. At dusk we were under the guns of Fort Morgan.[12]

Maffitt anchored off Melrose. Against all the odds he had got his ship home. In his journal he wrote: "Soon visited by the officers. Colonel Powell says the scene was brilliant, and he considers it one of the most dashing feats of the war. Sharkey, captain forecastle, and Billups, quartermaster, were at the wheel during the cannonading, and did well; in truth, everybody acted well their part."[13]

At Melrose, Maffitt buried his dead. Then he went up to Mobile to report, and to raise a new crew. The *Florida,* still racked with yellow fever, was put into quarantine. On 6 September a small steamer, the *Areal,* was sent to act as a hospital ship. Maffitt returned on the eighth to discover that Stribling had come down with fever. Dr. Barrett was attending to him, and the other sick members of the crew. Also seriously ill was Midshipman Sinclair, whom Maffitt had at first disparaged, this being his first voyage. Sinclair had demonstrated his worth, though, in the dash into Mobile. Maffitt now attended to Stribling personally over the next few days, but on the evening of 12 September, Stribling died, never having recovered consciousness. He was buried at Melrose, near Mr. Stone's country seat. Maffitt recorded of him, "He was a good Christian and excellent officer." Sinclair, whom Maffitt also attended, recovered. Over the next few days the *Florida*'s replacement crew began to arrive. As before they were a mixed bag; some had experience, some were totally unfit for service. It was a month before repairs to the *Florida* were begun. The carpenters and other craftsmen had been afraid to come onboard, even though the quarantine flag had been hauled down some two weeks previously. There were long delays, accompanied by personal criticism of Maffitt. He recorded the following in his journal: "I doubt not but that there will be much criticism and condemnation among the restless spirits of the service, who are always finding fault, yet most faulty themselves. 'Tis a curse in military as well as naval life that gossiping is carried to such reprehensible extremes, and as a general rule it belongs to the weak-minded, shallow-pated persons, living in glass houses, but always throwing stones."

In the end, naval secretary Mallory acted, and despite Maffitt's tireless work in getting his ship ready for sea, he was replaced by a Lieutenant Joseph N. Barney. Maffitt protested at this injustice, and his immediate superior, Admiral Buchanan, outraged at the duplicity involved in getting Barney the command, appealed directly to President Davis of the injustice done to Maffitt. Davis wrote a curt note to Mallory, ordering Maffitt's reinstatement. Maffitt was reinstated. The delays continued, and it was not until 15 January 1863 that the outfitting of the *Florida* was completed. The log of the *Florida* lists her officers by name, rank and address, just prior to sailing:

J.N. Maffitt, Lieutenant commanding	North Carolina
S.W. Averett, Second Lieutenant & Executive Office	Virginia
J.L. Hoole, Second Lieutenant	Alabama
C.W. Read, Second Lieutenant	Mississippi
S.G. Stone, Second Lieutenant	Alabama
F. Garretson, Passed Assistant Surgeon	Virginia
Jos. D. Grafton, Assistant Surgeon	Arkansas
J.J. Lynch, Assistant Paymaster	North Carolina
J. Spidell, Assistant Engineer (acting chief)	Alabama
R.S. Floyd, Midshipman	Georgia
G.D. Bryan, Midshipman	South Carolina
G.T. Sinclair, Midshipman	Virginia
J.H. Dyke, Midshipman	Florida
C.W. Quinn, Second Assistant Engineer	South Carolina
W.H. Jackson, Second Assistant Engineer	Maryland
E.H. Brown, Third Assistant Engineer	Virginia
T.T. Hunter, Jr Master's Mate	Maryland
Lionel Vogel, Captain's Clerk	South Carolina
W.H. Wilson, Paymaster's Clerk	District of Columbia

On the night of 16 January all was made ready for sailing. The *Florida* was provisioned and coaled. Her armament consisted of a 120lb. Blakely rifle gun amidships, and six broadside 68 lb. Blakely rifles. Fog delayed departure, but at two o'clock in the morning, the fog thinned, and the stars became visible. The *Florida* cautiously got underway, determined to run the blockade before dawn. Under sail alone, but with her engines in full steam, she eased out of Mobile, all lights extinguished. At two forty in the morning, she passed a Federal gunboat undetected. Unbelievably the enemy ship had no look-outs. On the *Florida* silently continued, past a second gunship; luck was holding. A third gunship loomed into view. As the *Florida* breasted the third ship, a flame from her funnel, caused by the ignition of coal dust, caused her discovery. The alarm was raised. Rockets were fired into the air, and lights from the nine blockaders lit up the night sky. The *Florida*, now under maximum steam and under full sail, made a dash for the sea. She was too fast for the blockaders lying at anchor. As dawn began to break she was well underway, her pursuers left far behind. The crew of the *Florida* were beginning to congratulate themselves when suddenly a Federal steam sloop of war, under topsails, came into view. She was heading directly for them. Many thought that it was the USS *Brooklyn*, a formidable opponent. The *Florida* sheered away from the enemy ship to avoid a collision, and her crew quickly went to quarters, preparing for an ill-matched fight should it come.

For some fifteen minutes they manned their guns, as the Confederate ship passed under the starboard guns of the more powerful enemy gunboat. Clearly the superior Federal ship saw the nearby steamer, for someone placed a light over the starboard gangway to prevent a collision. Unbelievably, on she sailed past Maffitt's ship, no doubt thinking that the *Florida* was just one of the many Federal gunboats patrolling off Mobile. The *Florida* now found herself in the midst of an enemy flotilla. To the east was another large armed ship, and on the starboard beam a fast gunboat passed by. Maffitt kept his nerve, and by late afternoon they were clear of the blockade. Steam pressure was lowered and preparations were made to continue under sail. Then barely three miles behind them, and approaching fast, the crew espied one of the ships from the blockading squadron in pursuit. It proved to be the USS *Cuyler*. The engine was reengaged, and more sail was quickly set. Gradually the *Florida* pulled away from her pursuer. As night fell, Maffitt changed course, heading westward, and by the following morning the *Florida* found herself alone in the vast ocean.

On 19 January 1863, the *Florida* captured her first enemy merchant ship. At daylight two ships in sail were sighted. One to stern was chosen, and during the course of the morning the *Florida* slowly but surely gained on her. About three miles distant, Maffitt ordered the Federal flag to be hoisted. The other ship responded by likewise raising the flag of the United States. All hands were called to stations as the *Florida* closed with the enemy merchant ship. At 500 yards the *Florida* put a shot across her bow. She immediately heaved to, and hauled down her colors. The *Florida* did likewise, and raised the flag of the Confederacy. Lieutenants Hoole and Stone, accompanied by Midshipmen Floyd and Bryan, boarded her. She proved to be the brig *Estelle* out of New York, on her maiden voyage from Santa Cruz, Cuba, to Boston. Her cargo consisted of sugar, molasses and honey. The officers and crew, eight in number, were taken aboard the *Florida,* where they readily signed paroles, negating the need to imprison them. Maffitt took what he needed from the *Estelle*, then just before dark the ship and its cargo, valued at $130,000, were set on fire. Maffitt then set in a course for Bahia Honda, Cuba.

By early afternoon the western end of the island of Cuba was in sight. A steamer was reported on the port bow, and Maffitt ordered all hands to quarters. As she approached, the steamer proved to be the Spanish gunboat *Morro Castle*. The men were stood down. Maffitt sailed his ship along the northwestern coast, and at twenty past seven on the evening of 20 January, the *Florida* approached the harbor of Havana. Not realizing that harbor regulations had changed, forbidding ships to enter after dark, Maffitt sailed into the harbor, in violation. The next morning, being made aware of his mistake, Maffitt apologized profusely to the captain of the port, and the apology was accepted. Maffitt gratifyingly noted in his journal for 21 January 1863: "The excitement in Havana on our arrival was intense; crowds were on the wharf, and a very strong Southern feeling was exhibited."

This was not a feeling shared by the United States consul, Robert Schufeld. He sent word to Key West of their arrival. News of this reached the ears of Major Helm, the Confederate representative in Havana, who informed Maffitt. At best Maffitt reckoned he had twelve hours to take on coal, provisions and clothing for the crew before the arrival of an intercepting Federal flotilla. As day dawned on the morning of the 22nd, with no enemy ships in sight, the *Florida* left the port of Havana. Annoyingly for Maffitt, the *La Coquena* from Portland, Maine, managed to dash past him and into Cuba's three mile limit, and safety. Then to his dismay Maffitt discovered that the so-called Cardiff coal that they had purchased turned out to be worthless. As the crew threw it overboard, the *Florida,* under sail, made for Cardenas. The disappointment of earlier that day was forgotten when a sailing ship came into view. She proved to be the American bark *Windward,* registered at New York and now out of Matanzas, Cuba, bound for Portland, Maine, with a cargo of sugar. Quickly overhauled, the *Windward* was boarded. Whatever provisions that were of use were taken from her before she was put to the torch. Her crew were permitted to man her boats and row safely to the nearby shore. Three hours later, at about four o'clock, not far from Cardenas, another U.S. vessel, the brig *Corris Ann* of *Philadelphia,* was captured. She too was set alight; but instead of sinking, she drifted into the port. That night at seven o'clock, the *Florida* was obliged to enter the same port of Cardenas in order to make adjustments to the valves of her engine. The *Florida* was in danger from Federal gunboats, and a squadron comprising the USS *Wachusett, Santiago de Cuba, San Jacinto* and *Sonoma,* under the command of Rear Admiral Charles Wilkes, was even then searching for her. All haste was made with the repairs. By nine o'clock she was at sea once more. Steering for Nassau, the *Florida* narrowly missed running aground at Green Cay, but arrived successfully at her destination early on the morning of 26 January. Unfortunately Maffitt fell foul of the port authority, for here too the law had changed, forbidding ships to enter during the night. The next day he made his amends, and, explaining the situation, was permitted a period of twenty-four hours to re-coal and take on any provisions necessary. During her stay the *Florida* received many visitors, including several officers of the West India Regiment and prominent citizens of the town. They expressed strong sympathy for the Confederate cause. In the harbor lay a dozen or more blockade-runners. Nassau was very much a Confederate stronghold, though the local authority somehow still managed to walk the tightrope of neutrality. Twenty-six of the American crew deserted while they were at Nassau, but Maffitt was of the opinion that the ship was better off without them. Only two of them were any great loss. Maffitt succeeded in recruiting some six sailors to replace them, but was careful both in his journal and the ship's log not to go into details over their nationality. It would seem that they were British.

By ten o'clock they had finished coaling, and by midday the *Florida* sailed out of the harbor. She lay at anchor some miles off, and here she remained until dark, when Maffitt set a course for Green Cay. Safely away from prying eyes, minor repairs and alterations were carried out, including the painting of the smokestacks a cream color in order to fool the enemy. By 29 January the *Florida* anchored off the sandbanks, some eight miles from Green Cay. Here she remained for a couple of days while everything was made "ship-shape and Bristol fashion." On 1 February, shortly after half-past four in the morning, she got under way once more. At eight o'clock the cry went up: "Sail-ho!" Away on the starboard bow, bearing down on them, was an imposing side-wheeled steamer, flying the Federal flag. All hands were called to quarters and the *Florida* was cleared for action. Maffitt believed the oncoming ship to be the *Santiago de Cuba,* of ten guns, reported to be sailing in the vicinity.[14]

They were no match for her, and Maffitt ordered a change in course to make an escape. Two broadside guns were moved to the stern to give some response should the Federal steamer close upon them. Steam was brought up to pressure, and with her engine now working to full capacity, the Confederate ship pulled away. The pursuit continued throughout the day and into the night. At daylight the other ship was still there, in the distance, away on the starboard bow. During the course of the day the *Florida* slowly pulled further away, until at midday there was no sign of her pursuer. Maffitt then changed course to elude pursuit.

A cyclone off Cape Hatteras now forced them southward and then eastward. Maffitt was obliged to use up precious coal to escape the storm. As the weather raged, two possible prizes eluded him, but there was little he could do. Maffitt then resolved to sail towards the West Indies to re-coal before continuing his assaults upon the United States merchant fleet. On the night of 5 February a Federal steamship was observed off the *Florida*'s starboard beam. She saw them, too, and changed course towards them. Rapidly closing, she was soon alongside the *Florida*. Maffitt ordered a small safety light to be hung over the side of the *Florida,* and this evidently fooled the USS *Vanderbilt* (as she was believed to be). Surely no enemy ship would advertise herself so. The *Vanderbilt* moved in for a closer inspection, then being satisfied, sheered off, evidently believing her to be a West Indies trader.[15]

As the weather abated, on the late afternoon of 8 February, a sailing ship was observed. The *Florida* pursued her for three-quarters of an hour, until she came into range. Maffitt raised the Union Jack of Great Britain in order to fool her; but rather than the suspected Federal flag, she raised the flag of Prussia. Maffitt broke off the chase and returned to his former course, set for the West Indies. Now very low on coal, the *Florida* was rigged for sail only. On the morning of the 10th a schooner approached. Seeing the *Florida* she raised the British ensign, and even saluted the Confederate ship. Maffitt continued on his course. On the morning of 12 February, away in the distance on the lee-side, a sail was seen. Though the *Florida* was low on coal, her propeller was lowered and the engine engaged. The *Florida* set off in pursuit. By late afternoon she was within two miles of her quarry. Maffitt ordered the Stars and Stripes to be hoisted, then fired a shot from his forward pivot gun. The other ship responded by raising the Federal flag, then heaved-to to await a boarding party. The ship proved to be the *Jacob Bell* of New York, from Foo Chow in China, bound for New York. Her cargo consisted of 1,380 tons of tea, 10,000 boxes of fireworks, matting, camphor and cassia (used as a laxative); the lot valued at an estimated $2,000,000. A cutter with Lieutenant Hoole, Midshipman Floyd and a crew of ten were sent over to her. Word came back that one of the forty-three passengers and crew, Mrs. Frisbee, the captain's wife, was heavily pregnant. Dr. Garretson was sent to ascertain the facts. With care, she and the other lady aboard, a Mrs. Williams, wife of the Customs House officer at Swatow, China, were brought aboard the *Florida* and housed, along with their "tons of baggage," as Maffitt relates, in his very own cabin. The others were likewise brought aboard, as were such provisions as were required. It now being late in the day, Maffitt ordered Lieutenant Hoole and his party to follow the *Florida* in the *Jacob Bell*. Wisely he decided not to set fire to her that night, as the flames would be seen for several miles, drawing Federal gunboats like moths. The next day, at about two o'clock in the afternoon, Maffitt ordered the *Jacob Bell* to be set on fire.

The *Florida*'s captain set a course away from the burning ship: northwards then westwards, eventually coming back onto his original course. A sail was seen and the chase began again. A warning shot across her bows brought the other ship to a halt. She raised the French tricolor and proved to be the brig *Leonce Lacoste* from Martinique to Le Havre. Maffitt sailed on for the West Indies. On the morning of 15 February, just after half-past five, a sail was seen. Maffitt altered course to pursue her. Throughout the day the chase continued. Maffitt ordered all sail to increase speed, but she kept well ahead of them by several miles. As night fell she was lost to view, and the pursuit was abandoned. Maffitt returned to his original course. On the 17th, shortly after midday a sail on the port bow was seen. The ship was sailing towards them. While still some four miles off, Maffitt ordered the Union Jack to be raised. The other ship responded by raising the Danish colors. Maffitt changed course to enable the other ship to come alongside. She proved to be the bark *Morning Star,* from New York, bound for St. Thomas in the Virgin Islands. Midshipman Floyd was sent over in a cutter to speak to her captain. He agreed to take the *Florida's* prisoners and their baggage on board. After five days Maffitt regained the comfort of his cabin.

Four days' further sailing passed without incident. Shortly before midday on 21 February, a barque in full sail was seen. Maffitt ordered a change in course to engage her. Closing, Maffitt raised the Union Jack; the barque likewise raised the British flag. Maffitt returned to his original course. Three days passed and shortly after dawn on the 24th, Barbados was sighted on the horizon. The *Florida* ran down the coast to the port at Bridgetown, following into port the U.S. flagged barque *Sarah A. Nickels.* The *Florida* anchored at ten o'clock that morning. The response to their arrival was most favorable, particularly, and perhaps surprisingly, among the Negro population, as Maffitt recorded in his journal. The *Florida* was the first Confederate ship to enter the port, and Governor Walker was at first concerned over his duties and obligations towards this belligerent ship. She had coaled at a British port within the previous three months, and strictly, under the Neutrality Act, was not permitted to enter a British port until three months had elapsed. Maffitt won him over, because in the detail of the act it was permissible to re-coal within the time period if the supply of fuel had been exhausted by stress of the weather. The precedent had allegedly been set by the Federal ship *San Jacinto,* commanded by Captain Wilkes of *Trent* infamy. Walker, his conscience clear, permitted Maffitt into the harbor to take on fuel and provisions.

Maffitt and his officers were invited to dine that night at Government House. The other diners were mainly British military personnel, who expressed admiration for the Confederate army, and in particular its two generals, Robert E. Lee and "Stonewall" Jackson. The following day the *Florida* played host to a constant stream of visitors, all of whom expressed Southern sympathies. In the harbor lay two American flagged merchant ships; and Walker, in accordance with the Neutrality Act, sought reassurance from Maffitt that he would not leave the harbor until twenty-four hours had elapsed following their departure. Maffitt readily agreed, for this gave him an extra day to reprovision and carry out minor repairs. The *Florida* took onboard one hundred tons of coal, supplied from Halifax by the Confederate steamer *Harriet Pinkney.* While in Barbados Maffitt appointed Mr. Robert Gordon of the firm of Gavan & Co. to act as the Confederacy's agent. That night Maffitt invited his former hosts to dine aboard the *Florida.* They dined and drank, perhaps too well, for the following day, 25 February 1863, Maffitt noted the following in the ship's log: "At 7 P.M. got underway and bulled among the shipping in the harbor. Carried away our starboard main brace and second cutter, the ship being at the time in charge of the captain." In his journal for that same date he elaborated: "Quite a number of gentlemen came off at dusk to call. All were full of zeal in their Confederate sentiment. Did the host to a late hour, and was not benefited thereby, for my piloting was not perfect, and I fouled one of the merchant vessels, parting our starboard main brace and lifting our second cutter from the fall hooks. Recovered the boat and proceeded out, steaming due east."

A little embarrassing for Maffitt perhaps, but at least he was honest enough to officially admit his own faults. The *Florida* stood out to sea that night, and the following morning ten men who had secretly boarded the ship (presumably British sailors) were signed on. Maffitt then set a northeasterly course, out into the Atlantic. The following day tragedy struck. Seaman Isaac White, in an attempt to unshackle the cable from the weather anchor, fell overboard, and not being able to swim, was drowned before help could arrive. It was a sobering reminder to all of the care and attention needed aboard ship.

That same day, 26 February, Rear Admiral Wilkes, as he now was, of the *San Jacinto,* and commanding the United States naval forces in the area, was actively looking for the *Florida.* He wrote to the naval secretary, Gideon Welles: "The fact of the Florida's having but a few days' coal makes me anxious to have our vessels off Martinique, which is the only island at which they can hope to get coal or supplies, the English islands being cut off under the rules of her Majesty's Government for some sixty days yet, which precludes the possibility, unless by chicanery or fraud, of the hope of any coal or comfort there."[16] Wilkes had overlooked something: that which had applied to him had also applied to Maffitt. So while Wilkes and his squadron made sail for the French island of Martinique, the *Florida* set a course towards the Azores and the main transatlantic shipping lanes. In the ship's log for 4 March, Maffitt notes that they covered 137 miles that day, taking him further and further away from his Federal pursuers.

On 6 March, at seven in the morning, a sail was discovered about seven miles to windward. The propeller of the *Florida* was lowered and, with steam up, the chase began. It was two hours later, at a closing distance of about four miles, that Maffitt ordered a shot across her bow. She immediately heaved-to in response. Coming alongside her, the cutter was lowered and Lieutenant Hoole and Midshipman Bryan and other crew members were sent aboard. She proved to be an American ship, the *Star of Peace,* registered at Boston, and traveling from Calcutta to her home port. What particularly pleased Maffitt was that her cargo, along with cowhides and goatskins, largely consisted of saltpeter destined for the DuPont munitions works where it would have been converted into explosives for the Federal army. It was true contraband of war. Captain Hinckley of the *Star of Peace* and his officers were transferred to the *Florida* and accepted parole. The rest of the crew were put aboard in single irons. Whatever rations and other supplies were onboard were transferred to the Confederate steamship and divided equally among all members of the crew. The *Star of Peace* was set on fire, and when at a distance of eight hundred and fifty yards, she was used for target practice. Of some twenty-two shots, six struck her. Maffitt observed that the accuracy was not up to his expectations, but put it down to the roll of the sea. At half-past nine that night, at a distance of some twenty miles, they could still see the ignited saltpeter aboard the burning ship, sending flames shooting high up into the nighttime sky.

Northeasterly the *Florida* sailed for three days without sight of any other ship. At half past three on the afternoon of 9 March, a small sail was seen off the weather bow. Maffitt turned and set off in pursuit. Barely an hour later he overtook her. He raised the Federal flag to see how she would respond, but she raised the tricolor. She was French. To make sure, Maffitt ordered a boarding party to inspect her papers, but she proved to be what she had proclaimed, a French fishing schooner. Maffitt returned to his original course. A squall got up, and heavy rain lashed the *Florida*'s deck that night and into the early morning. At about ten past five, as day was dawning, away in the distance on the leeward side a sail was seen. Due to the bad weather the chase proved futile and was eventually given up as a lost cause. Onward the *Florida* sailed on her northeasterly course. The 11th and 12th of March passed without incident. On the morning of the 13th, at half past eight, another sail was sighted. All canvas was put on as the *Florida* began the chase. Shortly before midday she was in range, and the *Florida* fired a blank charge. The quarry heaved-to, and Lieutenant Averett and a boarding party sailed over to her. She proved to be English, and was allowed to continue.

This disappointment was forgotten when, soon after, a schooner of American design was seen off to the north. The *Florida's* engine was engaged, and with steam and sail she ran the quarry to ground. Maffitt ordered the British ensign to be raised, to which the other ship responded with the Stars and Stripes. Without a shot being fired, the American ship heaved-to, and awaited a boarding party of inspection. Lieutenant Averett and his party took possession of the ship, the *Aldebaran* of New York, bound for Maranham in Brazil. Her master, Captain Hand, felt hard done by. He professed himself a Southern Democrat and was opposed to the war, which he saw as more a war over the Negro than maintaining the Union. His arguments availed him nothing. He was a Yankee trader — his ship was burned.

Three days passed without incident. At half past three on the morning of the 18th a barque passed to the leeward of the *Florida*, but Maffitt did not pursue her. As day broke two ships were seen. One proved to be the English brig *Runnymede,* sailing from Pernambuco (now Recife, Brazil) bound for Greenock in Scotland. Her captain agreed to take eleven of the *Florida's* prisoners if Maffitt would provide water and provisions for them. The incident had a follow up, as Secretary Benjamin Moran at the United States mission in London narrated in his journal:

> Mon. 6th April 1863: A curious case has arisen which seems to involve a delicate point in international law. An American vessel was burned some weeks ago by the British pirate "Oreto" and the crew placed on board a British vessel by which they were carried to Glasgow. The owners have claimed the amount of about one hundred pounds as passage money for these men and ask the United States to pay it. Mr Underwood, the Consul at Glasgow has written to Mr Adams on the subject, and he has referred the owners to Washington. The point in this case is worthy of note altho' I think it easy of solution. The pirate fell in with this British ship and asked her captain to take certain prisoners he had on board to Europe, or to a port. There was no compulsion. The Briton took them, and by so-doing assisted the pirate in her cruise against American commerce and thus became in fact an aider and abbetter [sic] in her villainy. Now he claims compensation for this act from the very nation he aided to injure. I would not pay him. And I would do so on the double ground that by paying him I was giving a premium to such characters to assist the pirate, and also by so doing endorsing the right of an enemy to get rid of his troublesome prisoners by placing them on a pretended or real neutral. Once it is known that our Government won't pay such demands, these Britons will not be so ready as now to relieve these pirates of their captives.[17]

Perhaps Moran had a point. The actions of the captain of the *Runnymede,* in trying to obtain passage money after he had been supplied with provisions and water by Maffitt, can only be described as avaricious. But perhaps the actions of the American government are also open to question regarding the welfare of their citizens. Neither party came out of the incident too well. Later on in the day, after the *Runnymede* had taken off Maffitt's former prisoners, a sail appeared out on the weather bow. The *Florida* turned to begin the chase. It was a long haul, over eight hours, before the suspect ship heaved-to in obedience. She proved to be an English ship, the *Larra Mara,* from Rangoon in Burma, bound for Liverpool. Fruitless pursuits followed on the 19th when a day was wasted chasing two other ships which likewise proved to be British, and on the 23rd the *Florida,* having chased a ship all day, became becalmed, and watched as the quarry disappeared over the horizon. Maffitt relieved himself of more prisoners on 25 March when the *Florida* overhauled an Austrian barque bound for New York with coal for Cunard's Royal Mail Steam Line. Maffitt likewise furnished his former prisoners with water and provisions. Whether the captain of this ship also claimed passage money is not recorded.

On 28 March, at about half-past eight in the morning, the lookout espied a sail on the lee bow, about seven miles distant. Maffitt ordered up steam for a pursuit. At half-past eleven they overhauled and boarded her. She was the U.S. registered barque *Lapwing*, out of Boston, bound for Batavia in the East Indies. Her cargo was mainly smokeless coal. Maffitt decided to requisition rather than destroy her. He put aboard a crew consisting of Lieutenant Averitt in command, Lieutenant Read, Assistant Surgeon Grafton, Acting Midshipman Dyke and fifteen men. A 12-lb. Howitzer with ammunition was transferred to the *Lapwing*, which with a sense of fun Maffitt renamed the *Oreto*. The *Florida* set an easterly course, the *Oreto* following on behind. At daybreak on the following day the *Florida* had a march on the *Oreto* of some six miles. She heaved-to and waited for the *Oreto* to come up alongside. The sea, Maffitt recorded in the log, was smooth, there being little wind. He transferred ten tons of coal to the *Florida* and brought Lieutenant Read back to the ship, replacing him with Acting Master G.D. Bryan. On the afternoon of the 30th, the *Oreto* espied a sail directly ahead. She signaled the *Florida,* and both ships set off in pursuit. Being the faster ship, the *Florida* left the *Oreto* behind. At a quarter to nine, as the light was rapidly falling, the *Florida* overhauled her quarry. She proved to be the barque *M.J. Colcord* of New York, bound for Cape Town. Maffitt took from her what he needed in the way of provisions, and took prisoner her captain, his wife, and the crew of the ship. It was now dark. There was no sign of the *Oreto*. Maffitt fired a rocket to attract her attention, but she was nowhere to be seen. He put up two lights on the mast in the hope that she would see them. The next morning there was still no sign of the *Oreto*. Trusting that Lieutenant Averett would return to the original course, Maffitt, with the *Colcord* in tow, steamed southward in an attempt to rendezvous with him. That morning, at around ten o'clock, they fell in with a Danish brig, the *Christian*, sailing from Dublin to Santa Cruz. She agreed to take on board all of the *Florida*'s prisoners, with Maffitt providing an adequate supply of water and rations for them. Maffitt continued on, after burning the *Colcord*.

Meanwhile, the *Oreto* was also returning to the original course; but seeing a sail, she went after her, only to discover that she was an English brig. Late at night, the *Oreto* reset her course and sailed northeasterly. Days passed with no sign of the *Florida*. On the 6th, at around half-past ten in the morning, another sail was sighted; but the ship was too far to windward for Averett to overhaul her, so he had to watch as she sailed on. The young Averett, now fully aware of his isolation and the inadequacy of his armament, set his crew to making "Quaker guns," a euphemism for make-believe wooden guns, which from a distance looked like the real thing. This might deter a single Federal gunboat from attacking, but perhaps not a full squadron. The *Oreto* continued on. On 11 April, the *Oreto* set out after a sailing ship, which to Averett's disappointment ran up the Spanish colors. The following day it was an English brig. On 14 April, at about midday, now back on her original course, she saw the smoke of a steamer in the distance. It was the *Florida*. She had sighted them to the southeast shortly before eleven and was proceeding towards them. The two ships rendezvoused, to much mutual cheering, at three o'clock in the afternoon. In his journal Maffitt called it "a most fortunate meeting, for both had drifted some 30 miles away from the rendezvous ... commenced coaling and continued through the night. A more perfect Godsend we could not have had at the present moment, particularly as our bunkers were nearly empty. Found all on board in good health and living like lords on Yankee plunder. Mr Averett was unhappy that he had not captured a prize. His vessel leaks and does not hold a good wind: will have to burn her when we expend her coal."[18]

Coaling continued throughout the night and early into the next day. Averett was confirmed in his position as master of the *Oreto,* and was given orders to rendezvous with the *Florida* at Fernando de Noronha, Brazil, by 4 May, where Maffitt intended to take off the remaining coal. Maffitt now sailed westward in pursuit of further quarry. From early on the morning of 17 April, Maffitt stopped a number of ships, but upon examination they all proved to be neutrals. At twenty past ten Maffitt alighted upon the Federal registered *Commonwealth,* sailing from New York to San Francisco. She was boarded and searched. Cargo and ship together were reckoned at $370,000. Her cargo of tobacco alone was estimated to be worth $60,000. As Maffitt prepared to set fire to her, a French vessel approached and agreed to take her master, one Captain McClennol, along with ten others as passengers.

The *Oreto* meanwhile was having mixed success. Early on the morning of 20 April, at about six o'clock, she overhauled a ship which proved to be French. Half an hour later she obliged a second merchant ship to heave-to and be inspected. She was the American ship, *Kate Dyer,* seventy-two days out of Callao, bound for Antwerp, with a cargo of guano. Upon examination of her papers the cargo was proven to be neutral, so Averett could only bond her captain for $40,000, to be paid within thirty days of the Confederacy becoming a reality. She was allowed to continue on her journey. Two days later, on 22 April, the *Oreto* stopped a schooner, which in response to his colors raised the Spanish ensign. The following day she passed a second Spanish-flagged ship, and in order to confuse the enemy raised not her own, but the Federal flag. At six o'clock on the morning of 24 April Averett sighted Fernando de Noronha.

The previous day the *Florida,* likewise sailing towards Fernando de Noronha, captured the U.S. flagged *Henrietta* of Baltimore, under Captain George Brown, bound for Rio de Janeiro with an assorted cargo. She had a family of four as passengers— Mrs. Flories and her three children. Maffitt was obliged to give up his cabin for their comfort. Their sojourn aboard the *Florida* was brief however. Overhauling a French ship, the *Bremontier,* bound for Pernambuco, Maffitt persuaded her captain to take his "guests." On the 24th the *Florida* captured the *Oneida* of New Bedford, commanded by Captain Potter, returning home from China with a large cargo of tea. Her value was reckoned to be near $1,000,000. It had been a successful few days. On the evening of 27 April they espied in the distance the island of Fernando de Noronha, then used as a penal colony by Brazil. The *Oreto* was waiting. The *Florida* dropped anchor, and her thirty-two remaining prisoners were taken ashore. As the *Florida* was ever watchful for any sign of a pursuing Federal squadron, smoke from a steamer away on the starboard beam caused concern, but she proved to be no more than the Brazilian mail boat. On 1 May, to their considerable pleasure, an English barque which hove into view proved to be the *Agrippina,* the tender for the CSS *Alabama,* with a cargo of coal for her. These were happy days for Maffitt and his crew.

That same morning, 1 May, with the *Oreto* in tow, the *Florida* moved off to the shelter of the island and began coaling. Lt. Averett, Dr. Grafton and Acting Master Bryan were recalled to the *Florida*. Acting Master R.S. Floyd was sent to replace them. On 4 May the *Florida* upped anchor and moved out to sea. The *Oreto* likewise sailed from the island for a later rendezvous with the *Florida* at Rocas Island. At dusk the following day, the *Florida* came upon a barque, which proved to be Brazilian. The following morning, quite early, she crossed the path of the *Oreto,* and after a brief exchange of pleasantries, continued on. The *Florida* stopped a Spanish brig, which was allowed to continue unmolested, and at a quarter to ten that morning the *Florida* overhauled and forced to heave-to an American flagged brig, the *Clarence.* She was en route from Rio to Baltimore with a cargo of coffee. Maffitt transferred three hundred bags to the *Florida.* The *Clarence* was a good ship, and Lt. Read requested Maffitt that he be allowed to requisition her as an armed cruiser. Perhaps because there was something of himself that Maffitt saw in Read, and perhaps because of the plan of campaign that Read put to Maffitt, he acquiesced.

Charles W. Read, nicknamed "Savez" from his habit of using the word, as in "you understand?" to finish a sentence, graduated from the Annapolis Naval Academy in 1860. He served briefly aboard the USS *Powhatan* before offering his services to the South at the outbreak of the war. He was ordered to the CSS *McRae* and saw action with the River Defense Fleet at New Orleans and Island No. 10. When the commander of the *McRae* was wounded on 24 April 1862, Read took command of the ship. He later served as executive officer aboard the CSS *Arkansas.* He was intelligent, experienced, possessed a certain guile, and above all was ready for command. His plan was audacious and worthy of his mentor. The ship was accordingly converted to an armed cruiser and commissioned as the CSS *Clarence.* A howitzer and ammunition were transferred to her from the *Florida,* as well as cutlasses and small arms. Second Engineer E.H. Brown was seconded, as were a crew of twenty men. At six o'clock that evening, Read set his new command on a southwesterly course as ordered. Then when well out of sight, he headed north.[19] His mission as outlined to Maffitt was to run into Hampton Roads, capture a gunboat or steamer in Chesapeake Bay, and generally raise havoc in the very heart of the enemy's operations. In this he would be aided by the *Clarence's* original papers, which had been retained, and her Portland registration, which would get him past the Federal naval blockade.

On 6 June, off the United States coast, he captured his first prize, the *Whistling Wind,* commissioned by the Federal navy to deliver coal to Admiral Farragut's squadron stationed at the mouth of the Mississippi. Read took off her crew, then burned the ship. It was a good start to operations, and gave them all confidence. The next ship they stopped was the *Alfred H. Partridge,* from New York, sailing to Matamoras in Mexico with arms and clothing for, as her captain proclaimed, the Confederate army. It seemed unlikely; but stranger things had happened during the war, and Read gave him the benefit of the doubt. He bonded the ship for $5,000. The captain eventu-

Lt. Charles "Savez" Read, C.S.N., who in his short career as captain captured or sank fourteen enemy ships.

ally did deliver his cargo to the Confederacy. Read was on surer ground when he captured his next ship. She was the Boston registered barque *Mary Alvina*, with a cargo of provisions for the Federal army, as her manifest proclaimed. Read took what he needed, then torched the unfortunate ship. Among the plunder were some recently published newspapers, where he learned to his dismay that all ships entering Hampton Roads were stopped and searched, and only those with cargoes commissioned for the Federal government were allowed to dock.

His hopes were temporarily dashed, but the plan did not necessarily have to be abandoned. If he could capture a ship with the necessary clearance papers and cargo, then it could go ahead. What was now required was ingenuity, and Read was not short of that. On 12 June, Read spied the ship, six miles ahead, that might bring his plans to fruition. She was too far ahead for his six pound howitzer to make much impression, and given her lines Read knew that she could soon outdistance them. He hoisted the Federal flag upside down. A flag flown upside down was an international signal of distress. Aboard the USS *Tacony*, sailing from South Carolina to Philadelphia, notice was brought to the attention of its captain, William Munday, that the ship sailing astern appeared to be in distress. After some hesitation Munday ordered the *Tacony* to heave-to and await the slower ship. As it drew abreast, a boat was lowered from the ship in distress, and the ten sailors aboard it rowed over to the *Tacony*. They scrambled aboard and from within their jackets they produced revolvers, taking the crew of the *Tacony* completely by surprise. With little choice but to surrender, it was all over in seconds. The *Tacony* had become a prize of the Confederacy. The crew were led down into the hold. The Howitzer aboard the *Clarence*, and the other arms and ammunition, were loaded aboard a cutter for transference to the *Tacony*. As they were doing this, another ship, the schooner *M.A. Schindler*, also seeing their flag of distress, came alongside. The same procedure followed, and the *Schindler* too was captured. Her crew were transferred to the *Tacony*, and the *Schindler* was set on fire.

Into this abundance of riches came yet another ship, the *Kate Stewart*. She had seen the distress flag and the burning *Schindler* and came to offer her help. Read, with his howitzer and arms bobbing on a cutter between the *Clarence* and the *Tacony*, his crew dispersed on both ships and the cutter, had nothing but bluff remaining. Aboard the *Clarence* he ordered his "Quaker" guns (fashioned en route), to be run out, and ordered the *Kate Stewart* to surrender. From a distance they looked convincingly real. Captain George Teague, former master of the *Tacony*, thought so, and begged Read not to open fire. The *Kate Stewart*'s captain surrendered. With the *Tacony* secured, the *Schindler* ablaze, the *Clarence* abandoned, complete with 8000 bags of coffee beans, Read boarded the *Kate Stewart*. She had twenty female passengers. Read's dilemma was that he now had more prisoners than crew — including twenty women. He abandoned the idea of torching the *Kate Stewart*, and instead transferred all his other prisoners to her, permitting her to resume her journey. As she sailed away, the *Clarence* was then set ablaze, and with the smell of roasting coffee wafting on the breeze, Read sailed away in a better ship than he had started with.

Read sailed north. The next morning he stopped the brig *Arabella* and boarded her. Inspecting her manifest he discovered that her cargo belonged to a neutral. Accordingly he spared the ship, but bonded it to the tune of $30,000. While all this was going on, the *Kate Stewart* arrived at New Jersey, and Captain Teague, former master of the *Tacony*, reported to the authorities what had happened. He also told them of an overheard piece of conversation: a large Confederate fleet was on its way to bombard the eastern coast of the United States. This was but a story, a ploy, deliberately planted by Read to cause anxiety to the Federal authorities. In Washington naval secretary Gideon Welles was ordered to take whatever measures were required. He issued instructions that all available ships were to proceed to sea at once to hunt down the *Clarence*. He was unaware that Read had transferred to the *Tacony*. Within a matter of days thirty-eight armed Federal ships were scouring the Atlantic seaboard for a ship that no longer existed. Private ships were seconded, and, armed with two howitzers each and manned by a naval crew, they were sent out in pursuit of the pirate. Twice the *Tacony* was stopped by Federal warships, and each time Read claimed to have seen their quarry. He gave bogus directions, sending the Federals off on a wild-goose chase. Read again went on the offensive. On 15 June, some three hundred miles off the Delaware River, he captured and burned the United States registered brig *Umpire*. He stopped the *Isaac Webb*, an immigrant ship with seven hundred and fifty passengers. The numbers were too great. He bonded her for $40,000 and permitted her to go on her way. As he was doing this, a fishing schooner, the *Macomber*, came up to investigate. Read took her crew onboard, then set fire to her.

The following day the clipper *Byzantium* was hunted down and forced to heave-to, under the threat of being bombarded. Her hold was full of coal. Read was tempted to take her and her cargo as a prize, for fuelling the *Florida* and the *Oreto*; but realizing that she would slow them down, and undoubtedly attract attention, Read had her burned. Her crew were placed as prisoners in his hold, Read sailed on. Later that day the *Godspeed*, bound for New York, crossed their path, and she too was put to the torch. On 22 June three fishing schooners were burned. A fourth was bonded, and Read's numerous prisoners were transferred to her. The next day two more New England fishing schooners were captured and burned. From newspapers taken from one of them, Read discovered that the authorities now knew that he was operating from the *Tacony*. Nonetheless, he continued in his assault upon the United States merchant fleet. He next stopped the *Shatemuc*, from Liverpool bound for Boston. She had a cargo of iron plate. She was also overflowing with Irish immigrants, and this saved her from a fiery destruction. Read bonded her for $150,000.

His twentieth victim was the ninety ton mackerel schooner *Archer*. She was a good ship, and with adaptation might make a good fighting ship. Read had the howitzer transferred to her and whatever other provisions he could manage. The howitzer was now out of ammunition; any further captures would have to be by bluff or stealth. The *Tacony* was set on fire.

Now lying off Portland, Maine, in the hope of another conquest, Read picked up a mackerel in the shape of a drifting dory. The two fishermen manning her were made prisoner. Interrogating them Read discovered that the fast passenger liner *Chesapeake*, then lying in New York harbor, was about to sail. Read put forward a proposal to capture the *Chesapeake*, and fire the other ships in the harbor. Second Engineer E.H. Brown dissuaded him, doubting that he would have the expertise to manage the huge engines aboard the ocean liner. Thwarted, Read sailed into Portland in search of a quarry. Lying at anchor was the armed U.S. Revenue cutter *Caleb Cushing*. That night — leaving just three men aboard the *Archer* — with his remaining crew, nineteen in number, Read lowered two boats and rowed across to the *Caleb Cushing*. The night watch, consisting of two men, were overpowered, and the sleeping crew were captured. To Read's surprise, the captain of the ship was Lt. Dudley Davenport, a classmate of Read's at Annapolis.

Davenport was a Southerner who had taken the Union side. By daylight, the *Caleb Cushing* and the *Archer* were at sea. At first it was thought that Davenport had changed sides and stolen the cutter. Port collector Jebediah Jewett summoned troops from the Seventh Infantry, based at Fort Preble, and with a hastily raised crew seconded the civilian cruise ship *Forest City*. A six pounder field piece and a twelve pound howitzer were placed aboard her, and she set off in pursuit. The *Chesapeake* was also pressed into service. Two six pound field guns were lashed to her deck. An unarmed steam tug, with more soldiers aboard, followed on.

Twenty miles out to sea, a sailor aboard the *Caleb Cushing* espied the pursuing flotilla. At two miles Read ordered his thirty-two pounder to open fire on the leading pursuer, the *Forest City*. Though not accurate, the salvo was enough to persuade her captain to heave-to and await reinforcements. The *Chesapeake* came up and the Union ships continued their pursuit. Aboard the *Caleb Cushing,* Read had used up his available shot and Davenport refused to tell him where the spare shot locker was located. A frantic search ensued as the enemy flotilla fast approached. Fearing that the *Chesapeake* would ram them, Read ordered his men into the boats. The *Caleb Cushing* was set on fire, and the magazine exploded. The *Chesapeake* caught up with the lifeboats, and Read and his crew were taken prisoner. In so short a time Read had carved out a name for himself, capturing twenty-two U.S. registered vessels and bonding ships to the value of $92,000, payable to the Confederate States of America within thirty days of the ratification of a peace treaty. Read and his men were taken prisoner under armed guard to Fort Preble, and from there they went to a prisoner of war camp at Fort Warren on an island in Boston Harbor. Read managed to escape two or three times before being exchanged and sent south to the Confederacy in October 1864.[20]

Meanwhile, back aboard the *Florida*, and unbeknownst to Maffitt, on 6 May 1863, Maffitt was appointed a Commander in the Confederate navy. The citation read:

CONFEDERATE STATES OF AMERICA,
Navy Department, Richmond, May 6, 1863.
Sir,
You are hereby informed that the President has appointed you, by and with the advice and consent of the Senate, a commander in the Navy of the Confederate States, to the rank from the 29th day of April, 1863, "for gallant and meritorious conduct in command of the steam sloop Florida in running the blockade in and out of the port of Mobile against an overwhelming force of the enemy and under his fire, and since in actively cruising against and destroying the enemy's commerce." Should you accept the appointment, you will notify this Department thereof.
S.R.MALLORY,
Secretary of the Navy.

To Commander JOHN N. MAFFITT, C.S. Navy,
Commanding Steam Sloop Florida

It was not only the Confederate senate that appreciated what Maffitt had done. Admiral David Dixon Porter, of the Union navy later wrote of Maffitt in his naval history: "During the whole war there is not a more exciting adventure than this escape of the Florida into Mobile Bay. The gallant manner in which it was conducted excited a great admiration even among the men permitting it. We do not suppose there ever was a case where a man, under all the attending circumstances, displayed more energy or more bravery."

On 7 May, running down the Brazilian coast, *Florida* made contact with a glut of

Lt. Read sinking the *Caleb Cushing*, off Portland, Maine.

English flagged ships. There was the barque *Hindoo* of Liverpool, the brig *Amelia,* from St. John, New Brunswick, sailing to Pernambuco, and the English barque *Clara*, from Pernambuco to Liverpool. There was no sign whatsoever of an American registered ship. The following day the *Florida* anchored in the harbor at Pernambuco (Recife), Brazil. Here she remained for four days, refitting and provisioning, despite the protestations of the U.S. consul. In response to the consul's protest, the regional president informed him that there had been no infringement of the letter or spirit of international law in the course which had been pursued by the authorities, and that they could not agree with the consul that the *Florida* was a pirate. This defense of Brazilian neutrality was to have later ramifications. On 13 May the *Florida* left Pernambuco. She got the latest war news from a French mail steamer and barely an hour and a half later took prisoner the Federal flagged *Crown Point,* thirty-four days out of New York, bound for San Francisco. Maffitt took what stores he needed, and shortly before midnight put her to the torch. Nine of the crew of the Federal merchant ship signed up for service aboard the *Florida.* By 16 May Maffitt anchored off the Rocas Shoals near Cape San Roque, Argentina. He buried one of his crew, seaman John Johnson, on the 18th, with all due honors. The *Florida* remained at the shoals for a number of days. On the 20th a sail was reported to the east. The *Florida* sailed after her. She proved to be a Danish brig; and in exchange for some supplies, she agreed to take ten of Maffitt's prisoners. Maffitt then returned to the shoals to await a rendezvous with the now delayed tender *Oreto,* formerly the *Lapwing.* On the evening of 29 May, at about half-past five, a number of the officers got permission to go ashore, in a bid to relieve the tedium. Tragedy struck, though, when the cutter they were on was overturned in the breakers and assistant surgeon Joseph Grafton was drowned. He had given up an oar he was using to keep him afloat to a seaman who could not swim. After a short service of remembrance for Grafton, and fearing to remain any longer, Maffitt left a message for the *Oreto* ashore and made sail.

For whatever reason, the *Oreto* had arrived at a different location, and there waited for some thirty days for the arrival of the *Florida*. With supplies of food and water running low, Acting Master R.S. Floyd set a course for Barbados in the hope of crossing the *Florida's* path. He arrived off the coast on 20 June. There was no sign of the *Florida*, and with every expectation of being sighted by Federal warships, Floyd ordered the ship to be set on fire. He and the crew went ashore in the ship's boats and made contact with Robert Gordon, the Confederate agent appointed by Maffitt. Gordon booked them aboard a ship for Ireland, with instructions to contact Bulloch when they arrived. Eventually they rejoined the *Florida* at the port of Brest, in France.

Having left Argentian waters the *Florida* sailed north. On 6 June she came upon the 938 ton *Southern Cross,* carrying a cargo of timber. Maffitt took what he needed and set her on fire. Twelve days later the Boston clipper *Red Gauntlet* suffered the same fate. She was carrying coal, and Maffitt transferred as much of her cargo aboard the *Florida* as he could. Five of the *Red Gauntlet's* crew agreed to join that of the *Florida*. The capture of the Connecticut clipper *Benjamin F. Hoxie* led to ramifications. She had a mixed cargo of timber and silver bars, a value of $105,000. The timber was a legitimate target, but not so the silver. The manifest declared it to be a neutral cargo belonging to an English bullion house, F. Huth & Co. of London. The silver was loaded aboard the *Florida,* and it eventually found its way to Bermuda. From there its provenance was proved, and it was shipped to Liverpool. The *Benjamin F. Hoxie* was set ablaze. What happened next is taken up by the United States embassy's London based junior secretary, Benjamin Moran, in his journal: "Thurs. 20th August 1863: We had a visit from one of the partners of F. Huth & Co., who wanted Mr. Adam's cooperation in recovering a large sum in silver bars belonging to them which had been stolen by the Oreto from the Ben F. Hoxie, an Am. Ship burned by that pirate, and brought to Liverpool in the steamer Eagle from her yesterday. I am glad this property was British and am sorry it was not twice as much."

Events took a curious turn, as Moran recorded some four days later. In accordance with instructions the silver bars were dispatched to Huth's, but something happened: "Mon. 24th August 1863: Mr. Huth's partner has been here again. He says the silver was sent up to London by Fraser, Trenholm & Co., the very night it was landed at Liverpool, and forwarded hence by way of Southampton to Paris, where it was seized in a smelters. He hopes to recover, but has his doubts...."

Unaware of these ramifications yet to come, the *Florida* sailed on. She captured the Providence, Rhode Island, registered whaling schooner *V.H. Hill*. As a matter of expediency, rather than put her to the torch Maffitt bonded her for $10,000 and unloaded his fifty-four prisoners on her. On 17 July, after capturing the packet ship *Surprise,* Maffitt learned from the New York newspapers of Read's incredible success. He also read of navy secretary Gideon Welles ordering some forty ships to locate and destroy his own ship, the *Florida*. Audaciously, rather than turning and heading for some neutral port, Maffitt laid in a course for New Jersey. In a gap in the early morning fog, Maffitt chanced upon the USS *Ericson*, a four funneled side-wheel steamer recently requisitioned for naval purposes. He went after her, but in the swirling fog she somehow eluded him. The brig *W.B. Nash* was not so lucky. With a cargo of 650,000 pounds of lard she was set ablaze. The whaling schooner *Rienzi*, back from a whaling expedition in the Pacific, soon followed.

Maffitt by his successes had drawn attention to his whereabouts. With some forty armed federal vessels scouring the Atlantic seaboard for the *Florida*, Maffitt decided to head southeast for Bermuda, his ship badly in need of repair. He himself was suffering a mild form of yellow fever. The months at sea had taken their toll and the *Florida* was in urgent need of a complete overhaul. She entered the port of St. George's on 16 July 1863. Maffitt requested to be allowed to re-coal and undertake repairs. He was granted a stay of eleven days, but no more. Leaving a junior officer in charge of the day-to-day operations, Maffitt was able to recuperate at the home of Mr. D.B. Heyle, a British merchant living at Hamilton. As a way of thanking him, Maffitt presented him with an inscribed silver cup, dated 20 July 1863. To his host's son, H.C. Heyle, he gave the new Confederate flag, to replace an old design, that the son flew from a flag post in front of the house. The new flag, carefully looked after, was eventually donated to the city of Alabama in 1912, and it now forms part of the collection of the Alabama Department of Archives & History.

At Nassau, the U.S. consul sent word to the mainland of the arrival of the *Florida*. As the Confederate raider prepared to be put into dry dock, the Iroquois class screw sloop of war USS *Wachusett* sailed into port and anchored nearby. The British authorities acted quickly and warned the *Wachusett*'s captain of the neutrality law pertaining to belligerents. The United States ship would not be able to leave the port until twenty-four hours had elapsed following the departure of the Confederate ship. The presence of two Royal Navy warships in harbor at the time emphasized the governor's authority. Other U.S. warships, thanks to the vigilance of their consul, were now making their way towards Nassau. Maffitt realized that delay would mean probable capture and destruction. On 27 July the *Florida*, with engine problems and the copper sheets on her hull coming loose, steamed out of Nassau harbor on a course for Europe.

In strict accordance with British Neutrality Law, Maffitt knew that he could not enter a British port for a further ninety days. He might perhaps try, insisting that his ship was not seaworthy, but he had no guarantee that his request would be agreed to. So he set course for the French Naval Yard at Brest in Brittany.

By mid-August he was off the coast of southern Ireland. A clipper came into view, flying the United States flag. The *Florida*, not forgetting her mission even though she was in dire need of a complete refurbishment, set off in pursuit. Overhauling the ship, which proved to be the 868 ton clipper *Anglo-Saxon*, out of Liverpool, bound for New York with a hold of good Welsh coal, Maffitt took what he needed, then burned her. He brought the *Florida* to anchor just outside of Queenstown (Cobh), the port for Cork, and put ashore Lt. Averett and a couple of other crew members. Averett telegraphed the Confederate commissioner in Paris, John Slidell, requesting that he contact the French authorities to get permission for the *Florida* to dock for repairs. Then he proceeded on to France himself, by rail and ferry. Maffitt cautiously sailed round the Irish coast, fully aware that at least two Federal warships were operating this side of the Atlantic Ocean and were actively looking for his ship.

The sinking of the *Anglo-Saxon* did not go unnoticed, nor did the arrival of Averett. Word was quickly dispatched to the American embassy in London. Moran noted the following in his journal: "Tues. 18th August 1863: A telegram from Eastman at Cork fell like a bomb into the Legation this morning. He says the pirate 'Oreto' touched at a point near that port early today and landed three of her officers, having burned an American vessel just before. This arrival accounts for the rebel movement lately at Queenstown.... We telegraphed to Madrid news of the arrival of the 'Oreto,' so that the 'Kearsage' might be sent after her. But I fear it will amount to nothing, for our war ships seem to be under the command of those who fear to engage these pirates."[21]

Maffitt sailed into Brest Harbor on 23 August. Upon arrival he reported to the prefet maritime, Vice-Admiral Count de Gueyton, as previously arranged through John Slidell, informing him of the necessity of a thorough refit for the *Florida*. On 3 September Maffitt sent one of his officers with a letter to Bulloch in Liverpool. It detailed the defects of the *Florida* and the requirements to make her seaworthy. Maffitt explained: "We must dock, relieve our shaft, which has got out of line, and replace some of our copper. We want also a blower to get steam with the bad coal we are often obliged to put up with.... Since leaving Mobile we have been under a constant pressure without a friendly port in which to overhaul or give ordinary attention to the engines."[22]

Bulloch approached the builders of the *Florida*, William C. Miller & Sons, of Toxteth, and arranged for representatives of that firm to go over to France and inspect her, then report on her condition. As there was no commercial dock at Brest, gentle pressure was exerted to use the government naval dock. An initial assessment estimated that the work would take five to six weeks. Meanwhile, possibly breaching French neutrality laws, the *Florida's* guns were taken ashore for refurbishment. An application was made to land some of the gun carriages for the same purpose, but this request was denied. However, a secret arrangement was made for a firm in Nantes to make new carriages, and these were later delivered to the *Florida* off the island of Belle Isle, together with other articles of contraband of war. Once underway, the repairs at Brest, rather than taking weeks, were taking months. Maffitt was obliged to discharge a large number of his crew. He paid them off and sent them with a letter to Bulloch at Liverpool, asking him to find them work. Their arrival did no go unnoticed. The ever efficient American consul at Liverpool, Thomas Dudley, wrote to the American ambassador in London, Charles Francis Adams, of their arrival. Benjamin Moran, the under secretary at the Legation, wrote in his Journal: "Thurs. 10th September 1863: Mr. Dudley reports the arrival of 75 of the crew of the pirate Oreto at Liverpool to join Laird's rams. These men had a letter from Capt. Maffitt to Bullock, asking him to employ them. They were no doubt sent to man the ironclads."[23] Moran need not have worried about the ironclads being constructed at Laird's. The British government had decided that the rams by their very construction were not mercantile, but warships. Lord Russell wrote to Adams that instructions had been issued to prevent the departure of the two ironclad vessels.

As the *Florida's* refurbishments were nearing completion, Maffitt applied to the French authorities for permission to raise a new crew. Strictly, such a move violated French neutrality, but Maffitt argued that the remaining crew were so few in numbers that he was unable to put to sea. The request went to Paris, where the Imperial Cabinet decided that Maffitt should be allowed to raise a new crew. The American ambassador, William L. Dayton, vigorously objected, but he was overruled. M. Drouyn de l'Huys, the French minister of Foreign Affairs stated to Dayton, that, having made enquiries, he "had ascertained that seventy or seventy-five men had been discharged from the Florida at Brest, because the period for which they had been shipped had expired, and that the Government had concluded not to prohibit an accession to the crew, inasmuch as such accession was necessary to her navigation."[24]

The argument was a fine point of international law, which Dayton saw as a breach of French neutrality. As a sop, Drouyn de l'Huys pointed out to him that Maffitt could not recruit French nationals for service in the Confederate navy. Maffitt, however, did not want Frenchmen, he wanted English-speaking sailors; and these were readily available just the other side of the Channel. Bulloch and his agents began recruiting English sailors, who were engaged in small numbers to avoid attracting the attention of the vigilant American consuls based at England's major seaports. The sailors were taken by couriers to Calais and the other Channel ports, then by rail to Brest. In order to avoid a breach of British neutrality laws, which were now being vigorously enforced, the sailors were not told what they were wanted for until they were aboard the *Florida*. There were few objections when they were told, and fairly soon the Confederate ship had a new British crew.

Shortly after the arrival of the *Florida* at Brest, Maffitt's health gave out. The attack of yellow fever at Cardenas had left him in a weakened state. Exposure at sea brought on rheumatism of the heart. The constant worry and exertions to get the ship ready for sea had also taken their toll. It seems that Maffitt then suffered a mild stroke. He accepted that physically he could no longer captain the *Florida* and would need a period of convalescence to recover his strength. He wrote to the naval secretary, via Commander Maury, then in Paris: "I regret to inform the Department that in consequence of impaired health I shall be under the necessity of applying for a detachment from this vessel."[25]

It was Maury who responded to Maffitt's request to be relieved from duty:

HOTEL DE'L'AMIRAUTE, RUE NEUVE, ST. AUGUSTIN, PARIS

September 9, 1863.

Sir,

I have received your letter of the 5th instant, enclosing the surgeon's certificate with regard to your health, and asking to be relieved from the command of the Florida on that score.

I am grieved to learn that your health has given away under the severe trial it has undergone in the Florida, and I am sure our countrymen will also learn with regret that they have to lose, even for a time, the services of an officer who has done so much to spread the fame of their flag over the seas. Let us hope that your health may be speedily restored.

An officer will be sent as early as practicable to relieve you. In the meantime I would be glad to know your wishes as to the length of your leave to remain in Europe, or as to orders for returning home.

Respectfully, etc.,

M.F.MAURY.

Commander, C.S. Navy.[26]

Maffitt's replacement was Joseph N. Barney, the self-same Barney that had temporarily been put in charge of the *Florida* back in Mobile. Though it is not stated in the official records, the suggestion is that Maffitt was not too pleased with his replacement. He need not have worried though, Barney had health problems too and never took the *Florida* to sea. On 6 January 1864 Barney was relieved of command, which passed to Lt. Charles Manigault Morris. Though lacking Maffitt's flare, Morris was more than capable of continuing the *Florida's* successful career. Charles M. Morris was born in South Carolina, and was appointed a midshipman in the United States Navy in December 1837. He was promoted to the rank of lieutenant in 1851. He resigned his commission in January 1861, and two months later he was appointed first lieutenant in the Confederate States Navy. Morris served on the Savannah Station from 1861 to 1863 before being appointed to the *Florida*.

Touchingly, the surviving members of Maffitt's original crew, as an undoubted mark of respect to the man, wrote a petition requesting to be transferred with him to his new vessel:

Brest, September 16, 1863.

Sir,

We having heard that you are about to leave us to take command of another Confederate States vessel, and having received so much kindness and consideration from you, most respectfully desire to be transferred to the vessel you are to command.

Hoping sir, that you will not consider our writing to you any breach of discipline, but as a desire to be again under your command, sir, we are,

Very respectfully,
Your most obedient servants,

Wm. Boynton	Wm. Wilson
Coxswain	Seaman
John Ross	Thos. F. Brown
Quartermaster	Seaman
Wm. Sharkey	Thos. Kehoe
Seaman	Quartermaster
Wm. Patten	Wm. Covel
Seaman	Quartermaster
James McDonald	John Hogan
Seaman	Fireman
John McDonald	Matt. Woods
Seaman	Fireman
James Hawthorn	James Hewett
Seaman	Ordinary Seaman[27]

Maffitt, however, due to ill health, was some months away from taking up a new command.[28] While repairs continued aboard his former ship, American spies at Brest kept the U.S. naval secretary up to date regarding progress. After the widely publicized havoc caused by Maffitt and Read to American shipping, and the savage criticism of himself in the American press, Gideon Welles was determined that the *Florida* should not escape. The USS *Kearsage,* under Captain John Winslow, was sent to Brest to keep watch. She entered the port on 17 October in order to take on coal. This appears to have been but a pretext for her to take a closer look at her adversary, for the amount she took on was minimal. The *Kearsage* left the dock, but remained at anchor in the bay, her fires banked, ready to sail immediately should the *Florida* depart. On 30 October the *Kearsage* left, reputedly for Queenstown in Ireland, but she returned on 27 November. Again, her fires banked, she lay at anchor until 4 December, when Winslow received intelligence that the CSS *Georgia* had been sighted off the coast of Cherbourg. He set off, sure in the knowledge that the *Florida* was still in dry dock and far from seaworthy. The rumor was true, the *Georgia* had entered the port for major repairs and would be detained there for some time. Winslow decided to return to his blockade off Brest, and anchored there on 11 December.

The *Florida*, meanwhile, had completed her major repairs and was moved from the government dockyard to the merchant harbor. On 27 December, now largely refitted, she was moved to the harbor entrance, barely half a mile away from where the *Kearsage* lay at anchor. On the afternoon of 29 December the *Florida*'s crew watched as the *Kearsage* upped anchor once more and left Brest for an unknown destination. She returned on 3 January 1864, but after steaming about the bay for a few hours, departed once more. The constant wear and tear on the fabric of the *Kearsage* began to tell, and Winslow was obliged to take his ship in for repairs before a replacement Federal ship could arrive. He apparently applied to the authorities at Brest, but was turned down. He was therefore obliged to sail to Cadiz, in Spain.

Former officer of the *Florida*, Acting Master's Mate Lionel Vogel, returning home to South Carolina on leave, gave a brief interview concerning this period, which was later produced in the Atlanta newspaper, *Southern Confederacy* (10 December 1863):

> The Florida, two months ago was at Brest, in France, undergoing repairs. The officials of that city and of the French Government rendered every facility to the authorities of the ship, and for two months she occupied the Government dock, while her officers and men were the recipients of the hospitalities of the people of the city. An indication of the sympathies of the French Government may be found in the fact that the commander of the United States gunboat Kearsage made a similar application to that of the Florida, but was refused.... The discipline on board is like that of a man of war. Her complement is one hundred and thirty men and eighteen officers. All live well, clothe well, and feed well. Oysters, turkeys and delicacies of every description captured on the prizes supply their larder, and these are served in the commonest messes of the ship, with silver knives and forks. Think of that ye hungry landsmen! Captain [John Newland] Maffitt, the former commander of the Florida is now in a Confederate port, in command of a steamer owned by the State of Georgia—one of the fastest vessels afloat and in every way adapted to the purposes of a blockade runner. Lieutenant [Charles] Manigault Morris, of this state, is now in command of the Florida.

On 9 February 1864, his ship now repaired, the *Florida's* new captain, First Lieutenant Charles Manigault Morris, eased her out of the port of Brest. At Belle Isle he took onboard his new gun carriages, a slight breach in neutrality connived at by the French authorities. Exactly one week later, on 16 February, he sailed out into the Atlantic on a course set for Madeira. Two days later, the USS *Kearsage,* her repairs now complete, returned to Brest only to discover that the *Florida* had sailed barely eighteen hours earlier. Frantic telegrams were sent, and whether it was by good intelligence work at Brest, or just a good calculated guess, Commander Preble, now captain of the USS *St. Louis,* likewise set in a course for Madeira. His hope no doubt was to redeem himself of the indignity of his last encounter with the *Florida* at Mobile. The United States 300-ton sailing sloop-of-war entered the harbor of Funchal. Four days later the *Florida* arrived and docked. The ships of the two belligerent nations lay almost side by side. Diplomatic maneuvering went on apace, the Americans urging, then threatening, the locals not to supply the *Florida,* while Morris demanded his rights to restock provisions and re-coal. The governor ordered the *St. Louis* to sail, but Preble, in a bid to circumvent the neutrality law, took the curious course of unloading his guns, thus effectively turning himself into a merchant ship; as such, he was no longer subject to that law. The governor then ordered the *Florida* to sail; she had 20 tons of coal aboard. Morris wanted more, but the opportunity to escape while the *St. Louis* was incapacitated was too good to miss. The crew were summoned from ashore; word was given that they were intended for Cadiz in Spain. Steam was got up, and before the moon rose, the *Florida* quietly slipped past the *St. Louis* and out to sea. Preble discounted Cadiz, and checking his charts, banked on Tenerife in the Canary Islands as being Morris' likely destination. He was correct, but as he approached the island, the *Florida,* under sail and steam, was just leaving. Preble's was a sailing ship, and just at that moment he found himself becalmed. He watched as the Confederate ship steamed away into the distance.

Morris now crossed the Atlantic with a view to cruising through the West Indies and up the American coast. His first victim was the American-flagged ship *Avon.* He took onboard her captain, his wife, and their two children, as well as her officers and men. On 4 April the lookout saw a ship to the north. The propeller of the *Florida* was lowered and she set off once more in pursuit. Overhauling the barque, Morris discovered that she was the British ship *Frances Milly*, out of London, returning to her home port from the island of Mauritius. Its captain agreed to take some of Morris' prisoners.[29] Raising his propeller, Morris made sail once more. As daylight was breaking on 7 April, the cry went up "Sail-ho!" In the distance off the port bow Morris made out a large sailing ship. At half-past six, with the weather clearing, she proved to be a large four-masted ship, flying no national colors. With sail and steam, the *Florida* began the chase. By eight o'clock she was sufficiently close to be able to hail the other ship, which revealed herself as the *Sarah Sands* of Liverpool. Morris asked them to take some of the former crew of the *Arden*, but the *Sarah Sands'* captain refused. Not being able to compel him, Morris returned to his original course. Dead ahead was another ship. The propeller was lowered and the pursuit under steam began. By half-past three the *Florida* caught up with her, and she was boarded. She proved to be another British ship, the bark *Excelsior* registered at London and sailing to her home port from Algoa Bay, South Africa. Fortunately for Morris, she agreed to take four of the *Florida's* prisoners. At seven o'clock that evening the Spanish ship *Margarita*, sailing from Manila for Cadiz, was boarded, and her papers checked. With nothing being untoward, she was allowed to continue. For much of the following day, 8 April, it was quiet. At about half past two that afternoon, the *Florida*, flying the Stars and Stripes and pretending to be a Federal warship, overhauled the *Englishman*, a Liverpool registered ship. After examining her papers and cargo, Morris allowed her to resume her journey.

Days passed without sight of another sail. On the night of 12 April, at a quarter to midnight, as an unexpected drill, Morris called all hands to quarters. In five minutes all hands were at their stations, but it was not until almost a quarter past the hour that they were ready. It was something that Morris knew needed to be improved. His men needed to be in a constant state of preparedness. At twenty-five past twelve they were stood down. The 13th passed without incident. In the early afternoon of the following day a sail was sighted. It was another British ship, the schooner *Belle*, from Granville, Nova Scotia. She was sailing from New York to Pernambuco, Brazil. The British merchant marine seemed to be everywhere, taking over the trade which formerly would have been shipped aboard United States ships. The Confederate raiders were succeeding in their mission to drive the American flag from the sea. The best part of a week followed without Morris seeing a sail. At twenty-five past six on the evening of 20 April, two ships came into view. The first, the *Aerial*, Morris ordered to heave-to. The second ship came towards them, and she too was halted. She was the brig *Mary*, from Barbados. Both being British, they were allowed to continue. The following morning the *Florida* overhauled the Danish bark *Thetis*. Mor-

Captain Charles M. Morris succeeded J.N. Maffitt as captain of the *Florida*. (*Harper's Weekly*)

ris flew the Federal flag once more. For a Portuguese ship that he stopped the following day, he flew the British red ensign. By these deceptions Morris kept the *Florida's* location a secret.

On the morning of 26 April the *Florida* anchored in the bay of St. Pierre, on the French island of Martinique, in the Windward Islands. For four days they remained, recoaling and taking on fresh fruit, water, and other provisions. The *Florida* set sail at half-past five on the evening of 30 April. Heading north, Morris sailed for Bermuda. Off the coast at Five Fathom Hole, he received a pilot who took the ship into an anchorage. There Lt. Averett and another sick officer were put ashore, with dispatches for the Confederacy. By eight o'clock that evening Morris was again at sea and heading for the enemy's coast. The hunting resumed on 18 May, when, in the northwestern Atlantic a few hundred miles south of Newfoundland, the *Florida* captured the schooner *George Latimer*, sailing from Baltimore to Pernambuco, Brazil, with a cargo of bread, flour and lard. Presenting an opportunity for target practice, the ship was badly damaged before she sank in flames. Turning south once more, Morris made for Bermuda. He anchored at St. George's Bay, and though he was within the ninety day limit, he was given permission to remain after he was able to demonstrate that the *Florida* needed to make necessary repairs to make her seaworthy. Lt. Averett was waiting upon her return, with five new engineers and a draft for $50,000 Confederate. Seven days later, as the *Florida* prepared to embark, James Butler (first-class fireman), lately escaped from the enemy after being captured on the CSS *Atlanta*, joined the crew.

On 30 June Morris laid in a course for the enemy coast, cutting across the routes of outward bound Federal merchant shipping. His first prize was the American barque *Harriett Stevens*, which he stopped the following day. Registered at New York, she was out of Portland, bound for Cienfuegos, Cuba, with a crew of captain and eight men. Taking her crew aboard, Morris sank her. That evening he was able to off-load his prisoners aboard the Danish bark *Maria Frederica*, sailing from Haiti to Cork in Ireland. On 8 July he captured and set on fire the American whaling barque *Golconda* of New Bedford. She was laden with 1,800 barrels of whale oil. He took her twenty-three man crew as prisoners. The following day he captured and burned the schooner *Margaret Y. Davis*, from Port Royal in ballast, bound for New York. She had a crew of seven. Later that day the barque *Greenland* fell prey to the marauder. She was bound from Philadelphia to Pensacola with a cargo of coal. Morris took her crew of fourteen as prisoners, and burned their ship. The next morning it was the turn of the barque *General Berry*, of Baltimore, bound for Fortress Monroe, New York. She was laden with 1,100 bales of hay destined for the Federal cavalry. Morris burned her.

As the morning wore on, he stopped and captured the barque *Zelinda* of Brunswick, bound from Matanzas to Philadelphia. He likewise sent her to the bottom of the sea. Morris' third ship of the day was the schooner *Howard*. Instead of sinking her, he bonded her for $6,000 and transferred all his prisoners, some sixty-eight in number. All this he accomplished in one morning. That afternoon, at about half-past one, off the Capes of Delaware, a brig-rigged screw steamer, to the southeast was sighted. The propeller was lowered into the sea, and in full sail the *Florida* set off in pursuit. By two o'clock, close enough so that she would see, Morris raised the British blue ensign. The other ship responded with the United States flag. All hands were piped to quarters aboard the *Florida* as the chase intensified. At about half a mile's distance Morris ordered a shot to be fired across the craft's bow. She ignored it, and continued on with all haste. Two more shots from the

Florida flew over her, and realizing the imminent danger she was now in, her captain brought her to a standstill and hauled down her colors. Lt. S.G. Stone with a boarding party clamored aboard. She was the U.S. mail steamer *Electric Spark* of Philadelphia, out of New York, bound for New Orleans, with forty-two passengers and a crew of thirty-nine. Before Morris had time to make any arrangements a British schooner, the *Lane*, came into view. With the newly captured prize steamer following on, Morris set off after the new arrival. The *Florida* overhauled her, and after firing a blank round, she came to. After some negotiation, the captain agreed to take all of the *Florida*'s prisoners, and in exchange Morris agreed to pay $720 for the *Lane*'s deck cargo of fruit. Among the prisoners taken aboard the *Electric Spark* were Lt.-Col. James Hopkins and Lt. Waterman of the U.S. Army, and Master W.P. Gibbs of the U.S. Navy, all of whom Morris paroled. Mail from the steamer was taken aboard the *Florida* for perusal of intelligence. Later that night, as it was growing dark, the Federal mail ship's pipes were cut, her valves and ports were opened, and she slowly sank beneath the waves. It had been a good day for the *Florida* and her crew, but a day tinged with sorrow. A cutter returning from the *Electric Spark* was swamped, and Midshipman William B. Sinclair, being able to swim, gave up his place on the upturned boat to another. He was never seen again. It was believed he was taken by a shark, seen swimming near the ship. Such a day would inevitably bring a response from the Federal navy. Morris set a course for Tenerife, in the Canary Isles. Arriving there on 4 August, he re-coaled at Santa Cruz, and by two o'clock that afternoon was once more at sea. Morris set a course for Bahia in Brazil.

Down the coast of Africa, then southwest into the vastness of the Atlantic Ocean, Morris steered the *Florida*. Eighteen days out they sighted the *Southern Rights*, an American flagged ship. She was carrying a cargo of 18,000 sacks of rice owned by British merchants. As rice was a neutral cargo, Morris bonded the Union ship for $35,000, and let her continue on her way. Over the next two weeks a dozen ships were stopped and searched, but all proved to be neutrals. Bulloch in his account glosses over this period, with the phrase "Officers and crew were in fine spirits, and hoped to accomplish a good deal of work still, although American ships were fast disappearing from the high seas, or at least they were rapidly sheltering from capture under the British mercantile flag."[30] The reality was far darker. The crew, many without shore leave since leaving Brest some eight months earlier, were close to mutiny. Several were arrested and faced charges. In addition two others faced a charge of sodomy. They were fined three months' pay and discharged when a neutral ship agreed to take them.

Off the coast of Brazil, on 26 September, the *Florida* captured her last victim. She was the Baltimore registered *Mandamis*, in ballast. Morris sank her. Under Morris as its captain, the *Florida* had captured thirteen enemy ships, six of them taken in just three days. He had bonded two, and a number of others clearly American but serving under the British flag and with dubious accreditation, he had allowed to continue.

At nine o'clock on the evening of 4 October 1864, the *Florida* anchored at San Salvador Bay, Bahia. Lights were lit, and with the promise of shore leave the next day, the crew settled down for the night. The night watch observed a small craft approach, which hailed them and asked who they were. They responded that they were the Confederate States steam ship *Florida*, then asked in return who their enquirers were. The craft replied that they were from Her Britannic Majesty's steamship *Curlew*. The next morning, much to his surprise, Morris discovered that the USS *Wachusett* was at anchor nearby. Her master was the colorfully named Commander Napoleon Collins. There was no sign of a Royal

Navy steamer. The boat that had hailed them the previous night was undoubtedly from the enemy ship. Later that morning the *Florida* was visited by a Brazilian officer, and Morris stated his needs: coal, provisions and the time to make some minor repairs. The officer agreed to report the same to the president of the Province of Bahia, His Excellency Antonio Joaquim da Silva Gomes; but in the meantime, until Morris received an answer, neither he nor his crew could go ashore or hold any communications with shore. Morris agreed to this.

At midday Morris received a response that the president would receive him. Subsequently Morris was informed that just forty-eight hours would be allowed him to refit and repair. However a government engineer would be sent onboard, and if he deemed it necessary, further time would be allowed. The president was at pains to remind Morris of the neutrality laws appertaining. He sought Morris' assurance that he would not attack the *Wachusett* while in port or in Brazilian waters. He added that he had received a most solemn assurance from the United States consul, Thomas F. Wilson, that the U.S. ship would do nothing contrary to the laws of nations and Brazilian neutrality. Morris likewise gave his word. The Brazilian admiral present at the meeting instructed Morris to move the *Florida* between his ship, the corvette *Donna Januaria*, and the shore, to avoid any difficulties between the belligerents. This Morris agreed to do. Permission was also given for the crew to disembark for shore leave.

Returning to the *Florida* Morris found that the Brazilian engineer was already onboard and having inspected the engine agreed to an extension of four days in order for repairs to be conducted to the pipe of the condenser. Shore leave was granted to the port watch for a twelve hour period. That evening, at about half-past seven, a boat from the *Wachusett* came alongside. As passenger was the U.S. consul, with a letter for the commander of the *Florida*. It was received by First Lt. Porter, who, inspecting the envelope, found it addressed to Captain Morris, sloop *Florida*. It was a calculated insult, the inference being that the ship was not that of a recognized belligerent state, but rather the ship of a group of insurrectionists. Porter pointed out that the letter was improperly addressed. The vessel, he informed the consul, was the CSS *Florida*; and if the consul would care to correct the error, it would be received. The following day, a local businessman, a Mr. DeVideky, asked permission to come aboard the *Florida* to speak to its captain. As permission was granted, he informed Morris that he was there at the request of the U.S. consul, and presented Morris with a letter, still incorrectly addressed. DeVideky asked to be allowed to read a letter sent to him by the consul, which proved to be a challenge for the *Florida* to fight the *Wachusett*. Morris stated that he was at Bahia to re-coal and take on provisions, but should he encounter her outside of Brazilian waters he would gladly do his utmost to destroy the Federal ship. He returned the unopened consul's letter to DeVideky, who left.

That afternoon, the port watch having returned, Morris permitted the starboard watch to go ashore. In the company of several officers, Morris also took shore leave. At half past three the next morning, the 7th, Morris was awoken by the proprietor of the hotel where he was staying, and told that there was some trouble aboard the *Florida*, as firing and cheering had been heard coming from her. Fifteen minutes earlier, Acting Master T.T. Hunter, being in charge of the *Florida*, saw the *Wachusett* approaching at speed. Hunter hailed her, but getting no response, called the crew of the *Florida* to general quarters. Before the officers and crew could get on deck the *Wachusett* rammed the *Florida* on her starboard quarter, cutting her rail down to the deck, and carrying away her mizzenmast. Small arms fire broke out in an exchange between the two ships. The *Wachusett* pulled back, then demanded the surrender of the *Florida*. Lt. Porter, the officer in charge, refused. This refusal was followed by fire from two of the *Wachusett*'s broadside guns. Porter, fearing a great loss of life among his men, agreed to conditionally surrender, protesting violation of neutrality rights. The captain of the *Wachusett*, Commander Napoleon Collins, called for Morris to come on board. Lt. Porter informed Collins that his captain was ashore, but he as commanding officer would go aboard the Federal ship. A number of boats were lowered from the *Wachusett* with armed men to take possession of the Confederate ship. Some of the crew of the *Florida*, some fifteen in number, hearing Porter surrender, dived overboard and began swimming for the shore. The Federals opened fire on the men in the water, killing nine of their number. Others, including Acting Master Hunter, were wounded, but managed to make the safety of the shore. As cheers went up from the *Wachusett* at the success of the operation, a hawser was made fast to the foremast of the Confederate ship, and after slipping her cable, she was towed out to sea.

Now down at the landing, Morris could only stand and watch as events unfolded. He dashed over to the admiral's vessel, where he was informed that even as they spoke, the admiral was preparing a flotilla of ships to pursue the escaping Federal ship. Apparently shortly before the attack, noticing that the *Wachusett* was no longer at anchor, Commander Gervasio Macebo of the *Dona Januaria*, sent an officer over to the Federal ship to find out what she was doing. Collins was threatened that if he attacked the *Florida*, all the Brazilian ships, as well as the forts, would fire on the *Wachusett*. Collins replied that he would come to anchor once more, but as the Brazilian officer departed, Collins launched his assault. The Brazilians did fire one cannon shot loaded with ball at the *Wachusett*, but it was unsuccessful. Commander Macebo, fearful that the Federal ship would attack, had previously ordered the Brazilian sailing ship *Paraense* to be made ready

The *Florida* at anchor at Bahia, Brazil. Her seizure in a neutral port by the USS *Wachusett* caused an international incident. (*Illustrated London News*, 19 November 1864)

to sail. As soon as this was possible, she set off in pursuit. The yacht *Rio De Centes* also joined the chase. By seven o'clock, the *Paraense* was gaining on the escaping vessels, but then the wind dropped, leaving Collins in steam to make his getaway. By a quarter to twelve the *Wachusett* and her prize were out of sight. The two Brazilian craft gave up the chase and returned to Bahia. The admiral's vessel, which had also sailed, returned in late afternoon, having failed to catch up with the United States ship and her prize.

While they waited, Morris called together his men. He had four officers, Lt. Barron, Paymaster Taylor, Midshipman Dyke and Master's Mate King. Acting Master Hunter was incapacitated by his wound. In addition Morris had seventy-one men, including the six who had escaped by swimming from the *Florida* after her capture. Morris made a formal protest to the president, through the Confederate agent, James Dwyer. On the 10th, Dwyer was informed that the president did not propose to make a formal reply to Morris, as the Confederate government had not been recognized as a de jure state by Brazil. Any details, correspondence, etc., would appear in the local newspaper.

The *Florida*'s crew ashore, many of them English, expressed a desire to remain in the Confederate navy. Morris made arrangements for them to be taken to England, and there to be reassigned duties. They were taken to England aboard the English bark *Linda*, commanded by Captain Bray. Morris was charged £10 per man and £20 per officer; Morris also paid the expense of £80 for fitting up the berths. While this work was being carried out, Morris and Paymaster Taylor embarked on the British mail steamer, so as to arrive in advance and make arrangements for the arrival and disposal of his men. Before his departure Morris received a very apologetic letter from De Videky:

> Dear Sir,
>
> I feel bound to address you after the fatal affair of last night has happened. When I accepted to go on board your vessel, I did so firmly believing that the mission I had to you was meant honestly and in good faith. Had I only the slightest idea, that the man who sent me to you on a mission, as I thought of honor, at the same time mediating (as it appears now), such an infamous, blackguardly trick, as he played, I certainly never should have accepted it. How could I think such villainy to be possible? Be sure that whenever I shall meet the faithless scoundrel who calls himself a consul of the United States of America, and goes by the name of Wilson, I will take my revenge, and treat him as he deserves it. I am very sorry for what has happened, and I am still more sorry for having accepted that mission of carrying a letter or verbal communication from him. My services are at your orders if you should require them. I am still in possession of the two letters, which I did not deliver to him, as I could not find him after I saw you. He has not got your answer at all, which proves still more that miserable and lawless trick must have been mediated before and at the same time when he pretended to offer a fair engagement outside the jurisdiction of the Government of the Brazils.
>
> I am dear sir, your obedient servant,
>
> L. De Videky.[31]

The Brazilian authorities demanded an explanation from the American consul. The wording is colorful in its controlled anger:

> Sir,
>
> Having reached this Presidency the grave attempt committed by the steamer Wachusett, of the United States of North America, and which violating the neutrality of the Empire, treasonably and disrespectfully during the night set at defiance the respect due to the Empire, and in the harbor took prisoner the steamer Florida, setting aside the most sacred rights of people and civilized nations, that guards between nations belligerent any such acts, having this Presidency received the word of honor of the Consul, Mr. Wilson, to preserve the neutrality, that in explicit terms promised that the Commander of the steamer Wachusett should confine himself to his duties,

and respect the neutrality due to the Empire, and not practice any hostile act in these territorial waters. The President cannot refrain from solemnly protesting against the act referred to, the more so that the Consul is therein implicated....[32]

Consul Wilson never received the rebuke. He had abandoned his post and escaped aboard the *Wachusett,* fearing the ramifications of his actions. A similar letter of rebuke, in perhaps more diplomatic language, was addressed to the American secretary of state, William H. Seward. The president demanded the return of the *Florida* and its captured crew to Brazilian territory. Seward replied that the consul had admitted that he had advised and incited the captain of the *Wachusett,* and was active in the proceedings, and would accordingly be dismissed. Captain Collins would be suspended and brought before a court-martial. In his letter of explanation, Seward wrote: "You will also be pleased to understand that the answer now given to your representation rests exclusively upon the ground that the capture of the Florida was an unauthorized, unlawful, and indefensible exercise of the naval force of the United States within a foreign country in defiance of its established and duly recognized Government." Then in a somewhat arrogant tone Seward gave the president a dressing down: "This Government disallows your assumption that the insurgents of this country are a lawful naval belligerent; and, on the contrary, it maintains that the ascription of that character by the Government of Brazil to insurgent citizens of the United States, who have hitherto been, and who still are, destitute of naval forces, ports, and courts, is an act of intervention in derogation of the law of nations, and unfriendly and wrongful, as it is manifestly injurious, to the United States."[33]

In short, the actions of Commander Collins was Brazil's own fault for allowing an insurgent ship to use its territorial waters. Nevertheless, Napoleon Collins was brought before a court-martial as stated. He was tried, found guilty, dismissed from the service—and then with breathtaking hypocrisy was reinstated by the naval secretary, Gideon Welles. In so doing, the United States showed its complete and utter contempt for international law, and for Brazil in particular. As if that was not bad enough, American general Watson Webb added to the contempt by making a gratuitous and irrelevant insult to England. In a letter to the Brazilian minister for foreign affairs, which was later published in the Brazilian press, he expressed his regret that, if the irregularity had to occur, it had not happened in an English port. Such a remark did not go down too well in the British press, which pointed out that in those circumstances the outcome of Collins' adventure would have had a completely different ending. The "Special Relationship" had hit another low.

Secretary of state Seward wrote to the President of Bahia Province that although the captured crew of the *Florida* were enemies of the United States, they had been brought unlawfully to America, and therefore would be set free. Of the thirty-three prisoners, a number were stated to be British. These included:

Dennis Sullivan	Charles Ballinger
——— Considine	——— Conway
——— Doris	——— McNevin
——— McCabe	——— McGarroch
——— Welch	——— Taylor
——— Rivers	——— Rivers
——— Grover	——— King
——— Thompson	

The case was difficult to prove, because according to the *Florida's* papers all the men had joined the ship at Mobile and were listed as Americans. Freeing them partially acceded to Brazilian demands, but the return of the ship was a different matter. The *Florida* itself was not returned, having been accidentally sunk. The official report indicated that having been brought into American waters, she was anchored under naval surveillance and protection at Hampton Roads. While waiting for representation from the Brazilian government for her return (and her handing back to the Confederacy), she was accidentally struck by a transport carrier, badly damaged, and sank as a result. The alternative explanation was that she was deliberately sunk, rather than being returned. Lt. Porter, taken prisoner at the surrender of the *Florida,* was of that opinion. Later released, he and his men left Boston for England aboard the British and North American steamer *Canada.* Porter wrote to Morris, then in Liverpool, on 20 February 1865: "We saw the Florida before we left. She had lost her jib boom by a steam-tug running into her. A lieutenant commander told me that if the United States Government was determined to give her up, the officers of the navy would destroy her. Several other of our officers were told the same. While in Fort Warren we heard these threats were carried out."[34]

3

Semmes

Raphael Semmes, who was to become captain of the second of Bulloch's ships, had already earned a considerable reputation for his exploits against the United States merchant marine. Semmes was born on 27 September 1809 at Charles County, Maryland, in the United States.[1] He was the son of Richard Thompson Semmes, a member of an old Roman Catholic family that arrived in America with Lord Baltimore in 1640. His mother was Catherine Hooe Middleton, a descendant of Arthur Middleton, a signatory of the Declaration of Independence. Raphael had one other brother, Samuel Middleton Semmes. Their mother died when they were both very young, and in 1819 their father died. The boys were taken into care by their uncle, Raphael Semmes of Georgetown, in the District of Columbia. At the age of fifteen the young Raphael was appointed a midshipman in the United States Navy, and sent to learn his craft aboard the seventy-four gun training ship *North Carolina*. Upon leaving the training ship he was seconded to serve in an administrative function under Commodore Wilkes at his office on Capitol Hill, Washington. There then followed three years of practical experience, cruising in the Mediterranean, then the South Seas, under Commodore Wilkes' Exploring Expedition, and a cruise off the west coast of Africa, and around the Cape to the East Indies. Semmes' studies at this time included international and marine law. On 5 May 1837 Semmes, then a lieutenant in the United States Navy, married Anne Elizabeth Spencer, granddaughter of Oliver Spencer, a Revolutionary colonel in the War of Independence, and the couple moved to the Perdido River near Pensacola, Florida.

At the outbreak of the Mexican War, Semmes was placed in command of the brig *Somers*. He and his ship were ordered to join the American blockade off Vera Cruz, in the Gulf of Campeche. In a violent storm his ship capsized, and most of the crew were drowned. While Semmes and some other members of the crew were rescued by the Royal Navy ship, HMS *Endymion*, others succeeded in swimming ashore, only to be arrested by the Mexican authorities and charged with spying. With the threat of execution as spies hanging over the heads of these prisoners, Semmes was ordered by the secretary of the navy to proceed to Mexico City under a flag of truce, and there intercede for his captured men, which he did successfully. In 1849 Semmes and his young family moved to Mobile, Alabama. In 1856, after some thirty years at sea, he was appointed lighthouse inspector on the Gulf of Mexico. After two years he was appointed secretary of the Lighthouse Board, and was stationed once more in Washington.

At the outbreak of the Civil War Semmes was a commander in the United States Navy. He resigned his commission, and traveling south, offered his services to the Confederacy. He was appointed a commander in the infant Confederate States Navy. In those still unsettled days Semmes was sent back north to procure machinery, guns, munitions and the other accoutrements of war. This he did with some success. Returning to Montgomery, Alabama, the then provisional capital of the Confederacy, he learned that he had been appointed head of the Lighthouse Bureau. It was not a position he had sought, believing that he would be of more use in a more active capacity. Discovering that a board of naval officers at New Orleans were involved in procuring light fast steamships to pursue a campaign against the United States merchant marine, he requested a transfer. The naval secretary acceded to his request on a temporary basis. The board he discovered upon his arrival, had examined a number of vessels, but had discarded them all for one fault or another. Semmes read through the reports, then discovered one ship which might seem suitable following some modification.

Raphael Semmes, C.S.N., Captain of the Confederate raider *Sumter*.

She was the 437 ton, bark rigged screw steamer *Habana,* built at Philadelphia in 1859 for McConnell's New Orleans & Havana Line. Her speed was reported to be between nine and ten knots. She carried just five days' fuel, and had no accommodation for a crew. Semmes went to have a look at her, and saw the possibilities. Accordingly the *Habana* was purchased for the Confederate navy in April 1861. The next day the chief clerk of the Navy Department handed Semmes the orders Semmes had so eagerly looked forward to:

Confederate States of America

Navy Department, Montgomery, April 18, 1861.

Sir: — You are hereby detached from duty as Chief of the Light-House Bureau, and will proceed to New Orleans, and take command of the steamer Sumter (named in honor of our recent victory over Fort Sumter). The following officers have been ordered to report to you for duty: Lieutenants John M. Kell, R.T. Chapman, John M. Stribling, and Wm. E. Evans; Paymaster Henry Myers: Surgeon Francis L. Galt: Midshipmen, Wm. A. Hicks, Richard F. Armstrong, Albert G. Hudgins, John F. Holden, and Jos. D. Wilson. I am respectfully your obedient servant,

S.R. Mallory, Secretary of the Navy.[2]

Semmes returned to New Orleans on Monday, 22 April, along with Lt. Chapman, and took possession of his new ship. He then set about converting the little merchantman into a vessel of war. He set a gang of workmen to remove her upper cabins and clear her deck of all unnecessary encumbrances, then improvising as he went along, he strengthened her deck to take the battery, created new crew's quarters, put in protection for the engine, which was partly above the waterline, and altered the ship's rig so that she could be converted into a square-sailed barquentine. Guns, gun carriages and ammunition were ordered and fitted. For her armament the *Sumter* had an 8-inch shell gun, pivoted amidships, and four 32-pounders, two each broadside.

With her renovations and additions almost complete, Semmes now began choosing his crew. His lieutenants, surgeon, paymaster and marine officer had all arrived. He appointed an engineer and two assistants, a boatswain, a carpenter and a sailmaker. He then began selecting the men at a seaport full of sailors, discharged from ships laid up by the blockade. The full crew, 117 officers and men (including 20 members of the Confederate States Marine Corps), is listed on an original roll now housed at the Georgia Historical Society, Savannah[3]:

Officers
Raphael Semmes, Commander
John McIntosh Kell, Lieutenant
R.T. Chapman, Lieutenant
John M. Stribling, Lieutenant

Officers
William E. Evans, Lieutenant
Henry Myers, Paymaster
Francis L. Galt, Surgeon
William A. Hicks, Midshipman
Richard F. Armstrong, Midshipman
Albert G. Hudgins, Midshipman
John F. Holden, Midshipman
Joseph D. Wilson, Midshipman

Engineers
Miles J. Freeman, Engineer
William P. Brooks, First Assistant Engineer
Matthew O'Brien, Second Assistant Engineer
Simeon W. Cummings, Third Assistant Engineer

Quartermaster
Eugene Ruhl

Captain's clerk
William Breedlove Smith

Sailmaker
Melville P. Beaufort
Jerome Abrio, Sailmaker's mate

Carpenter
William Robinson
James Hughes, carpenter's mate

Landsmen
John Allen
Nicholas Allen, officers' steward
Thomas Barker
Patrick Curley
Ralph Darby, surgeon's steward

Seamen
Frank Alberg, ordinary seaman
Charles Bell, first class boy
Joseph Britton, first class fireman
Thomas Burnett, ordinary seaman

Seamen
John Burns, ordinary seaman
James Cotter, seaman
Thomas C. Cuddy, gunner
Frank Curran, coal heaver
John Davis, seaman/coxswain
George Dobson, seaman/quartermaster
Patrick Dougherty, fireman
George Downing, ordinary seaman
Owen Duffy, coal heaver
William Emmerson, quarter gunner
David Evans, ordinary seaman
John Farrell, ordinary seaman
James Flemming, ordinary seaman
George Forrest, seaman
William Forrestal, seaman
John Fredericks, boy
Richard Gilbert, ordinary seaman
James Graham, fireman
John Griffin, seaman
Henry Hainsworth, boy
Thomas Hambley, ordinary seaman
Joseph Heasalton, ordinary seaman
John Hickey, ordinary seaman
Samuel Higgins, coal heaver
Thomas R. Hiley, seaman
William Hilliard, ordinary seaman
James Horan, seaman/coxswain
John Howard, seaman/quarter gunner
John Jenkins, seaman
Thomas Johnson, ordinary seaman
Frank Kamp, boy
David Legget, ordinary seaman
Charles Longman, boy
Robert Maghan, seaman/quartermaster
Michael Malloy, seaman
William May, ordinary seaman
Benjamin P. McCaskey, boatswain
William McDonald, seaman

The officers of CSS *Sumter*. Clockwise from top: Lt. Chapman, Engineer Freeman, Paymaster Myers, Lt. Stribling, Surgeon Galt, Lt. Evans. Center: Executive Officer Lt. Kell.

Landsmen
Frank Drake, master at arms
John Halligan, officers' cook
Samuel Hutchinson, paymaster's clerk
Edward Lee, officers' steward
Albert Louis
Joseph Miller
William Saunders, officers' cook

Marines
Becket K. Howell, First Lt.
H.J. Thompson, Sergeant
William Hudson, Corporal
George Stephenson, Corporal
Richard Abbot, Private
William Boyle, Private
John Bryan, Private
Thomas Cleary, Private
Bernard Conroy, Private
Fred Reagan, Private
John Dunlea, Private
Michael McCoy, Private
Edwin McKeever, Private
Fred Morton, Private
William Ryan, Private
James Smith, Private
Patrick Tobin, Private
Benton Vanoken, Private
William Wallace, Private
James Wilson, Private
Richard Wilson, Private

Seamen
William McKensie, seaman
Charles Merkin, ordinary seaman
Charles Miller, ordinary seaman
Thomas Moore, boy
Stephen Mullen, ordinary seaman
Thomas Murphy, first class fireman
William Oliver, seaman
John Orr, ordinary seaman
James Palmer, coal heaver
Thomas F. Penny, ordinary seaman
Thomas Pratt, seaman/captain of the hold
Patrick Rafferty, fireman
Everett Sammon, seaman/captain of the top
William Sharkey, seaman/captain of the forecastle
Henry Spencer, seaman
George Stapleton, first class fireman
Peter Thompson, seaman
George Whipple, ordinary seaman

The makeup of the seamen was predominantly English and Irish. Barely half a dozen of the men were Southerners. Perhaps surprisingly, Semmes also had half a dozen Northerners. The officers and crew were housed temporarily aboard the tender *Star of the West*, while work continued aboard the *Sumter*. Semmes now suffered the loss of one of his young midshipmen, John Holden, and three of the men. While transferring an anchor from the *Star of the West* to the *Sumter*, the boat was swamped, and all four were drowned. It was seen as a bad omen. The work continued, and on 3 June 1861, the *Sumter* was formally commissioned into the Confederate States Navy. One of her officers noted the following in his private journal:

> NEW ORLEANS.—June 3, 1861.—This morning the Sumter went into commission. The Confederate tricolor with its eleven stars, each star representing a sovereign state, was raised at the peak of the vessel, and duly honored by a salute from her guns. For the past fortnight strenuous exertions have been used to get her ready to receive her armament, ammunition, stores, coals, &c., in order that she may get to sea before the mouths of the Mississippi are sealed by the blockading fleet of the United States Government. Already reports reach New Orleans that two ships of the enemy—the Brooklyn and the Powhatan, both steamers, and represented as having powerful batteries and being uncommonly swift—are lying off the mouths of the Mississippi. In the face of these discouraging rumors, the commander of the naval station and his subordinates have at length completed the repairs on the Habana, and christened her the Sumter—a cherished name to every Southron. Who knows but that this little steamer may bear the Southern flag to distant

seas, and win for herself an immortal name? Much is expected of her. Her model is perfectly symmetrical, her masts are long and raking, her spars slender and nicely proportioned. She is a propeller, barque-rigged, carrying five guns—four 32's, and one 68 on a pivot. Her complement of men is 114. She is to be commanded by Captain Semmes, a veteran officer of the old navy. All who know him represent him as being a skilful seaman, a good tactician, an excellent diplomatist, and a brave man.[4]

With her full complement aboard she now embarked upon trials. Semmes was a little disappointed in realizing that her top speed was only nine knots. Her coal bunkers were only large enough to take eight days' fuel, and when under sail, her propeller, which could not be raised, produced drag. Nevertheless there she was; Semmes had to make the best of her. On 18 June Semmes ordered the anchor to be raised, and the *Sumter* sailed down the river to the Barracks, just below the city. Here the *Sumter* received her powder, and an additional 12-lb. howitzer. Semmes remained here for three days, the time given over to stationing and drilling of the crew. On the 24th the *Sumter* moved down to the Head of the Passes. Beyond at anchor were two Federal blockaders, the *Powhatan* and the *Brooklyn*. Semmes sent for a pilot to navigate them beyond, should an opportunity present itself, but there was an unwillingness on their part to get involved. Semmes sent a letter to the Pilots' Association, threatening that he would arrest them for disloyalty to the Confederacy. This did the trick. The captain of the association and a number of pilots now answered the call. Semmes appointed one to remain onboard, dismissing the others. By and large, the pilots, Semmes discovered, were Northerners. In preparation for running the blockade, Semmes now sent men to each of the lighthouses to take away their lighting apparatus and break open the oil-casks. Semmes now could only wait for an opportunity to run the blockade. He wrote to Stephen Mallory, secretary of the navy:

> At present the worst feature of the blockade of Pass a L'Outre is that the Brooklyn has the speed of me; so that even if I run the bar, I could not hope to escape her, unless I surprised her, which with her close watch of the bar, at anchor near by, both night and day, it will be exceedingly difficult to do. I should be quite willing to try speed with the Powhatan, if I could hope to run the gauntlet of her guns, without being crippled; but here again, unfortunately, with all the buoys, and other marks removed, the bar which she is watching is a perfectly blind bar, except by daylight. In the meantime I am drilling my green crew, to a proper use of the great guns, and small arms. With the exception of a diarrhea, which is prevailing, to some extent, brought on by too free use of the river water, in the excessive heats which prevail, the crew continues healthy.[5]

At night, engineer Miles Freeman was instructed to keep the water in his boilers as near steam point as possible, in the hope of a dash to the sea. The hot weather broke at three o'clock on the morning of the 25th, with thunder and a heavy downfall of rain. The weather cleared and turned hot and sultry once more as the *Sumter* waited her opportunity. Sunday morning, 30 June, Semmes received fresh provisions and a hundred barrels of coal. As boredom set in, the pilot was sent ashore, but then word arrived that the *Brooklyn* had left her station in pursuit of a sail. Semmes gave orders to raise the anchor, and with steam at full pressure, she made her bid for freedom. All the time in her pursuit of the sailing ship, a telescope aboard the *Brooklyn* had been trained upon the *Sumter*. As black smoke started issuing from her funnel, the Federal ship gave up the pursuit, and turning, made her way back to her former blockading station. Both ships were equidistant as they both raced for the bar. Semmes had a slight advantage with a four knot current leading down to the sea.

"What think you of our prospect?" Semmes asked one of his officers who had formerly served aboard the *Brooklyn*, before the outbreak of war. "Prospect sir! Not the least

The *Sumter* running the Federal blockade, 30 June 1861.

in the world — there is no possible chance of our escaping that ship."⁶ Just then a boat shoved off from the pilots' station, pulled by four sturdy black men, a pilot in the rear steering the craft. As she approached, a towline was thrown to her, and the pilot was pulled aboard. Past a ship from Bremen, grounded on the bar, the pilot now steered the *Sumter* as she continued with all haste, watch being kept on the approaching Federal warship. It was touch and go. Outside the bar and out onto the high seas the Sumter sailed, the *Brooklyn* about three and a half miles distant. The Confederate ship was just beyond the range of the *Brooklyn*'s guns. She had won the race. The pilot was dropped, and the *Sumter*'s sails were unfurled. The *Brooklyn* responded, her sails filling on the starboard tack. It was not over yet. Rain started to fall, partially concealing the ships from each other. Through the rain, the *Brooklyn,* with superior speed, still continued to follow. Semmes greatly feared he would be caught. The broad flaring bows of the *Brooklyn* tore through the water, getting closer and closer.

Every now and again Semmes, his telescope trained upon the enemy vessel, caught sight of the Federal ensign, the Stars and Stripes, flapping in the breeze. On her quarter deck he saw her officers gathered, many with telescopes trained upon his ship. She was gaining on the little rebel ship. Semmes ordered the newly acquired howitzer to be thrown overboard, to lighten the *Sumter*'s, load. This was followed by 1,500 gallons of water. Engineer Miles Freeman now dashed up to the captain, informing him that steam pressure had been enlarged from 18 to 27 lbs. The engines were now working to greater capacity, giving the propeller several additional turns each minute. The *Brooklyn* was now perceived to be falling more and more behind as she passed into the *Sumter*'s wake. She was visibly slowing down. She furled her sails, now relying upon her engines alone. The *Sumter* was making ground. At half past three, after a four-hour pursuit, the *Brooklyn* gave up the chase and turned away. The *Sumter* had escaped the blockade.

South the *Sumter* sailed, away from the Confederacy, and into the Gulf of Mexico. As evening came on there was a feeling of relief, perhaps even tranquility, aboard the ship after the adventures of the day. Semmes reminisced some years later: "[T]he evening of the escape of the Sumter was one of those Gulf evenings, which can only be felt, and not described. The wind died gently away, as the sun declined, leaving a calm and sleeping sea, to reflect a myriad of stars. The sun had gone down behind a screen of purple and gold, and to add to the beauty of the scene, as night set in, a blazing comet, whose tail spanned nearly a quarter of the heavens, mirrored itself within a hundred feet of our little bark, as she ploughed her noiseless way through the waters."[7]

The following morning the sun rose in an unclouded sky. The *Sumter* was put on a southeasterly course. The awning was set as protection against the warming sun, and the crew were dispersed in idle groups about the deck. The ship maintained her course throughout that day, not seeing another soul. That night the brilliant comet once again lit a star-filled sky. Day dawned on the morning of 2 July, and by midday the *Sumter* was off Cape San Antonio, on the southern end of the island of Cuba, with a course set in for Cape St. Roque, Brazil. The following day, cloud set in as the *Sumter* ran along the Cuban coast. About three o'clock that afternoon, a cry went up: "Sail ho!" There were two ships directly ahead. Everybody aboard dashed to their designated stations as the *Sumter*, flying the British ensign, set off in pursuit. She gained upon the first ship, a brig, which hoisted the Spanish flag. Being boarded, she proved to be what she claimed to be, a Spanish ship from Cadiz bound for Vera Cruz. Leaving her, the *Sumter* began pursuit of the second ship. From her rig she was undoubtedly American, though she flew no flag. Semmes ordered a blank shot to be fired, which forced her to a halt, the Stars and Stripes being raised. She proved to be the *Golden Rocket*, out of Maine, a bark of some 700 tons, in ballast. The captain and her crew were brought aboard, with such provisions of cordage, sails and paint as were required by the *Sumter*'s sailmaker, Melville Beaufort. At ten o'clock that night the Federal merchantman was put to the torch. In his narrative Semmes goes into great detail concerning the burning of this his first prize. It is not something that came easily to him. The captain of the *Golden Rocket* was treated with great courtesy. He was invited to share the officers' mess. His crew were put up in a mess to themselves, with their own cook, who was allowed to serve up rations on a par with the *Sumter*'s crew. These were early days, and Semmes had not yet hardened his heart to the people of the North.

The 4th of July, American Independence Day, was a day that Semmes found impossible to celebrate. It was a day that celebrated the breaking of the chains of government that bound a people against their will. He captured two American ships that day. The wind was light, and there was no possibility of their escaping. Semmes ordered the Confederate flag to be raised, and for a blank shot to be fired forcing them to heave to. Boats were dispatched to both ships, the *Cuba* and the *Machios*, and their captains, along with their papers, were brought back to the *Sumter*. Both ships were recently out of Trinidad-de-Cuba, laden with cargoes of sugar and molasses, bound for English ports. As the cargoes were neutral, and both ships were sailing between two neutral ports, Semmes did not feel justified in burning the ships. He put prize crews aboard them, then took both in tow and set in a course for Cienfuegos.

While both Britain and France had issued proclamations forbidding both belligerents from bringing prizes into their ports, Spain, up to that time, had not. Speed was greatly reduced in towing the two heavily laden brigantines, so that night Semmes ordered the *Cuba* to follow on under its own sail. Soon the *Sumter* and the *Machios* were far ahead. The prize crew that Semmes had put aboard the *Cuba*, Midshipman A.G. Hudgins and four men, were later overpowered by the captured crew, who, taking control, changed course and escaped.[8] The next morning, skirting the Jardinillos reef, the *Sumter* and her existing prize continued on towards Cienfuegos lighthouse. As they approached, the cry went up: "Sail-ho!" Out to the southeast were two more ships, which by their rig were identified as American. Semmes cast adrift the *Machios*, ordering the prize crew to heave to and await his return. The *Sumter* then gave chase; it was late in the day. With steam and sail they eventually overhauled the two brigantines, which as was surmised earlier, were American. They were the *Albert Adams* of Massachusetts and the *Ben Dunning*, registered at Maine. Both had recently left Cienfuegos, with cargoes of sugar, documented in their papers as Spanish property. By now it was dark. Semmes put prize crews aboard both ships, and at anchor they waited until daylight.

As preparations were made to sail into Cienfuegos the next morning, a tug, smoke belching from its funnel, was seen leaving the town. It was towing three ships. The officer of the watch aboard the *Sumter* identified them as flying American flags. They were within Spanish territorial waters still, so Semmes knew that he could not attack them without causing an international incident. He must bide his time. By way of a ruse, he raised the Spanish flag, then the merchant flag, thus apparently requesting the pilot in the tug to take them into Cienfuegos when he was ready. Clear of the mouth of the harbor, the three American ships were let go, and their sails were unfurled. The pilot's tug steamed over to the *Sumter*, and completely fooled, the pilot boarded and requested in Spanish if Semmes wished to go into the harbor. To his surprise Semmes announced that they were Confederates, and being at war with the North, it was his intention to capture the three ships that were sailing away. Perhaps to Semmes' surprise, the pilot urged him on to capture them straightaway. Semmes declined, informing him that they were still in Spanish waters, and very properly, he would not infringe Spanish neutrality. Semmes and the pilot stood and watched as the ships sailed away. When it was agreed between them that the ships were some five miles from the coast, Semmes ordered all speed ahead in their pursuit. The Spanish flags were lowered, and the Confederate flag raised. A boom of the gun brought the American ships to a halt. With papers examined, and prize crews put aboard, the ships were revealed to be the barques *Louisa Kilham* from Massachusetts and *West Wind* from Rhode Island, and the brigantine *Naiad* of New York, all carrying cargoes of sugar, covered by neutral certificates.

Semmes shepherded his little flotilla towards Cienfuegos, collecting the *Machios*, *Ben Dunning* and *Albert Adams* on the way. The Federal flagged ships were allowed to enter the port, but to Semmes' consternation, the *Sumter* came under musket fire. The ship was ordered by gestures to come to anchor. Semmes dispatched Lt. Evans to the fort to talk with the governor. It transpired that the governor did not recognize the flag of the world's youngest nation; but when it was explained to him, he readily acceded to Evans' request that the CSS *Sumter* be allowed to enter the port with her prizes. Though only a week at sea, the *Sumter* had barely a day's supply of coal left. This was not good news. Semmes knew that if he had to re-coal every week, it would not take too long for some enterprising Federal naval captain to work out where he would be at a given time. For the moment he was given permission to take on more coal at Cienfuegos, while Lt. Chapman was dispatched to see the governor regarding the legal standing of the prize ships. Semmes wrote a very flattering letter, and in view of the unexpected bias of the pilot towards the Confederacy—or perhaps his bias against the United States—Semmes expected a positive outcome. Unfortunately, on the greater international stage, Spain decided to adopt the policy of both Great Britain and France. Belligerent prizes would likewise not be permitted to enter her ports. Much to Semmes' later disgust, the ships that the *Sumter* had captured were eventually returned to their original owners. The *Sumter* while at Cienfuegos took on one hundred tons of coal, five thousand gallons of water and fresh provisions. Upon their arrival, the United States consul had telegraphed his counterpart in Havana, Consul Shufeldt, of their arrival, a fact that came to Semmes' attention soon after. Semmes was well aware that Federal warships were often stationed at Havana. By rough calculation as to their probable time of arrival, he ensured the *Sumter's* departure occurred some few hours before their arrival, this being eleven o'clock that night. Semmes had perhaps given the Federal navy too much respect. It was two days later before the *Niagara* and the *Crusader* arrived in pursuit.

By the morning, the *Sumter* was well out to sea, sailing southeast on a course set in for Barbados. The day passed without incident, save for the frustrating pursuit of a brigantine that upon inspection proved to be Spanish. That night the *Sumter* sailed past the Cayman Islands, and on the morning of 9 July the Blue Mountains of Jamaica were seen on the distant horizon. With a trade wind now blowing against them progress was slow. The *Sumter* was making barely five knots. The sky began to darken; it was the start of the hurricane season. The *Sumter* carried on as best she could. The ship began rolling under heavy seas, and the wind whistled through the rigging. So it continued for several days. By 13 July Semmes realized that with six days' coal consumed, he could not make Barbados under steam. He altered course, raised his sail and used the wind to his advantage, turning towards the coast of Venezuela and the Dutch Island of Curaçao. On 16 July, late in the afternoon, having passed the island of Aruba, the *Sumter* arrived at St. Anne's, Curaçao. By now it was dusk. Semmes raised his jack and fired a gun to summon a pilot. When the pilot arrived he informed Semmes that it was too late to take the *Sumter* into harbor, but he would return the following morning.

Once the pilot returned to shore, it soon became common knowledge that the ship waiting to come into harbor was a Confederate ship. The U.S. consul visited the governor, demanding that she should not be allowed to enter. She was a pirate. Semmes was later given to understand that the consul even threatened the governor that if she were permitted, U.S. warships would shell Curaçao. The following morning the pilot returned and told Semmes that orders had been received from Holland that Confederate ships were not to be allowed to avail themselves of Dutch facilities. Semmes dispatched Lt. Chapman with a carefully argued letter, that the governor must treat both belligerent nations equally. The governor and the leading citizens went into conclave. The hours passed, Chapman waited. Semmes lost his patience. He ordered gun practice. The firing of guns soon brought about a decision. Chapman returned to the *Sumter* with word that she would be permitted to enter the harbor. Entering, she came to anchor, and within moments the *Sumter* was surrounded by thirty or more little boats, with friendly people wishing to trade and barter. Local washerwomen took away the seamen's clothing for washing and ironing, and there was general fraternizing both onboard and ashore over the next few days.

Repairs, painting, re-coaling and restocking of stores now filled Semmes' time. Curiously he was visited by the ex-president of Venezuela, who requested his help in restoring him to power. Despite the promises of riches and titles, Semmes was obliged to decline, reflecting upon Abraham Lincoln's response to his secretary of state: "One war at a time." Once ashore, Semmes discovered that, apart from the U.S. consul, a Boston man, there was a second American living there, a photographer by the name of John Smith, of New York. Cheekily Smith informed Semmes that he had taken photographs of the *Sumter,* for publication in the New York illustrated newspapers. On 20 July, the monthly mail packet arrived, bringing with it newspapers from America. When she sailed two days later, on 22 July, Semmes knew that it would be only be a matter of time before news of his presence on the island reached the Federal authorities. In an attempt at buying time he told the officers from the packet, in strictest confidence, that it was his intention to sail north and cruise off the coast of Cuba. During his stay on the island, Semmes lost just one member of his crew through desertion, Ordinary Seaman John Orr, whom Semmes described as "a simple lad."

The *Sumter* had remained for a week at Curaçao. By then she had been thoroughly overhauled and painted, her bunkers were filled with good English coal, and fresh provisions and fruit had been stored aboard. On the morning of the 24th the *Sumter* moved slowly out of the harbor and out into the open sea. Semmes resolved to cruise along the northern coast of Venezuela, between Laguayra and Puerto Cabello, a coastline he knew from memory. It had trading links with the United States. At dawn the following day a sail was sighted on the port bow. By half past six, the schooner *Abby Bradford*, out of New York, bound for Puerto Cabello, was a prisoner. Her captain had sailed before the *Sumter* had escaped from New Orleans, so he was totally unaware that such a ship existed. Now with another prize, Semmes decided to try his luck at a Venezuelan port. The following day, just before noon, with the Confederate flag flying, Semmes and his prize sailed into Puerto Cabello. He wrote a letter to the governor, requesting to be allowed to leave the prize vessel there for adjudication. The response was swift. The governor did not have the power to accede to the request, and therefore the *Sumter* and her prize must leave immediately. Reluctant to burn the ship, Semmes decided to run her through the blockade into New Orleans. Quartermaster Eugene Ruhl and a small party of men were ordered to do so; but as she approached the coast of Louisiana, the *Abby Bradford* was captured by the blockaders and her crew taken prisoner.

The *Sumter* moved off, but she was scarcely clear of the harbor when a sail was sighted. By her very construction, by the way she was rigged with white cotton sails, Semmes knew that she was American. For seven miles the pursuit was followed before she was overhauled and captured. She was the bark *Joseph Maxwell* of Philadelphia, out of Laguayra, bound for Puerto Cabello, with a cargo belonging to a neutral owner. With the intention of landing the cargo, Paymaster Myers was sent ashore at Laguayra to treat with the owners. Myers returned with an order from the governor that the prize ship should be brought into the port, because it was claimed she had been caught within territorial waters. Semmes detected the influence of the resident U.S. consul. He declined the offer, and putting Midshipman William Hicks aboard as prize master, ordered her to be sailed to Cienfuegos, and there left for adjudication by a prize court of the Confederate States. If that was not acceptable then Hicks was to take her a league out to sea and torch her.

Semmes set in a course eastward, along the coast of Venezuela to the British island of Trinidad. An American brigantine, hugging the coast and well within the nautical mile, slipped by unmolested. A second ship, a fore and aft schooner, stopped by the Confederate steamship proved to be Venezuelan and was permitted to continue on. By afternoon the ship ran by the island of Totuga, the sea beautifully clear. Day turned to night. Ahead of them, at about eleven o'clock, the twinkling lights of the island of Margarita were seen. Between the island and the coast of the mainland, the *Sumter* came to anchor in thirty-two fathoms. At daylight the *Sumter* resumed her cruise. Off the port bow, way off into the distance, were sighted the uninhabited islands of Los Frailes. Continuing eastwards, past Carupanu and the peninsula of Paria, the clouds thickened, and rain began to fall. In lightning flashes and heavy thunder, the rain more heavy now, the *Sumter* continued on. By nine o'clock that morning they entered the Gulf of Paria, and eased between the three islands that form the Bocas del Drago, the "Dragon's Mouth." Trinidad was just ahead. A little after midday the *Sumter* anchored off Port of Spain. A boat was sent ashore. A lieutenant went to see the Governor, while the Paymaster was dispatched to get a supply of coal, fresh provisions and fruit. The prisoners from the *Joseph Maxwell* were released ashore into the hands of the American consul.

During the afternoon officers of the garrison visited the Confederate ship. Semmes was amused at their caution. Rather than risk being seen to be less than neutral to both belligerent nations, they wore civilian dress. This aside, they showed warm support for the Confederate cause. The *Sumter* remained at Trinidad for four days, re-coaling. It rained off and on the whole time. On 5 August Her Majesty's steam frigate *Cadmus* entered Port of Spain. Semmes sent a lieutenant over to her to pay his respects to her master, Captain Hillyar. The two captains met and came away with a feeling of mutual respect for each other. A little later that day, with steam up, the *Sumter* eased herself out of the port.

Now several days out to sea, still hugging the coast, the *Sumter* crossed the path of a brigantine, which with a blank shot she obliged to heave to. She was Dutch, out of Dutch Guiana (Surinam), bound for home. Several days now passed without incident. On 15 August they anchored at the French penal colony of Cayenne. In the bay were four American schooners whose skippers had a monopoly on provisions. Coal and fresh provisions were thus denied to the Confederates. The main contractor here was the United States consul himself. *Sumter* sailed the next day, retracing her course to Surinam, anchoring off Bram's Point, at the mouth of the river. Not long after, black smoke out at sea was seen. It was a steamer, heading towards them. Semmes' first thoughts was that it was a Federal gunship. Daylight began to fail; the ship continued coming. Semmes ordered up steam and beat to quarters. His crew manned the guns, ready for anything. About ten o'clock the approaching steamer came to anchor about three miles offshore. Semmes ordered his men to stand down, but gave the night watch orders to keep a strict lookout for anything untoward. If she were a mail steamer, Semmes reasoned, she would have entered the port — if a packet steamer of some sort she would be brightly lit. The ship offshore was not. At daylight the steamer weighed anchor, and came on towards the mouth of the river. Semmes once again ordered all men to their posts. Steam was got up and the anchor raised. The *Sumter* was ready for combat once more. The approaching ship flew no flag. Semmes decided to see what nationality she was. He raised the French tricolor. To his relief she responded, not with the Stars and Stripes, but with a matching tricolor. She was French. After identifying each other it was agreed that the Sumter would follow her into port. The French ship was the *Vulture,* a somewhat aged side-wheeled steamer out of Martinique, carrying convicts, bound for Cayenne. Her only armament was carronades, obsolete naval guns with short barrels and large bore. The two ships anchored off the town of Paramaribo. A lieutenant was dispatched ashore to treat with the Dutch governor. Meanwhile the traders of the town arrived aboard the *Sumter* to take orders for provisions. Among the bidders for coal was, as Semmes described him, a *"gentleman of color."* It was he who was eventually given the order. Slavery was still practiced in Dutch Guiana, but as Semmes added, it "is held by a very precarious tenure, here, and will doubtless soon disappear, there being a strong party in Holland in favor of its abolition." To Semmes' surprise, hypocrisy upon hypocrisy, the American consul at Paramaribo, a Connecticut man, was also a slave owner. Worse was to come; after failing to prevent, by cajoling and threatening, the provisioning of the *Sumter,* he enticed away Semmes' servant, a former slave called Ned. Semmes later discovered that Ned had been whisked away upcountry and set to work on the consul's plantation. Ned escaped and returned to Paramaribo, where he was able to get a job aboard a Europe-bound ship. At Southampton he boarded the CSS *Nashville,* where he told his story. He was last heard of in one of the black suburbs of Washington, where he died of cholera.

While in port, the *Sumter* belowdecks was given an overhaul. The water tanks, which provided more water than was necessary, were shortened, and the coal bunkers enlarged. As a consequence the *Sumter* could then carry twelve days' supply of coal, as opposed to eight, formerly. A Dutch mail steamer came in with news of battles at home. The next day the French steam warship *Abeille* arrived. On Sunday morning, Semmes went ashore and attended Mass. The congregation was racially mixed, and there was no seating order. Everyone mixed freely. It was something of a revelation to the captain. Later that day Semmes learned from a Dutch naval lieutenant that the enemy steamer, the USS *Keystone State,* was actively looking for them. Their preparations were almost complete, when further news arrived that cheered the hearts of Semmes and his crew. There had been a great Confederate victory at Manassas. General Beauregard had defeated McDowell and Winfield Scott.

On 30 August, after ten days, the pilot boarded the *Sumter* and took her down to the coast. While they waited for the last arrangements to be made, Semmes availed himself of the opportunity of visiting a sugar plantation that lay close by. It was a happy place, and it opened his eyes to how things could be in the South. The following morning his paymaster and the remaining crew returned; the *Sumter* slipped anchor and steamed out to sea, heading north. Out of the sight of land, Semmes altered his course to east-southeast. Four days on, the *Sumter* passed the mouth of the Amazon, then crossed the equator into the Southern Hemisphere. On 5 September the *Sumter* approached the entrance to San Juan de Maranham, Brazil. There was no pilot available, so cautiously the *Sumter* proceeded on. Taking the middle ground of the Meio, she moved upstream. Then suddenly she came to a juddering halt as she found herself stuck on a sandbank. Her engines were brought to a halt. Having regained composure, Semmes ordered the engines to be reversed; and with the aid of the current, she slid off the sandbank. Onshore some fishermen had gathered, and Semmes persuaded one of them to act as pilot. Three hours later the Confederate ship anchored in the port of Maranham. Despite the strong objections of the American consul, a dentist by trade, Semmes and the crew of the *Sumter* enjoyed the warmth and hospitality of the officials and citizens of the town. The American objections were seen to be lies and half-truths, and Semmes reserves two pages in his book to the chicanery of this individual. It was while here that Semmes learned the fate of his former prize ship, the *Cuba.* Refitted and repainted, the *Sumter* got underway on 15 September. It had been Semmes' intention to run down the coast but with the weather worsening, Semmes pointed the *Sumter* north into calmer waters.

For ten days the *Sumter* sailed north and into becalmed waters. On the 25th a sail was seen to the northwest. The engines were brought once more to life, and the chase began after the distant brigantine, for so she proved to be. Approaching her, Semmes ordered the Federal flag to be raised. The quarry likewise raised the Stars and Stripes and waited to be boarded. The enemy flag was hauled down aboard the *Sumter,* and the Confederate flag was raised. A boat was sent across to take her prisoner. She was the *Joseph Parke* of Boston out of Permambuco, in ballast and returning home. Captain Briggs and his crew were transferred to the *Sumter,* along with whatever provisions were needed. Lt. Evans, two midshipmen and some seamen were put aboard the prize ship. After two days Semmes recalled his men, and the *Sumter*'s gunners practiced their craft before the brigantine sank in flames. Sailing on, Semmes crossed the traditional sea routes, but found no American merchantmen to pursue. Only neutral ships sailed these waters now. Semmes set in a course for the French island of Martinique.

On the voyage north they espied what they thought was an American-built ship. The telescope revealed that she was flying the British ensign, but Semmes had his doubts. The engines were engaged, and under sail and steam the *Sumter,* flying the United States flag, set off in pursuit. The quarry loaded on all the sail she could, and set off at a real pace. A blank shot was fired, but still she refused to heave to. The chase continued, the *Sumter* slowly gaining. A live round was fired, landing very close to the British flagged ship. Realizing that she could not escape, she gradually hauled in sail, and came to. A boarding party was sent over to her. She was the *Spartan,* registered at Halifax, Nova Scotia, hence her American look, out of Rio de Janeiro bound for St. Thomas in the West Indies. Her captain, believing them to be from a U.S. warship, was not happy at being stopped, and did not spare them the contempt he felt for their nation. He praised the Confederacy and its recent win at Manassas. As for their merchant shipping, it was scared to leave port. Asked why he was so antagonistic, he replied that he supported the Confederacy because they represented the little man, fighting against an overgrown bully. How the officers of the *Sumter* would have loved to disabuse him; but Semmes had given strict orders that they were to maintain the ruse that they were the hated Yankees.

For the best part of a month they continued northwards, not seeing an American flagged ship. The captain of the *Spartan* was right. On 24 October, flying the United States flag, they chased a French brig, the *La Mouche Noire,* forty-two days out of Nante, bound for Martinique. On boarding her they discovered that her captain had only a vague notion that there was some sort of disturbance in America. After a brief search, she was allowed to continue on her way. The following day the *Sumter* overhauled a Prussian ship, somewhat of a novelty, they being so rare. Sunday, 27 October, dawned. The crew breakfasted; Semmes was on the point of calling a muster, when the cry went up of "Sail-ho!" Steam was got up, and black smoke poured from the funnel as the *Sumter* began the chase. The quarry was a fore-and-aft schooner, with milky-white sails, typical of New England. From her main topmast she flew the Stars and Stripes. She was fast, and it was only after some six hours that the *Sumter,* flying the Confederate flag, got close enough to fire a blank round towards her. She hauled in her canvas, and gave up her flight. She was the *Daniel Trowbridge* of New Haven in Connecticut, out of New York, bound for Demerara in British Guiana. She was a veritable menagerie, with pens on deck for sheep, geese and pigs. Before the boarding party could proceed belowdecks, another sail was sighted. The *Sumter* set off after her, the prize crew aboard the *Trowbridge* ordered to follow as best they could. It was dark before the other ship was overhauled. She proved to be a British brigantine, out of Nova Scotia, likewise bound for Demerara. The Confederate ship returned to her prize. Together they rode out the night, side by side. In the morning, and well into the next day, animals and other provisions were transferred to the *Sumter*, enough supplies for five months. The Connecticut ship, her crew transferred, was then set on fire. That same day they chased and boarded the Danish brig *Una,* sixty days out of Copenhagen, bound for Santa Cruz. Flying the American flag, the *Sumter* was taken for a Federal warship. Over the next few days progressing towards the West Indies, the *Sumter* overhauled a number of ships, but all were neutrals.

On 2 November, the sky filled with rain. A sail was seen in the distance. Steam was got up for the chase, and at seven that morning, the ship heaved to and received a boarding party. It was another neutral ship, the English brigantine *Falcon,* out of Halifax, bound for Barbados. Semmes obtained some recent American newspapers from them. They revealed that the cruiser USS *Keystone State* had lately been at Barbados, but then sailed for Trinidad in pursuit of the *Sumter.* Another Federal ship, the USS *Powhatan,* commanded by Lt. Porter, had been at Marahan, barely a week after the *Sumter's* departure. At some time the two belligerent ships must have passed each other. The following day saw the brief pursuit of an English steamer. The *Sumter* approached her, but, ascertaining her status from a short distance away, did not seek to board her. The *Sumter* once again flew the Federal flag. Over the next three days the *Sumter* stopped and boarded several ships: the English brigantine *Rothsay,* from Bermuda bound for Liverpool, the French brigantine *Pauvre Orphelin,* from St. Pierre for Martinique, the *Plover,* from Barbados for London, the English schooner *Weymouth,* from Nova Scotia, bound for Martinique, and the French brig *Fleur de Bois,* out of Martinique, bound for Bordeaux.

The *Sumter* continued on, past the islands of Marie Galante, then Guadeloupe and the Saints. She sailed north of the island of Dominica, then south for some thirty miles or so, in the hope of crossing an enemy ship on its way home from the Windward Islands. All she saw was another English ship out of Demerara, heading home to Yarmouth. At eight o'clock the *Sumter* approached the island of Martinique, and the town of St. Pierre. She anchored off the coast that night, and in the morning ran along the coast to the little town of Fort-de-France, where she came to anchor. She had been nearly two months at sea. The following day Semmes visited the governor of the island, Rear Admiral Maussion de Conde. The admiral agreed to takes Semmes' prisoners, and to allow the *Sumter* to re-coal from the government dockyard. Discovering Semmes to be of French descent, and a Catholic, he invited him to attend Mass the following day. That Sunday after Mass, Semmes returned to the *Sumter,* to discover it crowded with visitors. During their stay the Confederate officers were wined and dined by the local gentry. While here, Semmes learned of the "Trent Incident" and Britain's demand that the four Confederate delegates be freed. The ultimatum of an apology within seven days or there would be war brought fresh hope of Britain joining the conflict, which would inevitably see the establishment of a Confederate state. The news that the British minister, Lord Lyons, and the staff of the embassy were on the point of leaving Washington added to Confederate hopes. While Semmes was still awaiting the outcome, the *Sumter's* water tanks were filled and the ship got up steam and proceeded to St. Pierre for coaling. That evening she lay at anchor at the man-of-war anchorage, south of the town. With the frequent passage of steamers among the islands Semmes was aware that it was only a matter of time before news of his presence reached the ears of some Federal naval captain. It was his earnest desire to be gone from Martinique within twenty-four hours.

At two o'clock that morning, the USS *Iroquois* appeared at the entrance to the port of St. Pierre. She was flying the Danish flag. Aboard the *Sumter,* the night watch was not fooled. They knew her by sight. On the quarter deck of the *Iroquois,* her officers, with telescopes, scanned the ships in the harbor for the *Sumter.* They spied the Confederate pennant. The Danish colors were lowered, and the Stars and Stripes were raised. By now everyone aboard the *Sumter* was awake and on deck. Without noise the crew of the *Sumter* were called to arms. The ship was cleared for action. On shore those who witnessed the arrival of the *Iroquois* thought that she would give battle there and then. The French authorities spoke to Captain Palmer of the *Iroquois,* warning him against anything foolhardy. Over the next couple of days a game of cat and mouse took place. The *Iroquois* moved out to sea and there stood blockading the port. Early the next morning at one o'clock, and again at three, the *Iroquois* entered the port and moved alongside the *Sumter.* Each time the Confederate ship was prepared for action. Each time the Federal ship withdrew. Later that morning the French gunboat *Acheron,* of eight guns, commanded by Captain Duchatel, arrived from Port Royal to enforce French neutrality. An officer was sent aboard the *Iroquois* to inform Captain J.S. Palmer that he must either come to anchor within the port or go three miles outside the harbor. The Federal ship withdrew a league beyond St. Pierre.

The harbor of St. Pierre is crescent shaped, the distance between the two points three miles. Throughout the day the *Iroquois* sailed backwards and forwards between those points. Within the port, alongside the *Sumter,* was anchored a Federal merchantman, a lumber schooner from Maine. Sending a man ashore, Palmer had arranged with her master, by an elaborate system of lights, to indicate if the *Sumter* started to move off and in which direction she was headed. It looked as if a battle was imminent. Crowds lined the harbor waiting for the fight. By the night of the 23rd, the game had gone on for nine days. By his calendars Semmes knew that the moon would not rise until seven minutes past eleven. This was the night Semmes decided he would either escape or be captured. The *Iroquois* was not only twice as heavy as the *Sumter,* she was also faster, and better armed.[9] Every man was assigned his station. Out at sea the *Iroquois* was visible by the aid of telescopes, watching for the *Sumter.* At eight o'clock the harbor gun was fired, to indicate that the harbor was closed for the night.

Now the *Sumter's* engines were engaged. She started to move off, to the accompaniment of deafening cheers from the assembled multitude around the marketplace. With no lights showing, she moved off to take up a course heading for the southern exit. Close past the *Acheron* she sailed, her French crew cheering on the Confederate ship. From the rear of the *Sumter,* an officer watched for a signal from the lumber schooner. Two red lights were lit, one above the other. Semmes interpreted them—one that his ship was under sail, the second that she was heading south. On for several hundred yards the *Sumter* sailed, and into the shadows cast by the mountains. With his telescope Semmes saw that the *Iroquois* was making for the southern channel. Now he quickly spun the wheel to take her to the northern exit. For the first half hour everyone held their breath, hoping against hope that the Federal ship, realizing her mistake, would not set off in pursuit of the *Sumter* by the northern channel. As if by a miracle, it began to rain, falling in torrents, offering further cover to the escaping ship. Then she was out of the harbor, hugging the coast for four or five miles as she ran down to the south end of the island of Dominica. Leaving the island behind, Semmes set in a course of NNW. By the time daylight came the *Sumter* found herself alone in an empty sea.

Monday, 24 November, flying the United States flag, the *Sumter* gave chase to an hermaphrodite brig. She responded by raising the British red ensign. The *Sumter* returned to her earlier course. That afternoon they had more luck. A large ship came on towards them. The Federal flag was raised aboard the *Sumter*. The other ship responded by raising the Stars and Stripes too. The Sumter waited until she approached close enough, then brought her to a halt. She was the *Montmorency,* of Bath, Maine, having sailed from Newport in Wales bound for St. Thomas, with a cargo of coal. Her cargo properly documented as being British, the ship was spared; but Semmes bonded her, and made her crew swear not to take up arms against the Confederacy. The ship continued on to St. Thomas, and the *Sumter* resumed her NNW course out into the Atlantic. On the morning of the 26th a ship was observed running in their direction. After some careful study she proved to be a somewhat antiquated wooden ship of war. On she came; Semmes ordered up the United States flag. She responded with the colors of Spain. By her course she was heading for Cuba. Dipping their colors the two warships passed each other.

Not long after, the cry went up again: "Sail-ho!"—perhaps with a little more vigor. This was real quarry. She was a schooner, and by her distinctive construction, American. The chase was on, steam aiding the pursuit of the hunter. In two hours the schooner was close enough for the *Sumter* to fire a blank round. The schooner took in sail, and heaved-to to receive a boarding party. She was the *Arcade,* of Portland, Maine, with a cargo of wooden staves, bound for Guadeloupe. With no documentation to indicate her cargo belonged to a neutral, she was judged a lawful prize, and she and her cargo were burned. The *Sumter* continued on NNE, a course set in for the Azores. The furnaces were banked down; half the *Sumter's* fuel had been expended. The remainder of the journey would be made under sail. The *Sumter* crossed through the accepted Atlantic trade routes from Europe, but saw no other sail. The crew were issued with winter clothing. November turned into December. On the 3rd the long awaited cry was heard: "Sail-ho!" The *Sumter* was not in steam—her funnel had been lowered—but the ship was heading slowly towards them. The wind was light. The French flag was raised aboard the Confederate ship. On came the quarry. She hoisted the United States colors in response. On she came, and when she was within close range the Confederate flag was raised aboard the *Sumter*, and a blank round was fired. The American ship took in sail and came to a halt. She was the *Vigilant* from Bath, Maine, bound for Sombrero in the West Indies to collect a cargo of mineral guano. Among her cargo in the hold was discovered a rifled 9-pounder, with a supply of ammunition, and some small arms. She also had a supply of newspapers, detailing among other things, the *Iroquois'* blockade of the "Pirate *Sumter*." Ten members of her crew of twenty-one were Negroes, who feared the worst, but they were reassured that nothing would happen to them. They would not be dragged off into slavery.

Five days passed in an empty ocean, and the weather closed in. Then out of nowhere emerged a sailing ship. Semmes ordered the Stars and Stripes to be raised, the other ship, a whaling bark, responded with the same. A boarding party was sent over to her. She proved to be the *Eben Dodge,* twelve days out from New Bedford, heading for the Pacific Ocean. She had been subject to a heavy gale, and was leaking badly. From her the *Sumter* took wet-weather wear—pea-jackets, whaling boots and sou'westers. Two whale-boats, so sturdy in stormy seas, were also brought onboard. Her crew of twenty-two transferred, she was put to the torch. With prisoners equaling crew, Semmes was obliged to take precautions. Where formerly prisoners had been given more or less free range of the ship, Semmes was now obliged to put half of them in single irons—manacles on one wrist only. The arrangement was that half would be manacled for twenty-four hours, then a change-over for the following period. Even the prisoners seemed to see the sense in such a precaution, and apparently did not view it as too great an indignity.

The weather became unsettled; the *Sumter* was sailing into a gale. Semmes changed course, but could not outrun the storm. Rain came down in torrents, the wind got up. The sails were hauled in. The *Sumter* would have to ride out the storm. Thunder and lightning raged; the sea became mountainous, tossing the little ship from side to side. The starboard bow was stoved in when a giant wave struck her, carrying away one of the stanchions that held the bow gun secure. A 32-pounder, it broke away, careering about the deck, until, risking life and limb, crew members secured it to the rail. Emergency repairs to the hole in the bow, with nailed planks and canvas, kept out the worst of the weather. Crew and prisoners alike took turns to man the pumps throughout the night. Just before daylight on the third day, the storm began to abate. The *Sumter* proved to be a better ship than anyone could have imagined. Semmes later discovered that his ship had passed completely through a cyclone with a diameter of 354 miles. Tossed uncontrollably by the sea, she had been taken wildly off course. He gave up the idea of sailing for the Azores in favor of Cadiz.

Christmas Day 1861 out in the Atlantic was a day of heavy rain squalls. Semmes called to mind all that had happened since they had left New Orleans. Several years afterward, safe upon dry land, he consulted the log for that day. Amidst the regular weather records and positions was the simple note "spliced the main brace." The crew celebrated Christmas with an extra mug of grog.[10]

The old year was ending. On 28 December, within striking distance of Cadiz, the masthead watch spied a sail in the distance. All hands stood to quarters. Steam was brought up to pressure and the *Sumter* gave chase. It did not take too long before she had overhauled the ship, the *Richibucto,* an English ship out of Liverpool bound for Vera Cruz. She had a cargo of salt. She also had some English newspapers of recent date. The newspapers, black bordered, announced the death of Prince Albert, husband and consort of Queen Victoria. Other news included the resolving of the Trent affair, and of special interest to Semmes, a report of the CSS *Nashville*, under the command of Captain Pegram, capturing and burning the *Harvey Birch* in the English Channel. Over the next two days the *Sumter* chased and boarded eighteen ships. All of them were neutrals. The American maritime fleet had been driven from the Atlantic trade.

On the 31st of December, the last day of the year, a couple of sail were reported, but being so distant, Semmes held on to his course. Cadiz was a day or two away. On 3 January, the light beginning to fail, the lighthouse at Cadiz beckoned. The *Sumter* had barely a day's supply of coal remaining. The storm had damaged her, and she was leaking badly through the sleeve of the propeller. As darkness descended, she anchored just beyond the maritime league. The next morning the crew fired a gun and hoisted a jack to summon a pilot. Upon his arrival the *Sumter,* her Confederate flag flying from the mast, entered the harbor. Through the anchored ships she proceeded to her mooring. A number of ships within the harbor raised their flags in recognition of the Southern ship, including, gallantly, one of the four American ships there.

As soon as they came to anchor, the *Sumter* was visited by a Spanish health officer who placed the ship and its crew in quarantine for three days. Semmes wrote a letter to the United States consul, one Mr. Eggleston, informing him that he held forty-three prisoners, which he wished to hand over to him. The next morning a letter from the military governor was delivered. Semmes was told that he must sail from the port within twenty-four hours. Semmes wrote a letter in reply, refusing to accept the decision. The *Sumter* was not seaworthy he maintained. To order her to leave was a flagrant violation of international law. The authorities eventually relented, and word returned that the *Sumter* could land her prisoners, and that she would be given sufficient time to carry out repairs. That night a large Spanish frigate steamed down from the inner harbor and anchored alongside the *Sumter*. Semmes interpreted this as an attempt to intimidate him. If that was so they had misjudged the man. As there were no private docks at Cadiz, Semmes requested use of the naval dock. In response to this request the *Sumter* was invaded by a number of Spanish officials who came to ensure that she was as badly off as Semmes had portrayed. Eventually permission was granted. Meanwhile the telegraph wires ran hot as the American consul, having received the prisoners, now summoned warships to the harbor. While this was going on the *Sumter* was placed in a dry dock. Upon examination things were not as bad as was feared. Some of her copper-bottomed plating had come loose, some planking was indented, and as previously surmised, the leak was coming from the propeller sleeve.

While repairs were undertaken, the crew was given shore leave. The American consul was soon at work encouraging dissatisfaction and desertion among them, and in particular the Northerners. To add to his difficulties, Semmes then discovered that he had little money left to pay for repairs and coal. He wrote to the Confederate "embassy" in London. While he waited, the United States minister in Madrid, Horatio J. Perry, was exerting strong pressure, to the point of bullying, on the Spanish government to order the departure of the *Sumter*. On the morning of 17 January Semmes was ordered to depart within six hours. Semmes went ashore to see the governor to protest, but his protests were futile. Rather than try to reason with the authorities, Semmes decided to run into Gibraltar, where he thought the British authorities would be more sympathetic. A Spanish emissary then arrived to say that the *Sumter* had been given a twenty-four hour extension. But Semmes had had enough of a weak and vacillating Spanish government that allowed itself to be bullied by the United States. Late that afternoon he set sail for the Rock, some eighty miles away.

Shortly before dawn the next day the *Sumter* passed through the Straits, the lights of Gibraltar beckoning. All around them were ships queuing up, waiting to depart the Mediterranean. It occurred to Semmes that some of them might be American. Using their telescopes the officers of the *Sumter* scanned the many ships. Two of them, by their construction, were clearly American. The first they went after was standing over on the African side of the Straits, some six miles from the coast. Raising the Confederate flag, a gun was fired towards her, bringing the American barque to a halt. The *Neapolitan,* of Kingston, Massachusetts, proudly flying the Stars and Stripes, had sailed from Messina in Sicily, bound for Boston. She had a cargo of fruit, both dried and fresh, and, interestingly, fifty tons of sulphur. Sulphur was clearly contraband of war. The prisoners were quickly transferred to the Sumter, and the ship was set on fire, much to the surprise of those who watched from both the European and African coasts. The *Sumter* then set off after the remaining American ship, whose captain was well aware of his intended fate. She was the *Investigator* of Searsport, Maine, out of Spain, bound for Newport in Wales. Her cargo was iron ore, and her documentation showed it to be a neutral cargo. Semmes, always scrupulous in his dealings, released her under bond. He now turned the *Sumter* back towards Gibraltar, arriving there at half past seven that evening. The *Sumter* anchored at the man-o'-war anchorage. Everyone on the Rock was well aware who she was. They had watched her at work that day. Within minutes of dropping anchor she was visited by a boat from the English frigate HMS *Scylla*, which had guard that day. In response a boat was sent from the Confederate ship to pay respects to the port admiral.

Sunday, 19 January, the officers of the *Scylla* boarded the Sumter to pay their respects. It was clear which way their neutral bias lay. That such a small ship should have created such a stir amazed them. In response Semmes, in full Confederate uniform then paid his respects to Captain Frederic Warden of the *Scylla*, and from there proceeded to the residence of the governor, Sir William Codrington. Formalities observed, Semmes and his officers were invited to dinner, and in fact were made welcome in the officers' messes and clubs on the Rock throughout their stay. Wherever they went, support for the Confederate cause was expressed by the officers of both the British Army and the Royal Navy. News eventually arrived from the outgoing Confederate commissioner in London, William L. Yancey, on 3 February, authorizing monetary withdrawals on the house of Fraser, Trenholm & Co., of Liverpool. The following day First Lt. John McIntosh Kell and Paymaster Henry Myers were sent ashore to purchase coal. Every merchant they approached turned them down. The American consul in Gibraltar had been at work.

These merchants also supplied American ships. The consul, Horatio Sprague, warned the merchants that if they supplied the *Sumter,* then they would not receive any further orders from American ships. So they refused. The consul had been busy. He informed the Spanish government that the *Neapolitan* and the *Investigator* had been captured in Spanish waters. A Spanish naval lieutenant from Algeziras was sent to remonstrate. Semmes, from his records, including statements from the captains of the two captured

The *Sumter* captures the *Investigator* and the *Neapolitan* off Gibraltar. In her six-month adventure she captured eighteen American merchant ships. (*Illustrated London News*, 1 February 1862)

ships, was able to demonstrate that the consul was lying. Still without coal, Semmes now approached the authorities to obtain coal from the government dockyard. A week later the reply came back that this was not possible. Confederate Thomas Tait Tunstall, former U.S. consul at Cadiz then resident in Gibraltar, suggested that Semmes should try Cadiz. He agreed to go with Paymaster Henry Myers to the Spanish port to make enquiries. The two men embarked aboard a small French steamer that operated between some of the Mediterranean ports and Cadiz, via Gibraltar and Tangier in Morocco. Stopping at Tangier for a couple of hours, the two Confederates decided to explore the town. Returning to the boat they were seized by Moorish soldiers, and, in accordance with an international agreement, they were turned over as prisoners to the American consul, James De Long, on a charge of treason against the United States. In irons they were shipped back to America aboard the USS *Ino*. Eventually the extreme charges were dropped, and both men were treated as prisoners of war.[11]

A week earlier, on 12 February, the USS *Tuscarora* of nine guns, under Captain T. Augustus Craven, entered the harbor at Gibraltar. She surveyed the *Sumter,* then, leaving the harbor, she sailed over to the Spanish side, where she lay at anchor. Accordingly she then had the right to leave at the same time as the *Sumter*, rather than having to wait twenty-four hours before departing. Semmes eventually succeeded in obtaining coal. However, as he prepared to move the *Sumter* over to a coaling ship, an accident occurred to one of the boilers, forcing them temporarily to postpone taking on coal. On 10 March the USS *Kearsage*, of seven guns, commanded by Captain Charles Pickering, and which had arrived at Algeciras on the 7th, steamed over and anchored astern of the *Sumter*. The *Tuscarora* lay a short way off, in Spanish waters. Having orders to leave the following day, the *Kearsage* sailed over to the Spanish side of the bay. Word now arrived of a third Federal warship, the USS *Flambeau,* which anchored off Tangier. Semmes conferred by letter with Mason in London. With the *Sumter's* boilers completely worn out, and the ship blockaded by three Federal warships, Mason agreed with Semmes that he should lay up the *Sumter* to the end of the war and pay off the crew. On 9 April, after several months of inactivity, the crew were paid off, with the exception of eleven men, who were to remain onboard to take care of the ship until other arrangements could be made. On the morning of 14 April 1862, having turned the ship over to Midshipman William Andrews, Semmes and his officers left the *Sumter* for the last time and caught a mail steamer for Southampton.

In her six-month campaign the *Sumter* had captured eighteen ships:

Abby Bradford	*Joseph Maxwell*
Albert Adams	*Joseph Parke*
Arcade	*Louisa Kilham*
Ben. Dunning	*Machias*
Cuba	*Montmorency*
D. Trowbridge	*Naiad*
Eben Dodge	*Neapolitan*
Golden Rocket	*Vigilant*
Investigator	*West Wind*

As a postscript, on 16 October 1862, Midshipman William Andrews was killed aboard the *Sumter* by his second in command, a man by the name of Hester, whom he had caught pilfering. Marine Sergeant George Stephenson then took command, the only Marine, Confederate or Federal, to do so aboard a ship of war during the American Civil War.

As Christmas approached, Commissioner Mason in London authorized the sale of the ship. On 19 December she was sold at auction to Mr. M.G. Klingender, an associate of Messrs. Fraser, Trenholm & Co., of Liverpool, who promptly renamed her the *Gibraltar*.

In London, Charles Francis Adams wrote a letter of protest to Lord Russell:

> My Lord,
>
> On the 19th of this month I am informed by the consul of the United States at Gibraltar, that a public sale is said to have been made of the steamer Sumter.... Having the strongest reason, from the known character and previous conduct of the alleged purchaser, to believe that this sale is effected solely for the purpose of rescuing the vessel from its present position, and of making use of Her Majesty's flag to convert it to new purposes of hostilities to the United States, I must pray for your lordship's attention to the necessity under which I am placed of asking the assistance of Her Majesty's government to prevent any risk of damage to the United States from a fraudulent transaction in one of her ports....[12]

Russell wrote back that he was aware of the sale, which was being reviewed as to its legality by the Law Officers. Adams interpreted this as prevarication, and on 3 January 1863 telegraphed the American consul at Gibraltar that Captain Bryson of the USS *Chippewa* should endeavor to capture the *Sumter* should she leave Gibraltar under the British flag. The consul telegraphed back on 21 January that the *Sumter* was coaling again. On 7 February, evading the Federal blockade, she put to sea, and arrived safely at Liverpool on the thirteenth. There she remained until 3 July 1863. Her armaments were removed, and she was converted into a blockade runner.

At Southampton, Semmes, First Lt. John McIntosh Kell and surgeon Francis Galt took a train to London, and there found rooms in Euston Square. They remained in the capital throughout much of the month of May 1862. Semmes called upon James Mason, the Confederate commissioner, and made his report. In the company of Mason Semmes was introduced to English society. He also met Commander James D. Bulloch, who at that time was the designated captain of the Confederate States steamer then being built at Birkenhead. With no prospects of a command, Semmes summoned his officers with the intention of returning to the Confederacy. Bulloch made arrangements for them to return, by way of Nassau, aboard the blockade runner *Melita*. The voyage took twenty days, the *Melita* dropping anchor at Nassau on 13 June. Semmes, Kell and Galt found rooms at the Victoria Hotel. Here at Nassau Semmes met several Confederate naval officers, including Commander J.N. Maffitt, soon to become captain of the *Florida*, and Commander G.T. Sinclair, who presented him with new orders from the secretary of the navy. Mallory instructed Semmes to return to Europe, and there to take command of the new ship being built by Messrs. Laird, known as the "290."

4

The "290"

As the *Florida* (as she was about to become) sailed out of Miller & Sons yard at Toxteth, Liverpool, on 22 March 1862, nearby, at the extreme southern end of the rival yard of Messrs. Laird of Birkenhead, the ship known as "290" was under construction. At that time, Lairds were among the finest shipbuilders in the world. It was for this reason that Bulloch chose them to build the second of his ships for the Confederate navy. Other ships under construction in their yard were of iron, so the construction of a fine wooden craft attracted some attention from passersby as they traveled up the river Mersey to Tranmere.

The 290th ship built at Laird's yard was designed as a screw steamer of some 1,000 tons. She was a beautifully designed ship with graceful curves, 210 feet in length, with a beam of 32 feet. Built to British Admiralty standards of the finest English oak, she was barque rigged, for long distance cruising when not in steam. A little forward of the mizzenmast was placed the double steering wheel, inscribed with the Latin motto *Aide toi et Dieu t'aidera,* which roughly translated means "God helps those that help themselves." Just before the funnel was the bridge, either side of which hung the two principal boats. A further two were suspended from davits on either side of the quarterdeck, and a small dinghy hung over the stern. On the main deck she was pierced for twelve guns, with two pivot guns amidships. Regarding accommodation, there was in the stern, a semicircular cabin for her captain, with a small stateroom opening out from it. Forward of this was the companion ladder, and beyond this the wardroom for senior officers, with small cabins on either side. Beyond this was the gunroom, with allocation for midshipmen on one side and the engineers on the other. The engine room lay beyond, with coal bunkers and space for tools and other accoutrements. The berth-deck, or forecastle, had room for 120 men sleeping in hammocks. Below the accommodation, and divided into three sections, were the storerooms and shell room, the furnaces and fire-rooms, and the magazine hold and carpenter/sailmakers' stores. The "290" was given twin horizontal engines of 300 horsepower each; her iron bunkers stored 350 tons of coal, sufficient for eighteen days travel under steam. When not in steam her funnel could be lowered to deck level to cut down on wind resistance, and her propeller raised to cut down on drag.

There were delays to her completion, but at no stage did Bulloch criticize the makers, for he knew that they were building what would be one of the finest ships of her class in the world. A fixed price of £42,500 had already been agreed on for her construction, before work had even begun. In his book Bulloch noted the following:

> The builders were determined to turn out a first class ship, and feeling perhaps that their obligation to do so was, if possible, increased by my absence, and the fact that there was no one to look after the interests of the owner, they were especially critical and hard to please in the selection of

the timber for the most important parts, and had discarded two or three stern-posts after they had been partly fitted and bored to take the screw shaft, because of some slight defect. This creditable, satisfactory, and punctilious care had caused some delay in completing the hull, but all the other work was in an advanced state, and the engines were ready to go into the ship as soon as she was off the ways.[1]

On 14 May 1862 the "290" was launched into the Mersey. She was christened *Enrica*, her name being a variant of that of the lady who launched her. Even twenty-four years later Bulloch refused to name the lady who launched her, lest some of the "notoriety" of the ship should attach itself to her. Playfully, Bulloch remarked, "I hope her conscience has never upbraided her since, and that she has not felt in any way responsible for the bill of £3,000,000, which her Most Gracious Majesty had to pay on account of the 'Alabama Claims.'"[2]

Soon after the contract for the construction of the ship had been signed, Bulloch made arrangements for her armaments. The suppliers were not told the purpose of the arms, or how they were to be shipped. They were simply to be prepared, packed and stored and held by the companies until further notice. About the end of the month one of Bulloch's men was instructed to go to London and find a suitable craft fit for a voyage to the West Indies. She needed to be able to carry heavy weights. The agent found just the ship, a craft of some 400 tons, lately employed in bringing home old ordnance stores—cannons—from Gibraltar. She was the barque *Agrippina*, captained by Scotsman Alexander McQueen. Bulloch purchased her for the sum of £1,400. Notice was then given to the suppliers for delivery of their manufactured wares to the Port of London. These were then loaded aboard the new acquisition, without apparently raising the slightest suspicion.

Laird's Shipyard, Birkenhead, Liverpool. Both the *Florida* and the *Alabama* were launched from here.

In Birkenhead, following her launch, the *Enrica* was taken by two tugs to the graving dock, and there placed on the blocks, in preparation for outfitting. A powerful crane lowered her engines into place, and work was begun on converting what was a hull into a seagoing ship. The construction of the "290" standing out as she did, a wooden ship among those of iron construction, had come to the attention of the United States consul in Liverpool, Thomas H. Dudley, as early as 28 March. He employed a detective by the name of Matthew Maguire to make further enquiries. Maguire reported on the launch: "The gunboat launched from Laird's Yard on Wednesday, May 14th 1862, at which there was a very good attendance of gentlemen present, many Americans among them. There was no admittance to the yard, only those who were invited."[3] Two days later he had more detailed information, having apparently bribed a workman at Laird's, one Richard Broderick, a shipwright:

> The gunboat built by Laird's is a sister boat to the "Oreto" s.s. (gunboat) but is far superior. Her planks were caulked as they were put on; is built of the best English oak that could be obtained and that was picked. Every plank and timber of which she is built was strictly examined after being worked up. A large quantity of this oak was condemned, for what the carpenter says, was no detriment whatever. Every timber in her is fastened with copper bolts 18 feet long and 2½ and 3½ inches in circumference. The stern gear is all copper and brass, in fact the gentleman who supervised her construction says, "they could not turn out anything better from Her Majesty's Dock Yards."[4]

In his turn Bulloch was made aware of Maguire's snooping. He wrote of it in his *Secret Service of the Confederate States in Europe*: "I soon learned that spies were lurking about, and tampering with the workmen at Messers. Laird's, and that a private detective named Maguire was taking a deep and abiding interest in my personal movements."[5] So deep an interest was it that he was even following Bulloch. Maguire reported on 4 July 1862: "Captain Bullock went over to Tranmere in the same boat as I (Matthew Maguire) this morning (Wednesday July 2nd, 10 o'clock boat). Went to Laird's Yard and on board the gunboat, where he seemed to be giving orders to the men, who saluted him and who went and appeared as if they were carrying his orders into effect, whatever they were."

Such was Bulloch's concern that he consulted his solicitor to make sure that he was doing nothing illegal that would allow the British authorities to seize the ship. His solicitor assured him he was not. Nonetheless Bulloch was concerned. He then, in his own words, gained "the means of knowing with well nigh absolute certainty what was the state of the negotiations between the United States Minister and Her Majesty's Government." On 13 June the *Enrica* made her first trial, running up to the Formby lighthouse and back. Maguire watched from the shore, then duly reported to Consul Dudley: "The gunboat which was built at Laird's is in every respect similar to the "Oreto" S.S. (gunboat), with the exception, that she has only one funnel; she is also similarly rigged. About 40 or 50 gentlemen went out with her on her trial trip, which was to the Formby Lighthouse. The Byrnes were there also some from Messers. Fraser Tronholm & Co.'s firm. Everything connected with her, is kept a profound secret and her name is not known as yet to anyone in the yard. She went direct out of the dock and went direct in."

With the ship near completion, it was necessary to appoint a captain who held a board of trade certificate. It would be his duty to superintend the preparations for sea, to engage a crew, and complete all formalities with the relevant agencies. Charles Prioleau of Fraser, Trenholm recommended Captain Matthew J. Butcher, who was then serving as first officer aboard a Cunard steamship. It turned out that Bulloch and Butcher were acquainted, having met two or three years previously in Havana, when Butcher was chief officer aboard the Cunard steamship *Karnack.* Within an hour of meeting Butcher, Bulloch was able to introduce him at Laird's yard as the new master of the *Enrica.* Butcher was given strict instruction that he was "engaged merely to take the ship to an appointed place without the United Kingdom; and he was especially warned that no men must be engaged under any pretence whatever, except to navigate the ship to a port or ports in the West Indies, with the privilege of stopping at any intermediate port." By this exact wording Bulloch remained within the law relative to the Foreign Enlistment Act.

At the end of April, Lt. J.R. Hamilton arrived at Liverpool. Back in Savannah, after running the blockade in the *Fingal,* Bulloch was approached by Hamilton, who requested to serve under him. Bulloch, then designated captain of the second ship, the "290," had agreed. Then to Bulloch's immense disappointment he received a letter from the Navy Department. His hopes of sailing as the *Enrica*'s captain were dashed. Captain Raphael Semmes, late of the CSS *Sumter,* had been appointed her captain. The Confederate naval secretary, Stephen Mallory, had decided that Bulloch was doing too important a job in Liverpool to be replaced. Semmes, then at Nassau, was ordered to return to Liverpool. His old ship, the *Sumter,* the first Confederate armed cruiser, unable to be repaired, and blockaded in Gibraltar harbor by two Federal warships, had been abandoned. Orders now came for Bulloch to take charge and dispose of her as he saw fit. Bulloch put the *Sumter* up for sale in a somewhat spurious auction.. The purchaser was an Englishman by the name of M.G. Klingander, an agent for Fraser, Trenholm & Co.

Meanwhile, in Liverpool, Butcher began discreetly recruiting men. The officers fell under Bulloch's jurisdiction. Lt. John Low was appointed first officer. The second officer was George Townley Fullam. There were three more officers, surgeon David H. Llewellyn, paymaster Clarence R. Yonge, and chief engineer J. McNair. With the exception of Yonge, later to turn traitor, they were all British. The crew, appointed by Butcher, a man in whom Bulloch placed the utmost trust, were also British. They were mainly Naval reserve men.

The ever efficient detective Matthew Maguire was soon reporting to Dudley: "The engineers, cooks, stewards and officers are appointed (20th June).... Captain Butcher is to command her; Mr. McNair is to be Chief and Mr. Black second engineer (1st July).... Some person by the name of Barnett is shipping the crew by direction of Captain Butcher (4th July) ... Barnett, who is the shipping agent and servant at the Cunard Company, is shipping the crew of the gunboat, who are all picked men, from the Naval Volunteer Reserve Force." (15th July)." Diplomatic pressure by the United States Legation in London, was slowly bearing fruit. Previously, on 30 June the law officers reported to Lord Russell:

> The report of the United States Consul at Liverpool, besides suggesting other grounds of reasonable suspicion, contains direct assertion that the foreman of Messers. Laird, and the builders, has stated that this vessel is intended as a privateer for the services of the government of the Southern States; and, if the character of the vessel and of her equipment be such as the same report describes them to be, it seems evident that she must be intended for some warlike purpose. Under these circumstances, we think that proper steps ought to be taken, under the direction of Her Majesty's Government, by the authorities of the customs at Liverpool, to ascertain the truth, and that, if sufficient evidence can be obtained to justify proceedings under the foreign-enlistment act, such proceedings should be taken as early as possible....[6]

The Commissioner of Customs instigated an enquiry, then reported back to the Law Officers. They briefed Russell that the customs officers had been keeping a discreet watch upon the *Enrica,* and had at all times free access to the ship. As yet there not sufficient grounds to warrant the detention of the vessel. The proper course of action would be for the consul to submit evidence to the collector at Liverpool. By every means possible Consul Dudley collected evidence to confirm that the "290" was destined for the Confederate States Navy, and that she was recruiting a crew in defiance of the Foreign Enlistment Act. On 10 July the surveyor of customs ordered the vessel to be again "surveyed." No armaments were discovered. He wrote to Dudley notifying him of what had transpired, adding, "[I]f she is for the confederate service the builders and parties interested are not likely to commit themselves by any act which would subject them to the penal provision of the foreign-enlistment act."[7]

On 21 July, Dudley and his solicitor presented Maguire and four other men, William Passmore, John De Costa, Allen S. Clare and Henry Wilding, before J. Price Edwards, collector of the customs house at Liverpool. He received affidavits from them after taking their oaths. Passmore testified:

> I am a seaman, and have served as such on board Her Majesty's ship "Terrible," during the Crimean War. Having been informed that hands were wanted for a fighting vessel built by Messers. Laird and Co., of Birkenhead, I applied on Saturday, which was I believe, the 21st day of June last, to Captain Butcher, who I was informed, was engaging men for the said vessel, for berth aboard her. Captain Butcher asked me if I knew where the vessel was going. In reply to which I told him I did not rightly understand about it. He then told me the vessel was going out to the Government of the Confederate States of America. I asked him if there would be any fighting; to which he replied yes; they were going to fight for the Southern Government.... There are now about thirty hands on board her, who have been engaged to go out in her. Most of them are men who have previously served on board fighting ships....[8]

Price Edwards submitted the affidavits to the Commissioners of Customs, asking how he should act, as the ship appeared ready to sail. The comments relating to Captain Butcher in Passmore's statement are at odds with Bulloch's appreciation of the man. "Butcher," he wrote, "fulfilled all the requirements of the offices he engaged to perform, not only with tact, judgment and discretion, but with that nice and discriminating fidelity which marks the man of true honesty."[9] Butcher would not have jeopardized the mission by telling an ordinary member of the crew what was going on. The fact that he was selecting his crew with care, taking on men from the naval reserve, might have given Passmore a clue as to why such men were taken on. It would seem that Dudley coached Passmore in what to say, with the intention of implicating Captain Butcher. With his "evidence" Dudley went to see the American ambassador in London. Benjamin Moran noted his visit in his journal: "Dudley, the Consul at Liverpool, writes that the gun-boat built by the Lairds at Birkenhead for the rebels is being rapidly prepared for sea, and Mr. Adams has instructed him to get depositions of her guilty intentions and proceed against her in the Courts. Several persons have given information of so conclusive a character against her, that she must either be stopped or this Gov't will by refusal show the utter hollownes [*sic*] of its professions of neutrality. Our object is to put them on record as hypocrites and we shall do it, for no one in the Legation believes for a moment that either Gov't or courts will enforce their laws in this case."[10]

Word reached Bulloch that the British authorities might act. In his book he later wrote:

> On Saturday, July 26th, 1862 I received information from a private but reliable source, that it would not be safe to leave the ship in Liverpool another forty-eight hours. I went immediately to Messers.

Laird's office, and told them that I wished to have a thorough all day trial of the ship outside. Although the testing trial had already been made, and the delivery of the ship to me in accordance with the terms of the contract was complete, yet it had been verbally agreed that there should be another trial when coal and stores were all on board, if I desired it. Captain Butcher was ordered to ship a few more hands, and to have everything ready to come out of dock on Monday's tide. None of the crew had an inkling of the contemplated movement; but I informed Captain Butcher confidentially that the ship would not return, and directed him to get on board some extra tons of coal, and to complete his stores.[11]

On the evening of Monday the 28th, the *Enrica* left her dock and anchored off Seacombe. Preparations were made for leaving the harbor the next day. Security was not as tight as Bulloch believed however. Early on the morning of Tuesday, 29 July, Maguire met with Passmore once more. He informed him that the *Enrica* would sail that day. They would go out on a trial trip and not return. Her crew had been paid two weeks' money in advance, £2.5s. The crew, now between 90 and 100 men, had signed articles to go to Nassau, or any other port or ports. When there, anyone not willing to continue could return with Captain Butcher aboard the next mail ship, their passage paid. Writing up his report for Dudley, Maguire noted that on Friday, 18 July, he had been informed by a man named King that two dozen swords had been taken onboard. On the 26th the "290 (gunboat), had received," he wrote, "seven guns, viz:- two 32 pounders, two 96 pounders and three swivels." Allegedly there was also a hundred pounder onboard, as well as shot, shell, small arms and some coals. This statement was later proved to be patently false. Maguire's informants were embroidering the truth to make money out of him — and Maguire was believing what he wanted to believe, as indeed was Consul Dudley. Mr. Morgan, surveyor of Her Majesty's Customs at Liverpool, who had free and unopposed access to her at all times, wrote about this time to his superior: "I have only to add that your directions to keep a strict watch on the said vessel have been carried out, and I write in the fullest confidence that she left this port without any part of her armament on board. She had not as much as a signal gun or musket."[12]

To maintain the illusion that this was just another trial, the *Enrica* was dressed in flags, and a small party was invited to go out for a trip. At about nine o'clock, Maguire must have watched as the ship, accompanied by the tug *Hercules,* steamed downriver. Perhaps his information was wrong. He watched as the ship sailed several times, between the bell buoy and the northwest lightship. It looked very much like another sea trial. Onboard the *Enrica* at about three o'clock that afternoon, Bulloch announced that he wished to keep the ship out all night to complete her trials and arranged for the day-trippers and himself to go up to Liverpool in the accompanying tug. Aided by the Liverpool pilot, George Bond, Captain Butcher then set sail for Moelfra Bay, Anglesey. The next morning, by prior arrangement, Bulloch met the tug *Hercules* at the Woodside landing stage. Various articles for the *Enrica* were loaded aboard. Bulloch was then handed a telegram. The USS *Tuscarora,* under Captain T.A. Craven, had left Southampton, where she had lain in and about for several weeks, and was making, it was believed, for Queenstown, near Cork, with a view to intercepting the *Enrica.*

As he pondered the significance of the telegram, Bulloch was joined by shipping master Barnett and a crew of some thirty to forty men for *Enrica.* To Bulloch's horror their wives and girlfriends were also there. They would not be parted from their men until they had received some of their wages. Rather than draw attention, Bulloch got everybody aboard, and the *Hercules* set off. At about three o'clock that afternoon they arrived at Moelfre Bay and tied up alongside the *Enrica.* Everybody, women included, were now hungry, and they were invited aboard the *Enrica* for a hot meal. A moderation of grog was dispensed and tobacco provided for the men's pipes. Now in a mellow mood, the men were addressed by Bulloch. It was explained that as the ship was in good working order, it had been decided to proceed on the voyage without going back to Liverpool. Conditions of service were outlined again, and all but three of the men signed up for the voyage. It was agreed that each man could have a month's money paid to his female companion. With everything settled the women returned happily to the tug, and made the return trip to Liverpool.

Bulloch consulted with Butcher and the other officers of the *Enrica* as to how to proceed. If Craven and the *Tuscarora* were proceeding to Queenstown as believed, from there he could contact either Adams in London or Dudley in Liverpool for information regarding the *Enrica's* sailing. The logical sea-lane out into the Atlantic from Liverpool was to proceed into the Irish Sea, then south into the St. George's Channel. By waiting just off Tuskar Rock, some eight miles or so off the coast of Wexford, Craven knew that he could not fail but to intercept the *Enrica*. Well aware of this, Bulloch proposed that they sail north from Anglesey. Butcher agreed, and George Bond, the Liverpool pilot, who knew the route well, agreed to take them. At half past two on the morning of 31 July the *Enrica* weighed anchor and set off under steam, Butcher anxious to make progress as quickly as possible. The weather was as bad as the Irish Sea can be, with strong winds and lashing rain. By eight o'clock that morning the *Enrica* was off the Calf of Man, with Port Erin in the distance. With the sky clearing and the wind dropping, she proceeded at a steady 13½ knots. By one o'clock the *Enrica* was passing South Rock and steering along the northeast coast of Ireland.

In official circles information was moving ponderously slow. As the *Enrica* was passing South Rock, that Thursday, 31 July, Lord Russell, the Foreign Secretary, spoke to Mr. Adams concerning the *Enrica*. He regretted that a delay in determining the status of the ship was attributable to the sudden development of a malady by the queen's advocate, Sir John Harding, which had totally incapacitated him. As a result he was unable to give a verdict on the legal position of the *Enrica*. This necessitated the bringing in of other qualified lawyers, who determined that the *Enrica* should be seized. Unfortunately, by the time Adams was so informed, he himself was well aware, as was Russell, that the *Enrica* had sailed.

By eight o'clock that night, with the rain lashing down, the *Enrica,* having passed between Rathlin Island and Fair Head, was approaching the Giant's Causeway. The engines were stopped, and hailing a nearby fishing boat, Bulloch and pilot George Bond were taken ashore. The *Enrica* continued on to Inishtrahull Sound and out into the Atlantic. The following day Bulloch and Bond traveled into the nearby town of Portrush, and from there proceeded by rail to Belfast and by steamer and rail to Fleetwood and home to Liverpool.

Now the recriminations began, and lasted for nearly a month. At the American Legation in London, Benjamin Moran in his journal lashed out at the incompetence of Captain Craven, a man chasing after shadows:

> Wed. 30th July '62: The Tuscarora sailed at 8 P.M. last night from Southampton in search of the British pirate No. 290.
>
> Wed. 6th August '62: It is provoking that Capt. Craven blundered so greatly as he has in following this vessel 290. I am sure he would have caught her had he gone off the Western Coast of Ireland, instead of running into Dublin.
>
> Tues. 12th August '62: The vessel 290 is said to be still in the channel. This we get from Liver-

pool, together with the fact that 50 more men have been sent to her in a tug from that port. Wilson [the legation secretary] telegraphed the news to Craven at Dublin & he will doubtless go after her. I doubt the story, but think the men have been sent to join her at some rendezvous outside of British jurisdiction.

Thurs. 14th August '62: Capt. Craven has gone up to the Isle of Man after pirate 290.

Fri. 22nd August '62: Capt. Craven has missed the British pirate 290, and reports that he is coming into Falmouth. I can't but think that he has made a great mistake in not going right out to sea off the west of Ireland. And this trip to Falmouth will do no good.[13]

Returning to Liverpool on 3 August, Bulloch received word that the *Agrippina* under Captain Alexander McQueen, loaded with the *Enrica*'s armament, was now clear of the Channel, and sailing west into the Atlantic, to rendezvous with the *Enrica* at Terceira. With him McQueen had a letter from Bulloch with his orders:

London, July 28th 1862.

CAPTAIN,

You will proceed at once to sea with the barque Agrippina, now under your command, and make the best of your way to the bay of Praya, in the island of Terceira, one of the Azores.... The bay of Praya is open to the east, and is easy and safe of access, there being no sunken rocks or danger of any kind not visible to the eye. With a leading wind, stand boldly in for the middle of the bight until a small islet off the north point is in range with the point of the mainland of the island itself; then haul up for the town, which lies in the northern curve of the bay, and anchor by the lead in eight to ten fathoms of water.... You will be visited soon after anchoring by a health officer, to whom you will simply report that you are from London for Demerara, and have put in for supplies. It is hoped that the steamer will not be long behind you; indeed you may find her there. The name of the commander of the steamer is Butcher. He will have a letter to you with authority to take whatever quantity of coal and other articles of your cargo he may require, and we particularly desire you to give him your best assistance, and afford him every aid in your power to transfer what he needs from the Agrippina to his own ship, and you will proceed to any port he may direct, and land or deliver the remainder of your cargo. In fact you are to consider all orders from the commander of the steamer as being authorized by us.

At long last, Semmes and his officers arrived from Nassau, aboard the steamship *Bahama*. She docked at Liverpool on 8 August. While Lt. McIntosh Kell and the other officers reassembled members of the *Sumter's* crew, who had made their way from Gibraltar, Semmes himself went to stay with Bulloch at his home in Wellington Street, Waterloo. Here they could talk unobserved. Additional armaments were now brought to Liverpool by rail and loaded aboard the *Bahama*. Bulloch details them as "some extra stores and two additional 32-pounder guns."[14] The Federal report goes into more detail: "Fawcett, Preston & Co. shipped on board of her nineteen cases containing guns, gun-carriages, shot, rammers, &c., weighing in all 158 cwt. 1qr. 27lbs. There was no other cargo on board, except five hundred and fifty-two tons of coal for the use of the ship."[15]

On 11 August Bulloch wrote to the secretary of the Confederate navy, Stephen Mallory, that all was ready:

Liverpool, August 11th 1862

SIR,

I have already informed you by letter, as well as by private messenger, that the Alabama is safely clear of British waters, and that another vessel, with her battery and ordnance stores, had previously sailed for a concerted rendezvous. I have now the satisfaction to report that Commander Semmes, with his officers, has arrived here, and will sail tomorrow in a steamer chartered for the purpose, to join the Alabama. It has been deemed advisable that I should go with Commander Semmes as far as the rendezvous, to smooth away as much as possible his embarrassments and difficulties in assuming the command of an entirely new ship with a strange and untried crew. My absence will not be prolonged beyond one month, and I have arranged all other business so that there will be no delay or interruption in the progress of other work....

It will give me the greatest satisfaction to know that Commander Semmes is fairly afloat in the Alabama, and confident of his ability to do good service in her, I will watch with pride her coming success, although I cannot overcome the feeling of disappointment I experienced when first informed that I was not to command her myself.[16]

Thirty additional British sailors were induced to sail aboard the *Bahama,* ostensibly on a voyage to Nassau. One of them was John Latham, who lived at 36, Jasper Street, Liverpool. As he later recorded, "I signed articles at the Sailors' Home, Liverpool, to ship in the steamship Bahama, Captain Tessier, for a voyage to Nassau and back."[17] The *Bahama* left the Bramley Moore Dock, Liverpool, at near midnight on 12 August. She lay to in the river until the following morning, when about half past seven, Bulloch, Semmes and his officers boarded her from the tug *Hercules.*

In seven days the *Bahama* reached Praya, and there, waiting at anchor, were the *Alabama* and the *Agrippina.* Semmes now takes up the story: "On the morning of the 20th of August, we were on the lookout, at an early hour, for the land, and it was not long before we discovered the island, looking, at first hazy and indistinct in the distance, but gradually assuming more form and consistency. After another hour's steaming, Porto Praya, our place of rendezvous, became visible, with its white houses dotting the mountain side, and we now began to turn our glasses upon the harbor, with no little anxiety, to see our ships were all right. We first caught sight of their spars, and pretty soon, raising their hulls sufficiently for identification, we felt much relieved."[18]

The approach of the *Bahama* was a cause for some anxiety aboard the *Alabama.* For all they knew she could be an enemy steamship. They were still unarmed, and it seemed unlikely that the Portuguese authorities could give them any protection. As she approached, the *Bahama* was eventually recognized, and tension was dissipated. At half past eleven that morning she steamed into the harbor, and came to anchor. As a matter of security, the *Alabama* was registered with the Portuguese authorities as the steamship *Barcelona,* out of London bound for Nassau. Her master requested only to re-coal his ship in calm waters, and had no need to communicate with the town. Captain Butcher then reported to Bulloch. The voyage had been rough, and he had been obliged to consume most of his coal. However since their arrival, he had begun taking stores aboard the *Alabama.* The wind was getting up, and Semmes gave orders for Butcher to follow him with the two ships to the greater protection of Angra Bay, on the western side of the island. By mid afternoon, the transshipment of the armament and stores was recommenced. Now, for the first time since she had left Liverpool, Semmes boarded the *Alabama.* Everything was in a state of disorder, as the men had done their utmost to get the stores aboard as quickly as possible, placing such goods on the deck wherever space permitted. Semmes looked at his crew as they worked: "The crew, comprising about sixty persons, who had been picked up ... about the streets of Liverpool, were as unpromising in appearance, as things about the decks. What with faces begrimed with coal dust, red shirts and blue shirts, Scotch caps, and hats, brawny chests exposed, and stalwart arms naked to the elbows, they looked as little like a crew of a man-of-war, as one can well conceive. Still there was some physique among these fellows, and soap, and water, and clean shirts would make a wonderful difference in their appearance."[19]

By and large his men were ex–Royal Navy. They knew their business, and they were willing. That was a start. The transshipment continued throughout the evening and resumed in the morning. The American consul meanwhile made careful notes concerning the *Alabama*:

> [S]he reached [the Azores] on the 10th of August. On the 18th of August, while she was at Terceira, a sail was observed making for the anchorage. It proved to be the Agrippina of London, Captain McQueen, having on board six guns, with ammunition, coals, stores, &c., for the Alabama. Preparations were immediately made to transfer this important cargo. On the afternoon of the 20th, while employed discharging the bark, the screw-steamer Bahama, Captain Tessier (the same that had taken the armaments to the Florida, whose insurgent ownership and character were well known in Liverpool) arrived, having on board Commander Raphael Semmes and officers of the Confederate States Steamer Sumter There was also taken from this steamer two 32-pounders stores, which occupied all the remainder of that day and a part of the next.
>
> The 22nd and 23rd August were taken up in transferring coal from the Agrippina to the Alabama. It was not until Sunday (the 24th) that the insurgents' flag was hoisted. Bullock [*sic*] and those who were not going in the 290 went back to the Bahama, and the Alabama, now first known under that name, went off with twenty-six officers and eighty-five men.[20]

Bulloch records that by ten o'clock on the morning of 22 August the last gun of the battery was mounted, the powder and shell all stowed, and shot was in its racks. The *Alabama* was ready for action. As the American consul reported, the remainder of that day and the following day were taken up in coaling. On the morning of Sunday the 24th the *Alabama* and her tender moved out to sea, beyond Portuguese jurisdiction. Aboard the *Bahama,* Semmes, along with his officers, called the British sailors to the bridge where he addressed them: "Now my lads, there is the ship [pointing to the Alabama] she is as fine a vessel as ever floated; there is a chance which seldom offers itself to a British seaman, that is, to make some money.... [Y]our prize money will be divided proportionately according to each man's rank, something similar to the English navy.... I will put you in English ports where you can get your book signed every three months."[21]

Semmes and his officers and men, now crossed to the *Alabama,* and in full Confederate States naval uniform he addressed the men assembled there, on the aft quarterdeck. Semmes read out his commission appointing him a captain in the Confederate States Navy, by the authority of its president, Jefferson Davis, and of his authorization to take command of the CSS *Alabama*. A gun aboard the ship was then fired, and the British Union Jack was lowered. The Confederate flag and pennant were raised, and an impromptu band played "Dixie." The *Bahama,* lying at anchor close by, fired a gun in salute, its crew cheering the new flag. Semmes now spoke to his mainly British crew. He thanked them for what they had done. They had completed their contracts, and were free to return home to Liverpool with Commander Bulloch aboard the *Bahama,* if they so wished. Passage would be free, and they would continue to be paid until the ship docked. Semmes then gave a brief account of the war, of how the Confederate States had broken away and forged a new sovereign and independent state, and how the Northern states, much stronger than they, were attempting to force them back into the union against their will. He asked the men to join him in the struggle. He would, he told them, pay them double the ordinary wage for the risks they would run. They would also receive their share of prize money. John Latham, who had shipped out on the *Bahama* recorded this about it:

> When I got on board the Alabama, I found a great number of men that had gone on board of her from Liverpool. Captain Semmes then addressed us.... [H]e [hoped] "we should all content ourselves and be comfortable, one among another; but any of you that thinks he cannot stand to his gun, I don't want." He then called the purser, and such as agreed to serve signed articles on the

companion-hatch, and on signing the men received two months pay in advance, or one month's wages and a half-pay note. I took a month's wages and a half-pay note for £3 10s. A month in favor of my wife, Martha Latham, 19, Wellington Street, Swansea; the note was drawn on Fraser, Trenholm & Co., of Liverpool, but it was paid at Mr. Klingender's, in Liverpool; the note was signed by Captain Semmes, Yonge, who was the paymaster, and Smith, the ship's clerk. I sent £5 and this half-pay note ashore by Captain Bullock, and he forwarded it with a letter to my wife.[22]

Those who agreed were instructed to go to the paymaster and sign the articles. Eighty-five men agreed to serve:

Adolphus Marmelstein	I.G. Dent
R.B. Hobbs	W.F. Forrestall
James King	George Harwood
Brent Johnson	James Brosnan
Thomas Weir	William Crawford
Ralph Masters	George Appleby
George Addison	Frederick Jones
William Purdey	George Freemantle
Edward Rawse	James Smith
Peter Hughes	William Morgan
Thomas McMillan	James Higgs
A.G. Bartelli	R. Parkinson
Henry Fisher	Robert Wright
Henry Eustachia	Owen Duffy
James McFadden	Frank Curran
George Egerton	Charles Godwin
Michael Mars	Charles Seymour
Henry Tucker	Edgar Fripp
John Emery	H. Legris
John Doyle	John Duggan
Peter Henney	William McGinley
John Caren	F. Townsend
John Roberts	Samuel Henry
Joseph Connor	Edwin Jones
William Rinton	William Hearn
John Neil	Robert Williams
Thomas Williams	Joseph Pearson
Henry Yates	H. Cosgrove
James Wilson	Robert Egan
Thomas Parker	John Grady
John McAllee	John Latham
David Roach	Adam Shilland
James Mair	John Jack
Peter Laverty	John Harrigan
Patrick Bradley	Samuel Williams
Thomas Potter	John Reilly
Thomas Murphy	James Foxton
Martin King	William Levins
James Mason	Thomas Winter
Peter Duncan	Malcolm McFarland
Christian Pust	Edward Fitzmaurice
George Gnischhas	William Price
Thomas Walsh	

Some members of the *Alabama*'s British crew.

Of these, nineteen have been identified as Royal Navy Reserve, including Irish-Liverpudlian Michael Mars, Thomas McMillan, Charles Seymour, David Roach (R.N.R. 11919) and Peter Hughes (R.N.R. 10849) Some of the names may be aliases. With Bulloch and Butcher assisting, the paymaster and clerk began issuing half-pay tickets for the sailors' wives and sweethearts back in Liverpool, of those men who had signed up. Details of names and addresses were written down for Butcher to take back to Fraser & Trenholm so that payment could be made.

Just prior to departure, Dr. David Herbert Llewellyn, who had signed up as surgeon aboard the *Bahama* in her voyage from Liverpool carrying the officers of the "290," now requested to be allowed to join the crew of the CSS *Alabama*. Semmes readily agreed to this unexpected offer, and appointed him Assistant Surgeon Lieutenant. Llewellyn, who was of Welsh descent, was a native of Wiltshire in England, and had studied medicine at Charing Cross Hospital, London. He was the son of an Anglican bishop and grandson of Lord Herbert. The officers of the *Alabama* were now:

> Raphael Semmes, Commander
> John McIntosh Kell, First Lieutenant
> Richard F. Armstrong, Second Lieutenant
> Joseph D. Wilson, Third Lieutenant
> Arthur Sinclair, Fourth Lieutenant
> John Low, Fifth Lieutenant
> Francis L. Galt, Surgeon
> David Herbert Llewellyn, Assistant Surgeon
> Becket K. Howell, First Lieutenant, Marines
> Clarence R. Yonge, Paymaster
> Miles J. Freeman, Chief Engineer
> Irvine S. Bulloch, Acting Master

Eugene Anderson Maffitt, Midshipman
Edwin Maffitt Anderson, Midshipman
George Townley Fullam, Master's Mate
William P. Brooks, Second Engineer
Matthew O'Brien, Third Engineer
Simeon W. Cummings, Third Assistant Engineer
John Pundt, Fourth Engineer

In addition, Semmes brought with him reliable men from the *Sumter,* including William Breedlove Smith, his clerk, Thomas C. Cuddy, gunner, William Robinson, carpenter, and Benjamin McCaskey, boatswain. Additional men, not listed with the other seamen, include Henry Allcott, to replace sailmaker Melville Beaufort.

It was eleven o'clock that night before the administration was completed; then Bulloch, bidding his good-byes and wishing them the best of luck, finally returned to the *Bahama.* As she steamed away, Semmes, aboard the *Alabama,* was later to write: "I turned my ship's head to the north-east, set the fore and aft sails, and directed the engineer to let his fires go down. The wind had freshened considerably, and there was some sea on. I now turned into an unquiet cot, perfectly exhausted, after the labors of the day, and slept as comfortably as the rolling of the ship, and a strong smell of bilge-water would permit."[23]

5

The *Alabama*

His new ship in total disarray, following the hurried transference of armaments and supplies, with discomfort and confusion abounding, Semmes sailed the *Alabama*, as he himself described it, "from the beaten tracks of commerce." Over the next few days the detritus aboard was properly stored in logical fashion, the men properly berthed, mess arrangements completed, and teams allocated to their various stations. The crews were exercised in their various drills, and with an abundance of expertise from the men of the British Naval Reserve, rapid progress was made. Finally the upper decking, which had been expanding in the semitropical climate, was re-caulked. The *Alabama* and her crew were now fit for duty. Semmes set in a course for the whale fishery off the Azores.

By 4 September the *Alabama* was off Pico and Fayal in the western Azores. The weather was fine and clear, but the following day turned cloudy. A ship was discovered lying to, her topsails reduced. The *Alabama* moved slowly towards her. The Stars and Stripes were raised. As the *Alabama* moved to within a few hundred yards of her she languidly responded by raising a similar flag. The other ship was a whaler, and alongside her was a huge sperm whale, recently killed. Her crew were engaged in the grisly business of cutting up the leviathan. Semmes hauled down the old flag and raised the Stars and Bars. Now under the *Alabama*'s guns there was little that the captain of the captured ship could do. She was the *Ocmulgee*, of Edgartown, Massachusetts. She was obliged to surrender, and her crew of thirty-seven were transferred to the Confederate ship. Stores of pork and beef, and other necessary commodities were brought aboard. By now it was nine o'clock at night. Semmes decided not to set fire to her for fear of driving off any other whalers in the vicinity. The following day he set her ablaze; the smoke would, he hoped, be taken for that of some steamship. The *Alabama* sailed on, the whale-boats of the *Ocmulgee* towed at her stern.

As the morning turned to afternoon, another sail was seen. Semmes ordered the American flag to be raised once more and set off in pursuit of her. She was French with a neutral cargo. Semmes led her captain to believe that his was a Federal ship. Continuing on NNW the *Alabama* made Flores, the most westerly of the islands of the Azores, by late afternoon. The *Alabama*, her sails shortened, lay off the island that night. Sunday dawned, a muster was called, and the articles of war were read out to the crew. Semmes observed of the men, that they were "all neatly arrayed in duck frocks and trousers, well polished shoes and straw hats. There was a visible improvement in their health too. They had been long enough out of Liverpool to recover from the effects of their debauches, and regain their accustomed stamina." Later that morning, off the village of Lagens, Semmes paroled the crew of the *Ocmulgee*, and sent them ashore in their whale-boats, adequately provisioned from their own stores. On the neighboring island of Fayal lived the American consul, who would ensure their safe return to the United States.

The *Alabama* made sail once more, away from the island. Barely had she done so than the cry went up from the mast-head: "Sail ho!" Coming towards her and the island, way off in the distance, was a fully rigged schooner. Semmes ordered the British flag to be raised. An hour later, five miles out to sea, it was clear that the oncoming ship was American. Still she had not raised her colors. Her course began to change to avoid coming close to the British-flagged ship. Her captain was cautious; he was trying to get within the safety of the marine league. Semmes ordered a change in course to block her, and ordered a blank round to be fired. She did not give way, nor show her colors. She was making all sail for the safety of the island. The *Alabama* began to gain on her. Semmes knew that he had the beating of her. He ordered a live round from one of his 32-pounders. The shot passed between her masts, barely feet above the heads of her crew. Realizing that she was dead in the water, her captain hauled in sail and surrendered to his fate. He raised the Stars and Stripes. A boarding party was sent over to her, and the boat returned with her captain and his papers. She was the *Starlight,* registered at Boston, out of Fayal bound for her home port by way of Flores. The crew of seven Semmes put in irons, down in the hold of the *Alabama.* The infamous treatment of his paymaster, Henry Myers, and Confederate Thomas Tait Tunstall at the hands of the American consul at Tangier had hardened his heart. Yet for all that, the next day he paroled his prisoners, and landed them and the passengers at the little town of Santa Cruz.

Getting under sail once more they chased and overhauled a Portuguese whaler. That afternoon they had more success in taking an American whaler, the *Ocean Rover,* of New Bedford, Massachusetts, with a cargo of eleven hundred barrels of oil. Again Semmes put the crew of thirty-six in irons. Though he did not hold the captain or his crew personally responsible, for the ship had been at sea for three years and four months, they represented all that he had come to hate. Semmes wrote later of the incident: "[W]hen I came to reflect for a moment, upon the diabolical acts of his countrymen of New England, who were out-heroding Herod, in carrying on against us a vindictive war, filled with hate and vengeance, the milk of human kindness which had begun to well up in my heart disappeared, and I had no longer any spare sympathies to dispose of."[1]

The next morning the captain of the *Ocean Rover* approached Semmes. He had heard from the crew of the *Alabama* that Semmes had released the crew of the *Ocmulgee,* and had permitted them to row for shore. Could he and his men do the same? Though having professed that the milk of human kindness had been driven from his heart, Semmes readily

Raphael Semmes, C.S.N., captain of the British-built merchant raider *Alabama.*

The officers of the CSS *Alabama*. Clockwise from top: Lt. Sinclair, Midshipman Maffitt, Midshipman Anderson, Master's Mate Fullam, Lt. Howell, Acting Master Bulloch. Center: Lt. Armstrong.

agreed. Then curiously he expressed concern for their safety. They were some five miles from shore. Would they be safe? The captain of the *Ocean Rover* explained that such a journey in their small whaling boats was nothing new to them. Having been put under parole, the crew descended into their six whaling boats, and complete with provisions, were allowed to depart. Later in the Yankee press Semmes was to be vilified for his actions in casting adrift these men.

The *Alabama*, complete with her two prizes, now lay off the islands that night. About midnight the officer of the watch woke Semmes. There was another ship nearby, about a mile or so distant. Quickly dressing, Semmes ordered pursuit of the mystery ship. Seeing that she was being followed, she responded by putting on all sail. With dawn breaking, and flying the Royal Navy blue ensign once more, the *Alabama* was close enough to fire a blank shot. The other ship did not respond, until a 32-pounder from the *Alabama* convinced her that she should do so. She raised the Federal flag, and took in sail. She was the *Alert,* sixteen days out from New London, Connecticut, bound for the Indian Ocean by way of the Azores and Cape Verde Islands. Among her cargo was winter-wear for the whalers operating off the Navigators' Islands in the South Indian Ocean. There were also supplies of beef, pork, bread, soap and tobacco, which Semmes had brought aboard the *Alabama.* Sailing into the marine league of Flores, the captain of the *Alert* and his crew were paroled and sent ashore in their own boats. His three prizes Semmes now set ablaze.

After the prize crews had gotten back aboard the *Alabama,* the cry went up again: "Sail ho!" She was heading towards them, a large schooner of New England design. The United States colors were raised aboard the *Alabama*; the oncoming ship raised them too. Perhaps now seeing for the first time the cause of the three plumes of smoke, the schooner veered off from her course in order to escape the fast approaching ship that was the *Alabama.* Within half an hour's chase she was close enough. Semmes ordered the Confederate flag raised and a blank fired. The other ship heaved-to. She was another whaler, the *Weathergauge* of Provincetown, Massachusetts. Barely was her crew transferred to the *Alabama* when another ship came into view. It was late in the day. Leaving the *Weathergauge* under a prize crew, the Confederate ship set off after her. Darkness descended as the hunt continued. The moonlight on the white sails seemed to identify her as a New Englander. Dawn broke. The *Alabama* was closing in on her quarry. She was identified not as American, but as Danish. She proved to be the barque *Overman,* out of Bangkok, in Siam, bound for Hamburg. Semmes confessed that he was angry at the forced pursuit. Why had she run away, if she was a neutral? The attitude of her captain was why should he stop? The *Alabama* returned to the *Weathergauge,* lying off the coast of the island of Corvo. The crew of the Massachusetts ship were put ashore in their own boats, and the *Weathergauge* was burned.

The ***Alabama***'s English born assistant surgeon, David H. Llewellyn. (*Illustrated London News*)

Over the next two days just one ship, Portuguese in origin, was stopped. Semmes put in a course to the northeast, intending to skirt the islands at a distance of about forty miles in the hope of catching another whaler. On the third day he struck lucky. She was the hermaphrodite whaling brig *Altamaha,* five months out of New Bedford. Valued at $3,000, she was put to the torch. That afternoon it was a Spanish ship that was overtaken. Her cargo, like herself, was neutral, and she was allowed to continue. Night fell and Semmes turned in. About half past eleven he was summoned from his cot. Another ship had been sighted. By the time all sail had been spread, the ship was a good two and a half to three miles away. During the course of the night she slowly came up to the vessel. At about a mile's distance Semmes fired a blank round. The quarry failed to respond. The hunt continued, the *Alabama* gradually gaining. Semmes ordered a live round to be fired. The 32-pounder brought the sail to heel. Semmes sent over a boat to investigate. She was indeed an American vessel, the *Benjamin Tucker* of New Bedford, eight months at sea with three hundred and forty barrels of oil. Her crew of thirty were transferred to the *Alabama,* and the whaler was set on fire. The logbook of Lt. John Low reveals that she and her cargo were valued at $18,000.

Days passed. The men practiced at their guns and did essential maintenance. Recaulking of the decks and other tasks neglected in the pursuit of enemy shipping were undertaken. The course laid in now brought them back to Flores. As foggy morning broke, Semmes discovered that another ship was lying nearby. Almost leisurely, the *Alabama,* flying the Stars and Stripes, approached her. She languidly raised the American flag. Semmes tore down the enemy flag from his mast, raised his own colors, and ordered a blank to be fired. The other ship heaved-to and received a boarding party. Another whaling ship, a fore-and-aft schooner, proved to be the *Courser,* of Provincetown, Massachusetts. She was a good ship, and Semmes confesses a certain admiration towards her captain. Unfortunately, having read the American papers retrieved from the *Weathergauge,* which railed with various degrees of hatred towards the South and everything Southern, Semmes was in no mood to be generous. "There were too many white-cravatted, long-haired fellows, bawling from the New-England pulpits, and too many house-burners and pilferers inundating our southern land, to permit me to be generous, and so I steeled my heart," he admitted.[2] He now had some seventy prisoners aboard the *Alabama.* Running back towards the island, Semmes put them aboard the eight whaleboats he had in tow from the captured ships, and, putting them all on parole not to take up arms against the Confederacy, he put them ashore. The *Courser,* which Lt. Low valued at $7,000, was used as target practice by the gun crews.

With a course set in of north then westwards, the *Alabama* came across another ship, a whaler. Seeing them she set off, piling on all canvas to escape. Slowly but surely the *Alabama* overhauled her and forced her to come to. She was the American ship *Virginia,* twenty-one days out of New Bedford, under Captain Tilton. She had been fitted out for a long cruise, with warm clothing and provisions for her crew. Semmes took what he needed, including sails and cordage and soap and candles, brought her crew aboard as prisoners, then set fire to her. Her value was reckoned to be about $25,000.

The next morning, the weather turned and the wind got up to gale force. The papers of a French ship were examined and she was permitted to continue. As she pulled away another sail was sighted. The *Alabama* gave chase. The sail must have seen them too, for all sail was applied as she made a dash for freedom across the stormy sea. The *Alabama,* flying British colors, continued after her. A shot from the gun forced her to haul in sail and raise what Semmes described as that *"flaunting lie"* the *"old flag."*[3] With the sea akin to a maelstrom, Semmes maneuvered his ship towards her then lowered two boats. Her crew, chronometer, flag and papers were transferred to the *Alabama*. She was the *Elisha Dunbar* of New Bedford, twenty-four days out. Semmes set her ablaze.

The bad weather continued for several days, but it now being the beginning of October and the end of the whaling season around the Azores, Semmes put in a course for New Foundland, intending to sweep along the American coastline. His target was the grain-laden ships destined for Europe. The *Alabama* sailed northwest for several days without catching sight of a single sail. Into the Gulf Stream the *Alabama* passed, and a noticeable warmth was felt. Early on the morning of 3 October two sails were reported. Both were approaching in the *Alabama*'s general direction. All she had to do was remain on course and they would both deliver themselves up to her. Semmes did not raise any colors until both ships were nearly abreast of the steamship. Then he raised the Confederate flag and fired a blank, which brought both of the Yankee ships to heel. One was the *Brilliant,* of 839 tons, twelve days out of New York, laden with flour and grain, bound for London. The other was the *Emily Farnum,* of Portsmouth, New Hampshire, also out of New York, bound for Liverpool with a similar cargo. The cargo of the *Emily Farnum* being properly documented as neutral, Semmes spared her, but off-loaded all his prisoners, including those from the *Brilliant,* which he then set on fire. "Three of the crew of the *Brilliant*, (all Englishmen) volunteered on the *Alabama*."[4] The captain of the *Farnum* was then put on oath that he would continue on to Liverpool, but no sooner was he out of sight of the *Alabama* than he broke his word, and sailed for Boston to report the presence of the Confederate raider.

Back in New York, Captain Hagar, late master of the *Brilliant,* wrote to the editor of the *New York Journal of Commerce,* asking him to publish the enclosed description as a warning to others:

DESCRIPTION OF THE CONFEDERATE STEAM PROPELLER ALABAMA

The Alabama was built at Liverpool or Birkenhead, and left the latter port in August last; is about 1,200 tons burden, draft about fourteen feet, engines by LAIRD & SONS, of Birkenhead, 1862. She is a wooden vessel, propelled by a screw, coppered bottom, about 210 feet long, rather narrow, painted black outside and drab inside, has a round stern, billet head, very little shear, flush deck fore and aft, a bridge forward at the smoke stack, carries two large black boats on cranes amidships forward of the main rigging, two black quarter-boats between the main and mizzen masts, one small black boat over the stern on cranes. The spare spars on a gallows between the bridge and foremast show above the rail. She carries three long 32-pounders on a side, and is pierced for two more amidships; has a 100 pound rifled pivot gun forward of the bridge, and a 68 pound pivot on the main deck; has tracks laid forward for a pivot bow gun, and tracks aft for a pivot stern-chaser, all of which she will take on board to complete her armament. Her guns are of the Blakely pattern, and manufactured by WESLEY & PRESTON, Liverpool, 1862. She is bark rigged, has very long bright lower masts and black mast heads, yards black, long yardarms, short poles (say one to two feet) with small dog vanes on each, and appended to the main studding-sail booms on the fore and main, and has wire rigging, carries on her foremast a square foresail, large trysail with two reefs, topgallant sail and royal. On the mainmast, a large trysail with two reefs and a bonnet. No square main-sail bent, topsail two reefs, topgallant sail and royal. On the mizzen mast, a very large spanker and a short three cornered gaft topsail, has a fore and foretopmast staysail and jib. Has had no staysails to the main or mizzen masts bent, or royal yards aloft.

It is represented to go thirteen knots under canvas and fifteen under steam. Can get steam in twenty minutes, but seldom uses it, except in a chase or emergency. Has all national flags, but usually sets the St. George's Cross on approaching a vessel. Her present complement of men is 120, all told, but is anxious to ship more. Keeps a man at the masthead from daylight to sunset.

Her sails are of hemp canvas, made very roaching; the topsails have twenty cloths on the head and thirty on the foot. General appearance of the hull and sails decidedly English. She is generally under two topsails, fore and main topsails, fore and foretopmast staysails, sometimes topgallant sails and gib, but seldom any sail on the mizzen, except while in chase of a vessel. She is very slow in stays, generally wears ship. She was built expressly for the business. She is engaged to destroy, fight, or run, as the case may be. She took her armament and crew, and most of her officers on board near Terceira, Western Islands, from an English vessel. Her crew are principally English, the officers chivalry of the South.

All the water consumed on board is condensed. She has eight months' provisions, besides what is being plundered, and has about four hundred tons of coal on board.

The following are the names of her officers:

Captain SEMMES, Commander-in-Chief; First-Lieutenant KELL; Second-Lieutenant ARMSTRONG; Third-Lieutenant WILSON; Fourth-Lieutenant LOW; Sailing Master SINCLAIR; Lieutenant of Marines HOWELL, brother-in-law of JEFF DAVIS; Corporal FULLAM; Gunner CURDY; Captain's Clerk SMITH; Midshipman MAFFITT, SINCLAIR, BULLOCK; Chief Engineer FREEMAN; Carpenter ROBINSON; Boatswain McCASKIE; Doctor, Surgeon, &c, unknown.[5]

Oblivious of what was happening ashore, the *Alabama* continued on course, skirting the American coastline. Over the next few days she overhauled a number of neutral ships sailing from New York with cargoes of grain for European ports. Semmes got fresh news from them as to the progress of the war. On the afternoon of 7 October the *Alabama* chased and captured an American bark, the *Wave Crest,* out of New York, bound for Cardiff in Wales, with a cargo of grain and flour. They took what they needed, then used her for target practice. Just before nightfall a second ship approached, possibly to investigate the burning ship that was the *Wave Crest.* With presence of mind, her captain, seeing one ship ablaze and a second making all speed towards him, summed up the situation, and changing course made a dash for freedom. Through his night glasses Semmes studied the ship, a hermaphrodite — a cross between a brig and a schooner. Though she flew no flag, she was clearly American. Semmes feared losing her in the oncoming dark, but his ship had the speed of her. A blank shot brought her to a halt, and a boarding party was put aboard her. She was American, the *Dunkirk,* launched in 1861, out of New York, with a cargo of grain for Lisbon in Portugal. The cargo was American, and Semmes had no qualms about putting her to the torch. When her crew were transferred to the *Alabama,* one of them, George Forrest, an American, was recognized as a deserter from the *Sumter.* Semmes could have hanged him in accordance with the articles of war, but chose not to. In a court-martial he was dishonorably discharged from the Confederate navy, then put in the hold with the other prisoners until he could be landed somewhere.

The *Alabama* now running up the eastern seaboard in exceptionally fine weather, two days after the burning of the 298 ton *Dunkirk* another sail was sighted. She was a large ship, and after a chase of a few hours, and just before sunset, the *Alabama* approached her and obliged her to heave-to to receive a boarding party. A packet ship, her rails were lined by passengers, not knowing what to expect from the ship that now bore the Confederate colors. She was the *Tonawanda,* a vessel of 1,300 tons, out of Philadelphia, bound for Liverpool. While she and her cargo were American, and thus liable to be burned, she also had sixty passengers — men, women and children. Not wishing to burden himself with the women and children, Semmes bonded the ship for $80,000, and obliged her to sail alongside the *Alabama* for the next few days in the hope of coming across another ship that would take the passengers and prisoners, thus enabling him then to burn the *Tonawanda.*

It was early on the morning of the second day that a sail came into view — another grain ship by the look of her, and fast approaching. The *Alabama* only had to wait for her to deliver herself up. Semmes ran up the Federal flag, the oncoming ship did the same. When she was close enough Semmes ordered a blank shot to be fired. She came to, and Semmes put a boarding party on her. She was the *Manchester,* a ship of 1,075 tons, built in New Hampshire in 1861. She had sailed from New York and was bound for Liverpool with a cargo of grain. Eyeing up the ships and their cargoes for value, Semmes decided on putting all his prisoners, from the *Wave Crest* and the *Manchester,* aboard the *Tonawanda*. This done, she was allowed to sail away. From the *Tonawanda,* Semmes took aboard one of her passengers, a black boy of about seventeen, called David White. He was a slave, from Delaware. A little afraid at first, he was put to work as a mess steward in the ward room. His name was entered as a member of the crew, and he was paid according to his grade. Eventually he became an assistant to Dr. Galt, the medical officer. The Federal side put a different complexion on the account, based on uninformed opinion, as is borne out in the journal of Benjamin Moran in London:

> Tues. 28th October '62: We have a telegram from L'pool saying Philada. ship Tonawanda, Capt. Julius, has arrived there with about 200 prisoners from the pirate "290" which vessel captured the Tonawanda on the 9th Inst., and released her as a cartel on a bond of $80,000 payable after the war. Julius reports that Semmes had burned several other vessels.
> Fri. 31st October '62: We have a written statement from Capt. Julius of the Tonawanda thro' the Consul at L'pool. The Capt. says the pirates number nearly 100, nearly all of whom are English man o' wars men. Semmes stole a free Negro boy from the ship, and will no doubt carry him into slavery.[6]

Semmes wrote of the young man: "Dave served us during the whole cruise. He went ashore in all parts of the world, knew that the moment he touched the shore he was at liberty to depart, if he pleased, and was tampered with by sundry Yankee Consuls, but always came back to us. He seemed to have the instinct of deciding between his friends and his enemies."[7]

From the *Manchester,* Semmes gained a batch of the local New York papers. The *New York Herald* in particular was most informative. In its usual triumphalizing way the American authorities told the newspapers where all their warships were and what they intended. In Semmes' case it was a simple procedure of not being where they were. Semmes himself wondered at their stupidity—or was it arrogance? He wrote, "Perhaps this was the only war in which the newspapers ever explained, beforehand, all the movements of armies, and fleets, to the enemy."[8]

For the next three days the *Alabama* saw only neutral ships, to the extent that her crew could pick out from a distance the likely place of origin of each. Approaching, the appropriate flag would be raised, thus negating the need for a boarding party to go and investigate. It was the 15th of October before their next triumph. As with the *Manchester,* she sailed towards them. Upon boarding, she proved to be the barque *Lamplighter,* of Boston, from New York bound for Gibraltar, with a cargo of Virginia tobacco. Taking what tobacco he needed for his crew, Semmes burned her.

The weather now got up, and the waves increased in height. The *Alabama* found herself in the midst of a terrific storm. Semmes ordered her sail to be taken in, but before this could be completed, both the forestaysail and her main topsail were torn to pieces. Semmes would not risk his men further. All nonessential crew members were ordered below. In the three day gale that followed, the lee-quarter boat was wrenched from its davits and dashed to pieces, sails were torn to shreds, and seawater seeped through the

The capture of the U.S. flagged *Tonowanda*, out of Philadelphia bound for Liverpool. (*Illustrated London News*, 15 November 1862)

decking to soak bedding and clothes. Buffeted by the waves, all Semmes and his men could do was to ride out the storm. The *Alabama* was a good ship, Semmes knew. "She behaved nobly," he admitted. She could take it, and so she did. Laird's had built a fine ship. At the height of the storm, Arthur Sinclair wrote in his book of 1896, *Two Years on the Alabama*: "Lieutenant Low's superb seamanship and coolness in 'wearing' ship from port tack, without awaiting the commander's orders, doubtless saved the Alabama from foundering. Had he hesitated five minutes, the maneuver would have been impossible of execution, owing to the fury of the wind."

Then it was all over; they came out the other side of the storm. In the days that followed all hands were set to work repairing the damage—carpenters and sailmakers, and the gunners putting their battery in order. The sodden flags from captured ships were hung out to dry like washing. Semmes counted them, each one representing a captured enemy ship: seventeen flags, seventeen ships. The "flaunting lies" is how he described those flags.

The weather improved, and the *Alabama* continued her mission. Between 16 and 20 October they chased and boarded nine ships. All of them, in what was considered to be an American sea, were neutrals. "The American flag," Semmes observed, "was beginning to disappear from it."[9] On the 21st Master's Mate James Evans, a Charleston man, identified a large ship sailing off to the northwest of them as a Yankee. In full sail, she was running before the wind, a thing of beauty. Semmes moved to intercept her. He ordered the British ensign to be run up the mast and awaited her arrival. She made no change in her course and came straight on, without any fear. Once she was under the *Alabama*'s guns, Semmes ordered a blank cartridge to be fired. She responded by hauling in her sail, and gradually came to a halt, none too distant. Though Semmes had come to hate the American administration, he could not but help admire the seamanship of the men who were now his enemies. He wrote: "If the scene was beautiful before, it was still more so now. If she had been a ship of war, full of men, and with hands stationed at the sheets, halyards, and braces, she could not have shortened sail much more rapidly, or have rounded more promptly and gracefully to the wind, with her main topsail aback. Her cloud of canvas seemed to shrivel and disappear, as though it had been a scroll rolled up by an invisible hand.... I frequently had occasion, during my cruises, to admire the seamanship of my enemies."[10]

The ship was the *Lafayette,* a vessel of 945 tons, registered at New Haven, out of New York, and bound for several ports in Ireland with grain. Initially when her papers were perused, she appeared to be carrying a neutral cargo, but upon closer examination this proved false. The grain had been shipped by the New York company of Messrs. Montgomery Brothers, to their Ulster branch, Montgomery Brothers of Belfast, with the view of then selling it on. As it stood, the cargo was American, traveling aboard an American ship, destined for an American subsidiary company. The *Lafayette* and her cargo were legitimate prizes. This was a new phenomenon, papers forged to suggest that cargoes belonged to neutrals. Semmes trod warily, for he knew that the Confederacy could not afford to alienate nations that would, his government hoped, come to recognize it sooner than later as a de jure state among the nations of the earth. But these were Yankee tricks, and Semmes burned the *Lafayette* and her cargo accordingly. The barque *Lauretta* suffered a similar fate on the 28th of October; her papers too were forged to suggest that her cargo belonged to neutrals. Without any way of defending himself at the time, Semmes was vilified in the American papers for his actions against these two ships. Whether the editors knew that the account was based on a lie — or cared — is a matter of conjecture. By now government censorship in the United States was an actuality.

Three days after the capture of the *Lafayette,* having overhauled a number of neutral ships, a schooner was sighted, which Master's Mate Evans identified as a Yankee. She was ahead of them on a southeasterly course. The *Alabama* gave chase, but the schooner had a good few miles' start on her. Gradually she pulled back the distance, but evening was drawing on. Semmes feared losing her in the dark. At a distance of some four miles, Semmes ordered a live round from his rifled gun. It threw up a great spray, less than half a mile from her. There was some hesitation as to whether she should stop, but then she had nowhere to run to, and so hauled in sail. Coming quickly up now, a boarding party was dispatched from the Confederate ship. She was the 278 ton *Crenshaw,* an American ship, built in Baltimore, and three days out of New York, bound for Glasgow. Here was another ship with false papers to protect her cargo of grain. Semmes was to write: "I would have respected scrupulously any bona fide neutral ownership of property, but I knew all these certificates to be fraudulent. Fraudulent as the transactions were, however, some of the shippers might have imposed upon me, if they had only known how to prepare their vouchers. But they were such bunglers, that they committed the most glaring mistakes."[11] Invariably the other source of provenance, the bill of lading, would reveal that the property was consigned to the order of the shipper. Therefore, originating in the United States from an American company, it could not be a neutral cargo. Semmes took what he needed from the *Crenshaw,* then consigned her to the flames. One of her crew, an Englishman, joined the *Alabama's* crew.

News of these depredations were revealed to the great American public by *Harper's Weekly* (22 October 1862), again with information useful to Semmes:

> We have important news of the operations of the rebel steamer Alabama known as "290." The Cairngorm, an English vessel, lately arrived at Gravesend, from Sydney. She reports that when at Flores, Western Islands, three whale-boats' crews from the Alabama came alongside and reported that their ship, the Ocmulgee, of Edgartown, Massachusetts, had been burned by the Alabama, under command of Captain Semmes, late of the Sumter. The Ocmulgee had two hundred and fifty barrels of oil, and her crew (thirty-four men) were made prisoners. The Alabama had already burned four whalers. She also captured an American schooner (name unknown) in sight of the Cairngorm. The United States sailing sloop of war St. Louis left Lisbon to search, as was supposed, for the rebel privateer "No. 290" off the Azores, in consequence of her raid on American whalers.

Now long gone from the whaling grounds of the Azores, on the 29th of October, some two hundred miles from New York and in heavy rain, the *Alabama* captured her next prize. She was the brig *Baron de Castine,* from Bangor, Maine, bound for Cardenas in Cuba with a cargo of lumber. As Semmes reveals, she was an old ship and of little value. He released her on bond, and took the opportunity to unload all his prisoners on her, with instructions that she was to take them into New York. Engineer Miles Freeman now informed Semmes that fuel was low, about four days' coal remaining. Leaving the New England coast, Semmes set in a course for Martinique in the West Indies, to rendezvous with his supply ship in accordance with arrangements made with Commander Bulloch earlier at Terceira. On Sunday morning, 2 November 1862, shortly after half past eight, another sail was sighted from the masthead. The *Alabama* gave chase. Semmes ordered the United States flag to be flown, and upon firing a blank round, the pursued ship hoisted the same flag and waited upon a boarding party. She was the *Levi Starbuck,* a whaler out of New Bedford, on a voyage of thirty months, to the Pacific. With more than two years' provisions aboard, she was a veritable storeship. Semmes took what he needed, removed the crew, and burned her as night began to fall. Just four days out, newspapers aboard were fairly up to date, and thanks to the enemy's habit of informing its citizens of what it was going to do, Semmes learned that extra gunboats had been sent in pursuit of his ship.

Over the next few days they continued on a southeasterly course, the *Alabama* flying the Federal flag. Just before midnight on 7 November a schooner was sighted directly to the south. The *Alabama* altered course, and set off in pursuit. She was traveling at a fast pace. By dawn the *Alabama* was still five miles behind her. Just then another ship was sighted, off to the northwest. She was traveling at a slower pace; Semmes ordered a change in course to follow the new quarry. By ten o'clock that morning, they were within a mile of the ship. The *Alabama's* captain ordered a shot to be fired, which brought her to heel. She raised the American flag and waited to be boarded. She proved to be the *Thomas B. Wales,* registered in Boston, and returning to her home port from Calcutta in India. When examined, her cargo consisted of linseed, which belonged to the owner of the ship, and saltpeter, 1,704 bags of it, the property of Baring Brothers of Boston. It was true contraband of war. The captain of the *T.B. Wales* also had a number of passengers, including his own wife, and the family of the former American consul of Mauritius, George H. Fairchild. Traveling with Fairchild was his wife, an Englishwoman and daughter of a general in the British army, as well as their three children. The ladies and children were brought aboard and settled in the wardroom mess and the junior officers' rooms. Semmes' chivalry towards Fairchild and his family was later rewarded. Arrested after the war, despite being part of a group of amnestied officers, Semmes was threatened with a trial regarding cruelty to his prisoners. Fairchild wrote to the military commission in Semmes' defense. The main yard of the *T.B. Wales,* being more or less of the same dimension as that of the *Alabama*'s lost in the storm of 16 October, was brought aboard to replace it, along with other useful items. The ship was then consigned to the flames.

Back in England, Consul Thomas H. Dudley traveled up to London to see Mr. Adams with vital news. Secretary Moran at the American embassy wrote in his journal that "Mr. Dudley came up from Liverpool last evening in great haste to see Mr. Adams in order to get him to telegraph to the Kearsage and Tuscarora to go to the Western Islands where he had reason to believe Semmes was about to rendezvous to meet the Bahama and other rebel vessels now laden with arms at L'pool. He also stated that the Turkish steamer 'Schah Gehaad' had left Holyhead for Fayal with Dispatches for Semmes."[12]

The *Alabama* now sailed into the doldrums. Not wishing to waste his precious coal, Semmes could only wait for a wind. The men were put to work repainting the ship and burnishing the brass and steel; her guns were replenished with a new coat of "composition" and the decks scrubbed down. Becalmed around him were a number of British ships. To his disappointment none had recent American newspapers. He had come to rely upon them to tell him what his pursuers were up to, and where they thought he was. The Federal navy was not idle though, and unknown to Semmes the *San Jacinto* under Commander Ronckendorff was sailing for Martinique. On 16 November, wind fluttered the canvas, only to empty out almost as soon. Then the sails filled, and the *Alabama* was underway once more. On a parallel course, the *San Jacinto* was also under sail. On the 17th the *Alabama* made the island of Dominica. Now close, Semmes ordered the engines to be engaged, and with all speed they proceeded to their destination. On the following morning, they cautiously approached the harbor of St. Pierre, where aboard the *Sumter* they had been blockaded barely a year previously; but there was no sign of an enemy man-of-war. Sailing on, at about ten o'clock they entered the anchorage at Fort-de-France, Martinique, and there dropped anchor. After Semmes exchanged courtesies with the governor, the prisoners were landed; the Fairchilds took a very civil farewell. Soon the deck was crowded with inquisitive French people, most, if not all, aware of the *Sumter*'s incredible escape, under Captain Semmes, from a superior enemy craft. It was a feat of superb skill on the part of her captain and his crew.

Then, as things were going so well, Semmes was now faced by a minor mutiny. He ran a dry ship, apart from the regulated grog ration. Away from land for so long, some of the crew members went ashore and got drunk. Upon their return, an officer remonstrating with one of them had a belaying pin thrown at him. It was time for action on Semmes' part. He ordered a lieutenant to "beat to quarters." Drunk or sober, all the crew responded. His officers always appeared at quarters armed, as if going into battle. With thirty armed officers, the balance was changed. Semmes now proceeded among the gun crews, ordering the men to arrest any of their comrades who were drunk. With Semmes' authority reasserted, they followed out the order. In this way twenty men were isolated. They were put in irons. The quartermasters were then called upon to fill buckets with seawater. This done, and the water was thrown over the drunken men repeatedly, until the mutiny was drowned out of them. Released from their irons they were sent below to sleep it off.

The *Alabama*'s coal ship, the *Agrippina,* was lying nearby at anchor. She had been there waiting for some eight days. In so doing, she had attracted the attention of the American consul, who telegraphed the Navy Department. The *San Jacinto* was their response, now just a day away. Semmes quickly summed up the situation for himself. It would be dangerous to spend any time at St. Pierre, for fear that he would again be blockaded in port by a Federal warship. He ordered the *Agrippina* to sail to a new rendezvous. The very next morning Semmes was woken with the news that an enemy warship had appeared off the harbor. Midshipman Edward Maffitt Anderson, cousin to Eugene Anderson Maffitt, also serving aboard the *Alabama,* in a letter home to his father, vividly described what happened next:

> "We were all startled this morning by the cry that a Yankee Gunboat was coming into harbor. We immediately prepared for action, but on examining her, we found that she had 14 guns so we changed our mind, but we hope to run past her tonight and to give her a broadside as we go past. This is the same island and at the same time last year when the Sumter was blockaded last year, but we do not fear anything now, for we think we can ship her if we are put to the trial. All of our men are anxious for a fight. The Gunboat now blockading us is the San Jacinto. She is very heavily armed, having sixty eight pounders broadside, and 2 11 inch pivots. We have not learned who commands her, he refusing to give his name, when he was boarded by the Pilot.... The Captain of the French Man of War that was lying in harbor boarded the San Jacinto and told her either to come to an anchor or to go out three miles. She refused to do the former, so she was obliged to do the latter, so that as soon as it was dark, we put out all our lights, called all hands to quarters and loaded our guns with shot and shell, and started out. We did not have any trouble at all. The French showed us every kindness imaginable, giving us charts of the harbor, and inviting us up to their club rooms.... The night that we ran the Blockade from Martinique we made twelve knots, with only 11 pounds of steam on.... We are bound for some port where we can coal, the coal being sent from England for us.[13]

Semmes himself goes into a little more detail:

> There was a Yankee merchant-ship in the harbor, and just at nightfall, a boat pulled out from her to the San Jacinto, to post her, probably, as to the channels and outlets, and to put her in possession of the rumors afloat. The fates were much more propitious as to weather, than they had been to the little Sumter, when she eluded the Iroquois. The night set in dark and rainy. We ran up our boats, lighted our fires, and when steam was ready, got under way, as we would have done on any ordinary occasion, except only that there were no lights permitted to be seen about the ship, and that the guns were loaded and cast loose and the crew at quarters. In the afternoon, a French naval officer had come on board, kindly bringing me a chart of the harbor, from which it appeared that I could run out in almost any direction I might choose. I chose the most southern route, and giving my ship a full head of steam, we passed out, without so much as a glimpse of the San Jacinto! The next news that we received from the "States," informed us that the San Jacinto was perfectly innocent of our escape until the next morning revealed to her our vacant place in the harbor. Her commander was even more incredulous, and remaining cruising off the harbor for a day or two longer, until he could satisfy himself that I had not hauled my ship up into some cunning nook or inlet, and hid her away out of sight![14]

On the morning of 21 November Commander Ronckendorff was obliged to write to the naval secretary:

> Sir: I have the honor to submit the following statement with reference to the escape of the rebel steamer Alabama, or 290, from this port:
> I arrived here on the morning of the 19th instant, and finding the Alabama at anchor off the town and under the guns of the fort, I at once prepared to attack in case she attempted to escape. Of course I did not anchor, as that would have involved the necessity of remaining twenty-four hours. Shortly after my arrival a French steamer came out from the arsenal and anchored near the Alabama. The commanding officer came on board with a communication from the Governor of the island, a translation of which I herewith enclose, with my reply.
> I sent by a fishing boat an invitation to the captain of the brig Hampden, of Bangor, Me. (which is here discharging cargo), to cooperate with me by signaling during the night the movements of the Alabama. He came on board and took back with him several rockets with instructions to use them if the Alabama should get underway, firing them to the north if she should go by the north

shore of the bay and to the south if by the south shore of the bay. This was near evening. As soon as it was dark I dispatched two boats, one under charge of Acting Master Baker, the other under charge of Acting Master's Mate Keene, who were placed near the beach on each side of the bay with red and blue signal lights, so as to communicate the movements of the rebel vessel in the event of her going out. I kept the San Jacinto near the middle of the bay, so as to command both sides, if possible.

At 8:10 P.M. three rockets were sent up in a southerly direction. We immediately steamed over along the southern shore, opening the point so in case she passed I could see her. I would here remark that the bay is 6 miles wide where, by the direction of the governor's letter, I had leave to operate, and the land quite high on both sides.

Officers with glasses were stationed in the most favorable parts of the vessel, but were unable to see anything of the rebel steamer. The night was dark and cloudy, with a light rain falling, and the opinion of all was that she could not have been seen over half a mile, and not over 300 yards when covered with so dark a background of hills. The officers and men were kept at quarters during the night, and all seemed as zealous as possible, but from the width of the bay and the darkness of the night our efforts were fruitless. The enemy escaped, not withstanding all our vigilance.[15]

By the afternoon of the following day the *Alabama* had rendezvoused with her supply ship, and the two ran down to an anchorage at the little island of Blanquilla, off the coast of Venezuela. To his surprise Semmes saw an American whaling ship at anchor. As the *Alabama* had been flying the Federal flag, the captain of the whaler was fooled into believing she was a United States gunboat. In not too harsh a way Semmes quietly disabused him of the notion. Fearing the worst, he was reassured by the *Alabama*'s captain that, as his ship was within Venezuelan jurisdiction, it would not be put to the torch. However, he and his men would not be allowed to leave the island until the *Alabama* was ready to sail. In the meantime they could get on with what they were doing, filling their barrels with whale oil. This seemed to suit all parties. Re-coaling and reprovisioning took five days. While this was going on, the hold was cleansed and whitewashed, repairs were undertaken, and the boats were rigged with sails and fishing parties were formed. The crew went ashore on liberty. It was a welcome break. All too soon, though, it was over. The *Agrippina* was dispatched to rendezvous with the *Alabama* at the Arcas Islands in the Gulf of Mexico. Semmes had learned, courtesy of the American press, of General Banks' intended seaborne invasion of Texas, and resolved to disrupt the venture if possible.

The United States Army was fitting out a large expedition of some 30,000 men, consisting of cavalry and light artillery. They were to be transported by sea to rendezvous at Galveston, then in Federal hands. As there was but twelve feet of water on the Galveston bar, Semmes knew that they would not be able to enter the port, and therefore must anchor offshore and transport the troops in shallow draft boats. Amidst all the confusion Semmes decided to attack them at night. As usual the press had given details right down to the time of arrival off Galveston. It was an opportunity not to be missed; and if he could not destroy the enemy flotilla, then Semmes knew he could greatly disrupt it. It was now late November; the expedition was scheduled for 10 January. With several weeks on his hands Semmes' next plan was truly audacious. He resolved to waylay a California treasure steamer loaded with millions of dollars in gold. The place of ambush, Semmes decided, would be off the eastern end of the island of Cuba. This was the most likely route that the treasure steamer would take.

Under sail the *Alabama* progressed by way of the islands of Puerto Rico and Dominica, anchoring in the Mona Passage, on the night of 29 November. From her masthead the *Alabama* flew the Stars and Stripes. What struck Semmes as interesting was, in this busy channel, the obvious route for so many ships bound for America, that there was no Federal warship present to protect them. The next morning Semmes' men boarded a Spanish schooner, out of Boston bound for St. Domingo. She let them have the latest batch of newspapers. The Banks expedition was still being fully covered and in great detail, even down to the number of tents required and fodder for the horses. Portraying themselves as the USS *Iroquois*, Semmes asked to be remembered to all at St. Domingo. This the Spanish captain agreed to do.

Time passed, then the cry went up yet again: "Sail ho!" This was then followed with the description "Yankee!" All hands went to quarters as the hunt was renewed once more. A few short hours later the vessel was overhauled and boarded. She was the barque *Parker Cooke,* of Boston bound for Aux Cayes, Dominica. She proved to be a veritable delicatessen of a ship, with beef, pork, crackers, bread, butter and lots, lots more. Semmes restocked the *Alabama*'s larder. Transferring the provisions took most of the day, and it was dusk by the time they had finished. The job complete and the crew transferred and put in the hold, the *Parker Cooke* was set on fire. From the newspapers retrieved, Semmes learned from one New York paper of the impact that his ship was having on American shipping:

> The damaging effect of the Alabama's raid on our shipping upon the maritime interests of this port were as conspicuous to-day as yesterday. It was next to impossible for the owner of an American ship to procure freight unless he consented to make a bogus sale of his ship.
>
> Freights to Great Britain are rather more active under favorable foreign advices for breadstuffs, but rates by American vessels depressed: foreign bottoms most in favor, but even these now find it difficult to employ themselves profitably. To Liverpool, flour is 9d. @ 2s.[16]

The next day the *Alabama* continued on towards Cuba. During the course of the day she chased and caught two Spanish and one Dutch ship, but released them upon proof of their neutrality. That night the *Alabama* anchored off Cape Francois. During the course of the night a large warship under steam and sail passed by them, barely three hundred yards away. Seeing her well in advance Semmes had beaten to quarters to receive her should she be an enemy vessel. There had been no time to raise steam; he could only stand and fight should it come to that. She must have seen the *Alabama*, but took no interest. Semmes could only assume that she was a Spanish ship heading for Cuba. The men were stood down and sent back to bed. By 2 December the Confederate ship had reached Tortuga. As darkness fell a sail was seen, and the *Alabama* went after her. When within range she fired a blank cartridge, but the ship did not respond. The *Alabama* engaged her further with a live round, and this brought her to heel. The boarding party discovered that she was a French barque, and when questioned why she had not stopped, her captain asked why he should. France was not at war with anybody. Semmes marveled at his breathtaking logic. The *Alabama* turned and resumed her course. On 5 December the *Alabama* discovered that increasing rarity, a United States merchant ship. She was the *Union,* a somewhat decrepit schooner out of Baltimore. Her cargo was neutral and properly authenticated. Semmes bonded her, and putting his prisoners from the *Parker Cooke* aboard her, allowed her to resume her journey to Port Maria, Jamaica.

From the very accurate timetables of the arrivals and departures of ships, published in the New York newspapers, an incredible help to Semmes, he knew that the California treasure steamer was due the following day. Surprisingly, though, she did not show. The next day being Sunday, the crew were paraded on deck for inspection. Then suddenly the cry went up: "Sail-ho!" Out on the horizon, on the port bow, was a large steamer, brig-rigged and approaching fast. She could not be the treasure ship though, she was not approaching from the right direction. Nonetheless, the fires were stoked up, the propeller lowered, and within twenty minutes the *Alabama* was in full steam. At three miles' distance Semmes had the United States flag raised. Moments later the approaching side-wheeled steamer hoisted the same. For a moment there was some concern that she might be a Federal warship, but scanning the steamer, there was no sign of guns. She was evidently a packet ship. The *Alabama* moved to intercept her, but Semmes misjudged her speed. She passed ahead of them by two lengths at least. She was a fast ship. Onboard, lining the decks, he could see her passengers quite distinctly: men and women, many using binoculars to view his ship. There was a sprinkling of military men among them. They were clearly admiring the fine lines of this U.S. warship. Those in the know were aware she was not of American design, but she was very streamlined. Passing through her wake, the *Alabama* wheeled about, and set off in pursuit. Her quarry was some three to four hundred yards ahead.

The enemy flag was torn down from the *Alabama*'s mast, and the Confederate flag raised. Semmes ordered a blank shot to be fired. Onboard the steam packet there was consternation. The passengers fled from the deck to the safety of their cabins. The captain was not so easily intimidated. He ordered more speed, and she seemed to leap ahead. Semmes ordered more speed in response, but he knew that the packet could better him for speed. He ordered his rifled bow gun to be uncovered and prepared. Exercising caution, he wanted no fatalities, Semmes ordered a shot to be placed around her foremast. The shot cut through its target, sending large splinters flying. The game was up, her captain decided, and the great side wheels of the steamer stopped revolving. The *Alabama* now came swiftly up to her, and a boarding party was sent over. She was the Californian steamer *Ariel*, a sister ship to the treasure ship Semmes had hoped to capture. Outward bound, with five hundred men, women and children as passengers, the venture, as far as Semmes was concerned, had turned to farce. What to do with so many people he now had to decide.

Among them were some one hundred and forty military personnel, including a number of naval officers. These at least he could parole, extracting a promise from them that they would not continue in arms against the Confederacy. But what of the remainder? He could only hope that another ship might come along so that he could transfer them to it — and then sink the *Ariel*? That was a possibility. By now though there was near hysteria among the women passengers, who, having read the propaganda from the Northern press, now feared the worst. A charm offensive was required. Selecting a handsome lieutenant from his staff, and the most good-looking men from the crew, he sent them aboard the *Ariel* to reassure the ladies that they had nothing to fear. It was a complete propaganda victory for the Confederacy. One young lady, stepping forward, asked to be allowed to cut a button from the lieutenant's tunic as a souvenir. He agreed, and others followed, so by the time of his return, he had barely a button remaining. *Frank Leslie's Illustrated Newspaper* (10 Jan. 1863) commented: "The buttons of the officers are the best Birmingham manufacture." The Birmingham referred to was Birmingham, England. The company that made the buttons, Firmin & Sons, also supplied buttons to the Federal army. Boarding Officer George Townley Fullam in charge of twenty well armed men, after reassuring the passengers that none should be molested, informed them that their personal baggage and property would be respected. He then demanded the keys of the special locker, together with all the ship's private papers and letters. Money, amounting to $9,500, was removed from the safe and a receipt given. The engine room was temporarily taken over by two engineers from the *Alabama*.

Failing to overhaul another ship, and well aware that he was in dangerous waters, Semmes was obliged to bond the *Ariel*, the property of millionaire Jacob Vanderbilt, for $260,000, to be paid within six months of the establishment of the Confederacy. Now released, the *Ariel* continued on her journey. *Harper's Weekly* (10 Jan.1863) briefly covered the story:

A CALIFORNIA STEAMER CAUGHT BY THE "ALABAMA."

On 7th December the pirate Alabama came across the Ariel, bound from New York to Aspinwall, off the coast of Cuba, and brought her to by sending a 68-pound shot through her foremast. Captain Semmes then took off her captain, and held him prisoner for three days, expressing his determination at the same time to land passengers either at some point on the island of Cuba or St. Domingo, and then destroy the vessel. At the earnest remonstrance of Captain Jones, in behalf of the women and children on board, however, he consented to let her proceed. The Alabama started in pursuit of the Champion, then on her return voyage to New York, but failed to find her. Captain Jones carried the Ariel safe into Aspinwall, and arrived at this port on 28th, but brought no gold. With the fear of the Alabama before his eyes, he wisely left the treasure at Aspinwall.

In more depth was the report to the Naval Department by Commander Sartori of the U.S. Navy, a passenger aboard the *Ariel*:

PACKET STEAMER ARIEL,

Off Sandy Hook, December 27, 1862.

SIR: It becomes my painful official duty to inform the Department of the capture of this steamer, on board of which I was a passenger under your order to report to Rear-Admiral Charles H. Bell for a command in the Pacific Squadron. She was taken possession of by the steamer Alabama off Cape Maysi, Cuba, on the afternoon of the 7th instant, on her outward passage from New York to Aspinwall, under the following circumstances:

It appears that as the Ariel rounded Cape Maysi a sail was observed close under the land flying the United States flag; that little attention was paid her until she appeared to be heading toward this vessel, when Captain Jones, commanding the Ariel, made all speed. I, however, knew nothing of this until about 1:45 P.M., when one of the officers of the Ariel came into my cabin, where we were dining, and reported that the Alabama was close upon us. I immediately jumped to the deck and beheld a steamer not over 500 yards distant, rebel flag flying, and, having just fired a lee gun. Major Garland, commanding the detachment of marines (passengers on board bound to California), had them immediately formed in the waist and gangway. I at once say that nothing could be done. She was upon the Ariel with a heavy broadside, fully presented, and almost immediately two heavy broadside guns were fired, and a 68-pound shell struck the foremast just over the pilot house, cutting the mast more than half off. Captain Jones, seeing the utter impossibility of defending the vessel or injuring the enemy in any manner, with my advice and the advice of Major Garlands and the voice of all the passengers, surrendered his ship....

The Ariel was detained until about 10:30 P.M. on the 9th instant (fifty-six hours). Captain Semmes had, on the night of the 8th, sent word that he intended to land all the passengers at Kingston, Jamaica, and we had been steaming towards that point closely convoyed by the Alabama. When off Morant light-house the vessels were hove to for daylight, but about 10 o'clock a passing sail was boarded by a boat from the Alabama, from which material information must have been received by Captain Semmes, for he soon sent for Captain Jones, demanded and received heavy bonds, took from the Ariel his officers and men, and left her free to proceed to Aspinwall. This was at 11 P.M. of the 9th; the Alabama left us under sail, standing to the northward.[17]

With the assault upon Banks' expedition now very much in mind, Semmes withdrew from the main shipping routes to overhaul his engine. In the exertion to capture the *Ariel,* a valve casting had been cracked. As it would be needed in an intended assault where speed might prove critical, he decided to replace it. So for the next two days the *Alabama* continued under sail while a replacement casting was made. Bound for the west side of Jamaica, the *Alabama* sailed into bad weather. Three days later, the subject of the stormy weather, she had been pushed westward into the Gulf of Honduras. Proceeding north once more, the *Alabama* sailed up the coast along the Yucatan peninsular and back again into the trade routes. There being no sign of sail, by 20 December Semmes' ship anchored off Cape Catoche in Yucatan for the night. The next day they sailed westward into the Gulf of Mexico. A solitary sail passed by at distance. Semmes did not pursue her.

On 23 December a barque, British in design, was seen, sailing in the same direction. Semmes knew at once who she was; it was his own supply ship, the *Agrippina.* Catching up with her the two ships proceeded on to the three islands that make up Arcas Cays, a hundred miles or so west of the peninsular. For the next week the Alabama remained in the little islands, re-coaling, refitting and repainting. The upper deck, expanded by the sun, was re-caulked and made waterproof once more. Sails were repaired, and the *Alabama's* copper bottom was scraped clean. The *Agrippina,* her hold now empty of coal, was dispatched back to Bulloch in Liverpool, with a request for more. A future rendezvous was arranged between the two captains. Christmas was spent in this tropical paradise. Those not engaged in work passed their time in fishing and fowling and generally recuperating until ready to sail. Semmes now had a satisfied and motivated crew. It was now the 5th of January; Semmes had allowed himself five days to arrive at Galveston, and confront Banks' force. He put in a course for Galveston lighthouse.

The days passed without incident. No sail was seen, no ship overhauled. Arriving off Galveston on the afternoon of the 10th , the cry went up: "Land ho! ... Sail ho!" Telescopes scanned the coastline. There was no fleet, just five steamers, apparently ships of war. One of them opened fire upon the city. What to make of it? It could only mean that the city had been retaken by Confederate forces. What Semmes did not know then, devoid of news during his voyage from Jamaica to here, was that the city had been retaken by Confederate General Magruder, assisted by Captain Leon Smith with a couple of river steamers. The enemy's entire fleet had either been captured or driven off. Accordingly, the Banks expedition was diverted to New Orleans. All that remained were the five Union steamships that now lay off Galveston, occasionally shelling the city.

Dusk had now fallen. To attack the five ships would have been suicidal, but Semmes had promised his men a fight. If he were to turn and flee he would have lost face with his men. Hastily conferring with his officers, he was interrupted with the news that one of the ships, a side-wheeler, was approaching. She had been sent to investigate them. Quickly sizing up the situation Semmes decided to give her battle; but first he would have to lead her far enough away from her companions to make it anywhere near a fair fight. The *Alabama* began to veer away from Galveston, as if now trying to elude the Federal gunship. The propeller of the *Alabama* was lowered and her engine engaged. The pursuing ship came on. She was the USS *Hatteras,* a side-wheeled steamer constructed at Harland & Hollingsworth at Wilmington, Delaware, in 1861. She was of 1126 tons, 210 feet in length, and an armament of four 32-pounders and one 20-pounder. She was under the command of Commander Homer C. Blake.

Semmes now played a cautious game of cat and mouse, first speeding away, then slowing down for the enemy ship to catch him, gradually drawing his opponent twenty miles away from the coast. Darkness was rapidly falling. Though there was no moon, a star-lit sky enabled both ships to clearly see each other. Aboard both ships the crews had beat to quarters. On both ships the crews now manned their guns. By six o'clock that evening, the *Hatteras* was close enough to hail the mysterious steamer.

"What steamer is that?" the demand was made.

"Her Majesty's Steamer Petrel!" was the response. "What steamer is that?"

There was no reply. Twice more the call was made: "What steamer is that?"

The response was indistinct: "This is the United States Steamer...."

Though they did not hear the name of the ship, the *Alabama* crew had heard enough. Aboard the *Alabama* the Confederate flag was raised, and their own response was, "This is the Confederate States Steamer Alabama!"[18] As the name faded on the breeze, the *Alabama* opened fire with a broadside. The *Hatteras* responded with like, and soon it became a general melee. Closing to within forty yards, pistols and rifles were now engaged. Both ships were struck, the percussion shells from the *Alabama* tearing great rents of five and six feet in length in the side of the iron-hulled enemy ship. Barely seventeen minutes later the *Hatteras* ceased firing, and a lee gun fired, indicated that she had taken enough damage. Semmes ordered a cease-fire aboard the *Alabama,* then demanded to know whether his opponent had surrendered. The response was yes. The *Hatteras* was on fire, and sinking. Two of her crew had been killed and five badly wounded. Captain Blake went aboard the *Alabama,* and offered his sword in token of his surrender. Now all haste was made to save the crew. Commander Blake later filed an official report of the fight:

> UNITED STATES' CONSULATE,
>
> KINGSTON, JAMAICA, Jan. 21 1863.
>
> Sir:—It is my painful duty to inform the Department of the destruction of the United States steamer Hatteras, recently under my command, by the rebel steamer Alabama, on the night of the 11th inst. off the coast of Texas. The circumstances of the disaster are as follows:
>
> Upon the afternoon of the 11th inst., at half-past two o'clock, while at anchor in company with the fleet of Commodore Bell, off Galveston, Texas, I was ordered by signal from the United States flag-ship Brooklyn, to chase a sail to the southward and eastward. I got under way immediately, and steamed with all speed in the direction indicated. After some time the strange sail could be seen from the Hatteras, and was ascertained to be a steamer, which fact I communicated to the flag-ship by signal. I continued the chase and rapidly gained upon the suspicious vessel. Knowing the slow rate of speed of the Hatteras , I at once suspected that deception was being practiced, and hence ordered the ship to be cleared for action, with everything in readiness for a determined attack and a vigorous defense.
>
> When within about four miles of the vessel, I observed that she had ceased to steam, and was lying broadside and awaiting us. It was nearly seven o'clock, and quite dark; but notwithstanding the obscurity of the night, I felt assured from the general character of the vessel and her maneuvers, that I should soon encounter the rebel steamer Alabama. Being able to work but four guns on the side of the Hatteras— two short 32-pounders, one 30-pounder rifled Parrott gun, and one 20-pounder rifled gun —I concluded to close with her, that my guns might be effective, if necessary.
>
> I came within easy speaking range — about seventy-five yards— and upon asking, "What steamer is that?" received the answer, "Her Britannic Majesty's ship Vixen." I replied that I would send a boat aboard, and immediately gave the order. In the meantime , the vessels were changing positions, the stranger endeavoring to gain a desirable position for a raking fire. Almost simultaneously with the piping away of the boat, the strange craft again replied, "We are the Confederate steamer Alabama," which was accompanied with a broadside. I, at the same moment, returned the fire. Being well aware of the many vulnerable points of the Hatteras, I hoped, by closing with the Alabama, to be able to board her, and thus rid the seas of the piratical craft. I steamed directly for the Alabama, but she was enabled by her great speed, and the foulness of the bottom of the Hatteras, and, consequently, her diminished speed, to thwart my attempt when I had gained a distance of but thirty yards from her. At this range, musket and pistol shots were exchanged. The firing continued with great vigor on both sides. At length a shell entered amidships in the hold,

setting fire to it, and, at the same instant — as I can hardly divide the time — a shell passed through the sick bay, exploding in an adjoining compartment, also producing fire. Another entered the cylinder, filling the engine room and deck with steam, and depriving me of my power to maneuver the vessel, or to work the pumps, upon which the reduction of the fire depended.

With the vessel on fire in two places, and beyond human power, a hopeless wreck upon the waters, with her walking beam shot away, and her engine rendered useless, I still maintained an active fire, with the double hope of disabling the Alabama and attracting the attention of the fleet off Galveston, which was only twenty-eight miles distant.

It was soon reported to me that the shells had entered the Hatteras at the water-line, tearing off entire sheets of iron, and that the water was rushing in, utterly defying every attempt to remedy the evil, and that she was rapidly sinking. Learning the melancholy truth, and observing that the Alabama was on my port bow, entirely beyond the range of my guns, doubtless preparing for a raking fire of the deck, I felt I had no right to sacrifice uselessly, and without any desirable result, the lives of all under my command.

To prevent the blowing up of the Hatteras from the fire, which was making much progress, I ordered the magazine to be flooded, and afterward a lee gun was fired. The Alabama then asked if assistance was desired, to which an affirmative answer was given.

The Hatteras was then going down, and in order to save the lives of my officers and men, I caused the armament on the port side to be thrown overboard. Had I not done so, I am confident the vessel would have gone down with many brave hearts and valuable lives. After considerable delay, caused by the report that a steamer was seen coming from Galveston, the Alabama sent us assistance , and I have the pleasure of informing the Department that every living being was conveyed safely from the Hatteras to the Alabama.

Two minutes after leaving the Hatteras she went down, bow first, with her pennant at the mast-head, with all her muskets and stores of every description, the enemy not being able, owing to her rapid sinking, to obtain a single weapon.

The battery upon the Alabama brought into action against the Hatteras numbered seven guns, consisting of four long 32-pounders, one 100-pounder, one 68-pounder, and one 24-pounder rifled gun. The great superiority of the Alabama, with her powerful battery and her machinery under the water-line must be at once recognized by the Department, who are familiar with the construction of the Hatteras, and her total unfitness for a conflict with a regular built vessel of war.

The distance between the Hatters and the Alabama during the action varied from twenty-five to one hundred yards. Nearly fifty shots were fired from the Hatteras, and I presume a greater number from the Alabama.

I desire to refer to the efficient and active manner in which Acting Master Porter, executive officer, performed his duty. The conduct of Assistant Surgeon Edward S. Matthews, both during the action and afterwards, in attending to the wounded, demands my unqualified commendation. I would also bring to the favorable notice of the Department Acting Master's Mate McGrath, temporarily performing duty as gunner. Owing to the darkness of the night, and the peculiar construction of the Hatteras, I am only able to refer to the conduct of the officers who came under my especial attention; but from the character of the contest, and the amount of damage done to the Alabama, I have personally no reason to believe any officer failed in his duty.

To the men of the Hatteras I cannot give too much praise. Their enthusiasm and bravery was of the highest order.

I enclose the report of Assistant Surgeon E.S. Matthews, by which you will observe that five men were wounded and two killed. The missing, it is hoped, reached the fleet at Galveston.

I shall communicate to the Department, in a separate report, the movements of myself and my command from the time of our transfer to the Alabama until the departure of the earliest mail from this place to the United States.

I am, very respectfully, your obedient servant,

H.C. BLAKE.
Lieutenant Commanding

Hon. GIDEON WELLES,
Secretary of the Navy, Washington.

With the crew of the *Hatteras* now onboard, and the wounded attended to, Semmes ordered all lights on deck to be extinguished, in order to make his escape. Thundering towards them in fan formation, even as the *Hatteras,* a burning wreck, sank beneath the waves, was the remainder of the United States fleet, determined to seek and destroy the lone Confederate steamship. Once again, though, Semmes managed to elude his enemies and ran for the Yucatan Channel. United States propaganda, anxious to play down the loss of one of its warships, suggested that the combat was uneven, that the *Alabama* was the better armed. Semmes was later to compare the two ships and demonstrate that they were more evenly matched than the U.S. administration would allow. As to Blake himself, Semmes was magnanimous. "Blake behaved like a man of courage, and made the best fight he could, ill-supported as he was," he later wrote.

The following morning the watch aboard the *Alabama* scanned the horizon for any sign of pursuing Federal warships, but none were seen. They had returned to their bombardment of Galveston. Semmes set in a course for Jamaica, there hopefully to carry out repairs to his ship, some "two or three shot-holes the enemy had made above the water-line," and land his prisoners whom he had paroled under oath.

On the 20th of January, nine days after the action off Galveston, the *Alabama* approached Jamaica. During the following day she followed the coast up to Port Royal. At half past four that afternoon, off Plum Point lighthouse, at the mouth of the harbor of Port Royal, Semmes raised the French tricolor and fired a gun, the signal for a pilot to attend them. Within the hour they were at anchor beside the Royal Navy Squadron, consisting of the *Jason,* the *Challenger* and the *Greyhound*. The *Alabama* was then boarded by a Royal Navy lieutenant, who came to make enquiries. When news got out that she was the *Alabama,* with the officers and crew aboard of a Federal gunboat that she had sunk, the ship was invaded by well-wishers come to tender their congratulations. A somewhat biased neutrality was displayed by some of the younger British naval officers.

The following morning Semmes called on Commodore Dunlap, the commanding naval officer in Jamaica and there officially as a naval officer of the Confederate States, presented his compliments. Semmes requested permission to land his prisoners and make some slight repairs. Permission was granted. While the repairs were undertaken, Semmes

The sinking of the U.S. blockader *Hatteras*, off Galveston.

spent a few days in the country, the guest of an old friend, one Mr. Fyffe, at his country seat, Flamstead. Here Semmes settled into the life of an English country gentleman. From his sympathetic descriptions one can see that he had a greater affinity with the English than he did with his fellow countrymen in the North. On the fourth day of his sojourn, the ever reliable Lt. Kell sent word that the *Alabama* was nearly ready to return to sea.

Things were not well aboard the *Alabama* in respect of her crew. Their actions today would probably be described as posttraumatic stress following their action against the *Hatteras*. Drunkenness had become rampant among the men, but the worst offender was Paymaster Clarence R. Yonge. Yonge was born in Upson County, Georgia, in 1833. He had formerly worked for the Savannah, Albany & Gulf Railroad Company, but at the outbreak of the war he volunteered his services to the South. For a time he was assistant paymaster aboard the blockade runner *Lady Davis*. In November 1861, while serving at the naval paymaster's office in Savannah, he was appointed clerk to James Dunwoody Bulloch and returned with him to Liverpool in March 1862. Yonge attended to the day-to-day correspondence and acted as paymaster to the officers attached to the "290." Initially Bulloch found him to be "a quiet, modest young man, who was light and trivial in character and disposition, and whose conduct was most exemplary," or so he wrote in a letter to the secretary of the navy, Stephen Mallory. By August 1862, when Yonge had been appointed paymaster aboard the *Alabama,* Bulloch's opinion had changed.

When Semmes joined the *Alabama* in the Azores, Bulloch cautioned him that he now believed Yonge to be an "unsteady and unreliable young man, whose judgment and discretion were not to be trusted," but Bulloch added that he had no suspicion, "in regard to his integrity in money matters."[19] While at Jamaica Yonge began drinking to excess. One day when sent ashore with £400 to settle accounts, he did not return. He was found at a public house in the company of the United States consul and a number of recently paroled enemy seamen. He was arrested and returned to the *Alabama,* where on 25 January 1863 he was court-martialed on a charge of neglecting his duties and behaving in a most disreputable manner, by talking to the enemy. Refusing to remain onboard, he was confined to his room until they reached a Confederate port. He was deprived of his sword and sent ashore in disgrace. In his book, Semmes never once refers to the *Alabama*'s disreputable paymaster by name. Yonge then bigamously married a widowed Negro woman, took her to England with her mother-in-law and two teenaged children, swindled her out of all her money and property, and abandoned her in Liverpool. He tried to get money from American consul Thomas Dudley; but, Dudley being absent, he was referred to the American embassy in London. Assistant Secretary Benjamin Moran takes up the story:

> Wed. 1st April 1863: A young man of rather good manners and of Southern birth came into the Legation this morning at about half past 10, and expressed a desire to take the oath of allegiance to the Government. He announced himself as Clarence R. Yonge, said he was born in Washington, was a resident of savannah, was 29 years of age, and had until recently been paymaster on board the British pirate No. 290. We at once recognized him as the person mentioned in some of the papers sent up by Mr. Dudley on Monday, but not knowing how these had gotten into Mr. Dudley's hands, said nothing about them. Yonge's appearance at the Legation was a mystery, as he came from Southampton; and yet Dudley had sent documents from Liverpool. He took the oath, and then talked freely of the exploits of the pirate. I expressed myself very strongly against her and her crew, and thus drew from him the fact that he still had a good deal of the rebel in him. He came over with Capt. Bullock in March '62 to join the 290, which he will swear was built by Laird under contract for the rebels, sailed in her from Liverpool, went into Moelfre Bay in her, then up through the Irish Sea to a point near Londonderry, where the pilot and Bullock were landed, and on to Terceira. While talking to him Mr. Dudley very unexpectedly came in, having

just arrived from Liverpool; but he did not know Yonge. This confirmed me in the wisdom of my course in not having said a word about the papers, for it was evident Dudley had not obtained them from our man. Seeing we might get a good deal out of him, he was introduced to Mr. Adams, and Mr. Dudley finally took him to the Golden Cross Hotel, and provided him with money and whatever he needed. It was clear that his loyalty was the result in measure of empty pockets and partly a matter of revenge.... Yonge ... swears positively to the contract between Laird and Bullock for the "290," to the agreement on W.C. Miller's part with Fraser, Trenholm & Co. to build the Oreto for the rebels; to the fact that he and the other officers of the "290" knew on Sunday before this vessel left L'pool that it was the intention of the Gov't. to stop her; to the fact that the trial trip was a mere sham to get her out, and that Laird put his daughters on board as a blind that she was coming back; that of 115 men on board 9/10ths are English, and that many of them belong to the British Naval Reserve and get a pension from H.M.'s Govt. he also swears that the men get their pay off Fraser, Trenholm & Co. in L'pool; that the ship was armed and coaled from England; that she burned American vessels with the English flag flying, and that she was permitted to refit and repair at Port Royal, Ja[maica] And that her officers were feasted there by the Governor and she was saluted by a fort. He states distinctly that the vessel receives every assistance and courtesy from British officials; and that these openly expressed their sympathy and showed them favor where ever they met.

He says he does not know who gave Capt. Bullock [sic] and Laird notice of the intention of the Gov't to seize the ship on the Sunday night before she sailed, but it was no doubt some English official, as all of them at the port were friendly. He is quite certain the Collector connived at her departure.... Yonge is a man of talent, and has a large development of the perceptive faculties. Still he is a slippery fellow. It appears he was dismissed at Port Royal for marrying a Negro there, brought her to L'pool where he deserted her, and that it was from her Dudley got the papers before referred to. He was on his way home from Southampton when he got out of money, and determined to repent and become loyal.

Thurs. 2nd April '63: Yonge's deposition was completed & sworn to this Morning. Dudley brought it here. He took Yonge with him to L'pool this afternoon and is going to keep him for some weeks at $1500 per year.[20]

Yonge became one of a number of paid informers, but his former life caught up with him in the British courts, where he was thoroughly discredited. With the assistance of the U.S. minister, Yonge was smuggled back into the United States under the assumed name of James Edwards Davies. He partly redeemed his honor by enlisting in the Union army with the 25th Regiment of New York Cavalry, and later found employment as a clerk at the Department of the Interior, in Washington.

The *Alabama* at anchor, Port Royal, Jamaica. (*Illustrated London News*, 11 April 1863)

In Jamaica there was a degree of fraternization between the former enemies that made up the crews of the *Alabama* and the *Hatteras*. They drank and ate together while on shore. It was as if there was no war. The British authorities took an easy line in their duties towards the belligerents, there being no obvious animosity between the two sides. There was also fraternization between the British and Confederate officers, a number of whom were acquainted from their days in Nassau. So while dining aboard HMS *Greyhound* it seemed only natural that the band be instructed to strike up "Dixie" in honor of their guests. In England this particularly catchy tune (lacking any political significance) was very popular at the time, particularly in the music halls. But the "Puritans," as Semmes called the people of New England, saw it in a different light. Captain Blake wrote to Commodore Dunlap to complain. Dunlap saw the incident for what it was, and accordingly, in a sense of fun, instructed the bands of the fleet that in future when one played "Dixie" it should be followed by "Yankee Doodle," which was also popular in the English music halls. The next night the band aboard the *Jason* played "God Save the Queen." This was followed by the *Greyhound's* band playing "Dixie," and the band of the *Challenger* then playing "Yankee Doodle Dandy." Honor was thus satisfied, and everyone had a laugh at Blake's pomposity. Perhaps Blake himself had a laugh at his own foolishness.

At half-past eight on the night of the 25th of January, repairs complete and provisions laid in, the *Alabama* steamed out of Port Royal, bound for the coast of Brazil. The next morning the *Alabama* bowled along under sail; it was a particularly fine day, with a good breeze. Soon after midday the cry went up: "Sail-ho!" Business had been resumed. Directly ahead of them was a recognizable Yankee ship. The Stars and Stripes was raised aboard the *Alabama* as she set off in pursuit. The ship ahead of them ran up the Federal flag in response. Coming up in sail and steam, the *Alabama* tore down the "old Flag" and raised the Confederate flag. She ordered the other ship to heave-to and receive a boarding party. The ship proved to be the *Golden Rule,* of the Atlantic & Pacific Steamship Company, out of New York, bound for Aspinwall. She had an assorted cargo, including replacement masts and a complete set of rigging for the USS *Bainbridge*. As she was carrying pure contraband of war, Semmes put the ship to the torch at six o'clock that night.

Sailing along the coast of St. Domingo (present-day Haiti and Dominican Republic), at three o'clock in the afternoon of the next day they arrived before the guano island of Alta Vela, fifteen miles south of the main island. As dusk fell a ship was halted, and a boarding party sent over to her discovered that she was a neutral Spanish brig, out of Montevideo, bound for Havana. She was released. The anchor was raised again at about midnight, when a hermaphrodite brig, positively identified as a Yankee, was seen. The gun boomed out, and she came to a halt. She was American. The *Chastelaine* of Boston, having carried a cargo of wooden staves to the island of Guadeloupe, was now on her way to Cienfuegos in Cuba in search of a cargo of sugar and rum. Semmes burned her. With two crews of prisoners, Semmes sailed up to the old town of St. Domingo to release them.

In the harbor were two ships, one of them a New York brig, the British ensign lazily flying from her mast. Semmes viewed the hypocrisy of it all in the following statement: "She had a 'bran-new' [*sic*] English ensign flying. Admiral Milne having failed to respond to the frantic cries of the New York 'Commercial Advertiser,' to protect the Yankee flag, the Yankee ship-owners, with many loathings and contortions, were at last forced to gulp the English flag. There was no other way of coaxing England to protect them. Being in a neutral port , I had no opportunity, of course, of testing the verity of this 'cross of St.

George,' as the Yankees were fond of calling the hated emblem of England — hated, but hugged at the same time, for the protection which it gave ship and cargo."

Following an interview with the Spanish commander of the port, Semmes was permitted to discharge his prisoners. Arrangements were also made for fresh provisions and other refreshments to be delivered to the ship the following morning. The business of the day now done, Semmes allowed himself the time to visit the church attached to the Dominican convent. His Roman Catholicism was apparently very important to him and quite often seems to have shaped his actions. His not naming of the traitor Clarence Yonge may perhaps be looked upon as an act of Christian charity on his part, to avoid further embarrassing Yonge or Yonge's family. But there was to be no Christian charity for what he saw as the hypocrisy of the self-righteous Puritanism of New England. He equated Puritanism with avarice and considered Puritans a people set on exploiting other people and bullying smaller nations.

At the opening of the war his views were quite moderate; but as the war progressed, and he read of the burning of towns, and the general laying waste of the South by the Union army, his views hardened. His hatred is perhaps not directed towards the ordinary man and woman in the North, but more to Lincoln's administration and to big business. The antiquity of the church at St. Domingo that he visited predated by one hundred years "that pestiferous little craft, called the Mayflower, [which] brought over the cockatrice's egg that hatched out the Puritan."[21] Later, from a rocky cliff, he looked down at the ships in the harbor and picked out the *Alabama*: "She is full of men, and a strange flag is flying from her peak.... It is a flag of a nation which has just risen above the horizon, and is but repeating the history of the world. The oppressed has struggled against the oppressor since time began. The struggle is going on still. It will go on forever, for the nature of man will always be the same. The cockatrice's egg has been hatched, and swarms of the Puritan have come forth to overrun the fair fields of the South, that they may possess them.... But away with such thoughts for the present. We came on shore to get rid of them."[22]

At eight o'clock the next morning, the *Alabama* raised her anchor, and under steam, left the harbor, heading east. The only sails were of fishing boats and small coasters laden with fish and fruit. Passing through the Mona Strait that night, the following morning under sail, they encountered only neutral ships. It was the 3rd of February before they captured another enemy ship. She was the schooner *Palmetto*, out of San Juan, Puerto Rico, bound for New York. The cargo had been assigned by an American company in San Juan to a Spanish company in New York. Either way it was a contraband cargo in an American ship. Semmes took aboard its crew then burned ship and cargo. The following day saw a fruitless pursuit of what Semmes believed to be a neutral ship. They pursued it until nightfall, the darkness eventually enveloping her.

On the night of Saturday, 21 February 1863, Semmes opened the journal that he had bought at the shop of Thomas Walmsley, Stationers, of 64, Castle Street, Liverpool, and entered the events of the day:

> Weather very fine; wind light from the southward and eastward. About 7 A.M. a sail was descried from aloft and others soon afterwards in succession until four were seen. We gave chase to the first one discovered, standing to eastward for an hour and more, but finding her well ahead and to windward we tacked and gave chase to two others, getting up steam, as one of the two showed United States colors and was too far to windward to be overhauled in the very light breeze that was blowing. At 1 P.M. came up with and captured the ship Golden Eagle — she stand-

ing a couple of shot before she hove to—from Howland Island, Pacific Ocean, for Cork, for orders. Threw a prize crew on board her, with directions to follow, and stood for the other, now some 15 miles distant. Came up with her at 3 P.M. She proved to be the bark Olive Jane, from Bordeaux for New York. Captured and burned her and then stood back to meet our first prize, with which we came up at about dusk. Got on board from her a few provisions, and then burned her and filled away on our course. The former was laden with a partial cargo of French wines and knicknackeries, and the latter (the latter one burned) with guano. Latitude 29 28', longitude 44 58'.

In his expanded account, published as *My Adventures Afloat,* at London in 1869, Semmes continued his tirade against the Northerners, and referred to the cargo of the *Olive Jane*: "There were the richest of olives, and pates de fois gras, going to tickle the palates of the New York shodyites, and other nouveau-riche plebeians, destroyed in that terrible conflagration."

The *Alabama* sailed on into wet and windy weather. Four ships were seen, all neutrals, bound for Europe. The first was a French barque, the other three English; one was a packet ship sailing from Melbourne in Australia, back to Liverpool. Late at night on the next day they pursued a Portuguese ship, which fled in panic. After several shots, some live, she eventually heaved-to and awaited her fate. Her papers checked, she was allowed to continue, much to the relief of her crew, who thought they all would be murdered. The next day the crew of the *Alabama* boarded a Dutch barque and an English brig. Later that night it was the four-masted *Sarah Sands*, sailing from the East Indies, bound for Falmouth in Cornwall. Then there were seven ships the next day, all neutrals. The boredom was broken as Semmes detained one of them, a ship from Hamburg, whose surly captain refused to show his colors until Semmes threatened him with a live round. In complete contrast, on the following day, 27 February, an English ship saluted the *Alabama's* Confederate colors. Just behind the English ship came an American. She fought shy of an introduction and took to her heels. Semmes ordered a pursuit, and it took a live round to bring her to heel. She was the *Washington* of New York, with a cargo of guano from the Chincha Islands, bound for Antwerp in Belgium. Her captain was Joseph G. White. As it was a neutral cargo, consigned by the Peruvian government, Semmes bonded the ship for $50,000. He unloaded all his prisoners on her, the let the *Washington* continue her journey.

On the 28th the *Alabama* overhauled two English ships sailing home from the East Indies, and a French ship, from Batavia to Nantes. The weather continued fine over the next few days. On the morning of 1 March the watch were pleasantly surprised to see an American ship sailing close nearby. Without much exertion she was persuaded to heave-to. She was "just out from Yankee-land," as Semmes described her, the *John A Parks* of Hallowell, Maine, out of New York with a cargo of white pine lumber, destined for Buenos Aires. Her papers were fraudulent. Examining the post aboard her, a letter was discovered revealing the fraud. The consignee, one Davidson, could not help revealing how clever he had been in fooling the local British consul into certifying that the cargo was the property of British subjects. Semmes derived a certain pleasure in telling the American captain what he had discovered, then burned his ship. Semmes was further delighted when reading the newspapers from the *Parks* and he discovered that the *Florida* had succeeded in escaping through the Federal blockade off Mobile. As the *John A. Parks* went up in flames, an English merchantman approached, and Semmes persuaded her to take the American captain, his wife and two nephews as passengers to London.

Two further American ships were boarded within hours of each other, the *Bethiah Thayer* and the *Punjaub*. The first, under master Thomas Mitchell McCartney, was registered at Rockland, Maine. Her cargo of guano, used as a fertilizer, was owned by the

Peruvian government. Under the rules of war Semmes could not burn her; but he could bond the ship itself, and this he did for $40,000. The *Punjaub* passed right by them, a few minutes before midnight. The night was foggy, and she was almost on top of them before she was sighted. All canvas was piled on, as the *Alabama* set off after her. By now the *Punjaub* had a good start, and it was a quarter past three before she overhauled the other ship. Semmes ordered a blank to be fired, which brought her to a halt. Dawn was just breaking as the boarding party sailed over to her. The *Punjaub*, under master Lewis Miller, was registered at Boston, and under sail from Calcutta to London with a cargo of jute and linseed oil. The cargo was properly documented, going from one British port, Calcutta in India, to London. There could be no doubt that it was neutral. Her transporter was not though. Semmes bonded the ship for $50,000.

Within hours the *Alabama* was in pursuit of another vessel, but she proved to be British, transferring a cargo from Mauritius to Cork. From her master, Semmes learned what he had long suspected, that the few American ships still at sea were no longer using the main sea-lanes, but were taking circuitous routes to avoid his ship and the *Florida* and traveling up to four hundred miles out of their way. The *Alabama* now fell in with three neutral ships, all heading in the same direction. On 23 March, with rain falling, another sail was sighted. Off the *Alabama* raced in pursuit of her. She proved to be the *Morning Star* of Boston, out of Calcutta bound for London with a verifiable neutral cargo. Semmes bonded her. Later that day he overhauled a whaling schooner, the *Kingfisher*, registered at Fairhaven, Massachusetts. She had a crew of twenty-three — twenty of whom were Portuguese. She was contraband, and Semmes ordered her to be burned.

Approaching the equator, the *Alabama* passed through a veritable traffic jam of ships, heading in all directions. There were so many that they could not all be stopped. By their very design the spotters could identify them. Most were neutrals. Two days after the burning of the *Kingfisher*, the *Alabama* stopped two Yankee vessels, sailing in convoy. As the Confederate ship approached, they began to maneuver away from each other. They were obviously suspicious. Semmes ordered all sail to be clamped on as he set off in pursuit of the closest ship. As the *Alabama* approached, she ran up the Stars and Stripes. The other ship did likewise. Semmes ordered them to heave-to. The first was the *Charles Hill* of Boston. The second was the *Nora,* also a Bostonian. The *Nora* was covered by an affidavit, supposedly authorized by the mayor of Liverpool. The affidavit had not been signed though, and therefore had no legal binding. Then, in the ship's mail a letter from the ship's owner to her master, Captain F. Percival, was discovered. It read: "Dear Sir, I have received your several letters from Philadelphia. As a rebel privateer has burned several American ships, it may be as well if you can have your bills of lading indorsed as English property, and have your cargo certified to by the British Consul."

Here was the proof that the whole thing was a lie. The cargo was American. Semmes, with a great deal of satisfaction, burned both vessels. Out of the two crews, half a dozen decided to throw in their lots with the *Alabama* and signed on.

On the evening of 29 March, in the midst of a fierce downpour of rain, the *Alabama* crossed the equator, in pursuit of a sail. With the light rapidly deteriorating, the ship managed to escape as darkness finally descended. For the following week the Confederate ship continued south, the skies overcast and filled with rain. On 3 April, during the morning watch, the cloud lifted to reveal a tall ship in the distance, and like the *Alabama,* heading south. With a good wind behind her the *Alabama* set off in pursuit. The chase continued, but at midday the wind dropped and it came on to rain once more. By degrees the Confederate ship closed the gap, but by five o'clock that evening, she was still two miles off. Fearing that he might lose her in the gathering gloom, Semmes dispatched a whale-boat after her. The quarry was boarded, and the ship brought to a halt to await the oncoming commercial raider. The ship was the *Louisa Hatch,* of Rockland, Maine, out of Cardiff with a cargo of Welsh coal, bound for Point-de-Galle, in Ceylon (Sri Lanka). The bill of lading indicated that the cargo belonged to a steamship company, the Messageries Imperiales. Not certified, it had no legal standing. Semmes declared it to be a prize. He now had 1,000 tons of good coal, but he was not in a position to transfer it aboard his own ship. Leaving a prize crew aboard the *Louisa Hatch,* he gave orders that she should accompany him to his destination, the island of Fernando de Noronha, off the coast of Brazil, where he had arranged a rendezvous with his service ship, the *Agrippina.*

The following day they fell in with an English barque, which offered them newspapers. The day after, they chased what they thought was an American whaling schooner. After several hours they caught up with her, only to discover that she was Portuguese. Somewhat annoyed at the waste of time, Semmes returned to his original course. Four days on, Semmes, taking the prize in tow, applied steam. The following day, 10 April, they approached the island. There was no sign of the *Agrippina.* In his book, Semmes is a little hard on Captain Alexander McQueen. He wrote: "The Agrippina had not arrived; nor did I ever see her afterwards. Captain Bulloch had duly dispatched her, but the worthless old Scotch master made it a point not to find me, and having sold his coal in some port or other, I have forgotten where, returned to England with a cock-and-bull story, to account for his failure. The fact is, the old fellow had become alarmed lest he should fall into the hands of the Yankees."[23]

The reality was a little different, as Bulloch relates. Returning home to England the *Agrippina* damaged a mast, which had to be repaired. This caused some delay, and by the time McQueen got to the rendezvous at Fernando de Noronha, Semmes had sailed for Bahia. McQueen arrived at Bahia on the 1 of June, only to discover that Semmes had sailed on 22 May. At anchor in the harbor were two United States warships, the *Mohican* and the *Onward.* They were watching another British-flagged ship, which the American consul suspected was a supply ship for either the *Alabama* or the *Florida.* When the *Agrippina* entered the harbor she immediately fell under suspicion too. The USS *Onward,* McQueen discovered, was ordered to seize his ship should he leave the safety of the harbor. The Scotsman sought the advice of the British consul. The consul advised him to sell his cargo of coal and take another cargo home to England. Thus he would be protected, carrying a certified British cargo. This he did, and was given a consular certificate verifying that the port of "Bahia had been for some time virtually blockaded by the United States ships *Mohican* and *Onward.*" Arriving back in Liverpool, the cargo was sold for £437. 15s. 3d., and added to the Confederacy's European coffers. As a suspected Confederate supply ship, Bulloch decided not to use the *Agrippina* again, and she was sold at auction for £860.

At Fernando de Noronha, a Brazilian prison island, Semmes presented his compliments to the governor and requested to be allowed to purchase provisions. This was permitted. No restriction was placed upon his bringing his prize into harbor, contrary to the laws of neutrality, and in the absence of any prohibition, Semmes then proceeded to re-coal from the *Louisa Hatch.* While the loading was underway, Semmes and acting paymaster Dr. Galt were entertained onshore, the guests of the governor. The absence of a

U.S. consul ensured that friendly relations went beyond those permitted in the dealings of a neutral power and a belligerent. When reprovisioning was almost complete, two American whalers entered the harbor with a view to exchanging some whale oil for supplies. They anchored alongside the *Louisa Hatch,* and their captains got into a conversation with the English officer in charge of the prize. Turning their attention towards the *Alabama,* they enquired who she was. A Brazilian packet steamer come over to the colony to bring some convicts, they were informed. But they were not to be fooled. Looking along the ship, one of the captains espied a small Confederate flag, a boat's ensign, that had been thrown over a boom to dry. Quickly summing up the situation, both whalers moved out of the harbor. Their departure coincided with Semmes' return. He ordered up steam, and set out after them. By now they were some four or five miles away, well beyond the maritime league and safety. Coming up on them quickly, a gun was fired, and they heaved-to. As whalers, Semmes did not have to worry whether their cargos belonged to a neutral. They were both American ships, the *Lafayette* out of New Bedford, and the *Kate Cory* of Westport. The *Lafayette* was burned, the *Kate Cory* saved, and Semmes transferred his prisoners, 110 by then, aboard her. That night the two ships anchored at Fernando de Noronha. The following morning a Brazilian schooner entered the harbor and anchored nearby. Her captain agreed, subject to being promised supplies of flour and pork, to take all of Semmes' remaining prisoners and sail them down to Pernambuco and freedom. This gave Semmes the opportunity to burn the *Cory,* too. With no sign of his supply ship, the *Agrippina,* Semmes set sail once more. It was 22 April 1863.

The *Alabama* steamed down the coast for some forty miles before Semmes cut the engine, and she continued under sail. Soon another whaler came into sight. She was a barque, the *Nye* of New Bedford, thirty-one months at sea. She had previously sent home two cargos of oil, but now was on the return trip herself, with 425 barrels of oil. While Semmes could acknowledge the hardship these men had undergone in their two and a half year voyage, she nonetheless was a Northerner. Taking onboard her crew, Semmes set the *Nye* ablaze. The following day under a fresh wind, the *Alabama* continued her voyage down the coast of Brazil. A ship was sighted, and flying the enemy's colors, the *Alabama* gave chase. The other ship showed no colors, until a shot from the pursuing craft obliged her to raise her flag and come to for a boarding party. She was American, and her papers showed her to be the *Dorcas Prince,* forty-four days out of New York, bound for Shanghai. Her cargo was coal. Having sufficient coal aboard, and after transferring the crew, including the captain's wife, Semmes had no doubts over sinking her. He used her as target practice, firing shot and shell into her, then set her ablaze. It was dusk as the *Alabama* sailed away. Later that evening they boarded a British ship thirty-eight days out from Liverpool, destined for Calcutta. Semmes managed to procure some newspapers, but there was little news about the war at home. Over the next few days the *Alabama* overhauled nothing but neutral shipping. A British ship out of St. John's, New Brunswick, provided them with more newspapers. On 27 April they captured the *Tycoon,* after a two and a half hour pursuit. She had sailed from New York thirty-six days earlier, bound for San Francisco by way of Cape Horn. In his original journal Semmes wrote: "We received from the prize a number of Yankee newspapers, filled with the usual evidence of their insanity." Taking what supplies he needed, including warm clothing, Semmes burned the *Tycoon* after transferring her crew.

The 3rd of May was a squally day. At about eleven that morning a square-sailed clipper was seen. With her bright white sails, she was identified as an enemy ship. An hour and a half later they came up to her, obliging her to raise her flag, the Stars and Stripes, as was suspected. A boat crew was put aboard her, and her papers were examined. She was the *Union Jack,* of Boston, bound for Shanghai. As her cargo was being checked, away in the distance another sail was seen. Leaving a prize crew aboard, the *Alabama* dashed off to investigate. Semmes quickly overhauled the second ship, and she too proved to be American. The second prize was the New York registered *Sea Lark,* bound for San Francisco. Among his prisoners from the *Union Jack* were three women and two small children. There was also a New England parson, the sort Semmes had come to fervently dislike: "He had Puritan written all over his lugubrious countenance." He was the Rev. Franklin Wright, who was going out as American consul to Foo Chow. Semmes continues: "We deprived him of his Consular seal and commission, though we did not molest his private papers, and of sundry very pretty Consular flags, that had been carefully prepared for him.... I am pained to see, by that 'little bill' of Mr. Seward against the British Government, for 'depredations of the Alabama' ... that the Rev. Mr. Wright puts his damages down at $10,015. I had no idea that a New England parson carried so much plunder about him."[24]

The two ships were burned. Reading the captured newspapers, Semmes was angered by the report of a speech made by Governor Wright of Indiana. Of the land laid to waste by the invading Federal army, Governor Wright said, "Scripture teaches us that no people can live long where there is no grass. The question then is only, whether they can live thirty or sixty days." This was greeted with laughter and jeers by his audience. Semmes simply could not comprehend how these people could gloat over the prospect of starving women and children. He felt more justified than ever in what he was doing, but yet in all honesty he could swear that he himself had never caused real suffering to others. He had never practiced the intentional cruelty that the United States newspapers accused him of. His main concern now was to land his prisoners.

The *Alabama* ran into Bahia, in Brazil, on the evening of 11 May. The crews of the four captured crews, including women and children, were put ashore. The following day Semmes was visited by the local governor's aide-de-camp bearing with him a newspaper. Within it was a proclamation from the regional president ordering the *Alabama* to depart. Semmes believed that the American consul at Pernambuco was behind it. He wrote to the governor, calling his bluff, and indicated that he only wanted to take on a little coal, and then he would depart. The governor agreed to his request. Ashore, Semmes and his officers were feted by the local British community. A ball was given in their honor by Mr. Ogilvie, a British merchant. Several Brazilian dignitaries and foreign consuls were present. It was a show of solidarity for the Confederate cause. Noticeably there were no citizens of the United States present.

The following morning, back aboard the *Alabama,* an officer informed Semmes that a strange steamer of war had entered the harbor during the night. As yet the steamer had not shown her colors. Semmes gave orders for the Confederate flag to be raised from the masthead. Semmes, from the deck, waited for a response. To his intense delight the other ship also raised the Confederate colors. She was the *Georgia,* under the command of Commander Lewis F. Maury. She had arrived to meet her coal ship, the *Castor*. The American consul then began to badger the president of the Province of Bahia, indeed even threatening him with U.S. intervention should he allow the *Georgia* to enter the port. Maury and Semmes meanwhile both argued that Maury was legally entitled to re-coal, under the rules of neutrality agreed to by the Brazilian government. The *Georgia* and her tender were reluctantly allowed to enter the port. Word then arrived in Bahia that the CSS *Florida* had docked up the coast at Pernambuco.

With three Confederate ships in Brazilian ports the authorities became alarmed. They ordered the *Alabama* to depart, but Semmes informed them that he was still loading coal. Ignoring the requests to leave, Semmes and some of the officers from the *Georgia,* including old shipmates from the *Sumter,* Lieutenants Chapman and Evans, took a trip upcountry by rail, the guests of the British company that owned rail line. A few days later the *Alabama* left, followed a few days after that by the *Georgia*. The *Florida,* arriving at Bahia a little later, was to become an example of what happened when neutral countries refused to be bullied by the United States. With a complete disregard for her national integrity, the *Florida* was illegally removed from Brazilian territory and taken prisoner, with her crew, to America. When the Brazilian president protested, he was treated with studied contempt. Semmes himself held the people as a whole in equal contempt for their weakness of character. He refers to the population as "The effete Portuguese race ... ingrafted upon a stupid, stolid, Indian stock, in that country. The freed Negro is, besides, the equal of the white man, and as there seems to be no repugnance on the part of the white race — so-called — to mix with the black race and with the Indian, amalgamation will go on in that country, until a mongrel set of curs will cover the whole land."[25] Every hero has a flaw, and in this Semmes is badly flawed. His statement is so utterly racist, but very much of its time. It was part of Confederate thinking; the superiority of the white man. It was also a belief held by north–Europeans, and especially Great Britain. It was a view held by many in the United States. Slaves might be freed by their armies, but that did not make them the equal of the white man. The 100 year struggle for equal rights that followed in America shows how deeply rooted was the belief.

From Bahia the *Alabama* continued south. On the 25th of May the cry went up from the masthead: "Sail-ho!" No sooner was the ship prepared for the chase when a second sail, not far from the first, was reported. It would be a wealth of riches if both ships proved to be American. In a heavy sea, but with a good breeze, the Confederate cruiser set off after her first discovery. It was not long before she came upon the first, and glancing over at the second, it was obvious that both were Yankees. Overhauling them, both showed their colors, confirming what everybody aboard the *Alabama* already knew. The first ship boarded was the *Gilderslieve* from New York, out of London with a cargo of coal, allegedly for the Oriental Steam Navigation Company. Her cargo was not certified as neutral, so both ship and cargo were condemned. The second ship, the *Justina,* was from Baltimore, with a partial neutral cargo. This saved her, and Semmes put his prisoners from the *Gilderslieve* aboard her, then burned the New York registered ship. The next evening, as Kell records in his book, *Recollections of a Naval Life,* "We began a chase that consumed the night and amounted to nothing, being only a Dutchman!" Thus was one of the world's former naval powers contemptuously dismissed. The next three ships fell in quick succession: the *Jabez Snow* of Buckport, Maine, with a cargo of Welsh coal for Montevideo, the *Amazonian* of Boston, also bound for Montevideo, and the *Talisman,* out of New York bound for Shanghai. All three were burned. From the *Talisman,* Semmes removed two 12-pounder rifled guns., destined for some Chinese war lord. Among the letters discovered aboard the *Jabez Snow* was one from the owner to the master of the ship. It read: "We hope you may arrive safely, and in good season, but we think you will find business rather flat at Liverpool, as American ships especially are under a cloud, owing to dangers from pirates, more politely styled privateers, which our kind friends in England are so willing should slip out of their ports, to prey on our commerce."[26]

Such letters delighted Semmes. They were confirmation of the success of his little ship. The day after the capture of the *Amazonian,* the captain of an English ship was persuaded to take Semmes' prisoners. The captain drove a hard bargain before he would accept them, including accepting a chronometer from another captured ship. Semmes described him: "Virtuous Briton! Thou wert near akin to the Yankee." The next vessel captured was a former American ship, built in Maine. Due to the activities of the *Alabama* and her sisters, she had been sold to a British interest. Her master and crew were all English. On 16 June two more American ships were overhauled. Both were sailing under British colors. One was the *Azzapadi,* formerly the *Joseph Hale,* built in Portland. The second was the *Queen of Beauty,* formerly the *Challenger.* Both transfers to British owners were genuine. It was further confirmation of Confederate success in the maritime commercial war.

By the middle of June the *Alabama* had entered the winter season in the Southern Hemisphere. Winter clothing was provided for the crew. On the 20th Semmes captured the American barque *Conrad.* He was impressed with the sailing qualities of the 350 ton ship, and resolved to press her into the services of the Confederate navy. Lieutenant Low was put aboard in command. Midshipman George Sinclair was promoted to First Lieutenant to assist him. Adolphe Marmelstein, a quartermaster, born in Baltimore but resident in Savannah at the opening of the war, was appointed second lieutenant. A few intelligent seamen were likewise promoted, and a crew of ten was assembled to serve aboard her:

The Crew of the Tuscaloosa

Officers

John Low, Captain	George Sinclair, First Lt.
Adolphe Marmelstein, Second Lt.	James Minor, Third Lt.

Seamen

H. Legris	Edwin Jones
William Rinton	Robert Williams
Thomas Williams	Martin Molk
Samuel Brown	Robert Owens
Thomas Altman	John Duggan

Her armament consisted of the two 12-pounder rifled guns from the *Talisman,* as well as twenty rifles and half a dozen revolvers. She ran up the Confederate flag, and the newly commissioned ship was christened the *Tuscaloosa.* Shortly after five o'clock she sailed away, with orders to rendezvous with the *Alabama* at Santa Catherina, Brazil. In his orders to Low, Semmes wrote:

CSS ALABAMA

At Sea, June 21, 1863.

Sir: With the C.S. bark Tuscaloosa, a tender to this ship, under your command, you will proceed on a cruise against the commerce of the United States, with which States the Confederate States are at war. As most of the ports of the Confederate States are blockaded by the enemy, and as the maritime powers of the world have prohibited both belligerents from taking prizes into their ports, it will not be in your power for the present to send your prizes in for adjudication. This state of things is much regretted, but it can not be permitted, of course, to interfere with your right of capture. You will therefore destroy all the enemy's ships which fall into your power, discriminating, however, between such as have enemy's goods and such as have bona fide neutral goods on board. In the latter cases you will put the ships under ransom bonds and permit them to depart with their neutral cargoes, unless, indeed, the latter be contraband of war, in which case you may destroy both ship and cargo.

You will pay every respect to a neutral flag wherever you may find it; and in heaving a ship to bearing this flag, for the purpose of verifying her national character, you will cause her as little delay or molestation as possible.

The harbor of St. Catherine on the coast of Brazil, will be your first port of rendezvous. You will make the best of your way to that port and wait a reasonable time for my arrival, say one week. Should I not arrive within that time, you will proceed to Saldanha Bay, to the northward of the Cape of Good Hope, and there await me.

I have the honor to be, very respectfully, your obedient servant,

R. SEMMES
Captain, C.S. Navy

JOHN LOW,
Acting Second Lieutenant, Commandant.[27]

Later that evening the *Alabama* fell in with a British barque, the *Mary Kendall,* out of Cardiff bound for Point de Galle. Having sprung a leak she was heading back to Rio de Janeiro. One of her crew had been badly injured in a fall, and Semmes gladly sent over a surgeon to attend him. The master of the *Mary Kendall,* in response, agreed to take the thirty-two prisoners aboard the *Alabama* back to Rio with him. Sailing on for a few days more, before the intended rendezvous at Santa Catherina, Semmes was informed that weevils had got into the bread room and destroyed almost the entire supply. Realizing the impracticality of sailing across the Atlantic without bread, he put in a course for Rio himself. Over the next few days he stopped several ships; eleven on the 1st of July, all neutrals. That night, about eleven o'clock, the cry went up yet again: "Sail-ho!" There was a reluctance to bother with her, but as detail came down from the crow's nest as to her construction, it became evident that she was an enemy ship. All hands were mustered, and the chase began.

As day dawned she was still some miles ahead. Gaining gradually on her, a blank was fired to attract her attention, if she was not already aware of the *Alabama*'s presence. The crew watched as the enemy colors were raised, but still she did not heave-to. She was going to make a race of it. At less than three miles' distance, Semmes ordered a live round across her bows. This brought her to heel, and she hove-to and awaited a boarding party. She was the *Anna F. Schmidt,* registered at Maine, out of Boston bound for San Francisco, with a miscellaneous cargo of clothing and sundry items such as clocks, china, sewing machines, and patent medicines. She also had bread, thirty days' supply, in airtight containers. Semmes took what he needed, then set her ablaze. As they looted the ship another American-style ship passed by. Semmes now went after her. Upon boarding her it was discovered that she had been sold by her American owners to a British interest. She was now British, and so was her cargo. Her captain was Scottish, her crew English.

While investigating this ship, a large ship with square sails passed by at speed. She seemed not to care that there were three ships nearby, one in flames. Semmes and his officers were of the opinion that she was doing her best to get out of harm's way. She did not look American, but why should she run? Semmes decided to pursue her and find out who she was. By the time they got underway she was already three miles distant. Semmes ordered a blank round to be fired. To his surprise she responded with a round of fire. What to make of it — was it a bluff? Was she a New York clipper pretending to be a warship so that he would not follow up? He ordered up steam, in an effort to gain on her. She knew he was there, but she did not heave-to. If Semmes had then ordered up a live round, the *Alabama's* career would have ended there and then. About midnight they caught up with the mysterious craft. She was painted black, with a white band around her waist. The English sailors recognized her for what she was, a Royal Navy battleship. The officers aboard the *Alabama* were still unsure.

Lt. Kell called out, "What ship is that?"

"This is Her Britannic Majesty's ship *Diomede!*" came the reply. "What ship is that?" the officer of the watch demanded.[28]

"This is the Confederate States steamer *Alabama!*" Kell replied.

"I suspected as much," the Royal Naval officer responded, "when I saw you making sail, by the light of the burning ship."

Tensions now eased, Semmes did not demand to see the papers of the forty-eight gun British man-o'-war, and after exchanging pleasantries, the *Alabama* slid away to return to her original course.

Too late for his first rendezvous with the *Tuscaloosa,* Semmes now set in a course for South Africa. The 4th of July was celebrated with an extra glass of grog for the crew, but Semmes felt only bitterness that here again they were having to fight a war of independence. The day passed, and the *Alabama* sailed on through squally showers. A few minutes into 7 July, Semmes was awoken with the news that a sail had been sighted. He ordered up a pursuit, and when sufficiently close had a blank shot fired. She took no notice. Semmes ordered a second blank, and still she did not respond. A live round dropped just in front of her resolved the issue, and she heaved-to, raising the Federal flag, and awaited to be boarded. She was American, the *Express,* out of Boston, from Callao, Peru, to Antwerp, with a cargo of guano from the Chincha Islands. Though the cargo most probably was the property of the Peruvian government, who held the monopoly on guano, it was certified to an individual, with an unsigned authentication by the French consul at Lima. Semmes was unsure of what to do, but in the end, bearing in mind that the *Express* had refused twice to halt, he took the crew aboard and put the *Express* to the torch. East southeast the *Alabama* continued for several days, traveling seven or eight hundred miles and sighting but a single ship. On 29 July, shortly after nine o'clock in the morning, the Alabama sighted Daffen Island, situated a little to the north of the Cape of Good Hope.

Exercising caution, Semmes decided not to sail blithely into Cape Town, but to anchor in Saldanha Bay, a few miles up the coast, and there make enquiries as to the presence of Federal warships. Word came back that there had been no Federal warships in several months. Meanwhile, Semmes announced his arrival to the governor of the Cape and sent Paymaster Dr. Francis Galt ashore to buy fresh provisions for the crew. The *Alabama* was in serious need of repair and refurbishment, and during their week long stay in the bay, they were visited by members of both the British and Boer communities, who brought with them gifts of game and eggs, as well as various novelties. While the authorities had to maintain a strict neutrality, this was not the case with the people of the Cape, who expressed a strong sympathy with the Confederacy. While at the bay a schooner arrived, with letters from the local merchants, offering to supply coal and whatever other provisions were required. In the absence of the *Agrippina,* which, unknown to Semmes, was blockaded at Bahia, he accepted their offers.

During the refit, officers and crew not required aboard the ship were given shore leave. On the 3rd of August a party of four junior officers went ashore to go duck shooting. Returning to the boat at sunset, with well-filled game bags, Lt. Simeon Cummings accidentally struck the hammer of his gun against the gunwale of the boat. With a loud bang, it discharged a cartridge of buckshot into his chest. He was heard to say "Oh me!" before he collapsed and died. Placing his body in the boat, his companions rowed back to the *Alabama*. Semmes was visibly shocked at the tragic news. He later wrote of it: "This young gentleman had been very popular, with both officers and crew, and his sudden death cast a gloom over the ship. All amusements were suspended, and men walked about with softened foot-fall, as though fearing to disturb the slumbers of the dead." Arrangements were made for burying him in the graveyard of a neighboring farmer by the name of Pienaar, and the next day, with the *Alabama*'s flags flying at half mast, his body was brought ashore for burial at Kliprug Farm. A group of British naval officers stationed at Cape Town contributed funds to erect a simple memorial to his memory. Upon a plain unadorned stone, a Maltese cross bearing the arms of the Confederate States Navy was engraved. Below it were these words:

> Asst. Engr.
> Simeon W. Cummings
> CSS
> Alabama
> C.S.A.
> Aug. 3, 1863
> Aldanha Bay
> Republic of
> South Africa[29]

On the morning of 5 August, the weather being fine, the wind light from the south, the *Alabama* got underway and sailed down the coast to Table Bay. On the way

Above and following page: The ***Alabama*** in South Africa. A series of photographs reproduced as engravings in the ***Illustrated London News***, 10 October 1863.

she fell in with the *Tuscaloosa*. Low reported the capture of one enemy ship, the *Santee*. She was on a voyage from the East Indies, to Falmouth in Cornwall, with a cargo of rice. The cargo was authenticated as belonging to a neutral, so Low was obliged to release her on bond. Semmes now directed Low to take his ship further down the coast to Simon's Town. The *Alabama* meanwhile proceeded towards Cape Town. As the *Tuscaloosa* sailed away, from the *Alabama*'s masthead, the cry went up: "Sail ho!" Six miles or so out to sea was a ship with white sails, also heading towards Table Bay. Closer examination through a telescope identified her as American. Getting up steam the propeller was lowered, and the *Alabama,* a British ensign flying from her masthead, gave chase. Still well beyond the marine league, the other ship was forced to heave-to and was boarded. She was the *Sea Bride,* a Boston ship, out of New York on a trading voyage along the east African coast. Semmes transferred her crew, then put some of his own men aboard, with instructions to sail her to Saldanha Bay. The capture of the Yankee ship, within the view of the whole population of Cape Town, caused great excitement. The *Cape Town Argus* (6 Aug. 1863) threw aside any suggestion of impartiality, when it recorded the event:

Yesterday, at almost noon, a steamer from the northward was made down from the signal-post on Lion Hill. The Governor had, the previous day, received a letter from Captain Semmes, informing his Excellency that the gallant captain had put his ship into Saldanha Bay for repairs. This letter had been made public in the morning, and had caused no little excitement.... The news that the Alabama was coming into Table Bay, and would probably arrive about four o'clock this afternoon, added to the excitement.... About noon, a steamer from the north-west was made down by the signal-man on the hill. Could this be the Alabama?... Just after one, it was made down Confederate steamer Alabama from the north-west, and Federal bark from the south-east. Here was to be a capture by the celebrated Confederate craft, close to the entrance of Table Bay. The inhabitants rushed off to get a sight. Crowds of people ran up the Lion's Hill, and to the Kloof Road. All the cabs were chartered — every one of them.... The bark coming in from the south-east, and, as the signal-man made down, five miles off; the steamer coming in from the north-west, eight miles off, led us to think that the Kloof Road was the best place for a full view ... [and] as we reached the corner, there lay the Alabama within fifty yards of the unfortunate Yankee. The Yankee was evidently taken by surprise. The Alabama fired a gun, and brought her to.... This done, she sent a boat with a prize crew off, took possession in the name of the Confederate States, and sent the bark off to sea.... The Alabama then made for the port. We came around the Kloof to visit Captain Semmes on board. As we came, we found the heights overlooking Table Bay covered with people; the road to Green Point lined with cabs. The windows of the villas at the bottom of the hill were thrown up, and ladies waved their handkerchiefs, and one and all joined in the general enthusiasm.... At the central jetty it was almost impossible to force one's way through to get a boat. However, all in good time, we did get a boat, and went off.... On getting alongside the Alabama, we found about a dozen boats before us, and we had not been on board five minutes before she was surrounded by nearly every boat in Table Bay, and as boat after boat arrived, three hearty cheers were given for Captain Semmes and his gallant privateer. This, upon the part of a neutral people is perchance wrong; but we are not arguing a case — we are recording facts. They did cheer, and cheer with a will too....

Mr. Walter Graham, the American Consul at the Cape, did not share the sentiments of his fellow citizens. He dispatched a rather brusque letter to the governor, telling him what he must do. The governor replied, in a more courteous manner, that Captain Semmes' activities were in compliance with the activities interpreted under Britain's act of neutrality. The consul then declared that the *Sea Bride* had been captured within the marine league. Several thousand spectators, including the governor's own staff, were to verify that this was not the case. Captain Forsyth, aboard Her Majesty's Ship *Valorous,* after giving his deliberations, reported to the governor: "I have therefore, come to the conclusion, that the bark Sea Bride was beyond the limits assigned, when she was captured by the Alabama." The governor wrote back to Graham of his findings.

During their stay, Semmes and his men were treated like heroes. They were feted wherever they went; presents were thrust upon them. The officers were wined and dined, the crew were welcomed in all the taverns and whorehouses of the town. On 9 August, with great reluctance, the *Alabama* made sail. Scarcely out of the bay the cry went up: "Sail ho!" The chase was brief, the ship was halted. Filled with a cargo of rice, destined for Falmouth in Cornwall, the *Martha Wenzell* was indeed a Yankee. Though seven miles out from shore, she was just within the two points that made up the mouth of False Bay, so technically was within the proscribed league. From the shore the people watched to see what Semmes would do. To their surprise, and the surprise of the *Wenzell's* master, he released her. The *Alabama* sailed on, and taking on a pilot, entered Simon's Bay where the *Tuscaloosa* was already anchored. Upon dropping anchor, Semmes was visited by a lieutenant from the frigate HMS *Narcissus,* flagship of Rear Admiral Sir Baldwin Walker, commander in chief of British naval forces at the Cape. Courtesies were exchanged, and invitations to dinner were presented. Semmes recorded that "the English naval officers discarded all the ridiculous nonsense about our not being 'recognized,' and extended to us official as well as private civilities."[30]

The arrival of the *Tuscaloosa* had not gone unnoticed. The Federal consul, like some gadfly, was even then buzzing around the ear of the governor telling him what to do. His case was that the ship was owned by American citizens; she had been captured, but had not been condemned by a prize court. Therefore she should be returned. Semmes, a trained lawyer and able to argue from a point of law, said that, while it was true she had not been condemned she had been commissioned as a ship of war, which in its own way was a condemnation of the prize. Also in accordance with maritime law, no nation had the right to inquire into the antecedents of the ships of war of another nation. In a polite reply to the consul, the Colonial Secretary questioned him as to where in international law it was stated that captured vessels entering a neutral port should be handed back to their original owners, and as such, are forfeit by their captors. Claims of contending parties to vessels captured, the secretary argued, could only be determined by the courts of the captor's country. Failing to get his way in South Africa, Consul Graham wrote to complain to Charles Adams, the U.S. minister in London. Assistant Secretary Benjamin Moran wrote in his journal:

> Tues. 29th Sept. 1863: We have received a most interesting letter from Mr. Walter Graham, the U.S. Consul at Cape Town, narrating very clearly the doings there of the British pirate "No. 290." It seems she took as prize within three miles of the shore the bark Sea Bride of New York, and was cheered by a crowd from the land who witnessed the affair. Afterwards she anchored with this vessel in the bay, in unquestionable British jurisdiction and was permitted to remain with her prize in open defiance of the order in Council of June 1861, prohibiting either belligerent from bringing its prizes into a British port. And not only this but the barque Conrad of Philada., captured by this pirate and armed at sea, was received at Simon's Bay with honor as a regular man of war, and every facility given her to provision or refit.[31]

Adams wrote to Lord Russell to complain. A month later, having ascertained the true facts from South Africa, Russell wrote back to Adams, upholding the decisions taken by the governor. This was not to be the last of it however.

At Simon's Town five days later, on the 14th of August, the *Alabama* having been re-caulked, her copper about the waterline replaced and some slight repairs to her engine completed, raised anchor, and eased herself out of the port and into the open sea. The *Tuscaloosa* had sailed on the previous day. Low was instructed to take the *Sea Bride* from her anchorage at Saldhana Bay up to one of the uninhabited bays further north and there await the arrival of the *Alabama*. Some ten days later the *Alabama* rendezvoused with the other two ships and in convoy they sailed up to the Bay of Angra Pequena and anchored. This was unclaimed territory as far as European nations were concerned, and certainly beyond British jurisdiction. At Cape Town Semmes had been approached by a consortium of English merchants with a view to purchasing the *Sea Bride* and her cargo. Arrangements had also been made for the sale of the cargo of wool aboard the *Tuscaloosa*. Meeting with the Englishmen at Angra Pequena, the *Tuscaloosa*'s cargo was unloaded, and the *Sea Bride* was transferred to their ownership. Payment, made in English guineas, was transferred to the safe of the *Alabama*.

News of the arrival of the *Alabama* in South Africa would by now have reached the ears of the U.S. Navy secretary, Semmes reasoned. He would undoubtedly have dispatched a couple of warships. Semmes intended to be long gone by the time they arrived though. His plan was to sail eastwards into the Indian Ocean. Low meanwhile was ordered to take the *Tuscaloosa* back across the Atlantic, to cruise off the coast of Brazil. After a requisite time, Low was to return to the Cape to rendezvous with Semmes upon his return from the Far East.

The *Alabama* returned to Simon's Town. Upon anchoring Semmes discovered that the U.S. steamer *Vanderbilt* had been there just days before, searching for her. Failing to find her, she had sailed back to Cape Town on 11 September. It appeared that the two ships had passed each other without either being aware of the presence of the other. Semmes was now visited aboard his ship by Captain Bickford of HMS *Narcissus*. The American consul had been mischief-making, and reported that Semmes had disposed of the *Sea Bride* and the *Tuscaloosa*'s cargo off the island of Ichaboe, a dependency of Cape Colony. If this were true then Semmes was in violation of the Neutrality Act. Semmes, calling upon the English merchants to testify to the falsehood of this statement, was able to prove that the accusation was false, and was thereby exonerated.

Some five days later, on 24 September, the *Alabama*'s bunkers filled with coal, and with minor repairs to her distillation process completed, she prepared to sail. Leave had been given to the crew, but now Semmes discovered that fourteen of his seamen had deserted. Some had been induced to desert by Consul Graham, and later signed false affidavits to say that the *Sea Bride* had been in British waters when captured. Bending the rules of the Foreign Enlistment Act, Semmes was able to recruit ten men to replace them, on the basis that they were "passengers." With the *Vanderbilt* still in the vicinity, Semmes was anxious that the *Alabama* should not be blockaded in the bay. Late at night the *Alabama* raised anchor, and by three o'clock the next morning, she was safely at sea.

For five days the *Alabama* sailed south, then headed east at the 40th parallel, across the Indian Ocean, on what came to be recognized as the Cape Town to Hobart (Tasmania) route. Strong winds hurried the Confederate craft eastward at great speed. On the 12th of October the *Alabama* passed the small islands of St. Peter and St. Paul, the journey now halfway complete. A gale now set in; the waves were like mountains, the wind howling like a banshee. Into a dense snowstorm the *Alabama* now sailed, the temperature piercingly cold. Semmes set in a course northward, and two days later they were in a more temperate clime. The saturated bedding was brought up on deck to dry, and opened seams aboard the ship were caulked to prevent the sea getting in. The next day, continuing northward, they ran into another gale, which they had to endure for ten hours. On the morning of 21 October they crossed the Tropic of Capricorn. They had been twenty-four days out of Cape Horn, traveling under sail alone. The *Alabama* was a good little craft. She had exceeded all expectations. Now heading up into the tropics, they had sighted only three ships in their voyage, one of them an English steamer, which even under sail alone they had overhauled and boarded. Up to the 12th parallel and into the tropics the *Alabama* sailed. Semmes' intention was to make for the Strait of Sunda that separates Sumatra and Java.

On the evening of 26 October they overhauled an English barque. Her master informed Semmes that he had recently passed through the Strait, and advised him that the USS *Wyoming* and a three-master schooner acting as her tender were patrolling there.[32] Each evening she anchored off the island of Krakatoa. Two days later a party from the *Alabama* boarded a Dutch ship en route from Batavia to Amsterdam. Her captain said that he had been recently boarded by a party from the *Wyoming* off the town of Anger, in the Strait. As the *Alabama* continued on towards the Strait, she was met by an almost continual stream of ships. They boarded four ships, three British and one Dutch. Their captains corroborated the earlier stories of the presence of a Federal warship in the Strait. On 6 November the *Alabama* overhauled another English ship, out of Foo Chow, bound for London. She spoke of an American merchant ship, the *Winged Racer,* that had passed through the Straight with them. That afternoon the *Alabama* overhauled two more ships, but they too proved to be British. A third ship was now seen, and the *Alabama* set off after her. A blank shot saw her heave-to, and from her mast the Stars and Stripes was unfurled. She was the barque *Amanda,* from Boston, out of Manila bound for Queenstown (Cobh), Ireland, with a cargo of hemp and sugar. As her certificate that the cargo was British was an unsworn certificate, it was valueless. Semmes burned her. The next day the *Alabama* ran in and anchored under Flat Point, on the north side of the Strait, about one mile off the coast of Sumatra. Paymaster Galt went ashore to purchase fruit and vegetables.

As they lay at anchor, beneath a heavy cloud cover, a ship was observed far off. She seemed to turn towards them. All her sail was taken in, yet she was still coming towards them. The same thought crossed everybody's mind. Was she the steamer *Wyoming?* Orders were given to stand to, and steam was got up. Closer and closer she came until she was recognized for what she was. Not an enemy gunship but a Dutch barque, her topsails furled in the face of a squall. She was coming into the bay to take shelter for the night. Everyone was stood down.

Early the next morning the anchor was raised and the *Alabama* got underway to sail through the Straits. She passed through the generally unused narrow passage between the islands of Beezee and Soubooko, then hugged the shoreline, under sail and steam. Swiftly progressing, the *Alabama* sailed into the Straits just after one o'clock that afternoon, using the island of Thwart-the-Way to screen her. Beyond this they were in full view of the garrison town of Anger, but there was no sign of the *Wyoming.*

Through the Straits and into the China Sea, the *Alabama* sailed, right into a squally rain. The topsails were gathered in to aid her progress. Then right out of the dashing rain a tall clipper ship appeared. There was no mistaking her — she was American. Orders were shouted from the bridge, and everyone dashed to their designated stations. The *Alabama* gave chase, and in a few minutes forced her to heave-to with a shot. She was the *Winged Racer* the English captain had spoken of. A beautifully constructed ship, she was out of Manila, bound for New York with a cargo of sugar, hides and jute. Anchoring off the North Island, Semmes took what provisions he needed from her, then reluctantly set her on fire. The master of the captured ship, with his family aboard, was permitted, with his crew, to depart in his own boats, along with the *Alabama*'s other prisoners, and row to nearby Batavia (Jakarta), where he knew there to be an American consul. With the *Winged Racer* in flames, Semmes knew that any other American ships approaching the Straits would be warned off. The other probable route would take them through the Gaspar Strait. He set in a course.

By daylight the next day the *Alabama* was well beyond the coasts of Sumatra and Java. She passed beyond sight of the little island called North Watcher. The day was wearing on now, Semmes ordered the steam to be let down; the *Alabama* would continue under sail. As the order to lift the propeller was given, the cry went up: "Sail ho!" The order was countermanded, and steam was ordered up, as the quarry was identified as another American clipper. She was approaching them, a point or two on their lee bow. Cautiously, so as not to arouse suspicion, the *Alabama* slowly altered course to intercept her. She was a beautiful craft, with the grace of a swan. Lt. Arthur Sinclair takes up the story:

> We are under full sail, as much as our sticks can possibly carry, and with our screw down working as hard as our engineer dare let it turn. We know we must intercept and take this ship. We hoisted United States colors and can only hope she will take us for Wyoming, somewhat similar to us in appearance. But her captain smelt a rat and suspects us and proposes to be on the safe side and rather suffer the ignominy of being considered timid by his countrymen than take the least chance.
>
> She is much too valuable a prize for us to lose, but she throws to the breeze her studding-sails, and there can be no occasion now for further deception, for that point has passed. We shall have to get her by sheer steaming coupled with our sailing qualities. We lower the enemy flag and in its place hoist the white colors of the Confederacy, recently adopted by our Congress, and not unlike the St. George's cross of England, and our commander orders one blank round to be fired; but the clipper ignores it entirely and proceeds on course.
>
> We are more excited now than before in the last few months. As a rule then the chase of a sail was a matter-of-fact and everyday occurrence, but not so now. Our rails are crowded. But her sailing qualities are clearly much superior than ours and it becomes grievously clear that we have met our conqueror at least in speed, and our day of humiliation is upon us. Steam pressure is forced to and beyond danger point, but still she leaves us standing. Our commander conceives the idea that we are out-of-trim by the head and orders our battery shifted aft and, in a further effort to make more speed, had all available officers and men aft also. It is a maneuver which unfortunately only serves to demoralize many of our men. I talked with Bulloch and we agree that if this breeze does not die out then night will overtake us and the prize elude us before dawn. But we manage to come within four miles or so of her and our commander orders one round of live shell to be fired. It struck the water hard by her and threw a shower of spray right over her deck, but still she kept course, evidently her master having made up his mind to be sunk rather than taken and burned. His determination causes our hopes to sag, and nothing seems left to us but chance shots from our hundred pounder to disable her.
>
> Suddenly, though, we discover we are gaining on her; the wind has gone down with the sun and we realize that the elements will finally win this race rather than our speed. We approach her rapidly and all hope is unexpectedly abandoned by our victim as she luffs into the wind and with maintop sail to her mast heaves-to and lays quietly awaiting her doom. Our boarding officer returns with her captain and his papers, and we find she is the Yankee clipper Contest, from Yokohama for New York, with an assorted cargo of Japanese tea, fine silks and spices. With her cargo, the ship is condemned. We have never taken so lovely a vessel and it is a sacrilege, almost a desecration, to destroy so perfect a specimen of man's handicraft.[33]

When her captain was brought on board, Semmes congratulated him on his skilful handling of the ship. With deep regret Semmes ordered her to be burned. Ship and cargo Semmes estimated at $750,000. She was the *Alabama's* fifty-ninth victim.

With his coal running low, Semmes now set in a course for the Karimata Straits. He fell in with the British merchant ship *Avalanche* of London, who agreed to take his prisoners and put them ashore at his next port of call. The *Alabama* was now badly in need of serious repairs. Semmes decided to take her to Singapore. On the way they stopped at Pulo Condore, a French dependency. While Lt. Kell took charge of necessary repairs, the officers and crew were given shore leave. The copper torn off in parts was refixed, thanks to a clever waterproof box affair, constructed under Kell's instructions. Two weeks elapsed in repairs, before once again the *Alabama* raised anchor and headed off in the direction of Singapore. On 21 December, she followed an English steamer to the mouth of the Strait, and there waited in heavy rain for a Malayan pilot to come out to take them into port. At about five o'clock that evening the *Alabama* dropped anchor at New Harbor, in the port of Singapore. Her fame had preceded her; among the Malayan population she was known as "Kappal Hantu," the Ghost Ship.

On the morning of 23 December, following a popular clamor among the citizens of Singapore, visitors were allowed onboard. There was tremendous good will and support for both the crew and the Confederate cause.[34] A report on the *Alabama* appeared in the Singapore newspaper, the *Straits Times*, for 26 December 1863:

> [T]he Alabama was open for inspection on Wednesday, and no doubt many availed themselves of the opportunity to inspect a ship that will possess a place in the history of the present age. The Alabama once seen will not be readily forgotten. She is not large, being, we should say, barely 1,000 tons register; but still she has the air of a dare-devil craft that would hesitate but little to test her strength against a much stronger enemy. She is very low in the water, extremely long, being according to our measurement at the wharf 215 feet from stem to stern; but the most remarkable feature of her build is her extreme narrowness, her beam amid-ship we should set down at very little if anything over 30 feet. She is barque rigged with long raking spars; but not full barque rigged, as her main and fore top masts and top gallant masts are of one spar. Her greatest spread of canvas is in her fore and aft sails, which are of gigantic proportions; she has no square mainsail, and she sets no royals. Under canvas alone she has gone as much as 132 knots. Her funnel is short and stumpy, having a considerable rake aft, and with steam pipes both before and aft — like her hull, her funnel is painted black.
>
> Early in the morning we were shewn over her deck, and the narrowness of her beam was again most strikingly apparent. Her armament consists of six 32 pounder smooth bore broad side guns, and two large pivot guns one forward and the other aft; the former is a rifled gun throwing 110 lb shot, and the latter a smooth bore 68 pounder. Everything on deck is in splendid order and of the very best material. Her engine room is also a picture of neatness; she has double cylinders, working transversely, and is nominally of 300 horse-power, but capable of working up to very considerably over that. Her speed under steam alone is between 14 and 15 knots.
>
> The impression which an inspection of the Alabama gives, is that she is essentially a handy craft, capable of the most rapid movements, and thoroughly effective to the extent of her strength. We had been accustomed to think that she was slightly built; and unfit to stand fire; but this is a mistake, she is wooden built and presents a side equal in strength, we should say, to that of any modern war vessel of her size, so that she can fight as well as run from her enemy; though the former is not her policy when she has the alternative left to her. Three or four places are pointed out where the fire of the Hatteras off Galveston took effect upon her, one is just under the main chains, one a little before the foremast — low down, one on the deck close beside her broadside gun on the starboard side, and another has torn a fragment out of her funnel. It will be remembered that in the this engagement she sunk the Hatteras, but not with one broadside as is generally stated; she fired eight broadsides before her enemy sank.
>
> Whatever may be our impression when we sedately view the mission of the Alabama it is impossible in the presence of this little craft not to be momentarily carried away by an enthusiastic sympathy for her cause. When talked to here of the hard push the South had for it, Captain Semmes, pointing to the Confederate ensign floating above him, said, "It is no matter, that Flag never comes down." It is a bold and confident boast; — time will tell us if it be a true one. No one who will visit her, can deny that the Alabama is officered by gentlemen, courteous and obliging.

Back in June 1862, Semmes had written to the Confederate secretary of the navy, Stephen Mallory: "I think well of your suggestion of the East Indies as a cruising ground, and hope to be in the track of the enemy's commerce in those seas as early as October or November next, when I shall doubtless be able to make other rich "burned offerings" upon the altar of our country's liberties."

Now, to his surprise, Semmes found the work already complete. Twenty-two American ships — large clippers — were dismantled and laid up at Singapore. The burning of the first ship in these seas had driven them into port for safety. News came from other ports in the Far East that American ships there were also laid up. There were two at Bangkok, two at Canton and three at Shanghai in China, one in the Philippines and two more in Japanese ports. Even if they had been brave enough to sail, no one would entrust a cargo to them. British ships took over their trade. One very avaricious American captain threw away all his respect and wrapped himself in the flag of a nation that most Northerners had come to despise. On the morning of 24 December, the *Alabama* sailed from Singapore. At about half past eleven a sail was seen, which unexpectedly appeared to be an American ship.

By one o'clock the *Alabama* was close enough to fire a gun, which brought the sail to a halt. She was the barque *Martaban*. From her mast she unfurled the British ensign. Master's Mate George Townley Fullam, an Englishman and a native of Kingston-upon-Hull, had his doubts. Upon boarding the ship, as soon as her master opened his mouth Fullam knew that he was no Englishman. His drawl betrayed him as a Yankee. When invited to accompany them to the *Alabama* with his papers, the captain refused. He claimed the protection of "his" flag. Somewhat annoyed at the proposition, Semmes was obliged to go over to the other ship. Upon examination it was discovered that the ship had formerly been the U.S. registered *Texan Star*. She had reregistered as a British ship just ten days before, and transferred to British owners. She was an American ship, and her captain was American, as were the crew. When her papers were examined, there was no bill of sale, nor any evidence of the transfer of property. Semmes condemned the ship and its cargo to be burned. Her captain leapt to his feet, and as Semmes records it, cried out: "You dare not do it sir; that flag won't stand it." As he had boarded the *Texan Star*, Semmes had admired the beautiful "bran new" [sic] English flag, of which her captain spoke. He replied, "[T]he flag that ought to be at your peak, will have to stand it." In half an hour the *Texan Star* was ablaze. Sometime later, when nothing could be altered, the master of the burned craft, Captain Pike, admitted that it had all been a fraud. On Christmas Day 1863, Semmes put his prisoners ashore at Malacca. Celebrations for the special day were modest. Semmes held a brief religious service, and the crew were allowed an extra tot of rum.

The next morning at six, the *Alabama* got underway once more. Semmes' plan was to return to the Atlantic via South Africa. The lookout had not been long at his task when the cry went up: "Sail ho!" Then it was repeated. There were two ships at anchor, waiting for a fair wind to take them through the Straits. They looked like Yankees. Unhurriedly the *Alabama* progressed towards them. They could not raise anchor and get underway before the *Alabama* reached them. There was no need for hurry, no need for deception. The Confederate flag was raised from the *Alabama*'s masthead. Soon she was upon them. They had not even time to raise the Union flag. Both were captured. They had mistakenly believed that the *Alabama* was cruising in the China Sea, so had taken the risk. Both were registered at Massachusetts— the *Sonora* and the *Highlander*. So close to land, Semmes permitted the crews of both ships to load their personal effects aboard their boats and row to shore. He took what he needed from both vessels, and within sight of the Straight of Malacca, he set them on fire. From the captain's cabin of one ship, Semmes found a copy of the *Straights Times* for 9 December 1863. One article caught his eye:

> From our to-day's shipping list it will be seen that there are no fewer than seventeen American merchantmen at present in our harbor, and that they include some of the largest ships at present riding there. Their gross tonnage may be roughly set down at 12,000 tons. Some of these have been lying here now for upward of three months, and most of them for at least half that period. And all this, at a time when there is no dullness in the freight market; but on the contrary, an active demand for tonnage to all parts of the world. It is, indeed, to us, a home picture — the only

5. The Alabama 133

The sinking of the *Martaban*, formerly the *Texan Star*, in the Malacca Straits. (*Illustrated London News*)

one we trust to have for many years to come.... [I]t is a picture quite unique in its nature; for the nation to which these seventeen fine ships belong has a Navy perhaps second only to that of Great Britain, and the enemy with which she has to cope, is but a schism from herself, possessed of no port that is not blockaded, and owning not more than five or six vessels on the high seas.

The British merchant marine were the benefactors of this situation around the world, and remained so up to the outbreak of World War I. Though eventually the British government, under the Geneva Arbitration of 1873, were obliged to pay the United States compensation of $15million (£3million), this was but a drop in the ocean compared to the money made by her shipping, both during and after the American Civil War. In 1862, a total of 117,756 tons of American shipping was sold, primarily to British buyers. In the following year an additional 222,199 tons of American shipping was sold. In all, U.S. marine insurance rose by 900 percent, and over 700 Union merchant ships were transferred to the British registry.

Now through the Straight, the *Alabama* overhauled another American ship. She was flying German colors, and when boarded proved to be the *Ottone*, registered in Bremen. She had been transferred from her American owners the previous May. Her papers were genuine, and her master and crew were German. She and her cargo of rice, destined for Rangoon, were permitted to sail on. New Year's Day 1864, the *Alabama* cleared the coast of Sumatra, and crossing the Bay of Bengal, set in a course for Ceylon (Sri Lanka). Along the way a number of neutral ships were overhauled, mainly British, including one taking pilgrims to Jiddah. Sailing around Ceylon the *Alabama* anchored off the coast of Malabar, India. On 14 January 1864, she captured the *Emma Jane* of Bath, Maine, out of Bombay in ballast. Taking what he wanted, Semmes put her to the torch. Her master, his wife and crew Semmes put ashore. The next day the *Alabama* anchored off Anjengo, on the extreme southeast coast of India. Having taken onboard fresh provisions, the *Alabama* set sail once more. Four weeks later, on 9 February, the *Alabama* arrived at the Comore archipelago off the east coast of Africa, and under steam ran into the port of Johanna. Here the *Alabama* remained for a week, primarily to refresh the crew and give them shore leave. At the time, the islands, inhabited by a mixture of races, were under the rule of an Arab, the Sultan Abdallah. There were no grog shops, as the sailors discovered, and well before the time their leave had expired on the first day, they were lined up on the beach waiting to be collected. When the *Alabama* next raised anchor, on 15 February, she had a relaxed and rested and sober crew. Down the east coast of southern Africa the little Confederate steamship sailed. She passed through an electrical storm of lightning and torrential rain before eventually arriving back at Cape Town on 20 March. Her cruise had lasted six months, bar one day.

Semmes was met with bad news. The *Tuscaloosa*, having returned to South Africa in December, had been seized by the authorities. In London the Secretary for the Colonies, the Duke of Newcastle, had overturned the verdict of the governor of South Africa, Sir Philip Wodehouse. Learned opinion in London had decided that the *Tuscaloosa* was an uncondemned prize, and therefore was not entitled to be regarded as a ship of war. Having been brought into British waters, in violation of the Act of Neutrality, she was ordered to be seized and returned to her original owners. Low's protests were overruled, and he was requested to draw up a list of the contents of the ship and the names of its crew. By then the crew of the *Tuscaloosa* had been enlarged to twenty-four men. Samuel Brown, an original crew member, does not appear on the subsequent list compiled by Low, on 30 December 1863:

List of Confederate Officers and Crew
Onboard the Bark *Conrad*, late *Tuscaloosa*

Name	Rank or Rating	Whence
J. Low	Lieutenant commanding	
W.H. Sinclair	Master	
J.T. Metier [Minor?]	Master's Mate	
A. Marmilstein	Master's Mate	
Martin Molk	Boatswain's Mate	*Alabama*, June 22, 1863
R. Owens	Boatswain's Mate	*Alabama*, June 22, 1863
H. Legris	Quartermaster	*Alabama*, June 22, 1863
E. Jones	Quartermaster	*Alabama*, June 22, 1863
T. Williams	Ship's cook	*Alabama*, June 22, 1863
R. Williams	Able bodied Seaman	*Alabama*, June 22, 1863
W. Jones	Able bodied Seaman	*Alabama*, June 22, 1863
W. Gibbs	Able bodied Seaman	At sea, Aug. 23, 1863
R. Morrell	Able bodied Seaman	At sea, Aug. 23, 1863
A. Anderson	Ordinary Seaman	At sea, Aug. 23, 1863
H. Anderson	Ordinary Seaman	At sea, Aug. 23, 1863
S. Roberts	Ordinary Seaman	At sea, Aug. 23, 1863
T. Altman	Steward	*Talisman*, June 1863
W. Renton	Able bodied Seaman	*Alabama*, June 21, 1863
S. Brewer	Able bodied Seaman	*Alabama*, June 21, 1863
J. Duggan	Able bodied Seaman	*Alabama*, June 21, 1863
J. Ross	Ordinary Seaman	At sea, Aug. 17, 1863
C. Carew	Ordinary Seaman	At sea, Aug. 17, 1863

Name	Rank or Rating	Whence
S. Robertson	Carpenter's Mate	At sea, Aug. 17, 1863
Ben Backstay	Ordinary Seaman	At sea, Aug. 17, 1863

Those seamen recruited at sea appear to be former crewmen from ships captured by the *Alabama*. The probability is that they were American, as opposed to the original crew, which was primarily British.

Upon discovering the situation, Semmes wrote immediately to Admiral Sir Baldwin Walker, protesting the decision. Baldwin conferred with the governor and the attorney general of the colony. The matter was referred to London. The point being made was that on her original visit she had been treated as a Confederate ship of war. Upon her return her position had not changed in any way, therefore her treatment should be the same. The subject was brought up in the House of Commons, and after debate, with further information and advice, the decision was overturned. Lord Newcastle was instructed to write to the governor that the *Tuscaloosa* should be returned to Lt. Low of the Confederate navy. By the time the order was received, Low and his men had sailed with Semmes aboard the *Alabama*.

Reaction to the decision at the American Embassy was curiously muted. Secretary Benjamin Moran noted the following in his journal: "During the evening it was announced that orders had been sent to Simon's Bay to restore the Tuscaloosa to the rebels. This did not surprise me. But the reason is childish. She should have been seized on her first visit. But as she was not then seized, the recognition given her could not be revoked, and her seizure on her return was an outrage. O holy, righteous England."[35]

On the morning of 25 March the *Alabama* had gotten up steam, raised her anchor, and eased herself out of Table Bay. As she was leaving, an American steamer was arriving. The *Quang Tung*, recently built for the China Trade, was well within the marine league as they passed. Undoubtedly that day she was the luckiest ship sailing the seven seas. As she sailed past the *Alabama* the crews of both ships lined the rails to view each other. Out to sea once more, Semmes let his fires go down, and under sail he set in a course for France, via the Azores. Reaching St. Helena, Semmes hovered about the island for several days in the hope of capturing an American ship, but none came his way. Sailing on, northwesterly, he fell in with a number of neutral ships. Then on the 22nd of April he met up with that increasing rarity, an American merchant ship. She was the *Rockingham*, from Callao, Peru, for Cork. Her cargo was guano, covered by an unsworn certificate that purported to show that it was British. The chase had continued throughout the night and into the early morning. Her flight, assisted by the raising of extra canvas once she had seen her pursuer, suggested that she had something to hide. As dawn broke a gun from the *Alabama* was fired, and raising the Yankee flag, the merchantman heaved-to. Semmes condemned her and her cargo. The crew were transferred, and the *Alabama*'s gunners practiced their trade with shot and shell. At five o'clock she was set fire to. The *Alabama* sailed on.

A few days later, on 27 April, at about three o'clock in the afternoon, a large sail was seen approaching. Both ships progressed towards each other, as if they were close friends meeting. Very close now, a sailor aboard the other ship was seen with the Stars and Stripes in his hand, preparing to raise them to the masthead. Semmes called for the Stars and Bars to be raised aboard the *Alabama*. Too late to do anything about it, the other ship heaved-to to await a boarding party. It had been a complete surprise. The other vessel was the *Tycoon*, out of New York, bound for San Francisco, with an assorted cargo. There was no pretense on her part. She was American, as was her cargo. Taking what he needed, and transferring her crew, Semmes fired her at nightfall.

On 2 May the *Alabama* recrossed the equator into the northern hemisphere. She was badly in need of a complete overhaul. The news at home gleaned from newspapers taken from captured ships was not good. A depression set in on Semmes, as he realized the cause was all but lost. The *Alabama* breasted the Azores, then headed northeast to the Iberian peninsula. On 10 June, the Lizard was sighted, and that night the *Alabama* anchored in a Cornish bay. The following morning the *Alabama* entered the English Channel, and at 10 o'clock she took on a French pilot at Cape La Hague, who took her into Cherbourg harbor.

Upon anchoring, Semmes sent an officer to call upon the port admiral to seek permission to land his prisoners from the last two ships captured. This was acceded to, but Semmes' next request was a little more difficult. He asked to be allowed to carry out extensive repairs to his ship. Cherbourg Dock was a government installation. It had the best facilities available, but being a government yard, there were international ramifications. Could accession to government facilities be seen to be favoring a belligerent ship? The matter was referred to the government for adjudication. As Semmes awaited a response, the *Alabama* lay at anchor in the harbor. Semmes now received news that his superior in Europe, Flag Officer Samuel Barron, was in Paris. From Cherbourg on 13 June, Semmes wrote:

> SIR: I have just been informed by the Hon. Mr. Slidell of your presence in Paris. I have the honor to report to you the arrival of this ship at this place in want of repairs. She will be required to be recoppered, refastened in some places, and to have her boilers pretty extensively repaired, all of which will probably detain her a couple of months. I shall have sufficient funds at my command to pay off officers and crew, but will require money for repairs. As soon as I receive permission from the admiral here to go into dock I propose to give my men leave for an extended run on shore, many of them being in indifferent health, in consequence of their long detention on shipboard and on salt diet. The officers also will expect a similar indulgence.
>
> As for myself, my health has suffered so much from a constant and harassing service of three years, almost continuously at sea, that I shall have to ask for relief.
>
> I have the honor to be, very respectfully, your obedient servant,
> R. SEMMES,
> Captain.[36]

Within hours of the arrival of the *Alabama*, the United States minister in Paris telegraphed Captain John A. Winslow of the USS *Kearsarge,* then anchored off Flushing in the Netherlands.[37] John Browne, surgeon aboard the *Kearsarge,* later wrote:

> On Sunday, the 12th of June 1864, the Kearsarge, Captain John A Winslow, was lying at anchor in the Scheldt, off Flushing, Holland. The cornet suddenly appeared at the fore, and a gun was fired. These were unexpected signals that compelled absent officers and men to return to the ship. Steam was raised, and as soon as we were off, and all hands called, Captain Winslow gave the welcome news of a telegram from Mr. Dayton, our minister to France, announcing that the Alabama had arrived the day previous at Cherbourg; hence the urgency of departure, the probability of an encounter, and the expectation of her capture or destruction. The crew responded with cheers. The succeeding day witnessed the arrival of the Kearsarge at Dover for dispatches, and the day after (Tuesday) her appearance off Cherbourg, where we saw the Confederate flag flying within the breakwater. As we approached, officers and men gathered in groups on deck, and looked intently at the "daring rover" that had been able for two years to escape numerous foes and to inflict immense damage on our commerce. She was a beautiful specimen of naval architecture. The surgeon went on shore and obtained pratique (permission to visit the port) for boats. Owing to the neutrality limitation, which would not allow us to remain in the harbor

longer than twenty-four hours, it was inexpedient to enter the port. We placed a vigilant watch by turns at each of the harbor entrances, and continued it to the moment of the engagement.[38]

On 14 June, following the arrival of the *Kearsarge,* Semmes wrote again to Barron:

DEAR BARRON: The Kearsarge is off the port, which I understand, of course, as a challenge. As we are about equally matched, I shall go out to engage her as soon as I can make the necessary preparations, which will probably be tomorrow. As the issue of combats is always uncertain, I have deposited 4 sacks of sovereigns, containing about £4,700, and the paymaster's last pay roll with Mr. Ad. Bonfils, of Cherbourg, a gentleman known to Mr. Slidell.

I have also deposited a package of ransom bonds (sealed), all of which please bear in mind in case of accident.

Yours truly, etc.,

R. SEMMES.[39]

The strong expectation that the *Alabama* would give battle was confirmed when Semmes wrote to M. Bonfils, the Confederate States commercial agent:

CSS ALABAMA,
Cherbourg, June 14, 1864.

Ad. BONFILS, Esq.,
Cherbourg.

SIR: I hear that you were informed by the U.S,. Consul that the Kearsarge was to come to this port solely for the prisoners landed by me, and that he was to depart in twenty-four hours. I desire to say to the U.S. Consul that my intention is to fight the Kearsarge as soon as I can make the necessary arrangements. I hope these will not detain me more than until to-morrow evening, or after the morrow morning at furthest. I beg she will not depart before I am ready to go out.

I have the honor to be, very respectfully, your obedient servant,

R. SEMMES,
Captain.[40]

Through intermediaries, Captain Winslow informed Semmes that he had come to Cherbourg to fight, and had no intention of leaving. Aboard the *Kearsarge,* Dr. Browne reported:

Preparations were made for battle, with no relaxation of the watch. Thursday passed; Friday came; the Kearsarge waited with ports down, guns pivoted to starboard, the whole battery loaded, and shell, grape and canister ready to use in any mode of attack or defense; yet no Alabama appeared. French pilots came on board and told of unusual arrangements made by the enemy, such as the hurried taking of coals, the transmission of valuable articles to the shore, such as captured chronometers, specie, and the bills of ransomed vessels; and the sharpening of swords, cutlasses, and boarding-pikes. It was reported that Captain Semmes had been advised not to give battle. He replied he would prove to the world that his ship was not a privateers [*sic*], intended only for attack upon merchant vessels, but a true man-of-war; further he had consulted French officers who had all asserted that in his situation they would fight. Certain newspapers declared that he ought to improve the opportunity afforded by the presence of the enemy to show that his ship was not a "corsair" to prey upon defenseless merchantmen, but a real ship-of-war, able and willing to fight the "Federal" waiting outside the harbor. It was said the Alabama was swift, with a superior crew, and it was known that the ship, guns, and ammunition were of English make.[41]

Cherbourg on Sunday morning, 19 June, was a fine day. The sea was calm, with a slight haze. The *Kearsarge* lay some three miles out, near the buoy that marked a line of shoals. At ten o'clock the crew were assembled for Sunday service. At twenty past, the officer of the watch reported a steamer approaching from the port. As she drew closer she was identified as the *Alabama.* A drum beat to general quarters, and the deck was cleared for action. As if in flight, the *Kearsarge* then headed seaward. But this was no flight; Winslow had assured the French authorities that in the event of an engagement he would move well beyond territorial waters. The *Alabama*, escorted by the French iron-clad frigate *Couronne*, approached from the western entrance to the port. Behind them came a small fore-and-aft rigged steamer, the *Deerhound*, flying the flag of the Royal Mersey Yacht Club. At three miles from the shore, the *Couronne* turned and returned to port. A short way off the *Deerhound* continued to follow the *Alabama*. Now between six and seven miles from the shore, the *Kearsarge* wheeled about and made all steam towards the Confederate ship. The *Alabama* came on until she was about one and a quarter miles from her opponent, then turned to present her starboard battery. At three minutes to eleven the *Alabama* opened fire with a broadside, at a range of about 1,800 yards. The *Kearsarge*'s rigging was torn, but by and large the broadside was ineffectual. The *Kearsarge*

John A. Winslow, U.S.N., captain of the USS *Kearsarge*, confronted the *Alabama* at Cherbourg.

came on with increased speed, receiving a second and third broadside, but again with little effect. The rate of fire was good, but erratic. Now within 900 yards, and with her fuses set at five seconds, the *Kearsarge* sheered away, and presenting her broadside, opened fire with her starboard battery. Her first shell went crashing through the forward rifle port of the *Alabama*, killing one man, and smashing the leg of another.

Winslow's intention was to place the *Kearsarge* between the *Alabama* and shore, so that if beaten, Semmes could not make a dash for neutral France. Winslow attempted to run under the *Alabama*'s stern, but because of raking fire from his opponent, could not without risking serious damage. Both ships were now forced to fight on a circular track, barely half a mile apart, going round and round a common center, as they drifted westward. The *Alabama* changed from solid shot to shell. Semmes later wrote a letter to Flag-Officer Barron: "Perceiving that our shell though apparently exploding against the enemies [sic] sides, were doing him but little damage, I returned to solid shot firing, and from this time onward alternated with shot, and shell." A broadside from the *Kearsarge* struck the spanker-gaff of the *Alabama*, causing the ensign to come down. To the crew of the *Kearsarge* it was seen as a good sign. Aboard the *Alabama* the pennant was quickly retrieved, and run up the mizzenmast. The *Alabama* now opened up with both shot and shell, determined to bring the engagement to a closure as soon as possible. It was rapid but erratic, as opposed to the *Kearsarge*'s slower but more accurate fire. Though the *Alabama*'s shot and shell struck the *Kearsarge*'s hull, little damage was inflicted. The reason for this was twofold. Masters of wooden hulled ships in the U.S. Navy now followed

Admiral Farraguts's example of fixing chain to the outer hull to give better protection to machinery, and this included Winslow aboard the *Kearsarge*. In order to hide the unsightly chain, a box cover of one inch deal boards was placed over the chain. Thus the ship was converted to a crude iron-plated vessel, though this was not immediately obvious. Secondly, Semmes was using his original shot and shell, now two years old, as were their fuses, and they proved to be ineffectual. Kell, in his article in *Battles & Leaders of the Civil War,* commented in a footnote:

> On the coast of Brazil we had had some target practice at one of our prizes. Many of our fuses proved defective. Upon visiting the target I found that one of the 100-pound shells had exploded on the quarter deck, and I counted fifteen marks from the missiles, which justifies me in asserting that had the 100-pound shell which we placed in the stern-post of the Kearsarge exploded, it would have changed the result of the fight. I at once examined every fuse and cap, discarding the apparently defective, and at the same time made a thorough overhauling of the magazine, as I thought, but the action with the Kearsarge proved that our entire supply of powder was damaged. The report from the Kearsarge's battery was clear and sharp, the powder burning like thin vapor, while our guns gave out a dull report, with thick and heavy vapor.[42]

This use of outdated and damp powder was confirmed by an unnamed English sailor who served aboard the *Alabama* during the battle. In an article that appeared in the *National Eagle,* published in Claremont, New Hampshire, on 9 July 1864, he described the situation: "About the same time our forward pivot gun sent two well directed shells, one of which struck the chains which protected the Kearsarge's boilers, penetrating the chain, but doing no such damage as was expected. We supposed then that her engines were knocked to pieces, and that the Kearsarge would soon go down. We gave three

First shots of the battle. The *Alabama* and the *Kearsarge* move in circles to gain an advantage. (*Illustrated London News*, 2 July 1864)

The eleven-inch forward pivot gun of the *Kearsarge* did terrible destruction to the *Alabama*. (*Century Magazine*)

cheers. The shell was fired from our hundred pounder forward rifle pivot, and would certainly have penetrated the chain, and entirely disabled the Kearsarge had our powder been good, as this gun would have carried the shell and taken effect at five miles with dry powder. Our powder had been a long time on board, and was dampened."[43]

Some of the *Alabama*'s shots were effective. Eighteen minutes into the fight, a 68-pounder Blakely shell from the *Alabama* passed through the starboard bulwark of the *Kearsarge* and exploded on the quarterdeck, wounding three of the crew. Two more shots from the *Alabama*, now more accurate, crashed through the ports where the *Kearsarge*'s 32-pounder guns were. Another shell exploded, causing a fire aboard the *Kearsarge*, but this was quickly dealt with by men designated for the task. The *Kearsarge* had fired 173 rounds of shot and shell, the *Alabama* almost twice that figure. Responding shots from the *Kearsarge* were very effective, tearing into the *Alabama*'s hull near the waterline, between the main mast and the mizzenmast, exploding within the heart of the ship. At the after pivot gun aboard the *Alabama*, two of her gunners were cut in two by shell from the *Kearsarge*. A shell cut away the *Alabama*'s rudder. A second penetrated the coal bunkers and destroyed the boiler. The vessel now filled with smoke and steam. All power of movement ceased. She began to slow down, then noticeably began to settle by the stern. She had been mortally wounded, but the battle might yet be won. Her salvoes were undiminished as she sought to impose maximum damage upon her enemy as quickly as possible. Her shots were largely ineffectual though. The after pivot gun of the *Kearsarge* did terrible damage. Semmes ordered his gunners to concentrate on that one gun and silence it, but already it was too late. The battle was lost, if Semmes but knew it. A shell-man aboard the *Alabama*, James Hart, was cut in two as he brought a shell to one of the guns. John Roberts, a young Welshman, had his guts torn open by a shell splinter. He staggered

Outdated and damp powder lost the battle for the Confederates, the executive officer of the *Alabama*, John McIntosh Kell, believed.

forward, and died at his gun. Midshipman Anderson, directing fire, had his leg blown off and fell overboard into the sea. Semmes was wounded in the hand by a splinter. Tying a handkerchief around the wound he continued at his station. It was turning into slaughter aboard the *Alabama*. Dead and dying lay about the deck. The following is from the unnamed English sailor's article in the *National Eagle*: "The dead, of whom there were about eight, and the wounded, numbering perhaps twelve, instead of being carried below, were lying about the deck. The carnage was awful, some of the men being literally cut to pieces. There was much confusion on board, though nothing like a panic, excepting on the part of one or two who were not Englishmen. One young Prussian stationed at a gun, having ran below and stated to the doctor that he was wounded, was ordered on deck, he not being wounded, and was immediately shot in the back by an old man named Hicks, an English seaman who had been long in the English navy. He shot him with his revolver, he died soon afterwards."[44] The Englishman who shot the Prussian for cowardice appears to have been James Higgs, rather than Hicks. He was a native of Liverpool.

The two ships completed seven rotations and were entering an eighth. The *Alabama* now sinking, her engine destroyed, sought to escape by setting all available sail. She left the circle, now fully exposing herself, unable to return fire as she did so. Another broadside from the *Kearsarge* produced great gaping holes in the hull of the *Alabama*, through which the sea poured in. Now again between ship and shore, the *Kearsarge* battered the *Alabama* with impunity. The *Alabama* was listing heavily. Kell, realizing that it was all over, urged Semmes to strike the colors as the vessel was sinking. As he spoke a shell from the *Kearsarge* struck the mast and broke the color halyard. The flag came fluttering down. When some of the English members of the crew saw this they were enraged that Semmes was considering surrender. He commended their courage, but the ship was sinking, and Semmes, not wishing to see more lives needlessly lost, refused to raise the colors. Kell then ordered a white flag to be shown. A boatswain leapt up onto the boom and waved it as a token of surrender. Aboard the *Kearsarge* Winslow ordered his gunners to cease fire. Two of the *Alabama*'s junior officers (one of whom was Irvine S. Bulloch, half brother to James Dunwoody Bulloch), refusing to surrender, pushed aside the gunners and fired two rounds at the *Kearsarge*, in direct violation of the rules of war. Winslow ordered fire to be resumed. Shot and shell went crashing into the already sinking ship. The *Alabama* lurched, and began to settle even further to her stern.

With no fire being returned, and with a white flag now clearly being displayed aboard the *Alabama,* Winslow gave orders to cease firing. The battle was over; it had lasted one hour and two minutes. Boats were lowered from the *Alabama.* Other sailors dived into the sea, so as not to be dragged down with the dying ship. Master's Mate George Fullam, with a boatful of badly injured men, came alongside the *Kearsarge,* and when asked if Semmes had surrendered, replied that he had. Fullam, unloading his wounded, asked if he could return with his boat to help rescue the remaining drowning men of his crew. Winslow agreed. What was said next is open to debate, though things are sometimes confused in the heat of battle. Fullam, it was alleged, then gave his word of honor that when the men were rescued from the sea, he would return onboard and surrender himself. He always maintained that this was not so. Coming up towards the *Kearsarge,* the *Deerhound* was hailed; her owner, Mr. John Lancaster, was requested to assist in picking up the men in the water. Meanwhile, aboard his boat, Kell picked up more men from the sea and took them to the yacht *Deerhound,* which was approaching. Aboard the *Alabama,* Semmes was assisting the last of his wounded and those who could not swim to descend into the remaining boats. With everyone over the side, Semmes threw his sword into the sea and jumped overboard. As the *Deerhound* approached, the *Alabama* gracefully sank, stern first, below the surface. It was twenty-four minutes past twelve. Aboard the *Kearsarge* not a single cheer arose at their victory. Lieutenant Commander James S. Thornton gave the command "Silence boys!" and in respect for the *Alabama* and her crew there was silence. She sank in forty-five fathoms of water, four and a half miles from the breakwater, off the western entrance of the harbor.[45]

The *Deerhound* had lowered her two boats and rescued Captain Semmes, First Lieutenant Kell, twelve officers and twenty-six crewmen. Meanwhile, boats from the *Kearsarge* were lowered, and the remaining forty men still alive in the sea were likewise rescued. To the surprise of those men the *Alabama*'s crew were treated with considerable kindness by the men of the *Kearsarge,* men who barely half an hour before had tried to kill them. The *Alabama* sailors were provided with dry clothing and given measures of rum to restore their spirits. Two French pilot boats also rescued men from the sea and took them back to Cherbourg. Of the crew at the time of the battle, nineteen different nationalities were represented, most Englishmen. Only six were native-born Americans.

Now aboard the *Deerhound,* with the men he had rescued, Lancaster asked Semmes where he should sail to. According to Kell's report, Semmes said, "I am now under English colors, and the sooner you put me with my officers and men on English soil, the better." Lancaster ordered his captain, Evan Parry Jones, to sail the yacht under steam to Southampton with all speed. Aboard the *Kearsarge,* a number of junior officers pointed out to Winslow what was happening. The *Deerhound* with its rescued men, including Semmes, was sailing away. They requested him to put a shot across her bows, to halt her. For whatever reason Winslow refused, and the *Deerhound* continued home to England. For Winslow it was an incomplete victory. Semmes was still free.

Seventy prisoners were eventually taken aboard the *Kearsarge,* including five officers, surgeon and acting paymaster Galt, Second Lieutenant J.D. Wilson, First Assistant Engineer M.J. Freeman, Third Assistant Engineer Pundt, and Boatswain Benjamin McCaskey.

Opposite, top: Stern first, the ***Alabama*** sank beneath the waves. *Bottom:* Master's Mate George Fullam asks the ***Kearsarge***'s crew for assistance to save the drowning crew of the ***Alabama***. (*Century Magazine*)

Second Lieutenant Armstrong was picked up by a pilot boat and landed at Cherbourg. Armstrong wrote a letter to Flag-Officer Barron in Paris:

> SIR: I have the honor to report for your information the circumstances attending my rescue from drowning by a French pilot boat after the Alabama went down. I was wounded in the side by part of a shell early in the action, and suffered so much pain in the water that had it not been for the exertions of the Alabama's crew I would most certainly have gone down. One of the Kearsarge's boats was very near me, but laid on its oars and made no exertion whatever that I could see to save me. The officer apparently looking for some particular person. I made great exertions to reach the French boat, and was finally pulled into her so benumbed by cold and suffering so much from my bruised side that I could not stand, and for two hours was as helpless as a child. I had on, while near the Kearsarge's boat, my uniform cap, which the Federal officer could certainly have seen.
>
> The officers who were saved with me were Second Assistant Engineer William P. Brooks and Acting Sailmaker Henry Alcott. What time they got on board of the boat I can not say. I found when my faculties returned the following men on board with me:
>
> Charles Godwin, captain after guard; James Welsh, captain top; George Edgerton, ordinary seaman; Thomas Murphy, fireman; William Robinson, seaman, and Morris Britt, boy.
>
> As I got on board of the pilot boat I saw Michael Mars (seaman) plunge from the Kearsarge's boat and swim to the boat which I was in. The Federal officer said nothing, attempted nothing, appearing stupefied by the bold action of this brave man.
>
> I am, sir, very respectfully, your obedient servant,
>
> R.F. ARMSTRONG,
> Second Lieutenant, C. S. Navy[46]

Assistant Surgeon Llewellyn, after getting all the wounded aboard boats, jumped into the sea. He was unable to swim, and was tragically drowned before a boat could be got to him. David White, the black boy, also drowned. He had not told anyone that he could not swim. In all, the *Alabama*'s total loss was nine men killed and twenty-one wounded. Ten others were drowned after the ship sank.

At ten past three the *Kearsarge* anchored in Cherbourg harbor, next to the French ship-of-war *Napoleon*. She landed her prisoners, who were later paroled. The *Kearsarge* had received twenty-eight shot and shell, of which thirteen were in the hull. Meanwhile on the other side of the English Channel the *Deerhound* docked at Southampton that evening. Even in defeat, Semmes and his men were treated as heroes; they were lionized by all, and received with a demonstration of sympathy and kindness wherever they went. Kell later wrote of it:

> The next day the Admiral [as he was eventually to become] and I, went to a tailor to buy some clothes. The tailor invited us back to his private apartments and insisted on our partaking of cake and wine. While we were enjoying the feast, the tailor, who had left the rooms, returned and said, "Gentlemen I shall have to request you to return to your hotel. Your presence here has completely blocked business on this street." When we went out we found that the street was packed with thousands of people who had come to catch a glimpse of us. Policemen had to clear a way back to the hotel for us. The English at heart, were undoubtedly with the South. During our stay in England, they showed us distinguished attention in a thousand ways. Many young men from the best families were anxious to join us in our "new ship."[47]

For Lancaster there was to be only vilification.

6

The Castigation of Mr. Lancaster

There was much rejoicing in the United States over the defeat of the *Alabama*. One song in particular, written by R.B. Nicol, captured the mood of the time:

The Fate of the Pirate *Alabama*

Air — The Heights of Alma

Ye jolly sons of the ocean blue,
I have a song to sing for you
Of the Kearsarge and her gallant crew,
    And the pirate Alabama.
These vessels met in the forenoon,
On Sunday, the 19th day of June;
And our Yankee gunners proved right soon,
    Too much for the Alabama.
In half mile circles round they went —
An hour and more broadsides were sent,
Till through and through great holes were rent
    In the hull of the Alabama.
Like blasts sent from the pit of hell
Was the awful storm of shot and shell,
Which from the guns of the Kearsarge fell
    On the fated Alabama.
Her boiler by a solid shot
Was burst, while steam was scalding hot.
And shells were searching every spot
    Through out the Alabama.
The crew pell-mell all rushed on deck,
Hauled down their flag, the fire to check;
Confusion reigned upon the wreck
    Of the sinking Alabama.

Then over board all hands did bound
The Captain swam for the Deerhound,
A British yacht which had come round
    To help the Alabama.
Captain Winslow hailed her then,
For help to save the drowning men,
Not thinking her the chosen friend
    Of the pirate Alabama.
Of course his aid was freely lent,
Boats were lowered and quickly sent
Then with a plunge to the bottom went
    The far-famed Alabama.
A number of the crew were brought
With Captain Semmes aboard the yacht,
Which away for a British harbor shot
    With her prize from the Alabama.
Had our Yankee boys their treach'ry guessed
They would not have stayed to save the rest,
But to Davy Jones, had her expressed
    Along with the Alabama.
Now the English channel long will be
Remembered for this victory;
Three cheers for the "Champion of the Sea"
    That sunk the Alabama.

Within the United States administration, the defeat of the *Alabama* was seen not so much as a defeat for the South, which was already beaten, if it had but known it, but a defeat for Great Britain — the true enemy. In its distorted way of thinking, the United States blamed Great Britain for prolonging the war, first of all by acknowledging the very existence of the Confederate States, and secondly by permitting the rebels to build and equip ships. The *Alabama* was seen as being an English ship, built in an English shipyard, by English workmen, constructed of English oak, armed with English guns, manned by English sailors trained by the British Navy, and sunk in the English Channel. John Lancaster's part was seen as the ultimate betrayal by Britain.

In reality, far from being complicit in the building of these ships, the British government was seething at the abuse of her neutrality. Expressing his anger, yet wrapped up in the diplomatic language of the day, Earl Russell wrote to the Confederate commissioners, Mason, Slidell and Mann:

> In the first place, I am sorry to observe that the unwarrantable practice of building ships in this country, to be used as vessels of war against a State with which Her Majesty is at peace, still continues. Her Majesty's Government had hoped that this attempt to make the territorial waters of Great Britain the place of preparation for warlike armaments against the United States might be put an end to by prosecutions and by seizure of the vessels built in pursuance of contracts made with the Confederate agents. But facts which are unhappily too notorious, and correspondence which has been put into the hands of Her Majesty's Government by the Minister of the Government of the United States, shows that resort is had to evasion and subtlety in order to escape the penalties of the law; that a vessel is bought in one place, that her armament is prepared in another, and that both are sent to some distant port beyond Her Majesty's jurisdiction, and that thus an armed steamship is fitted out to cruise against the commerce of a Power in amity with Her Majesty. A crew, composed partly of British subjects, is procured separately; wages are paid to them for an unknown service. They are dispatched, perhaps to the coast of France, and there, or elsewhere, are engaged to serve in a Confederate man-of-war.
>
> Now, it is very possible that by such shifts and stratagems, the penalties of the existing law of this country, nay, of any law that could be enacted, may be evaded; but the offense thus offered to Her Majesty's authority and dignity by the de facto rulers of the Confederate States, whom Her Majesty acknowledges as belligerents, and whose agents in the United Kingdom enjoy the benefit of our hospitality in quiet security, remains the same. It is a proceeding totally unjustifiable, and manifestly offensive to the British Crown.[1]

Semmes and most of his officers had escaped, and the man responsible for that was English businessman John Lancaster. The United States secretary of state, William H. Seward, claimed that Semmes and his men were prisoners of war. He demanded that they be handed over, and that John Lancaster be severely castigated for his actions. In a brief note after the battle, Captain Winslow had written to navy secretary Gideon Welles:

> An English yacht, the Deerhound had approached near the Kearsarge at this time, when I hailed and begged the commander to run down to the Alabama, as she was fast sinking, and we had but two boats; and assist in picking up the men. He answered affirmatively and steamed toward the Alabama, but the latter sank almost immediately. The Deerhound, however, sent her boats and was actively engaged, aided by several others which had come from shore. These boats were busy in bringing the wounded and others to the Kearsage, whom we were trying to make as comfortable as possible, when it was reported to me that the Deerhound was moving off. I could not believe that the commander of that vessel could be guilty of so disgraceful an act as taking our prisoners off, and therefore took no means to prevent it, but continued to keep our boats at work rescuing the men in the water. I am sorry to say that I was mistaken; the Deerhound made off with Captain Semmes and others, and also the very officer who had come on board to surrender.
>
> I learned subsequently that the Deerhound was a consort of the Alabama, and that she received on board all the valuable personal effects of Captain Semmes the night before the engagement.
>
> I have the honor to be, very respectfully, your obedient servant,
>
> JNO. A WINSLOW,
> Captain.[2]

No evidence was ever put forward to substantiate Winslow's last statement, that the *Deerhound* was a consort of the *Alabama,* and that Semmes' personal effects were placed aboard the *Deerhound*. In a letter written from the safety of Southampton, on 21 June

The *Deerhound* rescuing members of the *Alabama*'s crew. (*Illustrated London News*)

1864, Semmes wrote to Flag-Officer Samuel Barron in Paris, informing him that money, payrolls, ransom bonds and other miscellaneous material had been placed in the hands of a Cherbourg banker by Paymaster Galt. If Galt was not released from Federal imprisonment, then Semmes requested Barron and French commissioner Slidell to approach the banker and retrieve the said items.

It was further alleged that Lancaster had entered into an agreement with Semmes the night before the battle that, in the eventuality of the *Alabama* being sunk, he would rescue the captain and his officers and take them to a place of safety. In reality, as Lancaster was to later testify, the first time that he met Semmes was when he was brought aboard the *Deerhound* after the battle. Confirmation that there was no prior arrangement between Semmes and Lancaster is evidenced in a private letter between Semmes, then safely in Southampton, and his superior, Flag-Officer Samuel Barron. One would have expected, if there had been some sort of arrangement, that Semmes would have mentioned it. But he does not. Referring to his rescue he wrote as follows: "Some twenty minutes after my furnace fires had been extinguished, and the ship being on the point of settling, every man, in obedience to a previous order which had been given to the crew, jumped overboard and endeavored to save himself. There was no appearance of any boat coming to me from the enemy until the ship went down. Fortunately, however the steam yacht Deerhound, owned by a gentleman of Lancashire, England (Mr. John Lancaster), who was himself on board, steamed up in the midst of my drowning men and rescued a number of both officers and men from the water. I was fortunate enough myself thus to escape to the shelter of a neutral flag, together with about forty others, all told."[3]

Seward's demand was presented to Earl Russell through the U.S. minister in London, Charles Francis Adams. After due consideration Russell wrote back to Adams, with just the right tone of sarcastic put-down:

Foreign Office,
June 27, 1864

SIR: I have the honour to acknowledge the receipt of your note of the 25th instant, complaining of the interference of a British vessel, the Deerhound, with a view to aid in effecting the escape of a number of persons belonging to the Alabama, who you state had already surrendered themselves as prisoners of war, and calling my attention to the remarkable proportion of officers and American insurgents, as compared with the whole number of persons rescued from the waves. You state further that you can scarcely entertain a doubt that this selection was made by British subjects with a view to connive at the escape of these particular individuals from captivity.

I have the honour to state to you, in reply, that it appears to me that the owner of the Deerhound, of the Royal Yacht Squadron, performed only a common duty of humanity in saving from the waves the captain and several of the crew of the Alabama. They would otherwise, in all probability, have been drowned, and thus would never have been in the situation of prisoners of war.

It does not appear to me to be any part of the duty of a neutral to assist in making prisoners of war for one of the belligerents.

I shall however, transmit to the owner of the Deerhound a copy of your letter and its inclosures, together with a copy of this letter.

I am &c.

(Signed)   RUSSELL.[4]

Matters were not to rest there though. Unable to bully the British government, a campaign of vilification was directed towards Lancaster. A personal attack upon his

Above: Lord John Russell, British Foreign Secretary. *Right:* Charles Francis Adams, United States minister to Great Britain.

integrity was made in the letters column of the *London Daily News* by two anonymous American writers. Lancaster responded in the same newspaper:

THE DEERHOUND, THE ALABAMA, AND THE KEARSARGE

TO THE EDITOR OF THE DAILY NEWS. SIR: — As two correspondents of your journal, in giving their versions of the fight between the Alabama and the Kearsarge, have designated my share in the escape of Captain Semmes, and a portion of the crew of the sunken ship as "dishonorable," and have moreover affirmed that my yacht, the Deerhound, was in the harbor of Cherbourg before the engagement, and proceeded thence, on the morning of the engagement in order to assist the Alabama, I presume I may trespass upon your kindness so far as to ask an opportunity to repudiate the imputation, and deny the assertion. They admit that when the Alabama went down, the yacht, being near the Kearsarge, was hailed by Captain Winslow, and requested to aid in picking up the men who were in the water; but they intimate that my services were expected to be merely ministerial; or, in other words, that I was to put myself under the command of Captain Winslow, and place my yacht at his disposal for the capture of the poor fellows who were struggling in the water for their lives.

The fact is, that when we passed the Kearsarge, the captain cried out, "For God's sake, do what you can to save them," and that was my warrant for interfering, in any way, for the aid and succor of his enemies. It may be a question with some, whether without that warrant, I should have been justified in endeavoring to rescue any of the crew of the Alabama; but my own opinion is, that a man drowning in the open sea cannot be regarded as an enemy, at the time, to anybody, and is, therefore, entitled to the assistance of any passer-by. Be this as it may, I had the earnest request of Captain Winslow, to rescue as many of the men who were in the water, as I could lay hold of, but that request was not coupled with any stipulation to the effect that I should deliver up the rescued men to him as prisoners.... I should have deemed it dishonorable — that is, inconsistent with my notions of honor — to lend my yacht and crew, for the purpose of rescuing those brave men from drowning, only to hand them over to their enemies, for imprisonment, ill-treatment, and perhaps execution.

One of your correspondents opens his letter, by expressing a desire, to bring to the notice of the yacht clubs of England, the conduct of the commander of the Deerhound, which followed the engagement of the Alabama and Kearsarge. Now that my conduct has been impugned, I am equally wishful that it should come under the notice of the yacht clubs of England, and I am quite willing to leave the point of honor to be decided by my brother yachtsmen, and, indeed, by any tribunal of gentlemen. As to my legal right to take away Captain Semmes and his friends, I have been educated in the belief that an English ship is English territory, and I am, therefore, unable, even now, to discover why I was more bound to surrender the people of the Alabama whom I had on board my yacht.... Your anonymous correspondent further says, that "Captain Winslow would now have all the officers and men of the Alabama as prisoners, had he not placed too much confidence in the honour of an Englishman, who carried the flag of the royal yacht squadron...." Another reason assigned by your correspondent for that hero's forbearance may be imagined in the reflection that such a performance as that of Captain Wilkes, who dragged two "enemies" or "rebels" from an English ship, would not bear repetition.

And so the letter continues, with Lancaster addressing all the accusations leveled against him, and logically answering all charges. In short, what Lancaster said in his letter was that he was British, not American. His yacht and crew were British. He had not put himself under the command of Winslow, and thereby was under no obligation to hand over Semmes and his crew to the representatives of a foreign power. He had simply answered a humanitarian call to save lives. The last comment concerning Captain Wilkes is a teasing reference to the Trent Affair (when two Confederate diplomats were forcibly removed from a British steamer by a Federal captain), and perhaps the true reason why the *Kearsarge* did not open fire on the *Deerhound*. That event had brought both nations very close to war. Sinking a British flagged vessel engaged in saving the lives of drowning men would have brought a clamor from the British public for revenge. The two American letter writers, hiding behind anonymity, had completely misjudged British public opinion. Far from castigating Lancaster, the yacht clubs up and down the country wrote letters in support of him, many offering him honorary membership.

Confederate commissioner Mason wrote a letter of thanks to Lancaster. Again there is no suggestion of collusion whatsoever:

> 24, Upper Seymour Street, Portman Square,
> London, 21st June 1864.
>
> DEAR SIR: — I received from Captain Semmes, at Southampton, where I had the pleasure to see you, yesterday, a full report of the efficient service rendered, under your orders, by the officers and crew of your yacht, the Deerhound, in rescuing him, with thirteen of his officers and twenty-seven of his crew, from their impending fate, after the loss of his ship. Captain Semmes reports that, finding the Alabama actually sinking, he had barely time to dispatch his wounded in his own boats, to the enemy's ship, when the Alabama went down, and nothing was left to those who remained on board, but to throw themselves into the sea. Their own boats absent, there seemed no prospect of relief, when your yacht arrived in their midst, and your boats were launched; and he impressively told me, that to this timely and generous succor, he, with most of his officers and a portion of his crew, were indebted for their safety. He further told me, that on their arrival on board of the yacht, every care and kindness were extended to them which their exhausted condition required, even to supplying all with dry clothing. I am fully aware of the noble and disinterested spirit which prompted you to go to the rescue of the gallant crew of the Alabama, and that I can add nothing to the recompense already received by you and those acting under you, in the consciousness of having done as you would be done by; yet you will permit me to thank you, and through you, the captain, officers , and crew of the Deerhound, for this signal service, and to say that in doing so, I but anticipate the grateful sentiment of my country, and of the Government of the Confederate States. I have the honor to be, dear sir, most respectfully and truly, your obedient servant,
>
> J.M.MASON.
>
> JOHN LANCASTER, Esq., Hindley Hall, Wigan.[5]

As late as 1 August 1864, Under Secretary Moran at the American Embassy was recording in his journal: "ten dispatches from Washington. One of them (No. 1035) directs Mr. Adams to demand of the British Gov't the restoration of Semmes and his fellow pirates on the grounds that they are pirates and the carrying them by the Deerhound to Southampton was a hostile act towards the U.S."[6]

Russell's reply was breathtaking in its logic. As Semmes was never in their hands, how could he be restored to them? Mr. Lancaster had been asked to help save lives, and this is what he did. At no time were the rescued men in American hands, ergo, they could not be prisoners of war. Moran's response in his private journal is typically petulant. On the 27th of September 1864 he wrote: "Lord Russell has written a most insolent note under the date of the 26th Inst. To Mr. Adams in answer to his request for the censure by H.M.'s Government of Mr. Lancaster of the Deerhound, for his conduct in rescuing the pirates of the '290,' and bringing them to England; and also in reply to the demand for the restoration of Semmes and his fellows."[7] So for the moment the affair of John Lancaster and the *Deerhound* was shelved. It was to raise its head again at the Geneva Settlement of 1872, but again with the same results. John Lancaster had acted out of common humanity.

As for Semmes, he was feted wherever he went. At Southampton, as has previously been mentioned, he was mobbed in the streets. Everyone wanted to see the gallant captain of the *Alabama*. Dr. J. Wiblin, a distinguished surgeon and physician of Southampton, attended to Semmes and his men, free of charge. Semmes, Kell and other officers had their photographs taken at S.J. Wiseman's Art Repository in the city. Copies, displayed in the shop window, were sold to an eager public. Semmes initially based himself at Millbrook, Southampton, where his men had been accommodated, but London Society demanded his presence.

Semmes' throwing his sword into the sea was seen as something heroic rather than as having been taken by his enemies. The officers of the Army and Royal Navy set on foot a subscription for another sword to replace it. Their intention was published in the *Daily Telegraph* (24 June):

> Junior United Services Club, S.W.
>
> 23rd June 1864.
>
> SIR:— It will doubtless gratify the admirers of the gallantry displayed by the officers and crew of the renowned Alabama, in the late action off Cherbourg, if you will allow me to inform them, through your influential journal, that it has been determined to present Captain Semmes with a handsome sword, to replace that which he buried with his sinking ship. Gentlemen wishing to participate in this testimony to unflinching patriotism and naval daring, will be good enough to communicate with the chairman, Admiral Anson, United Services Club, Pall Mall, or, sir, yours, &c.
>
> Bedford Pim
>
> Commander R.N., Hon Secretary.

At a dinner party held in his honor, attended by officers of both the Royal Navy and the British army, along with a sprinkling of sympathetic politicians, Semmes was presented with a magnificent sword to replace the one abandoned. On another occasion, at a soiree of Confederate sympathizers, he was presented with a large Confederate flag, made in richest silk, by a "noble English lady," as he himself reveals. He was now moving in elevated circles within English society. He reputedly met the young Prince of Wales, later Edward VII, at a private reception. Miss Gladstone, sister of William Ewart Gladstone, chancellor of the exchequer and later prime minister, wrote a letter of sympathy to Semmes over the loss of his crew members killed or drowned. She offered aid to both Semmes and his crew, if it were needed. Semmes also received no end of offers from young Englishmen who wished to serve aboard his next ship. Letters came in from Eton College and other public schools offering support and congratulations at his escape out of the hands of a ruthless enemy. The eccentric clergyman the Rev. F.W. Tremlett (he was opposed to Socialism, vivisection and Yankees), vicar of St. Peter's, Belsize, London, renewed their acquaintance. He had first met Semmes in the previous year, after the *Sumter* was abandoned at Gibraltar. He now offered Semmes the comfort of his home, and also made arrangements for Semmes, himself, and a mixed party to vacation in Switzerland for a few weeks of recuperation. At the end of September Semmes returned to England and made preparations to return home to the South.

7

The *Georgia* and the *Rappahannock*

The third of the Confederate vessels obtained in Great Britain was the *Georgia*. In his *Secret Service of the Confederate States in Europe,* James D. Bulloch wrote that he "was the agent selected by the Confederate Government to manage and direct the general naval operations in Europe, and I was the chief representative of the Navy Department abroad, during the whole period of the war. All the ships that got to sea, except the Georgia, were despatched and equipped under my instruction."[1]

The man responsible for sending the CSS *Georgia* to sea was Commander Matthew F. Maury, who had an international reputation as a man of science. Nicknamed "Pathfinder of the Seas," Maury was born in Virginia in 1806. At the age of 19 he joined the United States Navy as a midshipman, and was seconded to the Frigate USS *Brandywine*. He was studious by nature; and following an injury to his leg, which left him unfit for duties at sea, he devoted his time to the further study of navigation, meteorology, winds and the influence of ocean currents. His work brought him to the attention of his superiors, and he was appointed superintendent of the Naval Observatory and head of the Depot of Charts and Instruments. Studying ships' logs and charts available to him, with references to currents and winds, he was able to accurately chart their positions for the beneficial use of sailors, to shorten ocean voyages. His findings were published in *Wind and Current Charts of the North Atlantic.* As a consequence, Maury's system of recording oceanographic data was widely adopted by navies and merchant navies around the world. Other books followed, including *The Physical Geography of the Seas and Its Meteorology.* Maury developed an international reputation, and was publicly recognized by several nations, including Great Britain and France. At the outbreak of the Civil War, much to the dismay of his naval colleagues, he resigned his commission and joined the Confederate navy.

Maury was sent to Europe to investigate the subject of submarine defenses, and the use of torpedoes and magnetic mines. As a subsidiary commission he was also given the authority to purchase ships for the Confederacy if the opportunity should arise. Using Captain North to negotiate the purchase, he acquired a 1150-ton iron screw steamer, almost completed, which North's daughter christened the *Virginia*. Built by William Denny & Bros. at Dumbarton, Scotland, in 1862, she was 212 feet in length, with a beam of 27 feet. Propulsion was by steam and sail. She was launched in March 1863 as the *Japan,* a name chosen to disguise her true purpose. She cleared Greenock in ballast, ostensibly for a voyage to Singapore, on Friday, 27 March. She was registered as being the property of Thomas Bold of Liverpool. The customs officers were to later certify that they saw nothing aboard her that would have led them to suspect that she was intended for warlike purposes. Her crew of fifty (sixty to seventy, according to some American sources) were shipped up from Liverpool by the firm of Jones & Co., and were a mixture of ex–Royal Navy and merchant marine. Near the lighthouse at the mouth of the Clyde, she took onboard more men and provisions. As she cleared the Clyde, a small steamer called the *Alar* cleared from Newhaven, in Sussex, bound for St. Malo in France, with the guns, ordnance stores and other provisions intended for the *Japan.*

The collector of customs at Newhaven, R.J. Dolan, reported with some concern the departure of the *Alar* to the commissioners of customs in London. He wrote to them:

> The steamship Alar, of London, 85 tons, owned by H.P. Maples, sailed on Sunday morning, 5th instant, at 2 A.M., bound according to the ship's papers, for Alderney and St. Malo. On Saturday at midnight, thirty men, twenty of whom appeared to be British sailors ten mechanics, arrived by train. Three gentlemen accompanied them, Mr. Lewis of Alderney, Mr. Ward and Mr. Jones. The men appeared to be ignorant of their precise destination; some said they were to get £20 each for their trip. A man rather lame, superintended them. Shortly after midnight, a man arrived from Brighton, on horseback, with a telegram, which for purposes of secrecy, had been sent there and not to Newhaven, it is suspected. Mr. Staniforth, the agent, replied to my inquiries this morning, that the Alar had munitions of war on board, and that they were consigned by ---- to a Mr. Lewis of Alderney. His answer was brief and with reserve, leaving no doubt on my mind nor on the minds of any here that the thirty men and munitions of war are destined for transfer at sea to some second Alabama. The telegram to Brighton intimated, very probably, having been reserved for the last hour, where that vessel would be found. Whether the shipment of the men, who all appeared to be British subjects, can, if it should be hereafter found that they have been transferred to a Federal or Confederate vessel, be held an infringement of the foreign-enlistment act, and whatever the clearance of the Alar, if hereafter found to be untrue can render the master amenable under the customs-consolidation act, is for your consideration respectfully submitted.[2]

The ever-vigilant Thomas Dudley, U.S. consul in Liverpool, heard of men being recruited, and set his agents to work. On Saturday, 4 April 1863, under secretary Benjamin Moran recorded in his private journal as follows:

> We have information of the sailing a few days ago of a rebel pirate from Greenock called the Japan by the connivance of Her Majesty's officers there, with a crew of 70 odd men who were shipped at L'pool for the purpose of serving in her. We have long been on the watch about this vessel, but could get no positive proof against her altho' the negative evidence was most conclusive. Mr Underwood, the Consul at Glasgow has not been vigilant as he should have been. Our information about her comes from Mr. Dudley, altho' she was not at all in his jurisdiction. The next thing we shall hear will be that she is burning American ships. Her guns were sent up to London from L'pool some days ago and will no doubt be put on her somewhere near neutral England, if not in British waters.[3]

There was additional, if not entirely accurate information, received on the 7th of April. Moran noted:

> We hear that the British pirate that left the Clyde on the 3rd of this month or thereabouts bearing the name Virginia alias Japan, has turned up at the island of Alderney, where she will take on board her armament from an English steamer which carried it to her from Newhaven. This information has been communicated to us by Mr Morse, the able, vigilant and invaluable Consul of the United States at London. Mr Dudley at Liverpool kept them in view and followed them to the Aller [*sic*]. This pirate Japan is owned, manned and armed by Englishmen, to say nothing about her having been built here. No effort was made to stop her, and there will be some tall lying to justify her departure by this Government.[4]

The vessels rendezvoused off the island of Ushant, Brittany. The two running into the calmer waters between the island and Brest, the armaments were transferred. They consisted of two 100-pounder cannons, two 24-pounder cannons and one 32-pounder cannon. On 9 April 1863, Commander William L. Maury (a cousin of Matthew F. Maury) and his staff of officers were rowed over from the *Alar,* and having boarded the *Japan,* Maury called all hands aft. There he read out his commission of authority, and ordered the Confederate flag to be raised, and announced that the vessel was now the Confederate States ship of war *Georgia.* The English crew were invited to join the Confederate struggle, and were promised prize money in addition to their pay. Many did; those who did not, were paid off and returned to England. American intelligence in the shape of its consuls in Britain was very active. Moran wrote on 11 April: "We got news this morning that the Alar had put into Plymouth and landed a number of the crew of the Japan, some of whom had refused to go in her when they found she was a pirate, while several who had been scalded by the bursting of a steam pipe had been sent back to hospital. The guns were put on board in St. Malo bay by the Alar. That vessel is glorified in the Times for the part she took in this piracy. Mr Adams doubted about bringing the matter to Earl Russell's notice at first, but finally did so. The pirate is gone out against our commerce under British colors."[5]

Thomas Dudley managed to find two of the crew who had returned to Plymouth aboard the *Alar.* They were Edward Thompson and John Mahon. He succeeded in getting them to swear depositions. The men testified that they were engaged in Liverpool by a company called Jones & Co. for a voyage to China. They were taken up to Glasgow and there put aboard the *Japan.* Sailing to St. Malo Bay, they helped to transfer the guns, but refused to become members of the *Georgia*'s crew. Too late to do anything about the rebel ship, which was now on the high seas, the Americans made representations to the British government concerning a breach of the Foreign Enlistment Act. Two men were arrested, Jones and Highatt. The charge against them was that they had induced British subjects to enter the Confederate service. The case was tried at the Liverpool Assizes before Lord Chief Justice Cockburn. Both defendants were found guilty and fined £50 each. It would seem that both men were reimbursed by Fraser, Trenholm & Co.

Maury sailed for the Azores. On 25 April, off the Cape Verde Islands, a ship was seen, the third of that day. The first two had been Dutch and British. It was just after four o'clock in the afternoon when the third vessel was sighted. Maury lowered the British ensign that he had been sailing under, and raised the Confederate flag. The other ship raised the United States colors. After a chase in sail and steam, she was overhauled and boarded. The ship was American, the *Dictator,* out of New York with a cargo of coal, bound for Hong Kong. Maury replenished his supply, and

William L. Maury, C.S.N., captain of the CSS *Georgia.*

on the following day burned his prize. Her estimated worth, complete with cargo, was put at $86,000. Fourteen of her crew agreed to sign on:

List of Men Shipped from The *Dictator*

John Benson, seaman	Walter Kroon, coal heaver
John Williams, seaman	Antonio Pentz, coal heaver
John Harty, seaman	Charles Grinnell, captain's steward
Charles Brown, seaman	Antonio Bass, captain's cook
John Ahlstram, seaman	Matthew Shean, boy
William Cullen, seaman	William Cox, boy
John Cain, second-class fireman	Alex. Ellis, coal heaver[6]

Taking on fresh supplies at the Azores, Maury then made sail for Bahia, in Brazil. On the morning of 29 April, the *Georgia* approached St. Vincent, one of the Cape Verde Islands, off the coast of west Africa. As she began the run in, a steamer of war, flying the United States colors, was seen at anchor. Maury gave orders to take the vessel back out to sea and set in a course south by east. On the afternoon of 3 May they crossed the path of an unnamed British man-of-war and exchanged compliments. On into the southern Atlantic, the *Georgia* overhauled a number of neutral vessels, English, French, Hamburg, Norwegian and Swedish. She arrived at Bahia, early on the morning of 13 May 1863. As dawn broke Maury sailed into the harbor, and discovered another steamer of war. She hoisted the Confederate colors, and proved to be the CSS *Alabama*, commanded by Raphael Semmes. Maury anchored his ship alongside her. His prisoners were put ashore. Over the next couple of days the *Georgia* took on coal from a Confederate tender, the barque *Castor*. Other supplies were obtained from ashore. The *Georgia* transferred some 528 pounds of powder to the *Alabama*. The news of the arrival of two Confederate cruisers was cabled to the Brazilian capital. On the afternoon of 22 May a Brazilian sloop of war entered the harbor. Pleasantries were exchanged, and that evening the *Georgia* put to sea once more.

The *Georgia* cruised around the Brazilian coastline for several weeks, stopping and searching. Maury was rewarded on 8 June, when he captured the *George Griswold,* an American ship but with a neutral cargo of coal, from Cardiff, bound for Rio. He could only bond her for $100,000, then sent her on her way. Maury then put in a course for South Africa. He chased and overhauled a number of vessels, but all proved to be neutrals. On the 13th of the month he captured the barque *Good Hope,* fifty-two days out from Boston, bound for the Cape of Good Hope. Ship and cargo were estimated to be worth $65,000. Maury took what provisions and stores he required, then, transferring her crew, he burned the unfortunate vessel on the following day. On the 15th, Maury captured the barque *J.W. Seaver,* out of Boston, with a neutral cargo of machinery for Russia. He bonded her for $30,000, and transferred his prisoners from the *Good Hope*. Maury put in a course for the West Indies. On the 18th they arrived at Trinidad.

On the morning of the 25th of June the *Georgia* got underway once more and shortly after half past ten that morning, just off Trinidad, overhauled the American ship *Constitution,* out of Philadelphia, bound for Shanghai with a cargo of coal. Taking what he needed, he set her on fire by shot and shell the following day. Her estimated value, with cargo, was reckoned to be $40,270. On 28 June the *City of Bath* was captured and bonded for $40,000. The crew of the *Constitution* were put aboard her. Six, however, agreed to join the *Georgia*'s crew:

List of Men Shipped from the *Constitution*

John Peterson, seaman	James Donovan, seaman
Francis Gray, seaman	Joseph Brown, seaman
Thomas Robinson, seaman	John Schmid, seaman

What surprised Maury, as it did both Semmes and Maffitt, was the absence of Federal warships. In Maury's case this was fortunate, for he found that the *Georgia's* sail power was insufficient to make her independent of her engines, and he frequently found the need for supplies of coal. Unlike the *Florida* and the *Alabama,* she was not purposely designed for warfare as they were. Maury now set in a new course for South Africa.

Over the next few days the Georgia overhauled a number of ships, the *Christobel, Diamond, Kent,* and *Factory Girl;* they were all British. In the mid South Atlantic, on 16 July, Maury's luck changed for the better. The *Georgia* gave chase to another American ship, the *Prince of Wales,* out of Bath, Maine. She had a neutral cargo. Maury released her on bond for $40,000. Back in the United States, on 22 July 1863, the New York Chamber of Commerce had cause to mention the *Georgia*: "...150 vessels, including two steamers, representing a tonnage of upward of 60,000 tons and a value of over $12,000,000 have been captured by the rebel privateers Alabama, Florida, Georgia.... The result is, that either American ships lie idle at our own and foreign ports, unable to procure freights, and thus practically excluded from the carrying trade, or are transferred to foreign flags."

The *Georgia* arrived at South Africa, and anchored in Simon's Bay on 16 August. Here she re-coaled and took on fresh provisions. During her visit, the cousin of Matthew Fontaine Maury and his officers were feted by the Royal Navy, aboard ship and ashore at the officer's club. The *Georgia* put to sea once more on the evening of 29 July, heading

The Scottish-built Confederate cruiser CSS *Georgia*. (*Illustrated London News*, 28 May 1864)

west, back into the southern Atlantic. Just one day out she captured another American ship, the *John Watts*. She had a neutral cargo of teak, and Maury could only bond her. Prize and cargo were valued at $30,000. The *Georgia* now cruised up the coast of west Africa. The ship's log indicates that she sailed for thirty-three days without making contact with another vessel. On 4 October she overhauled the Liverpool schooner *Ben McCree*, and later that day exchanged colors with another British schooner. Off the coast of French West Africa, on 9 October, Maury captured and burned the ship *Bold Hunter*. She had sailed from Dundee, bound for Calcutta with a cargo of coal. Maury took what he needed to enable him to continue. The stops were becoming more and more frequent as the *Georgia* hobbled north to Europe. Under a full head of steam she could only make six knots. She touched at Tenerife on the evening of the 14th of October, and on 28 October 1863 she hobbled into Cherbourg harbor, France. In her seven month cruise she had destroyed five ships and bonded three to the value of $200,000. Word reached London of her arrival. Under Secretary Moran noted it: "Friday 30th October: The pirate 'Japan' alias the 'Georgia,' has again made her appearance on the coast of Europe. She has been burning our ships, but through the imbecility of Mr. Welles [the United States naval secretary] there are no war vessels here to take her."[7]

By January 1864 three Confederate warships, the *Florida*, the *Rappahannock* and the *Georgia*, were in French ports. Rumors began that this was no accident. The American consul at Le Havre, James O. Putnam, notified Captain John Winslow of the *Kearsarge*, then anchored off Brest, that he believed it was the intention of the three ships to rendezvous for the purpose of attacking the *Kearsarge*. Permission was given by the French authorities for the *Georgia* to be repaired in the government dockyard at Cherbourg. Maury, who was in ill health, was given leave, and his executive officer, Lt. William E. Evans, who had formerly served aboard the *Sumter* under Raphael Semmes, was given command. As the repairs extended over several months, Flag Officer Barron went to inspect the vessel. He wrote to naval secretary Stephen Mallory that he felt that the *Georgia* was not fit for purpose, and proposed that she be transferred to other duties. Repaired, the *Georgia* sailed south for Bordeaux. On 14 April, Barron wrote to Bulloch. Disingenuously, in his book, Bulloch wrote: "Commodore Barron informed me by letter that he should send the Georgia to cruise off the coast of Morocco until short of fuel, then return to a European port and report to me."[8]

In reality the *Georgia*'s mission was to rendezvous with the *Rappahannock* off the coast of Morocco, and there transfer her guns. Though the *Georgia*, under Lt. Evans, made her way to the appointed place, the *Rappahannock*, for want of a crew, never left Calais. Though the mission was unsuccessful, the *Georgia*'s departure in April prompted speculation. United States navy secretary Welles wrote to Rear Admiral C.H. Bell that he had received intelligence that the *Georgia* was to rendezvous with the *Florida* in the South Atlantic and there proceed to Cape Horn in South America, to lie between the islands of Tierra del Fuego and the island of de los Estados (Staten Island), with a view to capturing California bound ships. Her return to Bordeaux was greeted by universal American relief. The *Georgia* remained at Bordeaux until the 28th of April, when Barron then formally turned the vessel over to Bulloch. He requested that the ship be sent to Liverpool. The *Georgia* reached the English port on 2 May 1864. She was taken into Birkenhead Dock, where her armaments were dismantled and landed. Her crew was paid off and discharged. Bulloch announced his intention of selling the *Georgia*. Word was received from the customs authorities in London of their concern that the sale, like that of the *Sumter*, might not be bona fide. If that was felt to be the case, then the *Georgia* would be ordered to leave the port straightaway. Consul Dudley at Liverpool instigated enquiries. He discovered in the register of shipping that the *Japan/Georgia* had been the property of Thomas Bold of Liverpool, a British subject, as late as 23 June 1863, two months after she been commissioned as a Confederate ship of war. The sale seemed highly dubious.

On 1 June 1864, just over a year later, the vessel was sold to Mr. Edwin Bates, a Liverpool merchant, who removed all war fittings. The ship was chartered by the Portuguese government. On 8 August 1864, with a British registration, and flying the British flag, she sailed from Liverpool for Lisbon. As the *Georgia* made Las Rocas, off the mouth of the Tagus, she was seized by the USS *Niagara,* under Commodore Thomas Craven, and condemned. A prize crew was put aboard, and she was taken to Boston. Bates, who had legally bought the vessel, entered a claim for damages before the Mixed Commission in Washington, but this was disallowed. The ship was later sold as a lawful prize by order of the United States government. She became the U.S. merchant vessel S.S. *Georgia* of New Bedford, Massachusetts, on 5 August 1865. She was later sold to a Canadian company, in 1870, and was wrecked on the coast of Maine in January 1875.

Commander Matthew F. Maury was also responsible for the purchase of a second vessel, the twin-funneled CSS *Rappahannock,* as previously mentioned. She began life as the Royal Navy's HMS *Victor,* a 1042 ton wooden-hulled, barque-rigged steam sloop of war. She was 200 ft. in length and 30 ft. 2 inches in breadth, with two 350 horsepower engines and a lifting screw propeller. Her original armaments had consisted of six 24-pounders. Launched in 1857 on the Thames, she had been converted to a dispatch ship; but by 1863, she and a number of other dispatch boats which had become worn out and unserviceable were put up for sale. Maury appointed Lt. William F. Carter to take charge of the purchase. He contacted Thomas Bold, the "paper" owner of the *Georgia,* who employed the British firm of Gordon Coleman & Co. to undertake the purchase. The price for the Victor, according to Benjamin Moran at the United States embassy, was just £9,000. It was a price that fitted her obsolescence. At the time, she had neither masts nor rigging onboard, but under existing practices was permitted to fit out and equip at the Royal Navy dockyard at Sheerness, under the supervision of Mr. Rumble, the government inspector of machinery. At no stage was any attempt made to put any warlike equipment aboard her. Early on the morning of 24 November 1863, Maury received word that the British authorities were about to seize the vessel. He dispatched Lt. William P.A. Campbell and a token crew to take possession of her and get her away to France, where he hoped to transfer the *Georgia*'s armament to her. With workmen still onboard, Campbell succeeded in escaping from Sheerness. On the point of clearing the Thames estuary her bearings burned out, and under incomplete sail, she was forced to put into Calais. While crossing the Channel she was commissioned as a Confederate ship of war. Under this status she was admitted into the port of Calais. Lt. C.M. Fauntleroy was then placed in command. Almost a week later, on 30 November 1863, the *Times* announced that "the screw gun-vessel 'Victor' recently purchased from the Admiralty, has as had been expected, passed into the hands of the Confederate Government."

The United States minister at Paris, William L. Dayton, made strong representations, but these were overruled in that the ship had sought the shelter of a French port, under extreme necessity, and therefore under international law could not be excluded. The government did, however, reassure the Americans that no armaments would be permitted to be brought aboard her. The American consul now got to work, with bribery and beer, to ensure desertions among the *Rappahannock*'s crew. The Consul secured depositions from three of them, William Wynn, Joseph Murray and Thomas Kelley, that they had been enlisted by William Rumble, chief inspector of machinery afloat, and a man named Wise, who was captain of the yard, in contravention of the Foreign Enlistment Act. The case did come to trial, on 7 February 1865, but the defendants were found not guilty. During the trial, charges of corrupting witnesses were brought against the American consul in London. Evidence was given to prove that all three witnesses were given money and a daily beer allowance to keep them compliant.

At Calais, Lt. Fauntleroy undertook a complete inspection of his new charge, and finding the boilers to be very unreliable, wrote off to Maury that he believed her to be, in her present condition, unseaworthy. Maury's response was to transfer her to the control of Flag Admiral Barron in Paris. The Americans continued to exert pressure on the French authorities. Discovering the plan to transfer the *Georgia's* guns, they intended, they said, to hold France responsible for any American ships sunk by the *Rappahannock* after she left Calais. Fauntleroy also had problems. The American consul had been so successful in bribing men to desert, and he now had only twelve deckhands.

From Liverpool, Bulloch advised Barron to sell the ship, and in this he had Fauntleroy's full support. Barron was reluctant, believing that he still could do something with her. Though Bulloch did not openly admit it, it would appear that he wrote a detailed report to Richmond. By a copy letter written to him on 16 December 1864, from the secretary of the navy, he learned that Barron had been recalled to Richmond. The letter read in part as follows: "Orders by this steamer go to Commodore Barron to return to the Confederate States and to direct all officers whom you may designate to report to you for ordered, and to send the others home. He is further instructed to turn over to you the control and direction of the Rappahannock.... Conference with Commodore Barron will enable you to judge correctly of the situation of the Rappahannock, and to reach a definite conclusion as to the course which the interest of the country requires in her case."[9]

In effect Bulloch had now been given complete control. On 31 March 1865, in a general dispatch, Bulloch wrote to naval secretary Mallory that on the 28th of that month Commodore Barron had resigned his command as senior naval officer on the Continent. Bulloch, now in charge, dispatched a reliable officer, Lt. William H. Murdaugh, to inspect the vessel in Calais harbor. Having received his findings, Bulloch instructed Fauntleroy to pay off and discharge the crew, detach the officers and send them to Liverpool for further orders, and strip and lay up the *Rappahannock,* leaving her in charge of a master's mate until her future could be decided. Eventually the ship changed hands under a nominal sale and was brought back to England, but by then the war was over. The ship, by now next to useless, was eventually claimed by the United States as their property.

The episode had been a complete farce from start to finish. Maury had no practical experience regarding the construction and outfitting of warships. The *Georgia* was not a commissioned warship, but an ordinary ship of commerce, later adapted. She was an iron vessel, it is true, but very lightly built. She had no magazine, and her cabins and interior features were not constructed of any unusual strength. When examined, the collector at Greenock, from his own observations testified that she was not heavily sparred, and in fact could not spread more canvas than an ordinary merchant ship. In essence she was a commercial ship, inadequately fitted out for warlike purposes. The *Rappahannock* was a former warship, but with design faults. She had been downgraded to a dispatch ship, and was now worn out and unserviceable. Her sale price of only £9,000 should have warned off her Confederate buyers.

In comparison, Bulloch was actively involved in the design process of both successful warships that he sent to sea. To see Maury waste money must have infuriated him. Both Maury and Barron in France were superior officers, but both were totally unfitted for the war that needed to be fought. What followed, regarding the *Alexandra* and the *Pampero* (the residue of Maury's inexperience) must have equally galled Bulloch.

8

The *Alexandra* and the *Pampero*

The *Alexandra* and the *Pampero* were two ships built for the Confederacy, one in England and one in Scotland. Both vessels were subject to greater government scrutiny under the Foreign Enlistment Act, partially due to the dogged determination of the American authorities, who were not above using perjury and exaggeration, but also due to the British government itself, which had become angered at the manipulation of the act by the Confederacy's agents. Both ships were eventually condemned, but only after one of them had succeeded in sailing to Nassau.

The *Alexandra* was commissioned by Charles K. Prioleau of Fraser, Trenholm & Co., of Liverpool, as a gift to the Confederate government. It was built through the firm of Fawcett, Preston & Co., at the yard of William C. Miller & Sons. The hull of this wooden screw steamer was launched on 7 March 1863, and she was named after the Danish princess Alexandra, soon to become the bride of the Prince of Wales (later Edward VII). From Miller's yard the vessel was taken up to that of Fawcett, Preston & Co. to have her engines fitted and to complete her outfit. As builders of the *Oreto* (*Florida*), both Miller's and Fawcett, Preston's yards were closely watched by Federal agents. On 28 March, U.S. consul Thomas Dudley made a formal affirmation (he being a Quaker) that he believed the *Alexandra* was intended for the Confederate States. With affidavits from other witnesses to back up his claim, he submitted the file to the United States minister in London. Mr. Adams in his turn submitted the evidence to Lord Russell. Extensive enquiries were made, including to the customs authorities in London and Liverpool, the Treasury, Home Office, Chief Constable of Liverpool, and the mayor of that city. Legal opinion was that there was a case to answer. On 5 April 1863, the surveyor of customs at Liverpool seized the vessel and all work upon her was suspended.

The trial was begun two months later, on 22 June. Ninety-eight charges were brought against Fawcett, Preston & Co. The gist of the charges was that they had built and equipped a ship of war for a foreign power (the Confederacy) whose purpose was to wage war on a friendly power (the United States). The trial took place before the Lord Chief Baron of the Exchequer, Sir Frederick Pollock. By and large the testimonies of the American witnesses, including John Da Costa (shown to be a liar), George Temple Chapman (who acted as an agent provocateur) and the Confederate traitor and thief Clarence Yonge, were completely discredited. Summing up, the judge directed the jury that they should consider whether the *Alexandra* was merely in the course of being built for delivery in pursuance of a contract, which was perfectly lawful, or whether it was the intention of her builders to equip, i.e., to furnish her with arms, as a vessel of war in Liverpool, or any other British port. The jury found in favor of the defendants. The Queen's Counsel, representing the government, then tendered a bill of exceptions, which forestalled the jury's verdict, so that all the points raised could be examined in the court of appeal. The four judges there could not agree, and split fifty-fifty. The case was forwarded to the higher Court of Exchequer Chamber, where the case was dismissed on a technicality. Final adjudication went to the House of Lords, the highest court in the land. They found in favor of the defendants. Perhaps surprisingly the United States accepted the decision, because it could see that the British government had tried its best under existing legislation to secure a conviction. Adams wrote to Lord Russell: "It is a source of great satisfaction to me to recognize the readiness which her Majesty's Government has thus manifested to make the investigations desired, as well as to receive the assurances of its determination to maintain a close observation of future movements of an unusual character that justifies suspicions of an evil intent."[1]

Even the U.S. secretary of state, Mr. Seward, expressed his satisfaction that the British government had done its utmost. He wrote to Adams: "You are authorised and expected to assure Lord Russell that this Government is entirely satisfied that Her Majesty's Government have conducted the proceedings in the case with perfect good faith and honour, and they are well disposed to prevent the fitting out of armed vessels in British ports to depredate upon American commerce, and to make war upon the United States. This Government is satisfied that the law officers of the Crown have performed their duties in regard to the case of the Alexandra with a sincere conviction of the adequacy of the law of Great Britain, and a sincere desire to give it effect."[2]

Fawcett, Preston & Co. made a claim for damages against the Crown. They were awarded £3,700. Work continued upon the *Alexandra,* but it was not until April 1864, long after she had been completed, that she was finally released by the government. In June 1864, she was "sold" to Henry Lafone, a Confederate secret agent based in Liverpool, and her name was changed to *Mary.* Her structure on deck and below was converted to make her more suitable as a commercial vessel. She sailed from Liverpool in July 1864, en route for Halifax, Nova Scotia, via Bermuda. The U.S. consul in Liverpool, Thomas Dudley, was convinced that she would be converted back to a warship and armed in Bermuda or Nassau.

Seward, while being happy to see that Britain had fulfilled its duty to the United States, was nonetheless not prepared to let the matter rest there. The American consul at Halifax, M.M. Jackson, telegraphed Seward that the steamer *Mary,* formerly *Alexandra,* had arrived at Liverpool, Nova Scotia, in ballast from Bermuda, with a crew of twenty-four. It was believed, he informed Seward, that she had four guns. The secretary of state wrote to the British embassy in Washington, a letter which was forwarded to the lieutenant governor of Nova Scotia, demanding that the *Mary* be seized. The governor's response was that the ship was British owned and flagged, and was in a British port. He could not interfere on mere suspicion. However he would make enquiries. The *Mary* quietly departed in December for Bermuda, and from there to Nassau. The U.S. consul there reported her arrival to Seward, noting that she was particularly slow, it having taken her eight days. On 13 December 1864, she was seized by order of the governor, and proceedings were instigated against her. On 22 May 1865 the court decided that there was insufficient evidence and she was accordingly released. The war by that date was over.

The *Pampero*, alternatively known as the *Canton,* the *Texas,* and "Sinclair's ship," was built at James & George Thomson's Clyde Bank Iron Shipyard, Glasgow. During her construction she was known as the *Canton,* and word was put about that she was destined for China. She was a screw steamer of 1,000 tons, 230 feet in length, and 32 feet in breadth. Her dimensions were similar to those of the *Alabama.* She possessed a lifting propeller for reducing drag when under sail, as had the *Alabama,* as well as a telescopic funnel. She was barque rigged with iron fore and after masts. Her construction was overseen by Lieutenant George T. Sinclair of the Confederate States Navy; when she was completed, was to take command of her himself.

Under Bulloch's auspices, Sinclair had been responsible for earlier overseeing the construction of the screw steamer *Georgiana* in the spring of 1862. She was brig-rigged, with a clipper bow, a jib and two masts. She had a 120 horsepower engine and iron propeller. Her hull and funnel were painted black. She was pierced to take 14 guns. Graceful in design, she was a swift ship, 205 ft. 6ins. in length, 25ft. 2ins. wide, with a displacency of 14ft. 9 ins. She was built in the Lawrie Shipyard at Glasgow, under subcontract from Lairds of Birkenhead. The vessel was registered as of Glasgow in December 1862, and allegedly employed by N. Matheson's Clyde Service. Fitted out, she ran down the Scottish coast and into Liverpool, and she sailed from there on 21 January 1863, under the command of "a British naval retired officer," with a crew of 140 men. She took on her armaments off Tenerife, in the Canary Islands, but did not fit them. Then, under Captain A.B. Davidson, she attempted to run the blockade through Maffitt's Channel, into Charleston, with an additional cargo of rifles. As she made the attempt, on 19 March 1863, she was spotted by the yacht *America,* whose captain signaled to the nearby warship USS *Wissahickon*. The warship opened fire upon the *Georgiana* with devastating effect, and soon the Confederate captain signaled his surrender. The *Wissahickon* ceased fire, but the *Georgiana* continued on and succeeded in beaching herself. In order to prevent the rebels from salvaging her, Lieutenant Commander J.L. Davis, commanding the *Wissahickon,* resumed his fire upon the enemy ship until she burst into flames. The *Georgiana* burned for several days, accompanied by large explosions every so often when a powder barrel ignited.

Now back in Scotland, Sinclair watched the completion of this replacement ship. The vessel was launched on 3 November 1863, and christened the *Pampero*. So fine a ship, she proved to be the victim of her own success. Word of her construction was featured in the local newspapers, and though it was not stated, it was hinted that she was destined for the Confederate service. The *Illustrated London News* for 2 January 1864 even featured an illustration of her, giving accurate dimensions of her construction. This set alarm bells ringing with the American consul in Glasgow, William L. Underwood, and with the ever watchful Mr. Dudley, consul at Liverpool, and even at the American legation in London. In an attempt to show that she was destined for the merchant marine, advertisements were placed by Sinclair in the local newspapers advertising her availability to take on cargoes.

As early as October 1863, Commissioner Adams wrote to Lord Russell over his concerns:

> My Lord,
>
> It is with great regret that I find it my duty once more to call your lordship's attention to the efforts making in this kingdom to aid the insurgents in America in carrying on their resistance to the Government of the United States. I have strong reason for believing that, in addition to a very formidable steam-ram now in the process of construction at the port of Glasgow, but not yet so far advanced as fully to develop her character, there is another steamer ready to be launched,

called the Canton, having all the characteristics of a war vessel, which is about to be fitted up and dispatched with the same intent from the same place. I beg leave to submit to your lordship's consideration some extracts from a letter addressed to me by W.L. Underwood Esq., the consul of the United States, giving some information in regard to this case. Mr. Underwood himself entertains no doubt of the destination of this vessel, although from the secrecy used in the process of construction and preparation, itself a cause of suspicion, he has been slow in gaining evidence on which to base a representation.

Not doubting that Her Majesty's government will take all suitable measures to ascertain the correctness of these allegations, I pray, &c.,

Charles Francis Adams.[3]

The extracts enclosed with the above note contained a description of the *Canton*. Russell instructed the appropriate authorities to pursue full enquiries. It appeared that, though she was being fitted out as a passenger ship, she displayed all the peculiarities in her construction of being a ship that could be easily converted to a warship. Renamed the *Pampero*, following her launch, the consul at Glasgow then made a formal application that she might be seized, supporting his application with depositions on oath. They were hearsay rather than proof, though. No hard evidence of her being constructed for the Confederacy was submitted at the time. Backtracking from the various owners living in various parts of the United Kingdom, the paper trails all led to a Mr. Sinclair. He was shown to be a citizen of the Confederate States. Commander Sinclair, not wishing to lose the vessel, contacted the law officers for Scotland of his intention to cancel the contract. It must be assumed that he had some intention of recovering her at some later stage through a bogus sale. The government, using the collector of customs at Glasgow, seized the vessel (intended to have been renamed the CSS *Texas,* if she could have been got away), on the 10th of December 1863, and retained possession of her until October 1865, when she was given up to her owners. With the war ended, so also was the reason for detaining her.

9

Laird's Rams and French Rams

Back in November 1861, having successfully run the blockade aboard the *Fingal*, Bulloch was summoned to Richmond to meet once more with the navy secretary, Stephen Mallory. Among the matters discussed, Mallory expressed an interest in acquiring ironclad vessels to counter the enemy's "Monitors," and to open up the blockaded ports. To this end he had already dispatched Lieutenant James H. North to England to explore the possibilities of acquiring such vessels. On the point of departure for England, Bulloch received a letter from the secretary of the navy:

> Navy Department,
> Richmond, January 14th 1862.
>
> SIR,
> I desire more particularly to direct your attention to the subject of constructing iron or steel clad ships in France or England than was done in my letter of the 11th inst. Lieutenant North has had this matter in charge, but has not yet been able to do anything with it. I earnestly desire to have an armored steam-sloop of moderate size, say of about 2,000 tons, and to carry eight or ten heavy guns, built in England upon the most approved plan and in the shortest time, and the evident change of feeling and opinion in England in relation to our country induces me to believe that we may now contract for the construction and delivery of such a vessel.... Many plans of such a vessel have been submitted, and herewith I send you the drawings, without specifications of the one devised by Naval-Constructor Porter and Chief-Engineer Williamson.... I submit this plan for your information only; but so anxious am I to have an ironclad ship built, that should you and Lieutenant North, with whom I associate you in this matter, be able to contract, or to make the preparatory arrangements to contract, for an armored, either steel or iron clad, ship, you will proceed with dispatch to prescribe the character of the vessel, and I will place the funds in England at once....
>
> I am, etc.,
> S.R. MALLORY.
> Secretary of the Navy[1]

Arriving in Liverpool in March 1862, Bulloch began exploratory talks with a number of Liverpool shipyards. Lt. North meanwhile, in May of that year, successfully negotiated the construction of an ironclad with the Scottish firm of G. & J. Thompson, up on the Clyde. She was the most up-to-date ironclad in the world at that time. As such she attracted considerable attention, including that of the American consul. He notified Adams in London, who contacted Lord Russell. It was impossible to disguise the fact that she was a ship of war. There was no ambiguity, and Russell, after a short enquiry, ordered the ship to be seized. North conferred with Commissioner Mason in London over what they should do. Mason's solution was to sell the vessel to the Danish government, then at war with Prussia, in the hope of regaining her at some later date. The sale went ahead, and the ship was delivered by the builders to the Danish government.

Bulloch's search for a discreet shipbuilder inevitably brought him back to Lairds of Birkenhead. Due to their position as one of the most prominent shipbuilders in the country, they were able to obtain official reports of all the latest experiments in shipbuilding. Taking Bulloch's specifications into account, along with the information they had gathered, they prepared drawings for his approval and had a model prepared. The ship they proposed was a dual-purpose ironclad, fitted with 5½ inch armor plating, capable of attack at sea or inshore defense. As such the vessel would be seaworthy, but with a shallow draft. For armaments, in line with North's ship, they proposed two central revolving gun turrets, capable of taking four 9 inch guns, rather than broadside batteries, removing the strain from the sides of the ship, and placing it centrally. Dimensions were for a vessel 230 feet in length, 42 feet in width and with a draft (with crew and stores for three months) of no more than 15 feet. The weight would be 1,850 tons, and the ship was to be fitted with 350 horsepower engines, giving a nominal speed of 10½ knots. This was not particularly fast, but speed was not necessarily her main objective.

In June Bulloch received a letter from naval secretary Mallory to the effect that he was to negotiate for the construction of two such ironclads, and to this effect one million dollars had already been placed with Messrs. Fraser, Trenholm, with a second million dollars to be dispatched soon after. The principals acting promptly, a contract was agreed upon, and with an order for two ships, Lairds agreed on a reduction in price of £1,250 on each ship. Completion of the first ship was promised for March 1863, and the second for May. The cost of each, fully operational but minus magazines and battery, was £93, 750. When complete they would be superior to anything in the United States Navy. But, like North's ironclad, there could be no mistaking their status. They were warships. Bulloch knew that it was only a matter of time before Consul Dudley received word from one of his many spies that Lairds were building ironclads. Bulloch accordingly set up a web of deception. He arranged with the Parisian mercantile house of Bravay & Co. that they should become the purchasers of the vessels, on behalf of the Viceroy of Egypt. To enhance the story, the ships were given the names *El Tousson* and *El Mounassir*. Upon completion the vessels would be got away, and at a suitable location handed over to the Confederacy.

By the middle of July 1862 work on the two ships, allocated the yard numbers 294 and 295, was well underway. At Shoeburyness in Essex, the turret guns for the ironclads were being tested. In a letter to Mallory, 11 August 1862, Bulloch revealed the following: "I have resolved to construct the turrets to revolve, and run the risk of being interfered with, and there will be two guns of the heaviest caliber practicable for actual service in each turret, mounted parallel to each other, and four and a half feet from center to center. The ports will be oval, large enough vertically to give twelve degrees of elevation and five degrees of depression, with just width enough to clear the chase of the guns, so that an object can be seen over the side sights."[2]

In his letter Bulloch asked Mallory not to send any officers or crew as yet. He would make the necessary arrangements nearer the time. The last thing he wanted was speculation, which obviously would have arisen, if Liverpool was suddenly overrun by known Confederate naval officers. He proposed that at the right time officers and bona-fide Southern sailors should be sent to the island of Madeira to wait. Any communications

9. Laird's Rams and French Rams

BRITISH PLUCK.

This cartoon is from Comic News an English magazine which is not well known and was of short duration. It refers to the building of ships for the Confederacy by the Laird Brothers in Liverpool.

Lincoln, licensed drover, stands before the small Russell. Both are in front of Laird's Yard. Lincoln has a threatening attitude.

Lincoln: "Now, drover boy Jack, if you let out them rams, I won't answer for the consequences."

Russell: (very humbly) "No, sir — please sir — I'll do whatever you tells me, sir — in course, Sir — yes, Sir — please, Sir."

The American government warns Great Britain against releasing the Liverpool-built ironclad rams, then the most technically advanced warships in the world, to the Confederate navy. (*Comic News*) should be through Captain William Arkwright of the British ship *Carnatic,* operating between the island and Liverpool. The officers, Bulloch suggested, might perhaps be transhipped to the island from the Confederacy, by the *Julia Usher,* a Fraser, Trenholm & Co. blockade runner, or possibly the *Giraffe,* which likewise had a good reputation. On the 7th of September 1862, Bulloch wrote that there had been delays due to bad weather, but this had been overcome by erecting sheds over the vessels, which were now illuminated by gas to enable the workers to continue their work. Six months later Bulloch received bad news. His security had been breached. He wrote to Mallory:

> Our transactions have become well known — Southern papers received lately publish them, and a letter in the "Times" from the South clearly indicates that armored ships are expected from this side to break the blockade. I have been aware that indiscreet persons who should have known better have written to private persons at the South on such matters.... Parliament meets February 5th, and I am reliably informed that the question of furnishing supplies to the belligerents will come up. I am consulting the best legal authority, but confess that the hope of getting the ships out seems more doubtful — indeed hopeless, unless there should be a change in the political character of the Ministry. I will of course go on as if no obstacle existed, so as to be ready to avail myself of chance circumstances.[3]

If he had but known it the ministry had already ordered the collector of customs to examine, and report back at frequent intervals, upon the construction of all vessels, and in particular ironclad vessels. This included Liverpool and the Lairds' yard. Delays mounted; in fact Bulloch himself commented that no armored ship for the admiralty had ever been delivered on time due to the new techniques required in their construction. This was at a time when completion as soon as possible was an overriding factor. Aware of the problems faced by Bulloch, Mallory suggested that the ships be got out as soon as possible and taken to France for fitting. Interestingly, he wrote, "I do not suppose that the French Government would give any formal assent to this proposition, but I do suppose that not only no obstacle would be offered, but that facilities would be extended.... I am not at liberty to state the reasons of this opinion, but they are sufficiently strong to induce me to press the subject upon your attention."[4]

Tentative negotiations, still at a low level, had begun between France and the Confederacy, for French intervention in the war. The price was to be Texas. Commissioner Slidell in Paris confirmed to Mallory in Richmond that the French, having fitted out the ironclads, would load them with supplies, allegedly for the French army in Mexico, but deliver them to the Confederates at Terceira, or wherever they wished. Bulloch was now extremely anxious. Any serious enquiry that the two ironclads were for the Egyptian government would quickly be disproved; but then a genuine offer for their purchase was made by the Russian government through Messrs. Laird. As friendly arrangements existed between Russia and the United States, Bulloch began to suspect a ruse. Perhaps the ships were to be purchased by them on behalf of the American Government.[5] As Bulloch, or rather Messrs. Bravay, was the owner, the offer was refused.

In June 1863 the first of the ironclad rams was launched. Consul Dudley in Liverpool reported to the American commissioner in London, Charles Francis Adams, that he had four affidavits to the effect that the rams were really the property of the Confederates. On 11 June, Adams wrote to Lord Russell, presenting his evidence. Russell acknowledged receipt. Unaware that Russell was making enquiries, Adams wrote again, presenting further evidence — still no reply. Adams wrote on 16 and 24 July, and on 14 August. Two weeks later, on the 29th of August, the second ram was launched. Matters, as far as Adams was concerned, had become intolerable. If his evidence from Dudley was correct, and he had no reason to doubt it, the Confederates would soon be in possession of two of the most formidable warships in the world. Having checked with Lairds, Russell responded on 1 September, and reiterated the fiction that Bulloch had prepared: the ships had been purchased for Egypt by a company in France. Adams now gave Russell an ultimatum (which apparently had no official backing) that unless he acted, Britain's actions, or lack of them, would result in war. The gist of Adams' letter Secretary Moran noted in his journal: "Mr. Adams has adopted a tone in his note suited to the gravity of the occasion, for if these ships go nothing will prevent a war between the two countries. It will be folly for us to permit war to be made thus upon [us] from ports of this Kingdom, and not resent it. We had better be in open hostilities at once, for then we will know what to expect, and who are our friends and foes, as well as end this bastard neutrality."[6]

Russell was not used to being threatened by underlings. On 5 September, unbeknownst to Adams, he wrote to the British ambassador in Washington: "We have given orders today to the Commissioner of Customs at Liverpool to prevent the two ironclads leaving the Mersey.... Mr. Adams is not yet aware that orders have been given to stop the vessels. You may inform Mr. Seward confidentially of the fact."[7]

From a British point of view, war with America was the last thing she wanted. She now controlled the greatest maritime fleet in history, thanks to the American Civil War. The two rams were seized, a guard was placed aboard them, and a naval squadron was sent to watch over them. On behalf of the British government, Captain Hore R.N. approached M. Bravay at his home in Paris. The two ironclads had been seized, and were unlikely to be released until full enquiries were made. This could, and would, take time. Hore then made Bravay an offer. The British government was prepared to purchase the vessels. Bravay at first refused, but on 20 May 1864, with no prospect of getting his ships out of Birkenhead, he eventually agreed. Bravay was paid about £30,000 in excess of their original contract price as compensation. The vessels were purchased by the Royal Navy, and added to the fleet as HMS *Scorpion* and HMS *Wivern*. Poor Mr. Adams was instructed by secretary of state Seward to thank Lord Russell for all that he had done. His letter to Russell concluded: "I am therefore instructed to inform your lordship that the [American] Government will hereafter hold itself obliged, with even more care than heretofore, to endeavor so to conduct its intercourse with Great Britain as that the war in which it is now unhappily involved may, whenever it may terminate, leave to neither nation any permanent cause of discontent."[8]

With Britain's more rigid approach to its laws regarding neutrality and the Foreign Enlistment Act, Bulloch was instructed to contact John Slidell, Confederate minister in Paris. Slidell indicated that he believed that the French emperor, Napoleon III, would not place any serious obstacles in the way of Confederate operations in France, as long as they were discreet. Through Slidell a contract with the prominent shipbuilder M.L. Arman, of Bordeaux, was arranged in early 1863 for the construction of four corvettes, and later, in July of that year, for the building of two powerful ironclad rams, each fitted with a 300-pounder Armstrong rifle, and two 70-pounders in the turrets. The clipper corvettes were to be of 1,500 tons with 400-horsepower engines, and equipped with twelve 6-inch rifled guns— the canon raye de trente — as used by the French navy. Two of the corvettes, known in the yard as *Yeddo* and *Osacca*, were later subcontracted to the firm of M.J. Voruz in Nantes. Designs and specifications were agreed to on 15 April, and by the middle of June work was underway.

M. Arman advised Bulloch that he had been "confidentially informed by the Minister of State [M. Rouher] that the Emperor was willing for him to undertake the construction of ships for the Confederate Government, and that when the vessels were ready to be delivered, he would be permitted to send them to sea under the French flag to any point which might be agreed upon between him and the representative of the Confederate States."[9]

Arman further reassured Bulloch that should American spies enquire, details of the construction of the corvettes had already been lodged with the appropriate government ministry. Their eventual destination had been given as China and Japan. They were armed as a matter of precaution against Far Eastern pirates.

In June Bulloch received a letter from Mallory of such importance that it was entrusted to a personal courier, Lt. G.S. Shryock. It revealed that, following a secret act of Congress, £2million had been allocated for the construction of ironclads. Bulloch himself was selected as the man to accomplish this charge. In his letter Mallory acknowledged Bulloch's incomparable knowledge and experience. He wrote: "The President has selected you as the agent of the Government to accomplish the important object thus provided for by the Government [because] ... of your thorough knowledge of the subject and your means of observation, it is deemed expedient to leave to your judgment, untrammeled by instructions, the size and details of the vessels, subject to the consideration that in draft of water, speed and power, they must be able to enter and navigate the Mississippi river; that their first trial must be a long ocean voyage."[10]

Bulloch could not have wished for more. On 16 July 1863 he completed the contract with Arman for the construction of the two ironclads. In a later letter Mallory reassured him that he had subsequently received additional assurances that iron-plated ships of war could be constructed in France by French builders and delivered, ready for service, anywhere upon the high seas.

In September 1863, the American consul-general in Paris, John Bigelow, began receiving information regarding the building of these vessels. The material was apparently supplied by the confidential clerk of the Nantes shipbuilder M. Voruz. Seemingly irrefutable evidence, with dates and signatures, linking government ministers to the construction of ships for the Confederacy, it was presented to the French government by the Americans. It was a clear breach of neutrality. In a face-saving gesture, blaming rogue elements within the administration, the French government was forced to act. Construction on the various ships was allowed to continue, but it was ordered that the vessels were to be legitimately sold to approved foreign governments. Of the four corvettes, two were bought by Prussia, and two by Peru. Prussia also bought one of the rams; the other, known as the *Sphinx,* went to Denmark, which Prussia was then at war with. Before her delivery, the war had ended, and Denmark, no longer having need of such a costly vessel, sold her, without inquiring too closely as to her purchaser, which proved to be James Dunwoody Bulloch. This was the official version. In fact, on 18 February 1864, Bulloch wrote to Secretary Mallory: "[T]he Emperor, through his Ministers of Foreign Affairs and of Marine, has formally notified the builders that the ironclads cannot be permitted to sail, and that the corvettes must not be armed in France, but must be nominally sold to some foreign merchant and dispatched as ordinary trading vessels.... M. Arman ... has proposed that a nominal sale of the vessels should be made to a Danish banker, and that there should be a private agreement providing for a re-delivery to us at some point beyond the jurisdiction of France."[11]

The "Danish" ironclad was retrieved at Copenhagen by the banker, one Mr. Rudolph Puggard, acting on behalf of Arman. The vessel was then offered to the Confederacy at a price of 375,000 francs for Arman, and a further 80,000 for Mr. Puggard. Using the alias "Mr. Brown," Captain Thomas Jefferson Page of the Confederate States Navy, accompanied by Lt. R.R. Carter, formerly seconded to Bulloch, was sent to take possession of her. Bulloch then contacted Lt. George S. Shryock aboard the CSS *Rappahannock,* then moored in Brest harbor, ordering him and the former crew of the *Florida* to proceed to Greenhithe, near the mouth of the Thames, there to join the blockade runner *City of Richmond,* which was to act as a tender for the ram, now for the first time given the name *Stonewall.*

With a temporary crew, the *Stonewall* sailed from Denmark on 17 January. She ran into a fierce snowstorm, and was obliged to take shelter at Elsinore until it abated. It was noted that alterations to the ship when she had briefly been in the hands of the Danish navy were now affecting her performance. She was also leaking slightly at the rudder heads, where the bolts were yielding under the pressure of the water. News reached Bulloch of the delay. He dared not leave the *City of Richmond* at Greenhithe any longer, for fear of attracting the attentions of the British customs. He ordered her captain, Lt. Hunter Davidson, an officer in the Confederate navy, to sail to Cherbourg without delay. From there Davidson sailed for the rendezvous point at Belle Isle, Quiberon Bay. He arrived on the 20th, and there waited for four anxious days until the 24th, when the *Stonewall* steamed into the bay. She was in a terrible state, and it took four days to clean her up before any supplies could be put aboard, Davidson revealed in a letter to Bulloch. Coal from Nantes never arrived, and alternate plans had to be made. Davidson was ordered to sail to San Miguel in Spain to order supplies. The *Stonewall* put in a course for Madeira, but out of sight of the land she changed course for San Miguel. On 29 January a storm blew up in the Bay of Biscay, and the *Stonewall,* now leaking badly, was forced to run into the Spanish port of Ferrol. Captain Page related the following:

> The usual visits of ceremony were made, and on calling on the Captain General, who was an "old salt" holding the rank of Admiral, the character of the Stonewall was stated, and the object of her visit to have certain repairs made and to procure a supply of coals. Permission was politely granted, and authority to employ such hands from the dockyard as might be required.... Ship carpenters were immediately at work repairing damages, and at the same time a supply of coals was being taken on board.... There were here, as in every other port of Europe, curious gentlemen, whose avocation was to find out other people's business. The wires soon flashed the news of this arrival, under a novel flag, to the American Minister at Madrid, who forthwith protested to that Government that the admission of such a vessel — a pirate, an enemy to all mankind, a reckless rover of the sea — was an infringement of international law.[12]

The American minister informed the Spanish government that the *Stonewall* had been illegally sold, and that the French government had sent warships after her. All facilities extended to the Confederate ship were now suspended until enquiries could be made of the French government. It was all a lie on the part of the American minister, to stall until American warships could arrive. Page was summoned to put his case. He pointed to international law. Ships of war in the service of a belligerent, entering the ports or waters of a neutral, are, by the practice of nations, exempt from the jurisdiction of a neutral power. A vessel becomes a public ship of war by being armed and commissioned. Customarily a ship is held to be commissioned when a commissioned officer appointed to her has gone onboard of her and hoisted the colors appropriated to the military marines.

All these functions Page had observed, and the Madrid government found in his favor. Work was resumed on repairs to the *Stonewall.*

Then the long awaited warships arrived. The USS *Niagara* put into Ferrol harbor. She hovered about the *Stonewall* for two days before departing to join the USS *Sacramento,* anchored at the nearby port of Corunna, barely two miles away and situated in the same crescent of the coast. From there the Americans could clearly see their adversary. In law, because they were not in the same port, they would not have to delay their departure by twenty-four hours after the *Stonewall* departed. On the 24th of March, all repairs completed, and "stripped to lower masts and standing rigging, in order that neither spars nor running rigging, if shot away, should entangle her propellers,"[13] the *Stonewall* left Ferrol harbor, escorted by a Spanish frigate, to beyond the marine league. Here she waited to engage the two American warships. As Page wrote for the *Southern Historical Society Paper,* fourteen years later, the "Stonewall had been built to fight, not to run." Telescopes were trained on the American ships lying in Corunna, with steam up, smoke issuing from their stacks. Curiosity had led thousands of people from both Ferrol and Corunna to line the mountain slopes to watch the forthcoming battle. The hours passed as the *Stonewall* waited, her steam up, her screws slowly revolving—but the American ships did not come. Commander Thomas T. Craven, in command of the two American ships, declined to give battle in the belief that the odds were too great—this despite the fact that the *Niagara* carried twelve 11-inch guns, and the *Sacramento* two 11-inch guns. He was later brought to trial by court-martial on the charge of "Failing to do his utmost to overtake and capture or destroy a vessel, which it was his duty to encounter." His defense was that it would have been imprudent for him to risk his wooden vessels against an ironclad ram. Found guilty as charged, Craven was suspended from duty for two years. He was eventually restored to duty, but by then the war was long over.

That night the *Stonewall* set in a course for Lisbon and steamed away. The two American ships, at a safe distance, limped after her, hoping to fall in with other American warships along the way, and thus even up the odds even more. Upon the *Stonewall*'s arrival, the authorities at Lisbon, while agreeing to her re-coaling, gave every indication that they wished her to leave as soon as possible. They had received information that the two Federal ships had sailed from Corunna in pursuit. As dusk began to fall, the *Niagara* and the *Sacramento* appeared off the entrance to the harbor. Then, to everyone's surprise, they entered the port and anchored. By doing this they had subjected themselves to the international rule prohibiting them from leaving port until twenty-four hours had elapsed following the departure of the *Stonewall.* At dawn the next day, her coaling complete, the rebel ship eased her way down the river to the open sea. As she passed the *Niagara,* Page saw upon her quarterdeck his former friend, Thomas Craven, with whom he had cruised the West Indies aboard the USS *Erie,* when they were both young men. There was no saluting, no acknowledgment, just a steady gaze, until the *Stonewall* steamed by.

As the *Stonewall* left the Tagus, bound for Tenerife, Commander Craven ordered a covert pursuit. Anchors were raised, and both ships prepared to embark. Realizing what was happening, in direct violation of the twenty-four hour delay proscribed by international law, the port garrison fired a warning shot. Both ships heaved-to and dropped anchor once more. Later the United States was to claim that the *Niagara* had merely been "shifting her berth in the harbor." This was clearly a lie, but amidst bullying threats, a weak Portuguese government later apologized for the incident and made reparations.

The *Stonewall* re-coaled at Santa Cruz, Tenerife. Then, under sail in order to econ-

9. Laird's Rams and French Rams 173

The French-built ironclad steam ram CSS *Stonewall*, leaving Lisbon Harbor. (*Illustrated London News,* 15 April 1865)

omize on coal, she continued on, her fires banked up, just in case she might fall in with any Federal warships sent out to look for her. Out into the Atlantic she came across a clipper built barque in full sail. Page ordered the French tricolor to be raised from the masthead to see what response she might make. The other ship responded with the Stars and Stripes. Ordering the Confederate flag now to be raised, a shot across her bows forced the other ship to heave-to. She was out of Baltimore, bound for Rio, with a cargo of flour. Her captain was brought aboard the *Stonewall*, and without equivocation admitted that she was an American ship with a contraband cargo. Page was all for burning her until he discovered that the captain had his wife and daughter aboard. There was no accommodation aboard the *Stonewall* for passengers, let alone ladies. Page bonded the ship, and let her continue on. In gratitude her captain offered Page and his crew whatever stores they might require, but Page declined the offer. The *Stonewall* sailed on until she reached Nassau, on 6 May 1865. Here she anchored off the island to receive more coal. There was a rumor that the war was over. Not wishing to believe it, Page raised anchor and sailed for his destination, Havana, in Cuba. The vessel was admitted into the port, and here Page received confirmation — the war was over; the Confederacy was defeated. As the news had not been officially confirmed through government channels, Page and his crew were treated with the utmost courtesy, as if they were still the accredited sailors of a belligerent state. Shortly after her arrival the USS *Connecticut,* under Captain Boggs, entered the port. Boggs, another old friend of Page, offered him and his crew terms of surrender. Page refused. The Confederate captain then approached the captain-general of Cuba and surrendered his charge. By a decision made by the queen of Spain, Page was advanced $16,000 in order to pay his officers and crew the wages that were due to them.

The *Stonewall* was later handed over to the United States Navy. In 1868, she was sold to the Japanese navy for $40,000 and given the name *Kotetsu* (Ironclad). As civil war was raging in Japan, and America had taken a neutral stance, delivery was postponed until February 1869. Her first action, along with Japan's seven other steam warships, was to sail to the northern island of Hokkaido, to fight the remnants of the Shogun's forces who were trying to form an independent republic with the help of French military advisors. In March 1869, at the Battle of Miyako, she successfully repulsed an attack from the rebel warship *Kaiten*. The *Kotetsu* participated in the successful invasion of Hokkaido, bringing the war to a close. In 1871 the *Kotetsu* was renamed *Azuma* (East).

10

The *Tallahassee* and the *Chickamauga*

On page 320 of the 2 April 1864 edition of the *Illustrated London News,* there is a very powerful image of the *Alabama* destroying the *Texan Star,* or *Martaban,* in the Malacca Straits. Interestingly, just above it is an engraving of a race in the English Channel between the *Atalanta,* a twin-screw steamer, and the Dover mail-packet *Empress.* The *Atalanta* easily outstripped the *Empress,* we are told, and crossed the Channel in seventy-seven minutes, leaving her rival far behind. Within a matter of months the *Atalanta* had been purchased by the Confederate States Navy for use as a commerce raider. The *Atalanta* was designed by Captain T.E. Symonds, R.N., as a twin-screw propeller steamship, and built by Messrs. J. & W. Dudgeon, of Cubitt Town, Millwall, for the London, Chatham, & Dover Railway Company. She was built of iron and had a burden of 500 tons. The vessel was 200 feet long and 24 feet wide, with a draft of 14 feet. The *Atalanta* had two engines, independent of each other, and each of 100 horsepower; her propellers revolved between 100 and 120 times a minute, producing a speed of 17 knots. Her twin screws gave her incredible maneuvering ability. By reversing one screw, she could turn about her center in a space little more than her own length. The *Atalanta* was low in the water, with two funnels and two sparsely rigged masts. She was fast, and even drew admiring compliments from the American consul in London. The L.C. & D.R. transferred her on 12 April to Jefferson Wallace, a merchant in Bermuda. One "Captain Horner," an Englishman, and former master of the *Flora,* a well-known blockade-runner, was appointed her master. Between May and July 1864 the *Atalanta* ran the blockade from Bermuda into Wilmington at least twice, with war supplies.

Her presence at Wilmington was brought to the attention of Naval Secretary Mallory, and after purchasing her for the Confederacy at a cost of £25,000, he had her converted to a commerce raider. While she was fast, she had limited space in her coal bunker, and had been designed for cruises of only 1,000 miles. With this in mind she was commissioned as the CSS *Tallahassee,* and John Taylor Wood, a nephew of President Jefferson Davis, was appointed her captain. His officers included Lieutenant William H. Ward, executive and boarding officer; John Tynan, chief engineer; and Charles Jones as paymaster. The *Tallahassee* was crewed by 120 men, most of them Southerners. Her armaments consisted of a rifled 32-pounder, a rifled 100-pounder, and a heavy Parrot gun in her stern.

After an unsuccessful attempt at getting away on the 4th of August, she succeeded two days later on the 6th. At ten o'clock that night the *Tallahassee* eased down the river past Fort Caswell and into the open sea. Under maximum power she raced past the inner cordon of slower Federal ships anchored around the mouth of the river. Beyond them was an outer ring of faster vessels. Two American ships lay directly ahead. Taking the helm, Wood steered his vessel between them. As they passed, the Confederates distinctly heard the officer of one of them ordering his gunners to open fire. Because she was so low in the water the shot passed between the *Tallahassee's* funnels. With her speed, one shot was all that was allowed, then she was gone. Three more enemy ships loomed up, but the *Tallahassee* was past them before they could take any action. Then she passed two more ships; one opened fire, but no damage was done. In all, Wood had outwitted eleven of the fifty ships that blockaded Wilmington. Then she was clear; Wood had run the blockade, and not one shot had he fired in defense. He had used only speed and surprise. Now the work began.

Wood set in a course right into the heart of enemy territory — New York. For three days the *Tallahassee* proceeded north. Several ships were stopped and searched, but all were British. The American merchant marine had all but been driven from the world's oceans. On the 11th of August, that rarity, an American flagged ship, hove into view, eighty miles off Sandy Hook, New Jersey. She was the schooner *Sarah A. Boyce*. Wood knew that if he set the ship on fire it would alert the U.S. Navy as to his presence; so instead he had his men chop holes in her hull, and then he scuttled her. Off the entrance to New York the *Tallahassee* fell in with a pilot boat. She was the *James Funk*. Rather than destroy her, Wood decided to use her to lure other ships to where he lay in wait. He put two officers and twenty men aboard the smaller vessel. The brig *Carrie Estelle* was Wood's first victim using this ploy. A further brig, the *A. Richards,* and the barque *Bay Estate* were also captured. The schooner *Carroll,* with a neutral cargo, was bonded for $10,000, and all of Wood's prisoners were transferred to her. With four captured ships in tow, it was not long before another pilot boat, the *William Bell,* approached, believing that they were waiting to go in. Becoming suspicious, she began to turn, to head back to New York. The *Tallahassee* was quickly on to her, and a warning shot brought her to heel. Her crew were transferred to the *Carroll,* and the remainder of Wood's prizes were put to the torch. With so many ships burning, it is curious that no one came out to investigate.

The following day, 12 August, six more prizes were taken. The barque *Suliote* was bonded when it was discovered she was carrying a neutral cargo. The 989 ton *Adriatic,* with 170 German immigrants, was stopped. Immigrants and crew were transferred to the *Suliote,* as were the prisoners captured aboard the 222 ton *Robert E. Packer* carrying a cargo of lumber. The *Atlantic,* the *Spokane* and the brig *Billow* all fell to the *Tallahassee.* With all his prisoners aboard the *Suliote,* the other ships were burned. The *Billow* somehow survived when the USS *Grand Gulf,* attracted by the burning ships, extinguished the flames and took her in tow into New York. Wood decided not to push his luck by remaining in the vicinity, and sailed north for New England. The next morning all of New York was aware of what had happened just off its coast. John D. Jones, president of the Board of Underwriters, sent a telegram to Naval Secretary Welles: "Confederate Steamer Tallahassee is reported cruising within 60 miles of this port. She has already captured six vessels. Will you please have the necessary measures taken, if not already done, to secure her capture?" Half an hour after receiving the telegram, Welles responded: "Three vessels left New York Navy Yard yesterday afternoon; more leave today. Vessels left Hampton Roads last night; more leave today. Several vessels leave Boston today and tomorrow. Every vessel has been ordered to search for the pirate."[1]

That same day, 13 August, the 789 ton *Glenavon* was boarded. She was out of Glas-

The London-built twin-screw steamer *Atalanta*, racing the Dover mail packet *Empress*. (*Illustrated London News*, 2 April 1864)

gow bound for New York, with a cargo of iron. Wood took her crew prisoner, then helped himself to provisions before scuttling her. His next victim was the schooner *Lamont Du Pont*, laden with coal. Wood ordered her to be burned. The next day as all-out efforts were made to discover the whereabouts of the "pirate," *Tallahassee* struck again. The 547 ton *James Littlefield* was taken. She had a cargo of Welsh coal. Bad weather conditions prevented Wood from transferring her cargo, which the Confederate cruiser could have made good use of. With her crew aboard his own ship, Wood then scuttled her. Hovering off the coast of Maine, on 15th of the month, like some predatory shark, Wood captured and scuttled the schooners *Mary A. Howes, Howard, Floral Wreath, Restless* and *Etta Caroline*. He bonded the *Sarah B. Harris*, and transferred all his prisoners to her. Unharmed, they were landed in Portland that very same day. With a dozen or so Federal warships

John Taylor Wood, C.S.N., nephew of President Jefferson Davis, was appointed captain of the *Tallahassee*.

searching for the *Tallahassee,* the merchant marine was given false hope. They felt safe at the presence of so many of their navy's ships in home waters. A number of them sailed on 16 August, and a number of them had their hopes dashed. Wood captured and burned the New England barque *P.C. Alexander* and the schooners *Leopard, Pearl, Sarah Louise* and *Magnolia.*

The *Tallahassee* was now low on coal, barely forty tons remaining. Wood set in a course for the neutral port of Halifax, Nova Scotia, where he hoped to refuel. On the 17th the schooners *North America* and *Josiah Achom* were destroyed. The brig *Neva* was overhauled, but with a neutral cargo she was saved. Wood bonded her for $17,500, and transferred all his prisoners to her. Two small fishing schooners were captured, and Wood generously let them go. They had neutral cargoes, their captain proclaimed, already sold to Halifax merchants.

On the 18th of August the *Tallahassee* put into Halifax. Pleasantries were exchanged, and Wood requested to be allowed to re-coal. Perhaps due to the close proximity to their sometime aggressive neighbor, the naval commander, Admiral Sir James Hope, rigidly interpreted the rules of neutrality. His instructions were that the *Tallahassee* should only receive sufficient coal to allow her to steam to her nearest home port. That was 100 tons. The U.S. consul, Mortimer M. Jackson, was very soon made aware of the arrival of the "pirate." He dashed off a telegram to the naval secretary. Welles' response was to order as many warships as were available to sail for Halifax immediately. In the meantime Jackson was ordered to delay the departure of the *Tallahassee* for as long as possible. He made protests to the governor, Richard G. MacDonnell, that she should not be re-coaled; that she was a pirate; that Wood had mistreated his prisoners. MacDonnell was not a man to be bullied or cajoled. He dictated a response to Mr. Jackson: "[H]is excellency does not consider it his duty to detain the Tallahassee, or any man-o-war of a belligerent state, on the chance of evidence being hereafter found of her violating international law, and in the absence of proof to that effect he can not withhold from her commander the privilege of obtaining as much coal as may be necessary to carry him to a port of the Confederate States."[2]

Wood, unaware of the diplomatic chicanery being attempted by the American consul, was well aware that Jackson would have summoned help. He knew that time was of the essence, and he too would have to practice a little chicanery. As night drew on he ceased coaling, announcing that he now had 80 tons loaded (whereas in fact he had loaded 120 tons), and would load the remainder of the prescribed tonnage the following morning. As emphasis of his remaining the following day, he requested time to conduct repairs and alterations to his damaged mainmast. As night descended Wood got ready to depart. At one o'clock on the morning of the 20th, with a pilot, Jock Fleming, guiding her, the *Tallahassee* made for the entrance of the harbor, and by two o'clock she was away, heading south. There was no sign of Federal warships as she left, but at a quarter past six, three and a quarter hours later, the USS *Pontusuc* arrived at Halifax. It had been a close thing, but nobody it seemed, could out-guess Wood. To add to the confusion Wood had let it be known that he was heading up to the St. Lawrence seaway, there to wreak havoc upon the Northern fishing fleet. Wood set in a course for Bermuda, with the intention of taking on extra coal if the authorities would permit. Later that day the *Tallahassee* espied a ship on the horizon, and made pursuit. The other vessel was quickly overtaken, and proved to be the American flagged, 286 ton brig *Roan*. Wood took what he needed in the way of provisions, took her crew aboard as prisoners, then burned her. On the

Tallahassee sailed. But when members of his crew began developing yellow fever, Wood changed his mind and made for his home port of Wilmington. As night descended on the 26th of August, Wood lined the *Tallahassee* up and drove straight into the harbor and under the safety of Fort Fisher's guns. His entry passed without incident. Wood's cruise had been a tremendous success, confirming Mallory's faith in the little ship and her captain. Assigned to other duties, Wood's recommendation was that his little ship should go to sea once more as a raider.

Overhauled and refurbished and given a new name, CSS *Olustee,* in honor of the Battle of Olustee, in north Florida, she again put to sea under a new master, Lt. William H. Ward. As she passed through the blockade off Wilmington on 29 October 1864, she suffered some damage from Federal guns, but got successfully away. Her reign as a commercial raider, sailing up as far as Sandy Hook, was short, but not without success. In the first three days of November she destroyed the barque *Empress Theresa,* the schooners *Vapor, A.J. Bird* and *E.F. Lewis,* the ship *Arcole,* and the brig *T.D. Wagner.* On 7 November she ran the blockade back into Wilmington, suffering some slight damage as she did so. More repairs followed, and her guns were removed. She was turned back into a fast blockade runner under her new captain, John Wilkinson, C.S.N., formerly master of her sister ship *Chickamauga* (see below). She was also given a new name, the *Chameleon.* As she was ever-changing, the name was apt. On Christmas Eve 1864, while the Federal fleet was preoccupied with bombarding Fort Fisher, she ran the blockade once more, with a cargo of cotton to be exchanged at Bermuda for supplies for Lee's army. Wilkinson waited for the best part of a month before, with his hold full of precious supplies, he made the dash back to Wilmington. Driven off, Wilkinson then tried to enter Charleston, but was again repulsed. He sailed for Nassau, and there awaited further orders. Mallory directed him to land and store his cargo, then sail his ship to Liverpool, where he was to surrender it to Fraser, Trenholm & Co. He was to place himself under the command of James D. Bulloch, to await further orders. The *Illustrated London News* for 21 April 1865 recorded her return:

> In our Journal of the 2nd of April, last year, was an Illustration of the race across the British Channel, from Dover to Calais, between one of the paddle-wheel steamers of that line and the Atalanta, a new steamer designed by Captain T.E. Symonds, R.N.... [She] was afterwards purchased by the Government of the Confederate States of America, and named Tallahassee, from a place in Florida.... In the autumn of last year she perpetrated a vast amount of damage to the commerce of the Northern States—hovering sometimes for weeks near the entrance of the harbors of New York and Philadelphia, thereby capturing, plundering, and burning a great number of American vessels, and even the pilot-boats of New York, while it was utterly hopeless for any of the Federal ships of war to attempt to catch her. This career of not inglorious mischief came to an end some two or three months ago, and the Tallahassee has been disarmed and disposed of once more to private owners. She was lately brought to Liverpool, and is now being refitted, under the name of Amelia, for ordinary commercial purposes."

Whether she was being upgraded as a blockade-runner following a rather dubious sale is now open to question. Lord Russell ordered her to be seized. It was 9 April 1865, the day that Lee surrendered. Technically she now belonged to the United States, which in the form of the ever capable Thomas Dudley, instituted a suit in law for her possession. On 26 April 1866, she was handed over to the U.S. consul in Liverpool. She was renamed the *Haya Maro,* and traded between the United States and Japan. On 17 June 1869 she struck a rock while on a passage from Yokohama and Hiogo and sank, with a loss of 21 lives.

The commercial raider *Tallahassee*, formerly the *Atalanta*, returns to England. (*Illustrated London News*, 21 April 1865)

The *Chickamauga,* originally the *Edith,* was a sister ship of the *Atalanta,* and likewise was built by Dudgeon's, on the Thames. She was launched in late 1863. Like her sister she was 220 feet in length, 24 feet in breadth, with a displacement of 14 feet for her 500 tons. Also like her sister, she became a blockade-runner. The American consul in London, Samuel Morse, who suspected that she was intended as a runner, had been keeping close observation upon her. On 11 March 1864 he wrote to Federal secretary of state, Seward: "The steamer Edith, the last double screw completed, left on Wednesday last for Bermuda. The Edith makes the ninth double-screw steamer which has been built for the rebel service in this port."[3] Having successfully run the blockade she, too, was purchased by the Confederate navy and converted as a cruiser. Renamed the *Chickamauga,* the successful blockade-runner Lt. John Wilkinson, formerly of the *Robert E. Lee,* was appointed her captain.

Wilkinson was born in Amelia County, Virginia, on 6 November 1821. He was the son of a sailor, Jesse Wilkinson, of the U.S. sloop of war *Hornet* and later captain of the frigate *United States.* The son was appointed a midshipman, and served under Captain David G. Farragut aboard the USS *Saratoga,* during the late 1840s. In 1850 John Wilkinson was promoted to lieutenant. With the outbreak of war he resigned his commission, and offered his services to the Confederacy. His talents were somewhat wasted when he was appointed instructor to the "young gentleman privates" at Fort Powhatan on the James River. With its near completion, however, Wilkinson was appointed first officer aboard the ironclad *Louisiana*. When Farragut's fleet forced its way up the river past the fort and into New Orleans, the *Louisiana* was destroyed by her crew rather than let her fall into the hands of the enemy. Wilkinson and his men were taken prisoner, but barely three months later Wilkinson was part of an exchange of prisoners. Back in Richmond, Wilkinson was dispatched to Scotland by the naval secretary to purchase fast steamers for the Confederacy. He purchased the *Giraffe* and ran the blockade into Wilmington with her. In his new ship, commissioned as the CSS *Robert E. Lee,* he ran the blockade twenty-one times, making a mockery of it.

A daring officer, Wilkinson's next mission was to capture the Federal sloop *Michigan,* operating on Lake Erie. It was an audacious plan, but one that might have succeeded if it had not been leaked to the Federal authorities. With Federal soldiers in pursuit, Wilkinson and his men fled to the safety of Halifax, Nova Scotia, and from there sailed to Bermuda. Here he was given the opportunity of running an English ship, the *Whispers,* through the blockade into Wilmington. He jumped at the opportunity, and though he came under Federal fire, he succeeded in his mission. Wilkinson now took command of the *Chickamauga* and assembled his crew. The deckhands appear to be a mixture of the *Edith's* original British crew and an assembled Confederate crew:

Officers of the CSS *Chickamauga*
(26 September–15 December 1864)

John Wilkinson, Lieutenant, Commanding.	J.C. Schroeder, Chief Engineer
W.G. Dozier, First Lt. and Executive Officer.	G.W. Tennent, First Assistant engineer
F.M. Roby, Lieutenant.	J.T. Tucker, Second Assistant Engineer.
Clarence L. Stanton, Lieutenant.	C.S. Peck, Third Assistant Engineer.
Clarence Cary, Passed Midshipman	J.W. Tomlinson, Third Assistant Engineer.
D.M. Lee, Passed Midshipman.	T.P. Barry, Assistant Paymaster.
T.M. Berrien, Passed Midshipman.	David Bradford, First Lieutenant Marines
B. Gibson, Acting Master's Mate.	Smith, Pilot.
J.J. Ingraham, Boatswain	Jenkens, Captain's Clerk.
Julius Durand, Gunner.	Bain, Paymaster's Clerk.
Wallace, Pilot.	Pascalle, Master's Mate.
Sermons, Pilot.	
Garrison, Pilot.	

On the evening of 28 October 1864, Wilkinson took his new ship, the *Chickamauga,* downriver to Smithville. At 7 o'clock she crossed the bar and headed out to sea in full steam. Through the inner blockade of Federal ships she maneuvered, catching them unprepared. Then suddenly a series of rockets were sent up from one of the more alert blockaders, which set out rapidly after her. Soon the blockader's guns were blazing away at the *Chickamauga.* Twelve shots came screaming towards the little Confederate steamer. They were accurate, but too high, flying over her and crashing into the sea beyond. The *Chickamauga* veered from one side to the other, seeking to put off the Federal gunners. Wilkinson ordered more steam, and by 8 o'clock, as darkness descended, she was clear of her pursuer. Wilkinson changed course, steering east by north, to confuse any ships that might come after him.

Wilkinson's mission was to attack Federal merchantmen in the run up to Long Island Sound. Two days later, on 30 October at 11:00 A.M., the mission began as the *Chickamauga* overhauled and forced to heave-to the barque *Mark L. Potter,* of Bangor, Maine, bound for Key West, with a cargo of bricks, lime and lumber. The crew of 13 were taken aboard, and the ship was burned. From her the *Chickamauga* acquired five new boats, three of them dinghies. The following day they gave chase to the New York barque *Emma L. Hall* carrying a cargo of molasses and sugar from Cardenas, Cuba. This ship was burned. A little later another sail was sighted, and the pursuit began once more. Brought to a halt, this one proved to be the *Shooting Star,* out of New York, bound for Havana with a cargo of coal (1,500 tons). After her master, Captain Drinkwater, his wife, the "redoubtable Mrs Drinkwater," as Wilkinson describes her, and the crew were transferred aboard the *Chickamauga* as prisoners, another sail was sighted. A prize crew was put aboard the *Shooting Star,* with orders to follow on, as the *Chickamauga* set out after this new quarry. A shot across her bows eventually obliged her to heave-to. She proved to be the *Albion Lincoln,* of Harpswell, Maine, with a neutral cargo of lumber. Wilkinson bonded her for $18,000, then transferred all his prisoners, then some forty in number. The *Shooting Star,* he put to the torch. As they were transferring prisoners, a ship passed to windward of them, but they were too busy to pursue her.

The next day, 1 November, at midday, they sighted the lighthouse on Montauk Point, Long Island. As the afternoon wore on a sail was sighted, which proved to be the neutral schooner *Reliance,* from Nova Scotia. She was allowed to continue on her way. As darkness descended, two more ships in close proximity were seen and overhauled. They were both Federal merchantmen — the Schooners *Godspeed* of Philadelphia, in ballast, and the *Otter Rock* of Boston, with a cargo of potatoes. Their crews transferred as prisoners, both ships were scuttled. The latest newspapers from Boston revealed that three Federal steamships had been sent after the *Edith/Chickamauga.* Later that night there was an alarm that a Federal steamer was bearing down on them. All lights aboard the Confederate ship were doused, as everybody was summoned topside and called to action stations. All lit up, closer and closer the other ship came. The *Chickamauga's* crew waited tensely as on she came, almost running them down, completely unaware of their presence. Then she passed them, this large schooner, and proceeded on her way. The Confederate crew were stood down.

On the morning of 2 November the barque *Speedwell* of Boston was captured off the New Jersey coast. She was bound for Philadelphia in ballast. She was an old ship, carrying passengers. Wilkinson bonded her for $18,000, and transferred all his prisoners to her. He obtained the latest newspapers from the *Speedwell.* More steamers had been sent out to look for the Confederate cruiser, including the formidable USS *Vanderbilt.* Not wishing to tempt fate further, Wilkinson set in a course for Bermuda. He arrived there late on the night of 7 November, but had to wait offshore until the next morning, when a pilot boat came out to take the *Chickamauga* into St. George's.

Barely had she dropped anchor than the U.S. consul started complaining to the British authorities that the *Chickamauga* was breaching one law or another. Wilkinson had requested permission to enter the harbor for repairs, which he estimated might take five days. He also asked to be allowed to take on 25 tons of coal, sufficient for him to run the blockade back into Wilmington. The repairs overran to seven days, and Wilkinson apparently took on more coal than he had originally requested. This was pounced upon by the United States consul to show British connivance. This alleged bias was far from the truth though. On 13 November, sixty-five members of the *Chickamauga's* crew, including the chief gunner, deserted. Seeking the governor's aid in having them arrested and returned, Wilkinson was informed that this was not possible, because the Confederacy was not a recognized power. His seven days of repair complete, and minus half his crew, on 15 November 1864, Wilkinson took the *Chickamauga* back out to sea. He set in a course for Wilmington.

The following day the *Chickamauga* overhauled two neutral ships, the *Christine,* of Kien in Norway, and the *Jacop Cappe,* a French barquentine from St. Thomas. Both were

10. The Tallahassee and the Chickamauga 183

CSS *Chickamauga*, formerly the *Edith*, sister ship to the *Tallahassee*, was commanded by Lt. John Wilkinson, C.S.N.

allowed to proceed. On the morning of the 18th two ships were seen — one of them a steamer, possibly a warship. Wilkinson ordered a change in course to avoid her. She apparently did not see them. Wilkinson had hoped to approach the entrance to Wilmington before 10 o'clock that night, before the moon rose, but in avoiding the steamer he was delayed by an hour. Under a heavy fog the *Chickamauga* made a dash through the blockaders yet again, but having incorrectly lined up for the entry into New Inlet, Wilkinson found himself, because of the poor conditions, entered in by the Masonboro Inlet. Realizing the mistake, Wilkinson took the wheel, and edged the *Chickamauga* down the coast to New Inlet. Now safely under the protection of the guns of Fort Fisher, Wilkinson was obliged to wait the tide. As he did so, on the morning of 19 November, shortly before seven, the fog lifted. Not too far distant, a small Federal gunboat espied them and opened fire. Aboard the *Chickamauga* Wilkinson raised the colors and returned fire. This in turn drew the attention of three more of the blockading squadron. They likewise opened up on the smaller Confederate ship. The guns of Fort Fisher now opened up, and the blockaders retired. Half an hour later though, at 8 o'clock, five of the blockading squadron returned and reengaged in combat. The tide was turning, and the *Chickamauga* got underway and crossed the bar to safety. By mid-morning she was in the river and making her way up to Wilmington.

Lt. Dennison, commanding the USS *Cherokee*, part of the blockading force, put in a report of the action:

> At 6.30 this morning, being on my station S.E. from the Mound and [in] 5 fathoms of water, the weather very hazy, the "Clematis" bearing N.E., the "Wilderness" N.E. by N., and the "Kansas" E.N.E., I saw the "Clematis" apparently blowing off steam. Thinking she was disabled, I stood for her with my hawsers ready to tow her off clear of the forts. After heading for her a few minutes the haze lifted and I saw a steamer apparently on shore near Fort Fisher. I steamed towards her into $4\frac{3}{4}$ fathoms of water. The "Clematis" commenced firing, which was returned by steamer inshore, who at that time ran up the rebel flag. I then opened fire, as did the "Wilderness," I using my two 20-pounder Parrotts. The effect of my shots I could not ascertain, as the light mist which surrounded the vessel prevented me from seeing them. In a short time after, the "Kansas" com-

menced firing, and then Fort Fisher, the Mound, and Flag Pond Battery opened, most of their shots going over us. Wishing to speak the "Kansas," I stood towards her, but seeing she was standing out towards a steamer coming in from the northward and eastward and [which] afterwards proved to be the "Santiago de Cuba," I stopped and turned inshore. A heavy fog setting in, all firing ceased. At 8 A.M. the "Kansas" came up, and the fog lifting, the firing was again resumed on both sides, the enemy's shell exploding all around the ship. In the meantime the rebel steamer had worked off and steamed in by Fort Fisher. At 8.30 A.M. stopped firing, as the enemy was then in the river.

The above-mentioned steamer was a screw boat, schooner-rigged, two smokestacks, painted a light lead color, and had a very large number of men on board. From the sound of the shots as they passed over our deck I judged her armament to consist of two Whitworths and a heavy rifle amidships. Her men were dressed in dark blue.[4]

A few months later, in February 1865, Fort Fisher was assaulted in a combined operation led by Rear Admiral Porter with a fleet of 59 warships. The attack lasted three days. At three o'clock on the afternoon of the third day, 8,000 soldiers and 2,000 sailors bravely assaulted the landward side of the fort. They were supported by fire from the naval vessels, and eventually, despite heavy losses, took the fort. During the course of their assault, the *Chickamauga,* now under the command of Captain William H. Ward, had fired upon them constantly. With the fort captured, Wilmington was effectively closed to cruisers and blockade-runners. On 25 February, amidst fresh assaults, the *Chickamauga* was scuttled and burned by her own crew.

11

The *Shenandoah*

In the autumn of 1863, Bulloch and his assistant, Lt. Robert R. Carter, went up to the Clyde in Scotland to view a steamer, the *Coquette*, for possible use as a blockade-runner. While there Bulloch caught sight of a particularly fine full-rigged vessel and steamship, with the necessary arrangement for disconnecting and lifting her screw. She was fully laden and about to depart on her maiden voyage to Bombay. Her owners, Messrs. Robinson, had in addition also contracted with the British government to take troops out to New Zealand. From there the vessel was to proceed to China, and return with a cargo of tea. She was expected to return to Scotland in eight to ten months; her name was the *Sea King*. The vessel was built by Messrs. A. Stephen & Sons, at their yard at Kelvinhaugh, Govan, and launched on 17 August 1863. She was 1160 tons, 230 feet in length, 32 feet wide, with a depth of 20ft. 6ins. and her speed under steam and sail was 13 knots (though later in the Indian Ocean she made 18 knots over four consecutive hours). She was iron-framed and teak-planked. The vessel was provided with two smooth-bore 12-pounders, which was usual for ships trading in the China Sea. Bulloch was quite taken with her. How to acquire her was the problem. As soon as he went anywhere near her, Adams' agents, and by now there were many of them, would be on to him, and the transaction would be thwarted. He found himself a go-between, an Englishman above reproach. Bulloch, with his usual discretion, does not name him in his account: "The gentleman who acted for me in the purchase of the above-mentioned ship bought her in his own name, ballasted her with coal, and had her cleared out for Bombay, giving the captain a power of attorney to sell her at any time after leaving London. For this service he declined to receive any remuneration whatever, and I promised that when she received her Confederate crew and armament, no prize should be captured until the captain who took her out had been allowed sufficient time to return to England and cancel the register."[1]

The person in question was Mr. Richard Wright, the father-in-law of Charles K. Prioleau, of the firm of Fraser, Trenholm & Co. Wright purchased the vessel on 20 September 1864. On 7 October, the day before the *Sea King* sailed, Wright gave Captain G.H. Corbett, a fellow Englishman, the power of attorney to sell the ship at any time within six months for a sum of not less than £45,000. It was all legal, though not necessarily aboveboard. Corbett was known to the American authorities as a blockade-runner. He had been captain of the runner *Douglas*, afterwards renamed the *Margaret and Jessie*.

Bulloch's next step was to acquire a tender to serve her. He was advised to have a look at a ship employed in the packet service between Liverpool and Ireland. She was the *Laurel*. Inspecting her by making a crossing to Ireland and back, Bulloch approved of the ship. She was strongly built, with lots of room, and a shallow draft; she steamed at thirteen knots an hour. She would make a good tender, but could also serve the dual purpose of a blockade-runner, when not needed. Using an agent, Bulloch also bought her. To allay suspicion, she was advertised as making a voyage to Havana, and would take on freight and a limited number of passengers. However, when companies or passengers enquired, they discovered that the allocation had already been completed, as was evidenced by details available in the shipping agent's office.

On 28 September 1864, Lieutenant Carter returned to Liverpool after a successful run of the blockade in the *Coquette*. He brought with him instructions from Secretary Mallory. The target for the latest commercial raider was to be the American whaling fleet in the Pacific. Carter and Commander John Brooke, lieutenants together in a scientific expedition conducted by the United States Navy Department some years previously, had put forward the project to Mallory. Bulloch already had a copy of Commander Maury's set of whaling charts, published in connection with his *Physical Geography of the Sea,* which identified where whales, and by the same token, whalers, were to be found. This was not to be some random cruise, but one with a very definite objective—the complete destruction of the United States whaling fleet. With all the information now assembled Bulloch prepared a draft memorandum, which included general instructions, to be issued to the *Sea King's* new master, Captain James I. Waddell.

By the 5th of October The *Sea King,* under the temporary command of Captain G.H. Corbett, was lying at anchor in the Thames. On 6 October Bulloch summoned Lt. William C. Whittle, then based in England, and gave him orders to proceed by the 5:00 P.M. train from Liverpool to London, and there register at Wood's Hotel, High Holborn, under the name "Mr. Brown." The following morning he was met by a Confederate agent who took him to view the *Sea King,* and later to meet Captain Corbett. It was decided at this time only Corbett would know his true identity. Early on the morning of the 8th, Whittle boarded the ship, which within a few minutes left the dock and proceeded down the Thames to the open sea. It was Bulloch's intention that Whittle, soon to become executive officer, should familiarize himself with the ship during the voyage to Madeira, and in particular the best way of utilizing the space available.

That evening the *Laurel,* under Lieutenant J.F. Ramsay, C.S.N., with the *Sea King's* armament and other supplies, was waiting in the Mersey. In her hold she carried four 8 inch smooth-bore cannons, two 32-pounder rifled cannons, and two 12-pounder cannons. Nearby at Princes Landing stage a group of men gathered. One of them, Irishman Dr. F.J. McNulty recalled the event in later years: "On the evening of the 8th day of October 1864 there met on Princesses [sic] dock, Liverpool twenty-seven men. They were nearly unacquainted with each other, and knew nothing of their destination. All were officers of the Confederate navy, by commission or warrant, and each had his distinct order to report to this place at the same hour. My commission was that of assistant surgeon.

A tug was waiting, and we were hurried upon its deck with great haste. In the stream lay the steam blockade-runner Laurel. In the shortest time imaginable we were hustled on board this craft, and were steaming down the stream."[2]

The *Laurel* reached Madeira on Sunday, 16 October, and anchored in Funchal Bay near Loo Rock. She was visited by Portuguese customs officers, and she requested to take on coal. On the night of Tuesday, 18 October, a ship was sighted by the *Laurel's* crew a few miles off. The new vessel showed her signal lights, then moved off once more. The following day she returned, and was revealed to be the *Sea King.* Now with her clearance papers from the Portuguese authorities, the *Laurel* raised anchor, and proceeded out to sea. Coming up to the new arrival, Waddell signaled that she was to follow them. The two Confederate vessels withdrew to the Desertas, a group of barren islands nearby, where the cargo and officers aboard the *Laurel* were transferred to the *Sea King,* and she was converted to a ship of war. The ships were lashed together and in the first twenty-four hours two of the 8 inch guns and one Whitworth 32-pounder were mounted. The next day two more 8 inch and a second Whitworth were mounted on their carriages, and on 29 October, eight days after leaving their anchorage at Las Desertas, all the ports were cut and the whole battery of six guns were fully equipped and in place. Bulloch put this down to the spirit of the crew: "[T]hey were full of pluck and that ingrained verve and aptitude for the sea which is characteristic of the Anglo-Saxon race, whether born and bred in Great Britain, or in any part of what Sir Charles Dilke has called 'Greater Britain,' meaning by that broad and inclusive designation the English speaking countries which have been colonized by Britons."[3]

This feeling of the universality of the British being part of a superior race was a theme shared by Raphael Semmes, former captain of the *Alabama.* Unlike the Northern states, which were made up of disparate peoples, the South, by and large, was still very British. This was a feeling shared by many in Great Britain, and goes a long way to understanding that, though the British were vehemently opposed to slavery, they were sympathetic towards their cousins of the South.

On 19 October 1864, Lt. Waddell assembled all the officers and crew on the quarterdeck, and read out his commission as an officer in the Confederate States Navy. He announced that the ship was now the CSS *Shenandoah,* and the Confederate flag was unfurled at the mast. With him Waddell had brought a number of officers and specialist crew members from the sunken *Alabama,* but to his great disappointment, only 23 of the 80 British sailors shipped out agreed to join him. No doubt the deaths of so many British sailors killed when the *Alabama* was sunk, in June of that year, was uppermost in the minds of many of them. At the end of the day Waddell found himself with a working crew of only 42, plus officers. He hoped to increase it later from the crews of prizes taken. Fortunately, among his officers were men like the master, Irvine S. Bulloch, Paymaster W.B. Smith and Chief Engineer Matthew O'Brien, who had vast experience from their time aboard the *Alabama.* Within the crew he had Liverpudlian George Harwood, a former chief boatswain's mate aboard the *Alabama.* Waddell had specifically requested him to serve aboard his ship, believing that he would be very influential among a mainly British crew. Harwood had been born at Portsea, Hampshire, in 1817. He served in the Royal Navy during the Crimean War, and then apparently moved up to Liverpool where he found work. He enlisted onboard the *Alabama* on 24 August 1862, for a term of six months. His

James I. Waddell, C.S.N., captain of the Clyde-built ***Shenandoah***, formerly the ***Sea King.***

time up, he was entrusted with private papers, including a list of the ships bonded by Semmes, which he presented to Bulloch. From then until his enlistment aboard the *Shenandoah,* he appears to have served aboard the blockade-runner *Southerner,* plying between Liverpool and Charleston. Waddell was very impressed with him and his apparent commitment to the Southern cause.

Those who had not volunteered to serve aboard the *Shenandoah* returned to the *Laurel* and were later landed at Tenerife. With a crew at just half strength Waddell prepared to embark. With so few men though, he had his doubts. He called together his officers and asked what they should do. With unanimity they responded, "Take the ocean."[4] Waddell set in a course for the Cape of Good Hope. From there his orders were to proceed across the Indian Ocean to Australia, then into the North Pacific, in pursuit of the American whaling fleet.

Officers of the CSS *Shenandoah*
(19 October 1864)

James I. Waddell, Lieutenant Commanding, North Carolina
W.C. Whittle, Executive Officer, Virginia
John Grimball, Lieutenant, South Carolina
Sidney Smith Lee, Lieutenant, Virginia
F.T. Chew, Lieutenant, Missouri
D.M. Scales, Lieutenant, Tennessee
Irvine S. Bulloch, Sailing Master, Georgia
C.E. Lining, Surgeon, South Carolina
Matthew O'Brien, Chief Engineer, Louisiana
W.B. Smith, Paymaster, Louisiana
Orris A. Brown, Passed Midshipman, Virginia
John T. Mason, Passed Midshipman, Virginia

F.J. McNulty, Acting Assistant Surgeon, Ireland
C.H. Codd, Acting 1st Assistant Engineer, Maryland
John Hutchinson, Acting 2nd Assistant Engineer, Scotland
E. Mugguffiny, Acting 3rd Assistant Engineer, Ireland
John F. Minor, Acting Master's Mate, Virginia
C.E. Hunt, Acting Boatswain, Virginia
Lodge Cotton, Acting Boatswain, Maryland
George Harwood, Acting Boatswain, England
John L. Guy, Acting Gunner, England
H. Alcot, Acting Sailmaker, England
John O'Shea, Acting Carpenter, Ireland

Petty Officers

Moran, Ireland
Bronnan, Ireland
Crawford, Scotland
Fenner, England
Fox, England

Warren, England
Hall, England
Wiggins, England
Griffith, Wales
Jones, Wales

Firemen

Marshall, England
Martin, England

Rawlinson, England
Clark, England

Seaman

Simpson, England
Oar , England

Rose, England
Jones, Wales

James Iredale Waddell, captain of the *Shenandoah,* was born at Pittsboro, North Carolina, in 1824. He gained a place at Annapolis Naval Academy in September 1841. After graduation he was assigned as a midshipman aboard the USS *Pennsylvania.* He later served aboard the USS *Somers* off Vera Cruz during the Mexican War, and aboard the USS *Germantown* during a tour off the South American coast. Promoted to lieutenant, he was appointed as an instructor at the Naval Academy, specializing in navigation. Waddell did a tour of duty in the eastern Pacific aboard the *Saginaw,* and went on to serve aboard the USS *John Adams* with the East Indies Squadron. At the outbreak of the Civil War he resigned his commission, and offered his services to the Confederacy. In angry spite he was listed in the U.S. Navy Register as having been dismissed from the service, on 19 January 1862. In March 1862, now back home, Waddell was appointed a Lieutenant in the Confederate States Navy. He briefly served aboard the ironclad *Mississippi,* until her destruction in April of that year, and in the absence of a ship to serve aboard, he did shore battery service at Drewry's Bluff, Virginia, and at Charleston, South Carolina, during the remainder of the year and into early 1863. In March 1863 he was sent to England to await the availability of a position aboard a seagoing ship. That availability presented itself with the command of the *Shenandoah.*

Waddell's executive officer was William Conway Whittle, born at Norfolk, Virginia, in 1840. He entered Annapolis in 1854, graduated four years later, and served in Gulf Squadron until 1860, when he was ordered back to the Naval Academy to sit an examination. He was appointed midshipman and later sailing master. At the outbreak of the war he tendered his resignation, and offered his services to the Confederate government. Like Waddell, he spent time training battery crews ashore, before being appointed as third lieutenant aboard the CSS *Nashville.* He sailed in her to England and back to Beaufort, North Carolina, where he was placed in charge until her purchasers could send a crew to take her over. He ran the blockade into Georgetown, and later at New Orleans. In March 1862, he was appointed third lieutenant aboard the CSS *Louisiana.* He was captured following the fight with Farragut's fleet off Forts Jackson and St. Philip, and sent as prisoner to Fort Warren, Boston. Whittle was exchanged in August 1862, and served aboard the gunboat *Chattahoochee,* before being sent to England. Here he acted as an assistant to Commander Bulloch at Liverpool, running the blockade with dispatches for Richmond. In October Whittle was appointed executive officer aboard the *Shenandoah.*

Ship's doctor F.J. McNulty now takes up the story of the first few days of the cruise:

> Although liable at any hour to meet the challenge shot of the enemy, we entered upon our duties without fear. There was work for every man to do, and every man put his heart in his task. Boxes, trunks, casks of beef and bread, coal and ordnance, lay promiscuous about deck and below. Then, when after days of toil and with blistered hands all was stored properly below, and while the carpenter and his mate cut port holes for the guns, the captain took his trick at the wheels, and the officers and men, regardless of rank, barefooted and with trousers rolled up, scrubbed and holystoned decks.... [A]ll felt the necessity of the hour, and lieutenant, assistant surgeon, boatswain, and foremost hands, of whom there were but seven in all, kept watch. But at length everything was put in shipshape.[5]

The great adventure was now begun. Sailing south, en route for the Cape, Waddell and his crew captured six prizes. Five of these were put to the torch or scuttled, after he had transferred passengers and crew. The sixth he bonded, and transferred his prisoners to her. From four of these ships Waddell gained sixteen recruits for his crew. His first prize fell to him on 30 October, south of the Azores and due west of Dakar (Senegal). She was the barque *Alina* of Searsport, Maine, under Captain Staples. She was on her maiden voyage, with a cargo of railroad iron. Waddell took what he needed: little things like wash basins, jugs and other such things, not considered at the time when the *Shenandoah* was being fitted out. Seven of the *Alina*'s crew of twelve agreed to ship aboard the Confederate cruiser. Reluctant to set her ablaze for fear of scaring off any other Yankee ships, Waddell scuttled her.

On 5 November the schooner *Charter Oak,* out of Boston, bound for San Francisco, under Captain Gilman, crossed their path off the Cape Verde Islands. Among her passengers was Gilman's wife and his sister-in-law, Mrs. Gage, and her son Frank. The passengers and crew were removed aboard the *Shenandoah*, as were quantities of fresh fruit and vegetables, then the vessel was burned. The *Shenandoah* remained with her until she was completely consumed by flames, then continued south to the Cape. Three days later the barque *D.G. Godfrey*, under Captain Hallett, was captured. She was bound for Valparaiso, out of Boston. Six of her crew agreed to join the *Shenandoah*. Waddell helped himself, and his crew, to her cargo of beef and pork, then put her to the torch. On the 10th Waddell captured and scuttled the brig *Susan*, southwest of the Cape Verde Islands. Out of New York, under Captain Hansen, she was carrying a cargo of coal. The coal had been purchased at Cardiff, and was being taken to Rio Grande do Sul, Brazil. Without proper documentation confirming it to be a neutral cargo, Waddell sank her. Two men and a boy agreed to join the crew. In his personal journal Waddell gave the impression that he was doing her a favor, rather like putting an old dog down. Perhaps tongue in cheek he exclaimed, "She leaked badly and was the dullest sailor I had ever seen; really she moved so slowly that barnacles grew to her bottom, and it was simply impossible for her crew to pump her out as fast as the water made."[6]

On 12 November two American flagged ships fell to the *Shenandoah*. They were the clipper *Kate Prince* and the brig *Adelaide*. The *Kate Prince* was out of Portsmouth, New Hampshire, sailing under Captain Libby from Liverpool to Bahia in Brazil, with what proved to be a neutral cargo. As a consequence she was bonded for $40,000. Waddell transferred his prisoners to her, including Captain and Mrs. Gilman and Mrs. Gage, formerly of the *Charter Oak,* who were profuse in their thanks for the kindnesses received while they were "prisoners." Later in the day the *Shenandoah* overhauled the *Adelaide,* out of Matthews County, Virginia, under Captain I.P. Williams. When she heaved-to she was flying the Argentinean flag. Boarding her it was quickly discovered that both her captain and crew were Yankees. Her papers indicated that she had been sold recently. Waddell was all for burning her. He was convinced that her papers were bogus. Her captain took him to one side and convinced him that the true owner was a Southern sympathizer. In the end Waddell bonded her too.

The following day, 13 October, just north of the equator, they captured the *Lizzie M. Stacey,* an American flagged schooner. Sailing under Captain Archer, she was out of Boston bound for Honolulu. After some lighthearted banter with the crew, three of them agreed to join the *Shenandoah*. A fourth sailor was impressed—forced to join against his will. This was perhaps a mark of desperation on Waddell's part. Though his crew was growing, they were still working long hours, and must have been close to breaking at times.

There were moments of lightheartedness though, to break up the long hours. "Crossing the line" was one such merry time. It was a naval tradition stretching back 100 years or more, inherited from the British. Any officer or man aboard who had never crossed the equator before was introduced to King Neptune and his retinue. These were other sailors in disguise, with false beards and big hats, with tridents and nets. The newcomer was surrounded by the retinue so he could not escape. He was asked where he came from, and woe betide the man who opened his mouth to answer. If he did so his mouth would be filled with a mixture of soap and grease, or possibly molasses. Poor Lieutenant Chew was seized first. When he failed to answer, his face was covered in soapy lather and he was shaved with a long wooden razor. Then he was dunked in a canvas bath of water. Dr.

McNulty followed, and when asked where he was from, answered "Ireland," upon which utterance his mouth was filled with soap and molasses. This was too much for McNulty; he knocked the barber the full length of the vessel. Whittle too, despite his rank, was shaved, as were the others. It was a means of letting off steam and bonding the crew.

Three weeks then elapsed before the *Shenandoah* took another prize. It was off the British controlled island of Tristan da Cunha, in the South Atlantic. Somehow it seemed a statement of intent. She was the whaler *Edward,* out of New Bedford, Massachusetts, under Captain Worth. The vessel had provisions for an extensive sea voyage. Waddell took what he needed in the shape of clothing and other goods, including two of her boats, which were new. Taking aboard her crew of 26 men as prisoners, Waddell burned the vessel. Now with twenty-nine prisoners, Waddell decided to put them ashore on Tristan da Cunha, along with sufficient provisions to last for three months. Just twelve hours later the United States man of war *Iroquois* steamed into the harbor and took onboard the prisoners, weighed anchor and sailed with all speed for Cape Town, where she hoped to intercept the *Shenandoah.*

Waddell's plan did not include stopping at Cape Town, a favorite of the *Alabama,* but to carry on across the Indian Ocean to Melbourne in Australia. On 29 December 1864, the *Shenandoah* having skirted the Cape and entered the Indian Ocean, a sail was seen in the distance. The *Shenandoah* set off in pursuit. As she approached, the other ship raised the United States flag. Waddell ordered the Confederate flag to be raised in response, and fired a round across her bows. Rather than heave-to she piled on more sail, and made a run of it. Dr. McNulty recalled that it was not until the third solid shot, which almost cut away her fore-rigging, that she come to. The ship proved to be the barque *Delphine,* out of Bangor, Maine, under Captain Nicholas. She was sailing from London to Akyab, in ballast. Her captain with his papers came onboard the *Shenandoah.* His ship was a lawful prize. In an attempt to prevent her being burned, he said he had his wife aboard, and she was seriously ill. The ship's doctor was sent aboard only to discover that the wife was in the ruddiest of health. Along with her was their six-year-old son, Phineas. Using the Boatswain's chair, mother and son were brought aboard the Confederate ship, and the *Delphine* was put to the torch. Some of the junior officers were moved out of their cabin to accommodate the little family.

As the old year ended Waddell wrote in his journal: "Thirty-first of December closed the year, the third since the war began. And how many of my boon companions are gone to that bourne from whence no traveler returns. They were full of hope, but not without fears, when we last parted." In his heart of hearts he must have known that the war was lost. But what happened soon afterward must have raised his spirits.

Having crossed the Indian Ocean, on 25 January 1865 the *Shenandoah* entered Port Philip Bay, Melbourne, her flag proudly displayed. Steamers, tugboats and yachts done out in bunting came out to greet them. Flags dipped, cannons boomed and thousands cheered as the *Shenandoah* moved slowly up the channel and dropped anchor. Australia had declared for the South. For days, telegraphs and newspapers had told of their coming. It was rumored that the great Raphael Semmes was aboard. Upon landing, the entire crew were treated as conquering heroes. Everyone, from captain to cabin boy, were given free rides on the railways and trams. The various clubs in Melbourne elected her officers as honorary members. The great Shakespearian actor Barry Sullivan, then playing *Othello,* gave a special performance in honor of the officers of the Confederate steamship *Shenandoah.* One hundred miles away at Ballarat, a red letter day was announced in honor of the *Shenandoah* and her crew. Seven of her officers attended a civic reception there. The whole town came out to greet them. Across the main street on a triumphal arch of flowers a message read, "Welcome to Ballarat." The correspondent of the *Ballarat Star* of Friday, 27 January, wrote an article about them: "I was much struck with the appearance of the crew — a finer looking set of fellows never trod a deck. Captain Waddell, before showing me around his vessel, invited me into his cabin. He is a fine gentlemanly looking man, about thirty five years of age, well set up, frank and polished in his bearing, and evidently very determined. His officers are all young looking men, evidently well educated, cadets of good Southern families. He described the "Shenandoah" as being 'comfortably fitted up, but with no pretensions to luxury or elegance.'"

The honored guests were given a tour of a major gold mine, even descending the shafts to the workings belowground. In the evening a ball was held at Craig's Royal Hotel, which included the most prominent citizens of Ballarat. Responding, an unidentified Confederate officer who attended the ball was quoted as saying, "Every attention that kindness and courtesy could suggest was shown us, and more than one heart beat quicker at such convincing evidence of the existence of sympathy in this country of the Antipodes. Many a gray uniform coat lost its gilt buttons that night, but we saw them again ere we bade a final adieu to Australia, suspended from watch guards depending from the necks of bright eyed women. God bless the gentle women of Melbourne and Ballarat." Even today there are photographs of the *Shenandoah* and her crew displayed in the foyer of Craig's Hotel in Ballarat, just outside of Melbourne.

Amidst all the celebrating there were practicalities that needed to be attended to. The *Shenandoah* had been at sea for 108 days. Upon dropping anchor she was visited by Commander King of Her Majesty's ship *Bombay*. He reported to his superior, Commodore Wiseman: "The crew at present consists of only seventy men, though her proper complement is one hundred and forty. The men almost entirely are stated to be either English or Irish. Captain Waddell informed me that the Shenandoah is fast under canvas, and steams at the rate of thirteen knots; that she is fourteen months old, and was turned into a man-o-war on the ocean. It is suspected that the Shenandoah was lately called the Sea King, and that remains of the old letters are still perceptible; but of that I cannot speak from personal observation. From the paucity [lack of numbers] of her crew at present she cannot be very efficient for fighting purposes."[7]

Waddell sent a note to the Governor of the Colony, Sir Charles Darling, requesting to be allowed to take on coal and make essential repairs. Upon preliminary examination it was subsequently discovered that this might take four weeks. Waddell asked to be allowed to use the government dry dock at Williamstown. The American consul, William Blanchard, naturally objected with some degree of vigor. He presented all the information he could, showing the illegal status of the vessel. As she had never entered a Confederate port she was not entitled to belligerent status. Many of her crew, he maintained, were British, recruited in violation of the law. The consul insisted that she should be detained until a proper investigation could be made. Waddell countered that under the law, a nation could not question the origin of a belligerent warship that had been commissioned by the authority of that belligerent state. In the end Darling agreed to Waddell's request. The governor then wrote to the U.S. consul: "whatever may be the previous history of the Shenandoah, the Government of the Colony is bound to treat her as a ship of war belonging to a belligerent Power."[8]

This naturally did not go down too well with the United States representative. He responded that Britain would be held responsible for the damages already done to American shipping by the *Shenandoah,* and hereafter any damage done if she was allowed to depart from Melbourne. When bullying failed to work, deception, deceit and desertion became the order of the day. Blanchard then announced that Waddell was recruiting men for his crew, in violation of the Foreign Enlistment Act. There were men already taken aboard. Darling was forced to respond to this, and sent members of the police force with a search warrant to search the ship. Waddell refused them permission to board, in that his vessel was a ship of war, and as such, as a nation's own territory, was inviolable. Thwarted, Darling decided on a show of strength, and sent a battalion of militia to the wharf. Waddell responded by declaring his actions to be tantamount to military aggression. In the end Darling backed down and removed his men. Now pressured even further by the U.S. consul, on 7 February 1865, Darling called upon Waddell to name the date of his departure. Waddell regretted that he could not, as repairs were still ongoing. The next week, on the 14th, Darling enquired again, and to his great relief, Waddell informed him that he could proceed to sea by the 19th, but he still had to re-coal and take in stores. Consul Blanchard retorted that this was prevarication, on account of Waddell's recruiting extra crewmen around the streets of Melbourne. At the same time, the consul and his agents were doing their best to get the established crew to desert. Two at least are known to have been induced to desert. One of them, John Williams, claimed in an affidavit that he had cooked for a number of men who had sneaked aboard. Two "witnesses" for the United States consul, Hermann Wicke and F.C. Behucke, also a deserter, then signed affidavits to the effect that at least ten new crew members, including a man named James Davidson, alias "Charley," had been smuggled aboard. When "Charley" and three other men were arrested onshore, they stated to the superintendent of police "that they had been on board a few days unknown to the Captain; and that, as soon as he found they were on board, he ordered them on shore."[9]

The case could not be substantiated that Waddell had been aware of their presence aboard his vessel, before throwing them off. A rumor was then put about, no doubt originating with the consul, that a number of men had been taken aboard who were in reality American soldiers, and when the time was right they would seize control of the *Shenandoah*. This was evidently to put Waddell off recruiting men, and in particular Americans, of whom there were a number in Melbourne. Blanchard then claimed that the *Shenandoah* had taken on more coal than she had been permitted. The coal, 400 tons of it, had been sent out from Liverpool aboard a Confederate tender, the *John Fraser,* named after the founder of the firm of Fraser & Co. of Charleston, the parent company of Fraser, Trenholm & Co. of Liverpool.

Amidst all these claims and counterclaims, the *Shenandoah* sailed at six o'clock on the morning of the 18th of February, much, no doubt, to Darling's relief. By this time he was fed up with the shenanigans of both belligerents. The British counter case in the later "Alabama Claims" neatly sums it up: "The circumstances of her visit and the conduct of her commander, Lieutenant Waddell, during her stay, placed the colonial authorities in a position of no little difficulty and perplexity, in which they seem to have acted with great discretion and vigor, though their conduct has not escaped much invidious comment in the Case of the United States."[10]

After the pilot was dropped beyond the marine league, forty-two men came out of their various hiding places and asked to enlist. It seems highly unlikely, but Lt. Whittle infers that he did not know that they were aboard: "forty-two men, who had stowed themselves away, some in the hollow bowsprit and some in the coal, all where the officers of the ship could not find them came on deck and wanted to enlist. We wanted men after our losses in Melbourne, but we were suspicious, after the intimated plot. The men were black with dirt. We drew them up in a line, took their names and nationality. Thirty-four claimed to be Americans and the other eight of various nationalities. We shipped them all, but watched them closely. They turned out to be good, faithful men."[11]

In addition, a Confederate officer by he name of Blacker (Blackar), from the *Saxonia,* also joined the ship. Below is a list of the new recruits, giving their true nationalities:

ENLISTED AT MELBOURNE

Lieutenant
John Blacker of the *Saxonia,* appointed Captain's Clerk

Petty Officers
Robert Dunning, an Englishman. Captain of Foretop
Thomas Strong, an American. Captain of the Mizzen-top
Charles Cobbey, an Englishman. Gunner's Mate
John James, an Englishman. Carpenter's Mate
John Spring, an Englishman. Captain of the Hold
Ernest W. Burt, an Englishman. Doctor's Steward
James McLaren, a Scotsman. Master-at-Arms
William Smith, an Englishman. Ship's Cook
David Alexander, a Scotsman Corporal of Marines
H.C. Canning, an Englishman. Died 29 October 1865

Firemen
Thomas McLean, a Scotsman. First-class fireman
William Brice, a Scotsman
William Green, an Englishman
William Burgess, an Englishman
Joseph Mullineux, an Englishman
Henry Sutherland, a Scotsman
James Stranth, a Scotsman

Seamen
John Collins, an American
Thomas Foran, an Irishman
Lawrence Kerney, an Irishman
John McDonal, a Scotsman
John Ramsdale, an Englishman
John Kilgower, a Scotsman
Thomas Swanton, an Englishman
John Moss, an Irishman
James Fegan, an Irishman
Samuel Crooks, an Englishman
John Simmes, an Englishman
John Hill, an Irishman
William Hutchinson, an Englishman
Thomas Evans, a Welshman
Charles H. Morton, an American
George H. Gifford, an American
James Ross, a Canadian
John Williams, an English boy
Duke Simmons, a Malay

Marines
Henry Reiley, a Canadian
William Kenyon, an Irishman
Robert Brown, an Englishman

In the papers relating to the Treaty of Washington, two further names are given — Exshaw and Glover — but there are no details regarding first names or nationalities. Both would appear to be English though.

The reality of what had happened was revealed by three of the local Melbourne newspapers, the *Herald,* the *Argus* and the *Age,* a few days later. They concurred in their stories that on the night prior to the *Shenandoah*'s departure, at about nine o'clock, three watermen's boats left the pier and rowed towards the vessel, each boat containing six passengers. A policeman, Constable Minto, who observed it, reported that a man, believed to be an officer from the Confederate ship, in plain clothes, superintended the embarkation. While the policeman went off to report the fact to his superior, three or four more boats were observed leaving the pier and heading for the *Shenandoah*. In this way forty-two men were added to her crew. Before anything could be organized by the authorities, the *Shenandoah* was out of the harbor and well beyond the nautical league.

That very afternoon the rebel ship, with an enlarged crew and in a pugnacious mood, steamed up on a suspected American schooner, further along the coast. As the *Shenandoah* bore down on her quarry, she raised the British ensign. The schooner did the same. She was British, the *Sir Isaac Newton*. The *Shenandoah* peeled away, and returned to her original course, due north.

Skirting the eastern coastline of the Australian continent the *Shenandoah* then headed north, past McAskill Island, and onto the Carolina Islands. The Confederate vessel approached Ponape Island, on the 1st of April, and looked in at the harbor. Four American whalers lay at anchor. The pilot who came out to take them in was a Yorkshire man, Thomas Harrocke. He was a former Australian convict who had served his time. Once in Lea Harbor, Waddell sent off four boats and boarded each vessel. He made prizes of the *Edward Carey* of San Francisco, the *Hector* of New Bedford, the *Pearl* of New London and the *Harvest* from New Bedford, but under false papers as of Honolulu. The papers from this last ship still showed an American register. There was no bill of sale and no change in name. Her captain and crew were American and she was American. From the ships he obtained vital charts showing the location of the whaling grounds most frequently used by American whalers. The ships were then drawn up on a reef beyond the bay, where the local native population were allowed to strip them of anything of value. Waddell then put the vessels, valued collectively at $116,000, to the torch. While they were at Ponape, they were visited by the king of the island, Ish-y-Paw. They wined and dined him, and gave him presents from the whaling ships. He agreed to take the prisoners, 122 in number, along with provisions. Eight men from the former whalers' crews agreed to join the *Shenandoah*.

By now the *Shenandoah* had passed beyond the reach of communication with the outside world. Back in Liverpool, with the inevitable defeat of the Confederate cause, Bulloch grew anxious. Later, when President Davis was taken prisoner and there was no longer a civil government, it was no longer credible for Waddell and his crew to continue their mission as a legitimate act of war. How to contact the ship was the problem Bulloch now faced. He wrote to the former Confederate commissioner J.M. Mason, then residing in the English Confederate enclave of Leamington Spa, in Warwickshire. From 20, Grove Street, Mason replied:

> Dear Sir,
>
> Recalling our late conversation about taking measures to arrest the cruise of the Shenandoah, I think the time has come when it should be attempted, and I know of no other mode than that you suggested, of proposing to the Foreign Office here that the order might be sent through that Department. If you concur, let me hear by note the several points to which the orders should be sent, and send me the form of the order, which, after examining, I will return to you.
>
> The order must of course be sent open to Earl Russell, and therefore worded accordingly. I think it should state that in the present posture of events in the Confederate States, and the difficulty of communicating with any authority there, it had been determined here, and with my full sanction as the representative of the Government, that the war should be discontinued on the ocean. You will know best what order to give as to the disposition of the ship and her materials. On hearing from you I will write to Earl Russell, enclose the orders, and inquire whether his Government will transmit them through their Consuls abroad.
>
> I am, etc.,
>
> J.M. Mason.[12]

Bulloch drew up an appropriate order for the cessation of attacks upon American ships, giving details and dates relating to the ending of the war. Mason submitted it to Russell with a request that copies of it be made and transmitted to Her Majesty's consuls around the world. At the Foreign Office Lord Russell agreed.

Meanwhile the *Shenandoah* continued northwards, sailing past the Ladrone Islands, Los Jardnes, Grampus and Margaret Islands to the west, then eastwards past Camira, Otra and the Marcus islands. They cruised a well-known trade route used by ships sailing from San Francisco and the western shores of South America to Hong Kong and China, but found not a single U.S. flagged ship. Skirting Japan to the west, the *Shenandoah* passed Moukouruski Island and through the Amphitrite Straits of the Kuril Islands and into the Ohkotsk Sea. The days grew longer as they sailed north amidst snowcapped peaks until they reached so far north it became continual day. Off the coast of Kamchatka, on 27 May, they encountered the American whaling ship *Abigail,* out of New Bedford, and commanded by Ebenezer Nye. He had been captured earlier in the war by the *Alabama,* which prompted a member of his crew to reputedly observe lightheartedly of him, "You are more fortunate in picking up Confederate cruisers than whales. I will never again go with you, for if there is a cruiser out, you will find her."

Here at the ends of the earth the last thing they would have expected was a Confederate ship of war. Waddell took prisoner her crew of thirty-five, and transferred them to the hold of the *Shenandoah*. The following day, after taking warm clothing and provisions, and a portable stove for his cabin, he burned the *Abigail.* Now as they sailed along the Siberian coastline and Sakhalin, they experienced thick fogs, pierced by an eerie light. Heavy ice slowed their progress. As they crawled towards Ghifinsi and Tausk bays, the fog lifted and they found themselves in a field of ice as far as the eye could see. The floes rose up to the height of their sails, and they feared being crushed. The timbers of the ship groaned under the pressure. The wind was bitterly cold, turning the rain that now fell into ice that formed a crust everywhere. Ice covered the sails and rigging, producing icicles of great length. If not despair, then certainly concern gripped both crew and prisoners. But then the sun, though low in the northern sky, broke through the cloud, bringing warmth, and raised spirits. As the ice surrounded them loosened, Waddell engaged engines and reversed out into the Bering Sea. In such trying circumstances friendships were made, and fourteen of the *Abigail*'s crew threw their lot in with the *Shenandoah*. Through the Aleutian Islands they sailed and into the whaling grounds. A sail was seen, and pursuit begun. As the *Shenandoah* approached the ship, she raised the Russian colors. When hailed she revealed that she was the *Prince Petropoliski,* on a cruise. Upon closer inspection though, she proved to be an English vessel, the *Robert Downs.* It seems that she was a British spy ship. Whatever her captain chose to call her, she was still a neutral and was permitted to continue on her way. On the 18th of June at St. Lawrence Island, almost at the Bering Straits that separate Russia from Alaska, they were met by Eskimos, who were permitted aboard to trade.

Between 22 and 28 June the crew of the *Shenandoah* captured twenty-four whaling vessels. The first two to be captured were working close together. They were both from New Bedford; the *William Thompson* and the *Euphrates.* As Waddell put a prize crew aboard the *William Thompson,* the *Euphrates* took to her heels. It was imperative to catch her, for if she escaped she would warn the others. After a two hour pursuit she was forced to come to and accept her fate. Waddell made her crew prisoner, stripped her of all essentials, then set her ablaze. Returning to the *William Thompson*, he did the same to her.

From these ships were brought copies of San Francisco newspapers, and in one of these for 17 April, Waddell discovered coverage of correspondence between Generals Grant and Lee, relating to Lee's surrender at Appomattox. Despair gave way to hope, when further on Waddell read that President Davis had moved his headquarters to Danville, Virginia, and announced his intention of prosecuting the war with renewed vigor. So it was not all over.

The *Shenandoah* crossed the international date line. On the morning of that day, Waddell captured the *Milo,* also of New Bedford. He talked to her captain, who revealed that he believed that the war was over. When pressed, he could not confirm definitely that it was so, and in the absence of newspapers of a later date than the 17th, Waddell thought that it might be some sort of trick. He bonded the *Milo,* but took most of her crew as prisoners. Later that day he came across two more ships, working in tandem. As the *Shenandoah* moved towards them, they turned tail and headed into the ice floe to escape. Under sail and steam the *Shenandoah* caught up with one of them, the *Sophia Thornton.* Waddell placed a prize crew aboard her and gave instructions that she was to lie close to the bonded *Milo.* Waddell then began the pursuit of the other vessel, the *Jerah Swift.* Her captain, a man by the name of Williams, was not prepared to give her up if he could help it, and it took a three hour chase before the *Shenandoah* ran her down. Transferring the *Jerah Swift's* crew to the *Shenandoah,* Waddell put her to the torch. Rejoining the other two prizes, Waddell transferred all the prisoners aboard the *Milo,* and set them on a course for San Francisco. The *Sophia Thornton* he set on fire. Later that day Waddell captured the *Susan Abigail,* out of San Francisco. Another newspaper told of the capture of Richmond, but again there was the counter of Jefferson Davis that the war was not over. Three of the *Susan Abigail's* crew joined the *Shenandoah,* which seemed to indicate that they did not believe the war was over either. After burning the whaler, the *Shenandoah* sailed on.

On the 24th of June Waddell captured and burned the *General Williams,* near St. Lawrence Island in the Bering Sea. The 26th was to prove a highly successful day. Just after half past one in the morning, beneath the midnight sun, the lookout aboard the *Shenandoah* espied three becalmed whalers. In short time, the *Nimrod, William C. Nye* and the *Catherine* were captured and put to the torch. Concerned at the large number of prisoners, Waddell did not dare bring them aboard, but put them in their boats and towed them behind his ship. To the north of them the lookout spied three more whalers. Just before noon they too became prizes. They were the barques *General Pike, Isabella* and *Gipsy.* The *General Pike* Wardell bonded, and sent aboard all his prisoners. The other two whalers he burned. Within two days, it was reckoned, Waddell had destroyed or ransomed $253,000 worth of shipping.

The 28th of June was to prove the most successful single day for the *Shenandoah.* Near the narrows of the Bering Strait, Waddell came across eleven American whalers. One of them, the *Brunswick* of New Bedford, was in distress. Her timbers had been stove in by the pressure of an ice floe, and she was in danger of sinking. The others had gathered to take on her oil and crew. In order to prevent them dispersing Waddell ordered the American flag to be raised. He entered the bay and positioned himself so that all of them were covered by his guns. Then he prepared five boats with men and arms. As they moved off to their respective prizes, the Stars and Stripes was lowered and the Confederate flag raised. Ten of the whalers surrendered at once. The captain of the *Favorite* of New Haven gave a brief resistance, but wisely gave in. Waddell bonded two of the vessels, the *James*

CSS *Shenandoah* in Arctic waters. Under Captain Waddell she circumnavigated the world.

Murray and the *Nile*, and put his 336 prisoners onboard for shipping to San Francisco. In a somewhat macabre twist, the *Nile* was spared because her master had died, leaving a widow and two orphans onboard. The dead man's body had been preserved in whisky. Waddell stripped the other vessels of supplies then put them to the torch. They included the *Hillman, Nassau, Brunswick, Isaac Howland, Waverley, Martha, Covington, Favorite* and *Congress*. From their crews he gained a further nine men for the *Shenandoah*. To date Waddell had destroyed 38 vessels valued at $1,361,983.

With no further prizes to be found, and with the many ice floes forming into one enormous ice field, threatening to trap and crush the *Shenandoah*, Waddell set in a course south for St. Lawrence, the island that lies between Russia and Alaska. As he approached the island a dense fog descended, obscuring everything beyond a few yards. Cautiously they proceeded through the massive ice floes, the crew almost blind in this wilderness of white. Heavy rope mats were placed about the prow to give it some protection. Onward they continued, engaging the engines to push an obstructing ice floe before them. Then at last they were out into the open sea. Once more, on the 3rd of July, a heavy fog descended, engulfing them for several days. Navigation by the sun and stars became impossible. Using dead reckoning, Waddell continued south, exiting the Bering Sea by way of the Amukta Passage in the Aleutian necklace of islands. Now in the North Pacific, enjoying the warmth of the sea once more, Waddell set in a southeasterly course to cross the sea-lanes of the eastern Pacific. While still within the Bering Sea Waddell had dreamt up an audacious plan — to attack San Francisco.

From a San Francisco newspaper of 17 April, obtained from the *Susan Abigail*, Waddell discovered that the only Federal warship anchored in the bay was the USS *Saginaw*, commanded by his old shipmate, Commander Charles McDougal. The plan devised by Waddell was to enter the harbor at night, ram, then board the unsuspecting U.S. vessel and take her. Then he proposed to shell the city until she agreed to discuss terms in the shape of a sizeable ransom. Cautiously Waddell proceeded down the western coast of the United States, hoping to fall in with a ship recently out of San Francisco so that he could find out the recent disposition of the Federal Navy in the area. On 2 August 1865, just thirteen days from San Francisco, they fell in with the English barque, *Barracouta*. Sailing Master Irvine S. Bulloch boarded her to examine her papers. Satisfied that she was what she purported to be, Bulloch asked her captain for news of the war.

"What war?" the captain asked.

"The war between the United States and Confederate States," Bulloch replied.

"Why the war has been over since April. What ship is that?" he asked.

"The Confederate steamer Shenandoah," Bulloch replied.[13]

The captain then told Bulloch of the surrender of all the Confederate forces, the capture of President Davis and his cabinet, and the total collapse of the Confederate cause. He provided recent newspapers as confirmation of what he had said. Dejected at this news, Bulloch returned to the *Shenandoah* and informed Waddell and his fellow officers. The crew, bereft of country, bereft of government, found that the newspapers revealed that most of the destruction wrought by them had unwittingly been done after hostilities had ceased. Lincoln's successor, President Johnson, had issued a proclamation of outlawry against them. The newspaper warned that Waddell and his crew would be treated as pirates when captured and summarily executed.

A council of officers was then held to decide what course to pursue. Some advocated sailing to Melbourne or New Zealand, others suggested Valparaiso, Chile, which was nearer. As captain, Waddell had the final say, and he decided on Liverpool. From England they had come — to England they would return. The journey would be extremely hazardous. The crew of the *Shenandoah* were then called aft, and Waddell addressed them. They responded with three cheers to him. He then ordered the guns to be dismounted and stowed below in the hold of the ship. The ports were closed and the funnels painted white, so that to all appearances she was a merchant ship once more.

The following day, 3 August, the U.S. Pacific fleet under Rear Admiral George F. Pearson was dispersed to locate and destroy the *Shenandoah*, if they should find her. In the Atlantic, the newly re-formed Brazilian Squadron, under Rear Admiral Gordon, whose station ranged from the river Amazon right down to the Straits of Magellan, were also put on the alert. On 16 September the *Shenandoah* rounded Cape Horn and entered the South Atlantic. Now again she faced gigantic icebergs, as she journeyed on through treacherous waters. On up through the Atlantic she continued, well out from the coast, crossing the equator, midway between South America and Africa, on 11 October. As she crossed the trade routes she fell in with many other vessels, but continued on under sail, barely acknowledging their presence, ever aware of the increased danger she faced from Federal warships. On 25 October, 500 miles southeast of the Azores, way out in the distance, but on a converging course, a steamship was seen. Waddell did not change course for fear of attracting her attention. It would be dark soon. He ordered the propeller to be lowered to slow her down, so that the other ship would pass before they reached the other's cruise path. When darkness fell they were barely three miles distant of one another. Waddell ordered up steam, and a slight correction in course to take them away. It was the first time that she had been under steam since they had crossed the equator in the Pacific Ocean, a journey of over 13,000 miles. The other ship, it would seem, was the USS *Saranac* under Captain Walker. She had sighted them, but had no reason to be suspicious. The *Shenandoah* was believed to be still in the Pacific.

On 5 November 1865, the *Shenandoah* skirted the southeast coast of Ireland, passed Tuscar Rock and its lighthouse, and entered the St. George's Channel. It was the first land they had sighted in 122 days, after sailing 23,000 miles. Lt. Whittle, the executive officer, gave praise to Irvine S. Bulloch, half brother of James D. Bulloch, for his navigational skills in bringing them to their destination. The voyage of the *Shenandoah* had been quite remarkable. She had been the only Confederate vessel to circumnavigate the globe; she had visited every continent, save Antarctica, covering 58,000 statute miles. There was not a single death as regards hostilities. In total she had captured 38 vessels; 32 were destroyed, 6 were bonded.

Up the Channel the *Shenandoah* sailed and into the Irish Sea. Approaching Anglesey, with Snowdonia and the Welsh mountains lying beyond, a pilot boat came out to meet them. The pilot asked them to show their flag. Whittle informed him that they had no flag; they had no nation. The pilot informed them that he could not board the ship if it had no flag. Whittle consulted with Waddell. His response was to order that the Confederate flag be raised from the masthead for the last time The pilot recognized it, and called for a line to be thrown. Upon boarding, he confirmed what the captain of the *Barracouta* had said. The war was over.

On the morning of the 6th of November, he took them into the Mersey, It was thirteen months after the departure of the *Sea King* from the Thames, and six months, bar four days, since the war had ended. By Captain Waddell's order, the pilot was directed to place the *Shenandoah* alongside H.B.M. ship *Donegal*, Captain Paynter, R.N., commanding, and her anchor was dropped. Soon after, a lieutenant from the *Donegal* went on board to inspect her papers and learn her name. He informed Waddell officially that the war had ended. The Confederacy had been defeated. At 10 o'clock on the morning of 6 November 1865, the last Confederate flag was lowered, and the last Confederate vessel, the CSS *Shenandoah*, was surrendered to the Royal Navy. Waddell handed a letter to the lieutenant, to be forwarded to Lord Russell. It gave details of their cruise. The point that Waddell stressed was that he was unaware, or rather lacked confirmation, that the war was over when he and his men attacked the whalers in June. Failure to prove this would undoubtedly lead to him and his men being tried for piracy, the punishment for which was death. Later that morning the gunboat *Goshawk* was lashed alongside the *Shenandoah*.

The *Liverpool Mercury* for Tuesday 7 November 1865 reported the arrival of the vessel:

11. The Shenandoah

The Confederate Cruiser
Shenandoah in the Mersey.

Considerable excitement was caused on "Change" yesterday morning by circulation of the report that the Confederate cruiser Shenandoah, of whose exploits among the American whalers in the North Pacific so much has been heard, was passed about 8 o'clock by the steamer Douglas at anchor at the bar of Victoria Channel, apparently waiting for high water. By many the report was discredited, it being thought that those on board the Douglas were in error, and had mistaken some other craft for the celebrated ex-Confederate cruiser. At half past ten however, all doubts on the point were set at rest, with the Shenandoah steaming up the Victoria Channel with the Palmetto flag flying from her masthead.

The proceedings of this cruiser have caused much anxiety among commercial men. After Richmond was taken, and when the Government of the Confederate States was considered a thing of the past, Captain Waddell startled those who trusted their merchandise on board American ships, by misbelieving, or affecting to misbelieve, that the Confederate States had been broken up; and continued his depredations upon peaceful merchantmen. This conduct caused much irritation among the American merchants and ship owners, and one or two of the fleetest ships in the United States navy were sent in pursuit of the Shenandoah.

She however succeeded in eluding the vigilance of her pursuers, and the last that was heard of her whereabouts was that she was off St. Lawrence in the Arctic Sea. And that in that locality she had destroyed 10 whalers, most of which had cargoes of oil, and were bound for the United States. She was then steering in a southerly direction, and there can be little doubt that she was tracing her course towards England.

The article then gives a brief history of the *Sea King/Shenandoah*, and concluded:

At the present juncture, when so many knotty points of international law are at issue between this Government and the United States, and when the maintenance of amicable relations between

The ***Shenandoah*** anchors in the Mersey and surrenders to the British. From her mast was lowered the last Confederate flag of the Civil War. (***Illustrated London News***, Supplement, 18 November 1865)

the two countries is so much to be desired, and is so essential to the welfare of both, the absence of the Shenandoah from this port was more to be desired than her presence. There can be little doubt that after the necessary formalities are gone through, the vessel will be handed over to the United States authorities. However, some question may arise as to the detention of her crew, a subject that may lead to misunderstanding that had better been avoided.

It is understood that a representative of the American Government at this port has been, since the arrival of the vessel, in communication with the customs authorities. It is also stated, that certain commercial houses, who were said to be deeply interested in the success of the Confederacy, were engaged yesterday in making enquiries in regard to the Shenandoah.

Adams, the United States minister, was informed by Consul Dudley at Liverpool of the arrival of the *Shenandoah* at the port. He then wrote to the British foreign secretary requesting the securing of the vessel with a view to her being delivered to the United States in due course. Adams' letter, with that of Waddell and other documents relating to the *Shenandoah*, was referred to the law officers of the Crown on 7 November. They gave their advice: "We think it will be proper for her Majesty's Government, in compliance with Mr. Adams' request, to deliver up to him, on behalf of the Government of the United States, the ship in question, with her tackle, apparel, etc., and all captured chronometers or other property capable of being identified as prize-of-war, which may be found on board her.... With respect to the officers and crew ... if the facts stated by Captain Waddell are true, there is clearly no case for any prosecution on the grounds of piracy in the courts of this country, and we presume that her Majesty's Government are not in possession of any evidence which could be produced before any court or magistrate for the purpose of contravening the statement or of showing that the crime of piracy has, in fact, been committed."[14]

On 9 November the *Liverpool Mercury* reported:

[A]bout 6 o'clock last night a telegram was received from Government by Captain Paynter, of her Majesty's ship Donegal, to whom the Shenandoah was surrendered, that the whole of the officers and crew, who were not British subjects were to be immediately paroled. Captain Paynter immediately proceeded to the Rock Ferry slip, and applied for a steamboat. The Rock Ferry steamer Bee was placed at his disposal by Mr. Thwaites, in which he immediately proceeded alongside the Shenandoah. Captain Paynter went on board and communicated to the officers the object of his visit. The crew were mustered on the quarterdeck by the officers of the ship, the roll book was brought out, and the names of the men called out as they occurred. As each man answered to his name he was asked what countryman he was. In not one instance did any of them acknowledge to be British citizens. Many nations were represented among them, but the majority claimed to be natives of the Southern States of America or "Southern citizens." Several of those however, who purported to be Americans, had an unmistakable Scotch accent, and seemed more likely to have hailed from the banks of the Clyde than the Mississippi. Captain Paynter informed the men that by order of the Government they were all paroled, and might proceed at once to shore. This intelligence was received by the men with every demonstration of joy, and they seemed to be delighted at the prospect of leaving the craft in which they had hoped to be able to assist the Southern Confederacy. They commenced to pack up their bedding and other articles as fast as possible, and conveyed on board the Bee, which was to take them to the landing stage. Before leaving the vessel, however, they gave three lusty cheers for Captain Waddell, their late commander. Captain Waddell, in feeling terms, acknowledged the compliment, and said that he hoped the men would always behave themselves, as brave sailors ought to do. The men then went aboard the Bee, and were conveyed to the landing stage. This separated the Shenandoah and her crew, and the vessel now rides at anchor in the Sloyne in charge of some men from the Donegal, under the command of Lieutenant Cheek.

12

Blockade-Runners

On 19 April 1861, just one week after the assault on Fort Sumter, United States president Abraham Lincoln announced the blockade of the Southern ports from South Carolina to Texas. Fifty Federal vessels with steam transport and 20,000 men were initially allocated to the task. In reality half of the 90 vessels listed in the U.S. Naval Register of 1861 were, upon their own admission, either unfit for sea or awaiting decommissioning. It was hardly sufficient to control 3,500 miles of coastline. On 26 April, within days of the announcement, the blockade was proved to be ineffectual when the USS *Commerce*, lying off Havre de Grace, Maryland, gave chase to, but failed to catch, a vessel laden with a cargo of arms and ammunition which safely ran into port.

News of the blockade reached England on 3 May. Ten days later, on the 13th, Queen Victoria announced British neutrality. The Act of Neutrality also forbade British subjects from attempting to break the blockade "lawfully and effectually established." The emphasis was very much on the word "effectually." In Liverpool the firm of Fraser, Trenholm & Co., now acting as bankers for the Confederate States, decided to prove that the blockade was no more than a "paper" blockade, ineffective, and therefore illegal. The company, a subsidiary of cotton traders John Fraser & Co. of Charleston, had been established at Liverpool in 1860, with Mr. Charles K. Prioleau as resident partner. The parent company had five ships, *Susan G. Owens, Eliza Bonsall, Gondar, Emily St. Pierre* and *John Fraser*. In normal times, each of their ships was capable of carrying between 3,500 and 4,000 bales of cotton between Charleston and Liverpool. Following the outbreak of the war this trade effectively ceased.

In Liverpool, Prioleau purchased three additional steamships, *Bermuda, Victoria* and *Adelaide*. His intention was to load these with arms and run the blockade in the furtherance of the Confederate cause. An experienced coastal pilot, Captain Penn Peck, was sent for to take the first ship into Savannah The ship that Prioleau chose for the first run was one of his new vessels, the *Bermuda,* commanded by Captain Eugene Tessier. She was loaded at West Hartlepool, County Durham, with 18 rifled cannon, one 32-pounder and two 168-pounder Lancaster guns with carriages and equipment, including powder and shot, 6,500 Enfield rifles, 200,000 cartridges, 60,000 pairs of army boots, 20,000 blankets, 180 barrels of gunpowder, and medical stores including morphine and quinine. The vessel sailed from West Hartlepool in August, and in an uninterrupted voyage breached the blockade, arriving safely at Savannah on 18 September 1861. A few days later she ran out of there with a large cargo of cotton, valued at $1million, eventually arriving safely back in Liverpool on 23 January 1862.

The example that Prioleau had set stimulated interest throughout Great Britain and Europe, and saw the establishment of a number of new companies devoted exclusively to blockade-running. Primarily, blockade-runners were divided into two groups: patriots and profiteers. By and large the British blockade runners were in it for the money. In addition there was sometimes a combination of both. On behalf of the Confederate government, Major Caleb Huse, then residing at 38, Clarendon Rd., Notting Hill, London, made arrangements with the Mercantile Trading Company of London for an advance of £300,000 in exchange for which the company was given one third of the cargo space aboard Confederate blockade-runners, running both into and out of the South.

Another Confederate agent, Charles Lemprieu, formerly seconded to London, but then based at Havana in Cuba wrote to a former business associate in London, solicitor George Burgess, concerning the purchase of armaments to be run into the Southern ports, by way of Cuba:

Havana, November 24, 1861.

Dear Burgess: Will any client of yours take a contract under the following copy? There is everything open here, and the return money in cotton will pay everyone well. I am on my way to Mexico, and shall be back here in January, when I could attend to any certification your client might require. I am able to recommend the present holders of this letter.

Charles Lemprieu.

George Burgess Esq.,
71, Lincoln Inn Fields, London.[1]

Enclosed was a list of requirements and prices to be paid by Major J. Gorgas, chief of ordnance for the Confederate government:

CONFEDERATE STATES OF AMERICA

War Department, Ordnance Office,

Richmond, Va., July 16, 1861.

Sir: This bureau will receive from you any or all of the following articles at any point within the Confederate States, upon the proper inspection and at the rates specified:

From 50,000 to 150,000 pounds rifle powder, 250,000 to 350,000 pounds musket powder, 50,000 to 150,000 pounds cannon powder, for which they will pay 30 cents, or $33\frac{1}{3}$ per cent above cost and charges; from 10,000 to 100,000 Minnie [sic] muskets, at $30, or $33\frac{1}{3}$ per cent above cost and charges; from 10,000 to 100,000 Enfield rifles, at $30 , or $33\frac{1}{3}$ per cent above cost and charges; 2,000 artillery sabers, at $10, or $33\frac{1}{3}$ per cent above cost and charges; 2,000 Colt's navy or army pistols, at $30, or $33\frac{1}{3}$ per cent above cost and charges; 200 carboys nitric acid, strong, at $33\frac{1}{3}$ per cent above cost and charges; 20,000 pounds block tin, in pigs, at 50 cents, or $33\frac{1}{3}$ per cent above cost and charges; 1,000 boxes common tin, larger size at $33\frac{1}{3}$ per cent above cost and charges.

Payment will be made either upon the certificate of the inspecting officer or quartermaster, or, in the absence of either the certificate of the custom-house officer of the Confederate Government at the point where the articles are delivered, or upon such certificates of delivery after inspection and approval. The Department will pay to the value of deliveries at New Orleans such drafts as may be drawn by you on the assistant treasurer of the Confederate States to cover such purchases and deliveries.

Signed, with the approval of the President.

J. Gorgas,
Major and Chief of Ordnance, Confederate States.[2]

The blockade was always "imperfectly maintained," as the British commissioners at the subsequent Arbitration of Geneva put it. Throughout most of the war the United States Navy employed a variety of vessels, most of them inadequate for purpose. It was inevitable that commercial blockade-running should spring up alongside the Confederate runners, carried on by speculators and investors. Enterprising British companies were established whose sole purpose was to make money out of the blockade. There was nothing anti–American in it, it was simply money — and it was there to be made. Successful blockade-runners, it was estimated, could make a 700 percent profit per trip (George McHenry, *Approaching Cotton Crisis,* Otley & Co., 1863). For the enterprise these new companies bought up fast coastal, cross-channel and river steamers. The *Times* (18 Sept. 1862) records one such transaction: "The favorite and crack steamer 'Iona' was withdrawn from her station between Glasgow and Ardishaig on Monday last, the beautiful saloon steamer 'Fairy' taking her place. We are told that this withdrawal is caused by the 'Iona' having been sold to the Confederates in America. It is also rumored that the fine Belfast paddle steamer 'Giraffe' and the West Highland steamer 'Clydesdale' have also been disposed of to the same parties."

George Trenholm, banker to the Confederacy. The Liverpool branch of his firm organized and equipped ships to run the blockade.

It is said that 111 ships were bought up for blockade-running in Britain; these ships were a total of over 60,000 gross tons, and cost £1.7million. These ships in the hands of private speculators were loaded with anything that would sell — arms and ammunition, coal, machinery and general merchandise, including luxury goods. Instead of running directly through the blockade, as the *Bermuda* had done, they sailed for the British colonial ports of Bermuda, the Bahamas, Halifax, Nova Scotia, and the neutral ports of Spanish controlled Cuba. These served as staging posts to the South. Here these speculators rented or bought warehouses, established offices, and made contact with Confederate purchasing agents. The colonial newspapers of the day, at Nassau and St. George, are full of advertisements, offering for public sale the cargoes of vessels arrived, or expected to arrive, from various British and French ports.

At the receiving ports, cargoes might be broken up for transshipment to various Southern ports; additional cargoes were taken aboard, and then under the cover of dark, their ships painted gray, to make them more difficult to see. Burning Welsh anthracite coal that produced little or no little smoke, the runners made the dash through the blockade to Charleston, Savannah or Wilmington. At the British ports the American consuls kept a close watch on likely blockade-runners and forwarded their names to the naval secretary of state. Gideon Welles, in a letter to Commander G. Gansvoort, patrolling off the Florida coast, mentions that "among the vessels that have been reported as having arms, munitions of war, etc., and as having sailed from Europe with the intention of violating the blockade or throwing their cargoes into the Southern States by transshipments, are the steamers, *Julia, Usher, Bahama, Malita, Sylph, Stanley, Leonard, Columbia, Merrimac, Memphis, Scotia, Herald, Sophia, Phoebe, Ann, Tubal Cain, Southwick, Economist, Minho, Londona* and *Adela.*"

In February 1862 the *Bermuda* again sailed from Liverpool, with a cargo of arms

A cartoon from *Harper's Weekly*, regarding the blockade. John Bull (England) is saying, "Looks like a good blockade." In reality it was quite ineffectual: 5,389 fast steamers, most of them British, breached it.

and ammunitions, but under a new captain, Charleston-born Charles W. Westendorff. Her destination was Nassau, via Bermuda. On the morning of 27 April, out at sea, she was stopped by the United States steamer *Mercedita*, who put a shot across her bows. A prize crew was put aboard her and she was taken into Philadelphia for adjudication. In her hold was a contraband cargo including a battery of 7 fieldpieces, with carriages and accoutrements, a number of heavier rifled cannon, 42,720 pounds of powder in barrels, 70 barrels of cartridges, and over 600 cases of shells. The case put by her owners in defense was to the effect that she was a British ship, owned by a British subject, laden in Liverpool by British merchants, and bound for Bermuda, a British colony. From there her captain had been given directions to proceed to Nassau, another British port. It was while she was sailing in a direct line between the two islands, some 415 miles from the nearest stretch of American coast, and well beyond the blockade, that she was captured. The United States Attorney contended that the journey to Nassau was merely a pretense. The cargo aboard her, arms and ammunitions, was destined for the rebels, and was to be discharged at Nassau for transshipment to Charleston. This was how the United States district court sitting in admiralty also saw it. The *Bermuda* was adjudicated to be a prize. Her name and previous history, detailed in her ship's log, was very much against her. The vessel was confiscated and eventually sold to the United States Navy Department.

The *Bermuda's* old captain, Eugene Tessier, was now in charge of Fraser, Trenholm's newest vessel, the *Bahama*. In addition, the British-based company had also purchased two other vessels, the *Melita* and the *Economist*. The *Economist* was dispatched to Hamburg in Germany to meet with Major Caleb Huse, the Confederacy's procurement agent in Europe. He had been sent to England at the outbreak of the war. Now here in Hamburg once more, his latest purchase, 100,000 rifles and ten field artillery batteries complete with harness, awaited shipment to the South. This consignment was so vital that Charles M. Fauntleroy, executive officer aboard the CSS *Nashville*, was seconded to take command of the *Economist*. The blockade was successfully run, and on 14 March 1862, the *Economist* arrived at the port of Charleston. This equipment was unloaded and dispatched to the armies in the field, which led directly to Confederate successes at Seven Pines and Chickahominy. At Charleston, the cotton aboard Bulloch's entrapped *Fingal* was transferred to the *Economist*, which once again ran the blockade and sailed for Liverpool, bringing with her the first cargo of cotton dispatched on the Confederate government's account.

Equally successful was the British blockade-runner steamship *Kate*[3] commanded by Captain Thomas Lockwood, which had run the blockade several times. On the night of Saturday, 6 April 1862, she ran into Charleston with a cargo of 1,000 barrels of gunpowder, plus rifles and pistols and accoutrements for 10,000 men. The next morning every single wagon and cart that could be discovered was pressed into the services of the Confederacy to haul the *Kate*'s cargo down to the rail depot for dispatch to General Johnson's army camped not far from the little wooden church in Tennessee known as Shiloh.

A month later, in May 1862, the *Bahama* again left Hamburg with a cargo of arms, and four 7-inch rifled guns, intended as armament for the commercial raider *Florida*. She put in at Nassau, in the Bahamas, arriving there on 7 June. Arriving there about the same time, aboard the *Melita*, laden with arms and munitions, was Captain Raphael Semmes, Lt. John Kell and Surgeon Francis L. Galt, all formerly of the CSS *Sumter*. Also here at the same time was successful blockade-runner Lt. John N. Maffitt, C.S.N., soon to be given command of the *Florida*. They all found rooms at the Victoria Hotel.

Nassau, New Providence, one of the Bahama Islands, was a British possession, barely 200 miles from the coast of Florida. By 21 June 1861, as British government dispatches reveal, it had became an important staging post for blockade-runners, both Confederate and British. The Confederacy established an agency here under Mr. Lewis Heyliger, and Fraser, Trenholm & Co. used the commercial services of the island firm of Adderley & Co. to further its aims. Commander Gansevoort of the USS *Adirondack* observed as follows:

> [N]early the whole population is in open and notorious sympathy with the rebels. Steamers in large numbers have arrived here from England loaded with arms and munitions of war, which are trans-shipped in some cases into vessels bound to the Southern ports; in others the goods are landed; in others they remain in the vessels in which they came from England. All the warehouses in town, and many private houses even, are stored with these goods. In the face of open day, in the presence of the authorities of every degree, and necessarily by their knowledge and consent,

guns and munitions of war, marked "C. S. A." and known by everybody to be the property of the rebels are hauled through the streets and put on board steamers notoriously bound to run the blockade. No concealment is made or attempted.[4]

Semmes confirms Gansevoort's description, and adds to it:

[Nassau] had already put on the air of a commercial city; its fine harbor being thronged with shipping, and its warehouses, wharves and quays filled to repletion with merchandise. All was life, bustle and activity. Ships were constantly arriving and depositing their cargoes, and light-draft steamers, Confederate and English, were as constantly reloading these cargoes and running them into the ports of the Confederate States. The success which attended many of these little vessels is surprising. Some of them made their voyages as regularly as mail packets, running with impunity, through a whole fleet of the enemy's steamers.... During my enforced delay at Nassau ... I amused myself, watching from windows, with the aid of an excellent glass, the movements of the blockade runners. One of these vessels went out, and another returned, every two or three days; the returning vessel always bringing us late newspapers from the Confederacy.[5]

The United States government quickly became aware of the significance of the Bahamas as an entrepôt for the Confederacy. A semi-blockade of Nassau by the Federal navy was established as early as 1861. How successful it was is summed up in a report from Commander A.G. Clary of the USS *Tioga*: "On the 17th [May 1863] chased a large sidewheel steamer, painted white, with one mast, running him to the south-east at night, and, as he had been steering N.N.E., took the back track, thinking I must head him by daylight. Failing to discover him, but made another steamer standing to the eastward, overhauling this fellow fast, when within 4 or 5 miles of her broke all the blower belts in succession (making two during chase). Gave up the chase.... The large white steamer that had been seen passing South West Point of Bahama is the Wm. L. Hughes, too fast for anything out here except the Vanderbilt. She does not hesitate to leave Nassau in open day."[6]

British-flagged vessels were regularly pursued and, if slow enough, they were boarded — within the Bahama channels. There were successes. The U.S. consul at Nassau, Seth C. Hawley, in a letter to secretary of state Seward, observed in June 1863 that he was aware of 28 vessels that had run or attempted to run the blockade since March of that year. Of these, 13 had not been successful. While the proportion of losses seemed too large to allow the business to be profitable, this view is deceptive. While there were losses over the five year period 1861–65, over 85 percent of the blockade-runners were successful:

Year	Attempts	Successful Attempts	Unsuccessful Attempts	Success %
1861	3,579	3,465	112	96.8
1862	858	568	290	66.2
1863	1,003	731	272	72.9
1864	723	522	201	72.2
1865*	153	103	50	67.3
Total	6,316	5,389	925	85.3[7]

*1 Jan–10 May 1865.

Second in importance to Nassau as a transshipment entrepôt was the town of St. George, Bermuda, some 700 miles off the coast of North Carolina. Here at what was to become the Globe Hotel in King's Square, Confederate agent Major Norman S. Walker set up his office. By 1862 he was joined by a second agent, Mr. S.G. Porter. Bulloch writes of Walker and his fellow agents in Nassau and Havana:

> The Confederate Government was represented at Bermuda, Nassau and Havana by three gentlemen of great energy, industry, and business capacity. Major N.S. Walker, after serving in the field during the campaign which resulted in the repulse of General McClellan from the advance upon Richmond in 1862, was sent to act as the representative of the War Department at Bermuda ... [and] the labor of receiving and forwarding supplies for every branch of the Government was soon heaped upon him. They [the three agents] had control and management of all the public business at their respective stations. Their office was to receive the supplies shipped from Europe, and then forward them to the blockaded port, and that included the supervision of the blockade runners, the distribution of pilots, the arrangements for keeping up the large quantity of coals required for the service; and there was much correspondence and much financing to meet the necessary expenditure.[8]

Havana, the capital of Cuba, was also an important entrepôt for the Confederacy. An agency was established there very soon after the outbreak of the war, under Major Charles J. Helm. The United States' response to its presence and its activities was perhaps not as proactive as it might have been. Angrily, on 9 November 1861, R.W. Welch, an American citizen, protested at the freedom enjoyed by blockade-runners and the lack of a strong Federal presence: "[S]everal rebel vessels are loading for southern ports ... [and] 40,000 stand arms [have] left yesterday and today. Why this place is left without a single steam vessel of war is unaccountable, as it certainly is the most important point upon the coast of the United States, and hardly a day passes that one could not be useful; a single fast steamer might be dispatched, and, no doubt, would intercept one or more of the rebel vessels constantly arriving at and departing from Havana everyday."[9]

Unbeknownst to Welch, one week earlier U.S. naval secretary Gideon Welles had already set the wheels in motion for a closer investment of Cuba. He ordered the USS *Santiago de Cuba,* commanded by Captain Daniel B. Ridgely, to sail for the Spanish island. In the preamble of his letter, he wrote as follows: "In view of ... the reported increasing intercourse between the rebel States and the island of Cuba, it has become a matter of imperative necessity that a war steamer should be stationed at or near Havana to protect legitimate commerce and suppress communication and traffic with or by the insurgents."

One ship alone, though, was insufficient to watch the coast of Cuba. The day after his arrival at Havana, Ridgely was writing back to Welles that three schooners, under the British flag and laden with contraband, had already eluded him. On 13 March 1863 he wrote of two steamers that had left Havana the previous night to run the blockade, one into the Mississippi, the other further up the coast at Sabine River, Louisiana. Both had returned safely with cargoes of cotton.

Halifax, Nova Scotia, was the fourth recognized entrepôt for the South. The Confederacy established an agency here, very early on in the war, under Benjamin Wier. Confederate commander Matthew F. Maury, there in November 1862, described Halifax: "This is a place of 25 or 30,000 inhabitants. They are strongly 'secesh' here. The Confederate flag has been flying from the top of the hotel all day, in honor I am told of our arrival. Hand organs ground out Dixie all day under the window...."[10]

Near the end of the war, in November 1864, Lt.-Commander Harris, of the USS *Yantic,* visited Halifax. He found in the harbor "at anchor two blockade runners, the Old Dominion and Charlotte, with valuable cargoes, the former all ready to sail.... Halifax swarms with secessionists and their sympathizers, and our arrival, I understand, has caused great excitement among them; in fact, after anchoring I was welcomed by jeers and remarks that certainly could not be construed into anything complimentary. As the twenty-four hour rule established by the proclamation of Earl Russell is still in force, and although the officials seemed disposed to place the most liberal construction upon it, I deemed my presence there longer unnecessary, and left ... on the morning of the 3rd."[11]

Initially blockade-running was carried out by Southerners; but by 1862, with the rising price of cotton, it began to attract British blockade runners. For the purpose of this trade it became necessary to procure or construct suitable vessels, differing internally and externally from ships employed in ordinary trade. A new kind of steam vessel, of four to six hundred tons, with low side-wheels, began to appear. They were small, rakish, of graceful lines, with slanting telescopic funnels that could be lowered close to the deck. These vessels were slick and slippery and of light draft. The hull, which rose only a few feet out of the water, was painted dull gray so that it could hardly be seen by daylight beyond two hundred yards. The forward deck was constructed in the form known as "turtle-back," to enable the vessel to plough through heavy seas. Their engines were realigned below water level, or with coal bunkers constructed on either side as protection. They were fast and bore such names as *Lynx*, *Badger*, *Fox*, *Ferret* and *Greyhound*—names indicative of cunning and speed.

Of the owners of this new breed of blockade-runners, Consul Morse in London wrote to Charles Francis Adams, U.S. minister to England, on 24 December 1862:

> The ownership of these steamers, the cargoes they carry out, and the manner of conducting the trade, is a question of much interest to Americans. During the early stages of the war the trade was carried on principally by agents sent over from the Confederate States, aided by a few mercantile houses and active sympathizers in this country.... But by far the largest portion of the trade, with perhaps the exception of that in small arms, is now, and for a long time has been, under the management and control of British merchants. It is carried on principally by British capital, in British ships, and crosses the Atlantic under the protection of the British flag.... There are good reasons for believing that a large proportion of the supplies more recently sent to the aid of the insurgents has been sent by merchants on their own account. Several will join together to charter a steamer, and make up a cargo independent of all contractors, each investing as much in the enterprise as he may deem expedient, according to his zeal in the rebel cause, or his hope of realizing profit from the speculation.... Both steamers and cargoes are often, if not generally, insured in England "to go to America with liberty to run the blockade."[12]

Known blockade-running companies included Fraser, Trenholm & Co. of Liverpool, M.G. Klingender & Co. (a subsidiary of Fraser, Trenholm), Charles H. Read & Co. of Liverpool, Crenshaw & Co., also of Liverpool, Alexander Collie of Manchester (owners of 20 blockade-runners, including the *Giraffe*, later renamed the *Robert E. Lee*), the Anglo-Confederate Trading Co. of London, the Albion Trading Co., the Universal Trading Co., Isaac, Campbell & Co. of London, the Steamship Pet Co. of Teeside, the European Trading Co., the Chicora Exporting Co., and the Mercantile Trading Co., London. There were many more, their names now long forgotten—companies got up by speculators to make money from America's terrible civil war.

Of the many companies that built the vessels that ran the blockade, the principal shipyards were on the Clyde, Mersey, Tees, Tyne, Wear, and Thames. Smaller companies existed too, such as Harvey & Co. of Hayle in Cornwall, who built the *Cornubia*, later renamed *Lady Davis*. In some cases companies can be matched to blockade-runners, but in many cases this is not possible, often because of the change in name of a vessel.

Clyde

On the Clyde there are known to have been eight shipyards involved in the construction of blockade-runners. Barclay Curle & Co. of Glasgow built the runners *Emma, Emma II, Gertrude, Minnie* and *Emily*. Caird & Co. Ltd. of Greenock built the *Lord Clyde* (later renamed *A.D. Vance*), *Lord Gough, City of Petersburg, Mary & Ella* and *Hattie*. William Denny & Bros. of Dumbarton built the *Memphis, Japan* (better known as the *Georgia* under Lt. Maury), the *Ella, Caroline, Emily,* and *Yangtze* (*Brasil/Enterprise*), and the *Tientsin,* alias the *Adventure/Imogene*. For Commander Bulloch, Denny's built the *Ajax* and the *Hercules,* proposed to be renamed the *Olustre* and the *Vicksburg* by naval secretary Mallory.

Scott & Co. of Greenock built a number of blockade-runners, giving them names based on the novels of Walter Scott. These include the *Kenilworth, Marmion, Talisman, Red Gauntlet, Ivanhoe* and *P.S. Constance*. William Simons & Co. constructed the *Mary Bowers, Stormy Petrel, Ada* and *Julia* at their Renfrew shipyard. Alexander Stephens & Sons Ltd. of Glasgow built the *Dare, Fergus* and the *Sea King,* which achieved international fame as the commercial cruiser *Shenandoah*.

J. & G. Thomson/John Brown & Co. Ltd. of Clydebank were makers of the *Giraffe,* later renamed the *Robert E. Lee,* as well as the *Wild Rover,* the *Jupiter,* Commander Bulloch's *Fingal,* the *Lilian, Little Hattie, Iona, Iona II,* and the *Emma Henry*. Todd & McGregor of Glasgow built the *Jupitere* and the *Alliance*.

Other known Clydeside-built blockade-runners include[13]:

Adela	*Cornubia*	*General McKenzie*	*Lord Raglan*	*Scotia*
Agnes E. Fry	(*Lady Davis*)		*Mary*	*Spunkie*
Alice (*Sirius*)	*Dare*	*Georgina*	*Mary Ann*	*Stag*
Amelia	*Dawn*	*Gertrude*	*Matilda*	*Star*
Amy	*Diamond*	*Granite City*	*Maude*	*Susan Beine*
Anna Bell	*Dieppe*	*Greyhound*	*Campbell*	*Susana Mail*
Antona	*Dolphin*	*Hawk*	*Memphis*	*Tartar*
Armstrong	*Edith*	*Helen Denny*	*Minho*	*Thistle*
Banshee II	*Ella*	*Herald*	*Neptune*	*Tristram*
Beatrice	*Elsie*	*Imogene*	*Nola*	*Shandy*
Blenheim	*Emily*	*Juno*	*Pearl*	*Tubal Cain*
Britannia	*Emily II*	*Katie Dale*	*Princess*	*Tuscar*
Caroline	*Evelyn*	*Laurel*	*Queen of the Clyde*	*Venus*
Charlotte	*Falcon*	*Leesburgh*		*Victory*
Columbia	*Fanny* (*Orion*)	*Lee Bonny*	*Ranger*	*Virgin*
(*Memphis*)	*Flamingo*	*Leopold*	*Roe*	*Vulture*
Condor	*Florence*	*Let Her Rip*	*Rose*	*Wave Queen*
Constance	*Florrie*	(*Victoria*)	*Rothesay Castle*	*Wave Queen II*
Coquette	*Gem*	*Little Ada*		
Corinth	*General Havelock*	*Little Hattie*	*Rouen*	
		Lizard	*Ruby*	

In a report of 27 Feb. 1864, to naval secretary Gideon Welles, Commander Preble, of the USS *St. Louis,* anchored off Funchal, Madeira, lists some of the above, then actually engaged in running the blockade:

> Sir,
>
> The following English [*sic*] Clyde-built steamers, supposed blockade runners, have recently coaled at this port and cleared at the date for the destination named:

January 4 — Steamer Florrie, for Nassau.
January 6 — Steamer Druid, for Nassau.
January 10 — Steamer Rose, for Nassau.
January 31— Steamer Little Ada, for Nassau.
February 11— Steamer Albion, for Trinidad.
February 26 — Screw Steamer Greyhound, side-wheel steamer North Heath, for Nassau.

These vessels, having proper clearances, can not be interfered with out here.... I have thought it proper to make this communication, that our cruisers on the blockade may be on the alert.[14]

The Clyde-built blockade-runner *Lizzie*. (*Illustrated London News*, 6 August 1864)

The blockade-runner *Banshee* was built at Jones, Quiggin & Co.'s yard, Liverpool.

Mersey

The three principal builders of blockade runners on the Mersey were Laird & Sons of Birkenhead, W.C. Miller & Sons and Jones, Quiggin & Co. of Liverpool. Lairds are known to have built the *Denbigh, Lark, Wren* and *Prince Albert* (later renamed the *Mary*). The *Chatham* was constructed by them, and, interestingly, was shipped in pieces for assembly in Georgia.[15] On the stocks as the war ended were two further vessels for Fraser, Trenholm & Co., the *Albatross* and the *Penguin*. The *Isabel,* also by them, was not completed until after the war. W.C. Miller & Sons built the *Alexandra* for Henry Lafone of Fraser, Trenholm in 1862. In 1863 the company built the *Phantom* for Fraser, Trenholm and the *Wild Dayrell* for the Anglo-Confederate Trading Co. The *Let Her Be* was built by them for the Chicora Exporting Company in 1864. The *Bijou,* later known as the *Mary Celestia,* was constructed for Crenshaw & Co., in 1864, and the *Lelia* likewise for Crenshaw & Co., in 1865. Also completed that year was the *Abigail* for Fraser, Trenholm. The war ended before the *Ray* and *Leopoldina* could be completed for the same company.

Perhaps the most prolific of the Merseyside builders was Jones, Quiggin & Co. They built the *Banshee* for the Anglo-Confederate Trading Co. in 1862 (registered under the ownership of Edward Lawrence & Co. of Liverpool). In the following year they constructed the *Lucy* for Fraser, Trenholm. The year after, for the same company, they built the famous *Colonel Lamb,* as well as the *Lynx, Owl, Badger, Fox, Bat* and *Hope,* and the *Georgia Belle*. It seems likely that they also built *Badger II,* for the same firm. On their stocks, incomplete as the war ended, were the *Curlew, Hornet, Plover, Rosine, Ruby III, Snipe, Wasp* and *Widgeon*, all apparently intended as blockade-runners.

Other known local builders of blockade-runners were W.H. Potter & Co., of Liverpool, who built the *Deer* and the *Dream* for Fraser, Trenholm in 1864; McAndrews of Preston, who built the *Night-Hawk* for the Anglo-Confederate in 1864, and Bowdler, Chaffer & Co., of Seacombe, who built the *Secret* and the *Stag* for Fraser, Trenholm in 1864, and the *Swan II,* which was incomplete at the end of the war.

In addition, two blockade-runners owned by Fraser, Trenholm are known, the *Adelaide* and the *Racoon*. A number of the vessels listed above under the "ownership" of Fraser, Trenholm were in reality built for Commander Bulloch, of the Confederate States Navy. These include:

		Tons		Builders
		Gross	h.p.	
Bat	Steel paddle	466	180	Jones, Quiggin & Co., Liverpool
Owl	Steel Paddle	466	180	Jones, Quiggin & Co., Liverpool
Badger	Iron Paddle	375	150	Jones, Quiggin & Co., Liverpool
Fox	Iron Paddle	375	150	Jones, Quiggin & Co., Liverpool
Lynx	Steel Paddle	372	150	Jones, Quiggin & Co., Liverpool
Deer	Iron Paddle	465	180	W.H. Potter & Co., Liverpool
Dream	Steel Paddle	466	180	W.H. Potter & Co., Liverpool
Let Her B	Steel Paddle	365	150	W.C. Miller & Sons
Secret	Steel Paddle	467	180	Bowdler, Chafer & Co., Seacombe
Stag	Steel Paddle	465	180	Bowdler, Chafer & Co., Seacombe
Swan	Steel Paddle	470	180	Bowdler, Chafer & Co., Seacombe

Tees

The River Tees and its port of Hartlepool comprised the third important center for the construction of blockade runners. Perhaps the most well-known of these was the *Bermuda*, launched at the yard of Pearce, Lockwood & Co., of Stockton-on-Tees, on 8 July 1861. The company was also responsible for building the equally well-known *Bahama*, the *Czar* and the *Gladiator*. The *Gladiator* was bought by Melcher George Klingender of Liverpool, an associate of Fraser, Trenholm. Under him she made one run to Nassau, where she unloaded her cargo. The following year the *Gladiator* was acquired by the house of Fraser, Trenholm. She made at least four successful, substantiated, runs of the blockade.

Richardson, Duck of South Stockton, built the *Patros,* and the *Modern Greece* for Stefanos Xenos, later bought up by Zachariah C. Pearson, a Hull shipowner, and mayor of that town. The firm also built the *Justitia* in 1862 for the Albion Trading Company. Probably their most prominent blockade-runner was the *Harriet Pinckney,* originally known as the *Anonyma*, built by the company at their yard at Middlesborough. She was acquired for the Confederacy by Lt. North, and registered with Thomas Sterling Begbie of London. She was later sold to Isaac, Campbell & Co.

Richardson Bros. of Hartlepool, a junior branch of T. Richardson & Sons, built *Rechid*, originally known as the *Sir Colin Campbell*. She was the first iron steamer built in Hartlepool, in 1855. They also built the *Ann* , later acquired by Zachariah Pearson, mentioned above.

Pile, Spence & Co., of West Hartlepool built the iron screw steamer *Lloyds*, launched on 11 April 1862. She was later renamed the *Sea Queen*. The company was also responsible for the runners *Petro Beys*, *Peterhoff*, and the *Gipsey Queen*. Their last ship to be used as a runner was the *Whisper*, described as an elegant 250 foot iron paddle steamer, capable of 14 knots. Her captain was the very capable John Wilkinson, who took her into, and out of, Wilmington, at the closing stages of the war.

Newly established shipyard Backhouse & Dixon of Middlesborough built one of the most successful blockade-runners of the war, the *Pet*, launched on 11 October 1862. Her engines were supplied by T. Richardson & Sons of Hartlepool. She was registered in London as the property of John Charles Purdue, a Dubliner, and under Captain Mason eluded the blockade at least sixteen times.

The *Sheldrake* was built at Stockton, and was acquired by the West Hartlepool Steam Navigation Co. She was involved in one abortive attempt to run the blockade, but, springing a leak, was forced into Lisbon for repairs, and there her blockade-running career ended. The barque *Agrippina*, tender for the CSS *Alabama*, was built at Scarborough.

Tyne and Wear

The development of iron-shipbuilding along the northeast coast of England is credited to Sir Charles Palmer of the Palmer Shipbuilding & Iron Co., Jarrow. Palmer, with his brother George, opened their shipyard on the Tyne in 1851. Initially they began building iron screw steam colliers, but with the outbreak of the American Civil War they turned their hand to building fast, shallow-draft steamships for the blockade run. Two

The blockade-runner *A.D. Vance*.

at least are known by name: the *Ranger* and the *Grapeshot*. The company later went on to build warships for the Royal Navy.

Along the Wear at Sunderland was the Deptford shipyard of James Laing. The company is known to have built at least one blockade-runner, the *Aires*, laid down in 1861 and completed in the following year. This iron-hulled screw steamer was sold to one Frederic Peter Obicino of London, who sold her to the Cuban firm of V. Malga & Cie, of Havana. She made at least one successful run through the blockade, sometime about February 1863, returning with a cargo of 740 tons of cotton. On another expedition she was pursued by a Federal warship and ran aground off the coast of Bull's Bay, South Carolina, on 28 March 1863. U.S. rear admiral Samuel F. Dupont described her as "the most perfect example of a blockade runner we have yet see."[16]

Thames

Shipbuilding here was in decline by 1860, though there were eight companies building ships along the Thames. Perhaps the most notable company was J. & W. Dudgeon of Cubitt Town. Between March 1862 and 1865, they built 20 twin screw vessels, 12 of which, with an aggregate tonnage of 6,421, were blockade-runners. Their most famous were the *Tallahassee,* originally the *Atalanta,* the *Edith,* later renamed the *Chickamauga,* the *Hansa,* and the *Don*. When the blockade-runner *Cornubia* was captured in November 1863, among her papers was a letter from Dudgeons to the Confederate Navy Department:

> IRON SHIPBUILDERS,
> Cubitt Town, London .
> 2nd October 1863.

Dear Sir,

In answer to enquiry, whether the contract I now send you in will be in force for three months from the 25th October 1863, I beg leave to say it will, and that I am prepared to build three steamers of same dimensions, at the same price, to be delivered to you ready for furnishing for sea at the expiration of four months from the date of my receiving deposit installment from you.

In handing you the model for the constructor of the navy in Richmond, I shall of course be fully prepared to adopt any suggestion he may make and to alter the boat accordingly.

The price which you paid me for the steamers now building, particularly the Nutfield, is dearer, considering that she is of less horsepower than the offer I am now making you, as well as being larger. And you must also take into consideration that I am binding myself for three months hence, which I would not do except for the desire I have of doing more business for you.

I am sir, yours faithfully,
James Ash.

Edgar Stringer Esq.

Also found was a letter from the Blackwall Iron Works, London, makers of marine engines, dated 3 October 1863:

Gentlemen,

I will undertake to supply you with marine screw engines for line of battle ships or rams from 200 horsepower to 400 horsepower for the sum of £48 10s. Per horsepower, to be made of the best material and workmanship, all the pipes to be copper, engine bearings moving in the best gun metal, or white metal, if approved to be finished to the entire satisfaction of any person the mercantile marine company or yourselves may appoint; and I also agree to make the engines from plans and specifications to be sent home from the Confederate Government's engineer, and to be finished in six to eight months from the date of the order.

I also agree to send out men, if required, to place the engines in the respective ships, at the Confederate Government expense.

I am, gentlemen, yours truly,
John Stewart.[17]

Bristol and the West Country

At least one Bristol built ship is known as a blockade-runner, though it would appear she was not unique. This was the *Alfred*, operating under the pseudonym *Old Dominion*, and later as the *Sheffield*. Harvey & Co. of Hayle, in Cornwall, built the *Cornubia*, which was sold to the Confederacy in 1863 and renamed *Lady Davis*.

Though it would appear that most of Britain's shipbuilders constructed blockade-runners, deliberately, or sometimes unintentionally, it was only with their capture that their names came to be known; and thus their makers. For all those that successfully beat the blockade, and thus remain unrecorded, we may only guess at.

13

The Men and the Ships That Ran the Blockade

"As a beginning, let me recall the famous old seaport.... Whole neighbourhoods of that town were inhabited by seafaring people and the commonest talk was about ships. The granite basins of the docks, the finest in the world, were full of them in shapes that steam was only beginning to displace: clippers and other full-rigged craft, barques and bargentines, brigs and brigantines, trafficking with the ends of the earth, all smelling of tea, coffee, palm oil, sugar, spices, hides, cocoanuts, cotton, spruce or pine. They came in on an eighteen-foot tide and departed on the flood with their crews singing chanties as they trotted round the old-fashioned, handle-barred capstan.... [T]he high winds noisily, the low winds with suave and insidious persuasion, reiterated in every boy's ear the lure of the sea, and boomed a whispered 'Come to me — Come to me — Adventure — Riches.'

"From a seat in the bay window I saw Captain Bebbington jauntily mounted on his glossy bay hunter going home to the fine house he had rented on the hill, which then looked down over meadows to the mouth of the river, with yellow sand hills on both sides, and the silvery grey Welsh mountains flickering in the haze beyond.... He had been one of my father's juniors in the Cunard service, but he had retired from that, and suddenly become a person of splendour. 'No better than a pirate,' my mother said.... He had made eight round voyages between Nassau and Wilmington, and the newspapers, which could be depended on then, said that his profits had been fully one hundred and fifty thousand dollars each trip. That is a matter of history — it is on record of him and other blockade runners."

So wrote the author of *A Boy's Ambitions,* published in 1912, vividly recalling the Liverpool of the 1860s. With the outbreak of civil war in America, a great swathe of the workforce of northwestern England was thrown on the scrap heap when the cotton mills were forced to close. Through no fault of their own they lost their livelihoods because of a war being fought on the other side of the Atlantic. The lure of the sea was always there, but in the midst of poverty, the lure was even greater.

One of the most famous — or notorious — of the blockade-running skippers was "Captain A. Roberts," one of the pseudonyms of Augustus Charles Hobart-Hampden, third son of the sixth Earl of Buckingham. In his book, *Never Caught,* he gives some idea of the rates of pay in pounds sterling for those willing to take the chance in running the blockade:

	£
Captain	1,000
Chief Officer	250
Second & Third Officer	150
Chief Engineer	500
Crew & firemen	c.50
Pilot	750

In the 1860s, at a time when the wage of an ordinary workingman was about £1. 2s. 6d. a week, £50 was a fortune. As a consequence there was no shortage of young men willing to sign up for such a voyage. If the young workingman was attracted by £50, how much more so was a man skilled enough to become a blockade-runner's captain. Many signed up, including British naval officers "temporarily retired from service." Perhaps the most famous, as previously mentioned, was Augustus Charles Hobart-Hampden.

He was born at Walton-on-the Wolds, Leicestershire, on 1 April 1822. In 1835 he entered the Royal Navy, serving aboard the *Rover* of 18 guns, and later the *Rose*. In 1842 he passed his examinations at Dartmouth Naval College, and was seconded to the *Excellent*, based at Portsmouth. Hobart-Hampden qualified as gunnery mate, and joined the *Dolphin*, then engaged off the coast of South America in the suppression of the slave trade. He appears to have enjoyed a full measure of adventures, chasing and stopping slave ships. His last adventure involved him in the capture and escorting of a slaver into Demerara, in May 1844.

Returning to England he was appointed to the queen's yacht as a reward. It was a prestigious post, but lacked adventure. The following year he requested, and was granted, a new posting, to HMS *Rattler*, then operating in the Mediterranean. The outbreak of the Crimean War saw Hobart-Hampden serving as a lieutenant aboard HMS *Bulldog*, in the Baltic Squadron. He was seconded briefly to command of HMS *Driver*, and in dispatches reference was made to his "ability, zeal and great exertion" while at Abo. In 1855 he commanded the mortar-boats at the attack on Sveaborg (Helsingfors), where he was again mentioned in dispatches. As a reward he was promoted to the rank of commander. At the end of the war Hobart-Hampden briefly resigned his commission to become an officer in the coast guard. In 1858, taking up his commission once more in the Royal Navy, he was appointed an officer of the guard ship at Malta, and subsequently was given command of the gunship *Foxhound*, which patrolled in the Mediterranean. He was promoted to Captain in March 1863, but, his life lack-

Augustus Charles Hobart-Hampden, R.N., in old age. The third son of the Duke of Buckingham, he was one of the most colorful of the blockade-runners.

ing any excitement, he retired on half-pay. The mechanics of how Hobart-Hampden became a blockade-runner are not explained. All we know is that he "joined some brother officers in running the blockade," according to his entry in the *Dictionary of National Biography*. His activities as a runner are recorded in a short autobiographical work, *Never Caught*,[1] which American authorities state are substantially accurate.

Hobart-Hampden's first vessel was the *Don*, built by Dudgeon's on the Thames. It was partly owned by the State of North Carolina, they having paid $115,000 for the privilege. In his narrative he describes the ship and its crew: "The vessel I had charge of, which I had brought out from England, was one of the finest double-screw steamers that had been built by D-----n; of 400 tons burden, 250 horse-power, 180 feet long and 22 feet beam; undeniably a good craft in all respects, lying in St. George's Harbor, Bermuda. Our crew consisted of a captain, three officers, three engineers and twenty-eight men, including firemen — that is, ten seamen and eighteen firemen. They were all Englishmen, and as they received very high wages, we managed to have picked men; in fact the men-o-war on the West India station found it a difficult matter to prevent their crews from desertion, so great was the temptation offered by the blockade-runners."

The date of his first run is not given in the account, but it would appear to have been in the autumn of 1863. The *Don*, with a mixed cargo, sailed from Bermuda, heading for Wilmington, a distance of 720 miles. The first twenty-four hours passed without incident, but as dawn broke on the second day, a Federal cruiser was seen, barely half a mile away. She, seeing them, turned and headed straight towards them, opening fire as she did so. The random shot and shell, though rapid, was inaccurate, passing over or wide of the *Don*. This may have been partly due to the heavy squall of wind and rain that prevailed, or perhaps the gunners lacked practice. The *Don*, which ran in full steam throughout the daylight hours, shot off like a startled rabbit. As they were windward to the enemy vessel, and having no top weight, they soon left her far astern. The pursuer, for her part, kept losing ground in the pursuit by yawing from side to side in order to fire her bow chasers at the blockade-runner. By eight o'clock that morning the *Don* was well beyond the range of the Yankee guns, and by midday all that could be seen of the enemy was a smudge of smoke on the distant horizon.

Throughout the day the lookouts aboard the *Don* kept careful watch, as the runner proceeded through dangerous waters. As steamers were observed in the distance, Hobart-Hampden altered course, sometimes allowing one to pass ahead of them or at another time turning back on themselves, but each time as the danger passed, returning to the original course set in for Wilmington. Night fell, they had survived the day. At one o'clock in the morning, to the horror of all aboard the *Don*, they discovered a steamer sailing alongside of them. Neither had been aware of the other until that moment. Then all was astir on both vessels, as the Federal warship ordered the *Don* to heave-to, with the added threat that she would be sunk if she refused. Hobart-Hampden responded, "Aye, aye Sir, we are stopped!"

The *Don* came to a halt, but she was still in full steam. The enemy cruiser was barely eighty yards away, her guns trained on the suspected blockade-runner. Aboard the *Don*, they heard orders given aboard the warship to man and arm, then lower quarter-boats for boarding. Over they came to the *Don*. The boats now touching the hull of the little English vessel, Hobart-Hampden whispered down the speaking tube to the engineer below: "Full speed ahead." Away she shot into the darkness. The expected cannon fire did not come. Perhaps the captain of the Federal warship was afraid of hitting his own men —

perhaps pursuit was delayed while he got them back aboard — but for whatever reason, the *Don* escaped into the night.

The next day was spent avoiding enemy cruisers, but always continuing on to their objective. As dusk fell they were just sixty miles due west of Fort Fisher. Before it lay the inner blockading force of enemy ships, thirty strong, arranged in crescent formation just beyond the range of the Confederate fort's guns. Rather than run through the center of the blockading force, the usual practice for runners was to approach from the side, then run down the coast to the entrance to the river. To assist the runners shore-lights were lit, which when lined up by the runner indicated that the way was clear to run straight in. Crawling along the shore was where a goodly number of runners fell afoul, when they accidentally beached. The boats and their crews would then be fired upon with shot and shell. This was not for Hobart-Hampden. He decided to run directly through the main body of the blockaders. It was audacious, the sort of thing that none of the blockaders would have conceived as possible. But Hobart-Hampden was not your average blockade-runner. He had that touch of madness about him, the sort of thing some call genius. Do what the enemy would never suspect. The sheer design of the *Don* favored such a bold plan. She lay low in the water, her masts lowered on the deck; she was to all intents and purposes invisible. The sound of the engines of this little English vessel was masked by the greater sound of the sea and wind. With every light extinguished she set off at speed. Lookouts called out to the helmsman as they approached the blockaders— so many points to starboard, so many points to port, to pass among them in safety. Then a blockader loomed up in front of them. She was so close that it was impossible to pass to right or left without being seen. Hobart-Hampden shouted his order down the speaking tube to the engineer below to reverse one engine. The response was instantaneous. She turned rapidly within the space of her own length, her Symons' twin screw engines proving that they were the best in the world. Now returned to their original position, the engine was shut off. Hobart-Hampden and his men waited. Eventually the cruiser moved off slowly into the darkness. The way ahead was clear once more. It was now about one o'clock. Slow ahead the *Don* proceeded, then shortly they made out the glimmer of a light ahead. Speed was gently increased, the crew straining their eyes for danger. Nearer the coast they approached. The outline of a vessel lying at anchor was observed. From information that Hobart-Hampden had gleaned, he knew that she must be the senior blockade officer's vessel. The light that they had seen belonged to her. One of the lookouts pointed out a gap between her and the vessel to her left, sufficient for the *Don* to pass; and through the gap she passed in full steam. The pilot now took charge to guide them into the river. There was a heap of sand called the mound, which marked the entrance. He showed a small light from the shoreward side of the vessel, which was answered by two from the shore. Lined up into one they revealed the channel entrance to the river. Soon the *Don* found her way into the channel, and safely came to anchor under the batteries of Fort Fisher.

The following morning, out to sea, the *Don's* captain counted twenty-five enemy cruisers. There was a great deal of activity among them. Ship's launches with guns in their bows were making for the northern shore. Through his telescope Hobart-Hampden saw the object of all this activity. It was a beached paddle-wheel blockade-runner. Their intention was to capture her. Out of range of Fort Fisher's artillery, her commandant had two 12-pounder Whitworth guns sent down to the beach. From here they opened up on the Federal launches. Out at sea the blockaders responded, and an artillery duel ensued.

Meanwhile, two of the crew of the beached blockade-runner managed to get aboard her. Her cargo had been removed the previous night, and they set her on fire. With the object of the exercise blazing away, the Federal gunboats withdrew.

Later that morning the *Don* steamed up the Cape Fear River to Wilmington, and tied up along the quay. Her cargo was unloaded. While the main cargo was armaments, blankets and shoes, each of the crew was entitled to speculate in some private venture. Hobart-Hampden's was, unbelievably, women's corsets—1,000 of them. Apparently, before leaving England, he had been in conversation with a Southern lady, and with an eye to a profit had asked her what was most in short supply in the blockaded South. Her reply was corsets. Now, curiously, here in Wilmington, there was scarcely a woman to be seen. Eventually attracting a buyer, he discovered that most of the womenfolk had been moved inland to safety. Hobart-Hampden, having bought in bulk at 1s. 1d a pair, now sold them for 12s each, making a profit of 1100 percent.

The *Don* was then loaded with a return cargo of cotton. The hold was tightly packed, and bales were placed twofold on deck on every available surface, until at last the vessel looked like one enormous bale of cotton. The average cost of cotton was 3d a pound, which sold in Liverpool at 2s. 6d. a pound, giving a profit of 600 percent. Down the river about twenty miles the *Don* steamed, anchoring at the river mouth about two o'clock in the afternoon. She was hidden by Fort Fisher from prying blockaders' eyes. Here she waited until dark. At a quarter to eleven that night the *Don* weighed anchor and steamed slowly down to the entrance of the river. The order was given, "Full speed ahead!" and out into the sea she shot. Her speed was fourteen knots. Barely had she cleared the bar when she almost crashed into a Federal rowing boat, placed there to signal by rocket any escaping runner. Hobart-Hampden swung the wheel to avoid running her down. He heard the sound of her oars breaking against the side of his vessel, as he swept by, to all intents and purposes ludicrously steering a huge cotton bale. Within a minute a rocket was sent up into the night sky. A gun was fired, but they could not make out if it was at them. Down the coast the *Don* ran, then sharply out to sea. Several guns were now fired in the darkness, but no shots struck the runner.

As daylight broke they found themselves engulfed in thick hazy weather. As the morning wore on it began to break up. Astern of them, about six miles, they saw a large paddle-wheel cruiser. She, seeing them, turned and began to give chase. After an hour's pursuit it was evident she was gaining on them. Bales of cotton were moved to the stern to ensure that the propeller remained below the water line at all times. Four hours into the pursuit, she was getting ever closer. Then a ripple on the sea ahead was noticed, and the miracle that everybody had been silently praying for materialized. It was the Gulf Stream. Here it ran from two to three miles an hour. Hobart-Hampden altered course to enter it, and soon they were swept along at even greater speed. The pursuing Federal cruiser also changed course, but a few miles before she reached the speedy current. Soon she was left trailing behind. She was some eight miles behind before she too gained the advantage of the Gulf Stream.

By five o'clock she had made up ground. Now she was just three miles behind. She fired off her Parrott gun in the bow, but the shot fell short. By half past six the shots were closer. The sun set at a quarter to seven. If they could outrun her until then, they might escape. As dusk descended the sky began to fill with clouds. All the time the cruiser continued firing sporadically at them. She was no more than a mile behind them as the sun set. Then it was dark. Hobart-Hampden altered course, steering two points eastward.

After a time the engine was stopped, and there she sat in complete darkness. They waited, and in a short time, away off in the distance they saw the enemy vessel steam past them, firing ahead as she did so. When all seemed quiet the engine was reengaged, and off they set once more. The *Don* was now low on coal. Hobart-Hampden consulted his charts, and put in a course for the nearest point of the Bahama Islands, the little island called Green Turtle Cay. They arrived safely, but one more tense incident awaited. A Federal cruiser approached them. She stopped barely a mile offshore and waited. Would she dash in and capture them? The *Don* was clearly a blockade-runner, but she was lying in an English port. The captain of the Federal warship clearly thought about it, then changed his mind. No one wanted a second Trent affair. The cruiser steamed away. The next day Hobart-Hampden sent to Nassau for coal to be delivered to them. With fuel aboard, the *Don* weighed anchor and island-hopped towards her home port. The voyage to Wilmington and back had taken sixteen days.

By Christmas 1863, as Hobart-Hampden himself informs us, he had breached the blockade for a second time. This time was equally fraught with danger. At a distance of about fifty yards the *Don* received a broadside as she attempted to dash by a Federal gunship. Fortunately, because she was so low in the water, all the shots passed over her, except one that went through the funnel. Now the blockader was joined by two other vessels who opened up on the *Don,* but to little effect. On she raced away from them and into the blackness of the night. Two days later she arrived back at Nassau, with her second cargo of cotton. The round-trip had taken eighteen days.

The third trip almost ended before it had begun, when a Federal cruiser breached the maritime league in an attempt to make the *Don* a prize. She put a shot across the blockade-runner's bow, obliging her to heave-to. Hobart-Hampden raised the British flag, and when boarded remonstrated with the officer that the officer was in breach of international law in that the *Don* was still in British waters. The officer reluctantly accepted the status quo and retired. The American warship remained where she was though, keeping a watch on Hobart-Hampden's little vessel. In the middle of the night she moved off, presumably in pursuit of some other runner. This was the *Don*'s opportunity. They weighed anchor, and were soon far out to sea. Three days later they were some sixty miles off the coast of Wilmington. On nearing the blockading squadron they heard the sound of gunfire, as the blockaders opened up on a runner that had just breached their lines. All eyes were on the runner under attack as audaciously Hobart-Hampden eased his vessel closer, following the blockader ahead as it moved closer to the shore. Nobody seemed to have noticed the *Don*. Suddenly the firing ceased, and the blockaders moved back to their original positions, leaving the *Don,* her engines cut and sitting there in the dark, all lights extinguished. The tide took her in, then all of a sudden there was a shuddering as she beached herself. She was stuck on the shore. As dawn broke, two cruisers made her out, and turning, came racing towards her. Hobart-Hampden ordered as much of her cargo to be removed as was necessary in order to float her off. One of the gunboats opened fire, and its shell splashed in the water not too far away. This, however, brought her to the attention of the gunners at Fort Fisher, who opened up on the two Federals, now well within the range of the fort's guns. Discretion being the better part of valor, they withdrew.

Now the *Don* was able to ease herself off the shore and into deeper water. As she eased her way down the coast towards the inlet, the fort gave her covering fire. Twenty minutes later she anchored safe, under the Confederate guns. Taking onboard a pilot, the *Don* proceeded upriver to Wilmington. Finding her cargo of cotton waiting on the quay, she quickly unloaded and prepared once more to run the gauntlet. Back down river she went there to wait under the fort's protection until nightfall. A fog descended, and, much against local advice, Hobart-Hampden decided to take advantage of it. He eased his ship out into the mouth of the river, and in full steam took off. He was gambling that, because of the fog, the blockaders would have dropped their guard, not believing anybody would be so foolhardy as to try it. He was right, and the *Don* once more ran through the blockade. By morning, as the fog cleared, the little runner was one hundred and twenty miles out to sea, with no sign of any other vessel. Seventy-two hours later she docked at Nassau.

No vessel had succeeded in getting into Savannah since the establishment of the blockade. The main contributing factor was that the Federal army occupied Fort Pulaski, which guarded the entrance to the river giving access to Savannah. As a consequence of this position of strength, there were few if any blockading ships. The Federal authorities were fairly confident that no blockade-runner captain in his right mind would even contemplate attempting the run. Call it madness—call it genius, Hobart-Hampden decided he would try. Intelligence indicated that the lightship off Port Royal, a few miles from the entrance to Savannah, was still in operation. By using this as a guide to the entrance of the river it should be possible to run into Savannah, provided he was not first blown out of the water by Fort Pulaski's guns. With a Savannah pilot aboard, the *Don* left Nassau. Two days later she was lying off the coast of Georgia, edging slowly towards the lightship. The pilot now took control. Closer and closer they steamed. The shape of the fort loomed large before them. Added to the danger of the fort's guns were sandy shoals that threatened to trap them. The pilot was nervous, but slowly ahead they continued, when all of a sudden the heavens opened up with a torrential storm. The rain was so heavy that it was impossible to see beyond the bow of the ship. The pilot's nerve failed him. Without him nothing could be achieved. Hobart-Hampden turned his vessel back out to sea. Twenty miles out they anchored and waited. The storm overtook them and for three days they were tossed by heavy seas. Luck did seem to be against them. On the fourth day the storm abated. That night Hobart-Hampden tried again. They steered towards the lightship, but no light was seen. She had been blown from her position by the gale, and was temporarily out of action. The pilot described it as madness to try to enter the river mouth without the lightship as a point of reference. Hobart-Hampden anguished, but there was nothing that could be done. They were low on fuel, sufficient only to take them back to Nassau. Reluctantly he turned the *Don* around, and headed back up the coast to cross at the narrowest point between Florida and the Bahamas, a distance of twenty-eight miles. Coal was now very low. They cut up every available piece of wood they could, to feed the furnace, before eventually getting back to Nassau. Hobart-Hampden was philosophical about the whole business. "Easy come, easy go," was how he viewed the venture.

In all Hobart-Hampden made six successful runs to Wilmington and back in the *Don*. While Hobart-Hampden was taking a vacation, command of the ship passed to his chief officer, Mr. Cory. Cory is described by his former captain as a "fine specimen of a seaman as can well be imagined—plucky, cool and determined." Who he was is open to speculation. There is no one in the Navy List that quite fits the time period. "Cory," like "Captain Roberts," appears to be another nom de guerre. Cory twice successfully ran the blockade into Wilmington. On his third attempt, on 4 March 1864, the *Don* was captured by the USS *Pequot*. She had a cargo of army uniforms, blankets and shoes, valued at $200,000. The capture of the *Don* is a story worth telling.

Late on the afternoon of her third day out of Nassau, she was waiting off the coast of Wilmington for nightfall. Thick, hazy weather that was masking them suddenly cleared. Almost as it did, a lookout espied a Federal cruiser, under sail and steam, bearing down on them. Cory quickly summed up the situation. There was insufficient time for the *Don* to get up steam and escape before the enemy gunship was upon them. Cory ordered up steam, then turned his vessel into the wind. She made no attempt to flee. The Yankee vessel, a large full-rigged corvette, was running along before a strong breeze. In order to bring her under control the sail would have to be furled. On she came, the little blockade-runner now almost under her bows. Aloft aboard the warship in her rigging the sailors were gathering in the sail. She was barely fifty yards off. Cory called for full steam ahead. Off she steamed!—right past the oncoming warship. Unable to get a shot off, the enemy ship continued on for nearly a quarter of a mile before she could turn and set off in pursuit of the fleeing blockade-runner. Now she opened up with her bow guns, but to little effect. Gradually the *Don* pulled away, and as darkness descended she lost her pursuer. The next morning as day broke Cory discovered that one of the more modern Federal warships, the *Pequot,* was barely three miles away and steaming fast towards them. Cory turned to flee, but the chase was soon over. The *Pequot* was a far faster craft, and the *Don* was soon captured. Taken into port, the *Pequot's* commander, Lieutenant Stephen P. Quackenbush, now aware of the earlier incident, went aboard the *Don* to shake hands with Cory and compliment him on his skill and courage. Cory and his crew were taken to New York for trial before the Admiralty Court. They were found guilty, and the *Don* was confiscated as a prize, later becoming a Federal blockader. Cory and his men were set free and returned to Nassau. Cory eventually found his way back to England.

Refreshed after his vacation, Hobart-Hampden traveled up to Scotland, where he took charge, on behalf of the Confederacy, of the Glasgow-built side-wheel steamer *Falcon Fisher.* He sailed her down to Liverpool, where she loaded. With a mixed cargo she arrived at St. George, Bermuda, on 4 July 1864. Observing her arrival, the American consul made further enquiries, and discovered that "she was commanded by a person who when formerly master of the *Don,* went by the name of Roberts." Curiously, Hobart-Hampden makes no mention of this vessel after that, and it may well be that he merely brought her out to Bermuda, rather than ran the blockade in her. The following month, August 1864, Hobart-Hampden took charge, again on behalf of the Confederacy, of a newly built side-wheel steamer, the *Condor.* Built on the Clyde, she was of 300 tons, 270 feet in length, 24 feet in breadth, and with a draft of 7 feet. She was ideal for running the blockade. By his own record we know he made two successful runs into Wilmington in her. On the first, following his arrival, he traveled overland by rail to Richmond, where he had an interview with President Jefferson Davis. He visited Charleston before returning to Bermuda with a cargo of 1140 bales of cotton. On the second successful trip, yellow fever broke out among the crew, and the *Condor* was diverted to Halifax, Nova Scotia, where the sick were landed. Hobart-Hampden himself appears to have contracted the disease, and handed over control of the *Condor* to his brother officer, William N.W. Hewett, R.N. (more about him later). Hobart-Hampden ends his story: "To my acquaintance and companions in blockade-running, who may perhaps recognize the writer of this little narrative, I can only say that I look back with pleasure to the jolly times we spent together, and that I shall be always glad to meet any one of them again, and over a brandy cocktail ... have a chat over times the like of which we shall never see again."

Vice-Admiral Charles Murray-Aynsley, R.N., Companion of the Order of the Bath and justice of the peace, died peacefully in his bed on 1 April 1901. He was a brother officer of Hobart-Hampden, and like him was also a successful blockade runner. He was born at Olveston in Gloucestershire, on 21 September 1821, the son of John Murray-Aynsley, and great grandson of Sir John Murray, third Duke of Atholl. In 1835, at the age of fourteen, Murray-Aynsley entered the Royal Navy as a midshipman. He became a lieutenant in 1845, and served aboard HMS *Terrible*. At the outbreak of the Crimean War he was appointed lt. commander of the *Lynx*, and served in the Mediterranean and the Black Sea operations. Murray-Aynsley was promoted to captain in June 1862, but in the following year he temporarily surrendered his commission. By 12 June 1863, under the alias of "Captain Murray," he was in Bermuda as captain of the blockade-runner *Venus*. She was a side-wheel steamer of 700 tons, with a draft of just 9 feet when fully laden. She made an unspecified number of successful runs into Wilmington, before coming to grief on 21 October 1863. Chased by the USS *Nansemond*, under Lt. R.H. Lamson, she was hit by four shots. The first struck her foremast; the second exploded in the cabin; the third killed a man; and the fourth struck near the waterline, driving in an iron plate. Taking in water, Murray-Aynsley beached her, and got his men off safe, but was unable to offload the cargo. Unable to capture her, Lt. Lamson ordered his guns to play upon her until she caught fire.

Murray-Aynsley's next vessel was the *Hansa*, a sister ship of Hobart-Hampden's *Don*. He was her third captain, following James Randle and Thomas Atkinson. The *Hansa* was a side-wheel steamer of 257 tons and a speed of 12 knots. There is an engraving in the *Illustrated London News* (23 Jan. 1864) depicting the *Hansa* running the blockade into Wilmington. This would have been when Murray-Aynsley was captain. He was still captain in December 1864, when Colonel Lamb, commander of Fort Fisher, records in his diary: "4th December: Hansa, Captain Murray came in from Nassau, about daybreak...."[2]

When the war ended, Murray-Aynsley took up his commission in the Royal Navy once more, and progressed steadily through the ranks. In March 1878 he was appointed Rear Admiral, and his services to his country were recognized when he was honored with the Order of the Bath. In retirement he maintained an active life, and took up the civic duty of a local justice of the peace.

The third of the Royal Navy's blockade-running brother-in-arms was William Nathan Wrighte Hewett. To his fellow blockaders, and the Federal spies, he was either "Captain Hewett" or "Samuel S. Ridge." He was younger than the other two by more than ten years. Hewett was born at Brighton on 12 August 1834, and entered the navy in March 1847. He served as a midshipman in the Second Anglo-Burmese War of 1852–1853. In 1854, while acting mate of the gunboat *Beagle*, he was attached to the naval brigade in the Crimea. On 26 October of that year he was in command of a gun in the battery before Sevastopol. Almost surrounded by Russians, the army commander sent down orders for him to spike his gun and withdraw with all speed. Hewett replied that as the orders had not come from his superior officer, Captain Lushington, he must refuse.

Breaking down the side parapet of the battery, he dragged the gun around and opened fire with grapeshot on the surrounding Russian column. His devastating action was decisive to the outcome of the battle. A few days later, because of his gallant conduct at the battle of Inkerman, he was awarded the Victoria Cross, the highest award possible within the British services. Hewett was one of the first recipients of this award for valor. Hewett was promoted to lieutenant, and given command of the *Beagle*. He was, incredibly, just 20 years old. In September 1858, as an additional reward for his bravery, he was appointed to the royal yacht, and promoted to the rank of commander. This staid form of life was not to his liking, and he applied for more active service. He was then successively commanded the *Viper* off the west coast of Africa, and the *Rinaldo* on the North American and West Indies station. On 24 November 1862 he was made captain. Without explanation, his entry in the *Dictionary of National Biography* then leaps to 1865 when he was appointed to command the *Basilisk* on the China Station. During the missing years in between, he was a successful blockade-runner. His activities in this profession are shrouded in mystery, and he has in fact been confused with Hobart-Hampden. Hewett may well be the mysterious "Captain Hewett" of the yacht *Hornet* that acted as a tender to the *Alabama* when she was at Cherbourg in June 1864. He took aboard the seventy or so chronometers taken by Semmes from the vessels that he captured, as well as Semmes' personal effects, and sailed with them to Liverpool. On firmer ground, we know that Hewett took control of the *Condor,* apparently in August or September 1864. On 26 September 1864, the U.S. consul at Halifax, Nova Scotia, Mr. M.M. Jackson, clearly identifies Hewett, rather than Hobart-Hampden, as captain. He wrote to naval secretary Seward:

> Sir,
>
> I have the honor to inform you that the British blockade running steamer Condor, which cleared from this port on the 24th instant, as previously reported, with a valuable cargo, including clothing for the Confederate Army, destined for Wilmington, is commanded by Captain [William N.W.] Hewett, late commander of the British ship of war Rinaldo, and is still an officer in her Majesty's service on half pay, under the assumed name of Samuel S. Ridge.
>
> The Condor is a new and superior vessel of about 300 tons, built expressly for running the blockade. She was built at Glasgow, where she is registered and insured by Donald McGregor, of London. She is of a rakish build; very long, narrow in beam, and furnished with three low funnels and two short masts. She is of light draft and great speed. Her hull is painted very light lead color.[3]

Hewett, having served in command of the *Rinaldo* on the West Indies Station, was the ideal blockade-runner. He had considerable knowledge of the strengths and weaknesses of the Federal blockade. While still a serving officer in the Royal Navy, perhaps deliberately emphasizing the weakness of the blockade, he wrote to flag officer Silas H. Stringham, aboard the U.S. Frigate *Minnesota*:

> H.B.M.S. Steam Sloop Rinaldo
> 7th September 1861.
>
> Sir,
> I beg leave most respectfully to represent to you the open state of the blockade of the ports, etc., under mentioned, off the coast of North Carolina, viz:
>
> Entrance to the Cape Fear river and port of Wilmington
> Port of Beaufort, off which place I was at anchor forty hours without sighting any United States cruisers.
>
> > I have the honour to be sir, your obedient servant,
> > W.N.W. Hewett,
> > Commander.
>
> Flag Officer Silas H. Stringham,
> U.S. Frigate Minnesota.[4]

On 2 April 1862, U. S. Naval Records reveal that he requested permission to officially proceed through the blockade in order to pass a communication to two British consuls then operating within the Confederate States:

> H.B.M.S. Rinaldo
> Off Fortress Monroe, 2nd April 1862.
>
> Sir,
>
> Having dispatches for the British Consul at Norfolk and Richmond from Lord Lyons, which I have been asked to transmit, I have the honour to request you will be pleased to allow me to send them by an officer belonging to her Britannic Majesty's ship under my command, under a flag of truce, tomorrow, the 3rd instant, at any hour most convenient to you, when you may have a steamer at your disposal suitable for such service.
>
> I have the honour to be sir, your most obedient servant,
>
> W.N.W. Hewett,
> Commander.
>
> Flag Officer Goldsborough,
> U.S. Frigate Minnesota, Hampton Roads.[5]

So Hewett was no stranger to the Blockading Force, nor indeed to the U.S. consuls. It was Hewett, not Hobart-Hampden, that Consul Jackson saw aboard the *Condor* that 24 September. Unbeknownst to the Federal authorities, along with the valuable cargo Hewett also had one passenger, the Confederate spy Mrs. Rose O'Neal Greenhow. She had returned from Europe and was allegedly carrying private correspondence for President Jefferson Davis. Around her neck she wore a drawstring bag containing three hundred golden guineas (approximately $2,000). Some say it was a gift for Davis from a well-wisher in England, but more probably the money was a royalty payment for Mrs. Greenhow — an authoress of a series of letters — from her English publisher. Late on the night of 30 September, in atrocious weather, the *Condor* prepared to make the dash for the New Inlet channel of the Cape Fear River. Suddenly a rocket was fired — the *Condor* had been discovered. With the alarm raised, there was nothing for it but to apply full steam, and make a dash through the blockade to the safety of Fort Fisher. As the rain lashed down the *Condor* weaved through the blockading force and it seemed as if she would escape. Then suddenly, quite near to the entrance to the inlet, she almost ran into the wreck of another blockade-runner, the *Night-Hawk,* caught the previous night. The helmsman swung the wheel to avoid crashing into her, but in the process he lost his line of approach, and the *Condor* ran aground on a hidden shoal. The vessel's keel was broken. There was no way of getting her off the shoal that night in such bad weather.

Fearing that they would be captured by the Federal navy and the secret correspondence discovered, Mrs. Greenhow implored Hewett to get her ashore. Much against his will, in the treacherous conditions prevailing, he acceded to her request. A skiff was lowered and Mrs. Greenhow and the pilot were rowed towards shore by two of the crew. As they approached, a wave caught them, capsizing the little boat. In the water the three men searched for Mrs. Greenhow, but were unable to find her. Saving their own lives, they swam for shore. Mrs. Greenhow, encumbered by her voluminous skirts and weighed down by the gold coins around her neck, was drowned. The blockaders did not attempt to follow the *Condor* into the shallows, and returned to their station back out at sea, beyond the range of Fort Fisher's guns. The following morning, with the storm abated, Hewett and his men lowered the boats and rowed ashore. Mrs. Greenhow's body was later discovered a little way down the coast.⁶ The correspondence had disappeared, and some of the guineas had been stolen, but the money was later recovered.

Hewett was still at Fort Fisher as late as 17 November 1864. Colonel Lamb notes in his diary for that day that "Captain Hewett, of *Condor*, stopped at the Battery Buchanan this afternoon." A few weeks later, on 4 December, it is evident that Hewett was back in Nassau, preparing to return home to England. Not forgetting the children at Christmas time, Hewett sent presents. As Lamb writes, "Hansa, Captain Murray came from Nassau, about daybreak. We received a lot of toys etc., sent by Captain Hewett of the Condor."⁷

The first verifiable British blockade-runner was the *Bermuda,* captained by Eugene Tessier, on behalf of Fraser, Trenholm & Co., for the Confederate army. Tessier was a Breton, born at L'Orient. He entered the French navy as a boy, and saw service in the Algerine campaigns. Later he was employed on dockyard services, and acquired knowledge in the construction of wooden vessels. Leaving the French navy, he found work in the French merchant marine, then later the American merchant marine. Tessier married, and settled in Charleston, South Carolina. With the outbreak of the Civil War he volunteered his services to the South. Tessier was dispatched to Liverpool for secondment as a blockade runner to the firm of Fraser, Trenholm. His first ship was the *Emily St. Pierre*. In a letter to the United States Navy secretary, F.W. Steward, the U.S. vice-consul at Liverpool, H. Wilding, writes of him: "He was a Frenchman by birth, knows the Charleston trade well, and is a most desperate fellow, capable of any venture."⁸

In August 1861, he was to prove how desperate a fellow he was. Tessier was given command of Fraser, Trenholm's newest vessel, the *Bermuda*. She was constructed at Stockton-on-Tees by Pearse & Lockwood, and left West Hartlepool, loaded with arms, on 18 August 1861. Flying the British flag, the *Bermuda*, under Tessier, crossed the Atlantic and entered Savannah, completely untroubled by the Federal blockade. With the *Bermuda's* cargo of arms unloaded, her hold was then filled with 2,000 bales of cotton. Tessier departed Savannah on the night of 1 November 1861, again passing untroubled through the blockade. Tessier dropped off Confederate correspondence at Nassau, re-coaled, and continued on to Liverpool, via Le Havre. He arrived back in England on 23 January 1862.

Tessier was then given command of Fraser, Trenholm's newest ship, the *Bahama*, registered in Liverpool as being owned by Edwin Haigh (Fraser, Trenholm's cotton broker). Like the *Bermuda,* she was built by Pearse & Lockwood, and launched on the banks of the River Tees, on Saturday, 18 January 1862. In March, fully fitted out, the *Bahama* entered West Hartlepool docks, where she was loaded with a cargo of ammunition sent up from London. Later that month she sailed for Hamburg where she received four 7-in. rifled guns intended for the Confederate cruiser *Florida*. Tessier then sailed for Nassau, arriving there on 25 May. While the *Florida* (or *Oreto,* as she still was) waited for adjudication before the Admiralty Court as to her status, the presence of the *Bahama*, a recognized blockade-runner, did nothing to help her cause. Tessier was ordered by the Confederate agents Adderley & Co. to unload his cargo and transfer it to the public warehouse. Then, taking aboard Captain Raphael Semmes and a number of his officers from the *Sumter,* Tessier returned to Liverpool. The *Bahama* docked on 4 August 1862. Semmes' new command, the *Alabama,* had sailed shortly before, and nine days after arriving, Tessier and the *Bahama* departed Liverpool to rendezvous with Matthew Butcher and the *Alabama* at Praya Bay, Terceira. Along with Commander Bulloch, Semmes and his officers, the *Bahama* also carried armaments for the new Confederate cruiser. These included two 32-pounders, gun carriages, small arms and money. The remaining arms were shipped out aboard the old Scarborough-built barque *Agrippina*. With the transfer of the arms, the *Bahama*, with Bulloch and Butcher aboard, returned to Liverpool. She docked there on 1 September 1862. Recognized as she was by the Federal authorities and her spies, the usefulness of the *Bahama* as blockade-runner or transporter had now come to an end. She was sent down to London, and on 21 March 1863, sailed for Hong Kong, where it was intended she would be sold for not less than £23,000.

Back in England Tessier oversaw the construction and outfitting of the *Alexandra*, a warship built by W.A. Miller & Sons, for Fraser, Trenholm. In July he was given the opportunity once more to run the blockade. As captain of the newly built *Phantom*, he took her into Bermuda, then ran into Wilmington. On his return trip he carried the Confederate spy Rose O'Neal Greenhow, previously mentioned, on her fund-raising trip to England. The following year Tessier accompanied Bulloch to France, where he acted as interpreter in the bid to have corvettes and rams built for the Confederate navy. At the end of the war there was no place for Tessier in America. He returned to England, and set up a business in wooden ship construction and repair in Liverpool.

Before taking command of the *Bermuda*, Tessier had been captain of the Fraser, Trenholm ship *Emily St. Pierre*. Upon his departure, Scotsman captain William Wilson was given command of his old vessel. Wilson made one particularly noted voyage. As the *Emily St. Pierre* approached Charleston Bar, on 18 March 1862, she was discovered and eventually captured by the combined blockading force of the USS *Florida, James Adger, Sumter, Flambeau* and *Onward*. The captains of each aspired to a share of the prize money. Most of the crew of the *Emily* were transferred as prisoners, but Captain Wilson, his cook, and a steward were left aboard to assist the prize crew of fourteen in its journey to Philadelphia for adjudication. Outnumbered more than four to one, Wilson nonetheless resolved to recapture his vessel. Early on the morning of 21 March, some thirty miles off Cape Hatteras, while prize captain Lt. Josiah Stone was on watch with three of his men, Wilson and his two men tied and gagged the master's mate, Mr. Hornsby, who was asleep in his bunk. They then proceeded to capture the engineer, John Smith, who was

Captain William Wilson became the toast of England and the Confederacy when, after having his ship seized, he recaptured her and with a crew of just two sailed her 3,000 miles back to Liverpool. (*Illustrated London News*, 17 May 1862)

JOHN BULL'S OCCUPATION GONE.

JOHN BULL. (*Coster-monger*). "My heyes!—Market shut up!—and I've got to trundle combustibles and other wegetables back 'ome again!"

A cartoon from *Harper's Weekly* (Jan. 1865). With the capture of Fort Fisher by the Federal army, Wilmington was effectively closed to blockade-runners.

likewise tied up and gagged. On his own, Wilson then approached Lt. Stone on the bridge, and persuaded him to go below to check a chart. As he descended, Stone was overpowered and tied up. Wilson returned to the bridge, and supposedly on Lt. Stone's orders, sent the three men below, where they were enclosed in the hold. Now armed, Wilson and his two men captured the remaining slumbering sailors, one of whom, in the struggle, was shot by Wilson, though not killed. Wilson then shackled his prisoners two by two, and took charge once more of his vessel.

What to do? Wilson had a choice: he could attempt to run the blockade once more, and risk capture, or he could return home to Liverpool. He decided to return home. It was 3,000 miles away. Wilson was the only sailor. Neither the cook, a 27-year-old German, or the steward, a small 28-year-old Englishman, had any practical experience. For the first few days he practically ran the ship on his own, grabbing snatches of sleep when he could. Wilson spoke to his prisoners, and persuaded some of them to help. As he never completely trusted them, they were always kept under armed watch but they helped sail the *Emily St. Pierre* back to Liverpool. The journey took over thirty days. On 21 April, dog-tired, Wilson sailed his ship up the Mersey and dropped anchor. The Scotsman who had put one over on the Yanks became the toast of London and Richmond.

On the evening of 10 May 1862, at the offices of the Mercantile Marine Association in Liverpool, Wilson's daring was acknowledged. Many of the principal merchants of Liverpool, Captain Inglefield of Her Majesty's Ship *Majestic,* then anchored in the Mersey, and both members of Parliament for Liverpool, were in attendance when Wilson was presented with a magnificence service of plate. In addition a gold chronometer watch with appendages was given to him; his own crew, released and returned from America, presented him with a new sextant. At the same ceremony the owners of the *Emily St. Pierre* presented the 47-year-old Wilson with the sum of £2,000, and purses, each containing 20 guineas, were given to the cook and steward.

More successful as a blockade-runner, but perhaps not so well known as Wilson, was Jonathan Walkden Steele, captain of the *Banshee*. Steele was born at East Harlsey, Yorkshire, in February 1826. He went to sea as a boy in the merchant marine, and at the comparatively young age of twenty-eight, became captain of the tea clipper *Crest of the Wave*. She was a fully rigged wooden clipper of 924 tons; 184 ft. 3 inches long, 32 ft. 3 inches broad, with a draft of 20 ft. 1inch. The vessel was built in 1853 by William Pile of Sunderland for the Liverpool firm of Brice, Friend & Co. On her maiden voyage the following year, Steele sailed her to Melbourne, Australia, in 73 days. From there he proceeded to Shanghai. He left China on 20 October, with a cargo of tea, arriving at Liverpool 120 days later, on 17 February 1855. By 1862, on his last voyage, he had reduced the sailing time to 108 days. Steele arrived back in Liverpool on 16 April 1863. He was approached by a representative of the Anglo-Confederate Trading Co. to take command of the *Banshee* in a blockade-running venture. With the promise of £1,000 a trip, it was an offer he could not refuse. Later that month, as master of the *Banshee*, he crossed the Atlantic.

The *Banshee* had been launched in November 1862, at the Liverpool yard of Jones, Quiggin & Co. She was one of the first steel ships constructed for the Atlantic trade. Of 533 tons, she was a side-wheel steamship, 214 ft. long, 20 ft. 4 inches broad, with a draft of just 8 ft. She was fitted with engines of 120 h.p. producing a speed of 11 knots. Her top speed, under sail and steam, was 15 knots. The *Banshee,* registered in the name of John Toulmin Lawrence, a Liverpool merchant, had attempted to cross the Atlantic in early March 1863 under another captain; but because of leaky plates in her innovative construction, she was forced to put into Queenstown (Cobh), in southwestern Ireland. After undergoing some modification back in Liverpool, she was offered to Steele.

Steele's first trip was from Liverpool to Wilmington, North Carolina, but thereafter he operated short-haul into Wilmington. In all he made fifteen successful trips, seven from Nassau and eight from Bermuda, according to an annotated watercolor depicting the *Banshee,* in the collection at St. George's Museum, Bermuda. He came close to capture on the morning of 22 September 1863. When hauling out of Wilmington with a cargo of cotton, the black smoke from his funnels was sighted by the blockader USS *Adger*. Her commander, T.H. Patterson, takes up the story in a letter to Acting Rear Admiral S.P. Lee, Commander of the North Atlantic Blockading Squadron:

> Sir,
> I have the honor to report that at 5:30 a. m. on the 22d. instant, when 8 miles E.N.E. of Frying Pan Shoal light boat we discovered the masts and black smoke of a steamer, hull down, ahead, standing to the southward and eastward. Started in chase, and in an hour made out the stranger to be side-wheel steamer, painted light lead color, with two smoke pipes, schooner-rigged, and without any bowsprit.
> For three hours we gained in the chase until within four miles of her, when she commenced throwing overboard bales of cotton (we passed 169 whole bales), and as she lightened gradually increased the distance between us, so slowly, however, that I was encouraged to continue the chase until 6 P.M. (running 120 miles), when, finding it impossible to overhaul her, I reluctantly gave up the chase.
> At no time did the chase show any colors. But for the weak and unreliable condition of the flues of our boilers, which prevented our carrying more than a pressure of 15 pounds of steam to the square inch, I am confident we would have captured the chase.[9]

It was only later that the runner was identified as the *Banshee,* presumably by the U.S. consul at Nassau. On 9 October, at Beaufort, North Carolina, Patterson wrote once more to Rear Admiral Lee:

> Admiral,
> After sending you the report of my chasing the Banshee, it occurred to me that I should have stated why I had not picked up the cotton on my return, which my duty and interest prompted me to, but all the cotton was thrown overboard while in the Gulf Stream, and on my return at night I had a moderate gale from the eastward, with thick, rainy weather, which made it impracticable to recover the cotton without cruising for it thereby keeping me from completing the work of mooring the light boat. It grieved me to lose both vessel and cotton, but under the circumstances it appeared to me to be my duty to make the best of my way back to the light-boat.[10]

It was a close run thing for Steele, but it did not put him off. He just had to be more careful in future. He appears to have been doing return trips on an almost a weekly basis. On 8 August 1863 he ran into Wilmington with a cargo of 7,200 Austrian rifles, 300,000 cartridges, various metals, and chemicals. On other trips he shipped 2,300 army blankets, grey army uniforms, shoes, leather hides, bacon, tools, woolen clothing, and even iron plate for the Confederacy's ships. By his own admission he shipped out of Wilmington over 3,500 bales of cotton. He made over 1,000 percent profit for his employers in just six months.

It had been an incredibly successful venture, but it all came to an end on 21 November 1863. Three days out of Nassau, the *Banshee* was preparing her approach to Wilmington. It was just after three o'clock in the morning, when quite unexpectedly she crossed the path of a troopship, the steamer *Fulton,* bound for New York. Her captain ordered the *Banshee* to heave-to. Steele swung the wheel, altering course, and took off. The *Fulton* replied with a live round. There then followed a seven hour chase, the *Fulton* firing whenever the runner presented a clear shot. Having escaped from the USS *Adger* after a fifteen hour chase, Steele was not particularly concerned. By nine o'clock he was three miles ahead of the pursuing transport steamer. Still just within range of their rifle gun, the gunners aboard *Fulton* opened up once more. The first shot fell short, but having gained the range the next two struck home. The first hit her forward, the second her aft. Despite the hits, Steele refused to surrender. Then aboard the *Banshee* the cry went up of "sail-ho!" Way out on the port beam was another steamer charging down upon them. She was the USS *Grand Gulf.* By half past nine, having narrowed the gap to four miles, the *Grand Gulf's* 100-pounder Parrott gun opened up on the fleeing blockade-runner. By ten past ten, with both Federal vessels gaining on them, now firing almost continually, Steele had no choice, if he was to save the lives of his crew, but to surrender.

The *Fulton* arrived first and took the surrender, putting a prize crew aboard the *Banshee*. Coming up, Commander Ransom of the *Grand Gulf* sent a boarding party over to the little blockade-runner. To his astonishment the boarding officer, Ensign Charles Cadieu, was refused permission to board. The soldiers feared, and quite rightly too, that the navy would lay claim to their prize. It all got somewhat unseemly, when the army officer aboard the *Banshee*, Lt. George Darling of the First Rhode Island Cavalry, threatened the Federal sailors that if they attempted to board, he would order his men to fire into them. Sensibly Cadieu backed off, and returned to the *Grand Gulf*. With the *Banshee* in tow, the *Fulton* sailed for New York with her prize. Final adjudication by the U.S. District Court in New York valued the *Banshee* and her cargo at $111,216. The Court took $6,268 as costs; the remainder was divided between the officers and crews of both Federal ships.

Captain Steele and his crew were sent initially to Ludlow Street County Jail, New York, but were then transferred to Fort Lafayette Prison. Details relating to the crew were revealed during subsequent questioning:

The Crew of the *Banshee*

Name	Position	Age	Place of Residence	Place of Origin	No. of Times Ran Blockade
Jonathan Walkden Steele	Captain	37	Liverpool	England	8
Robert McKeon	Second Mate	24	Glasgow	Ireland	3
Adam French	Mess Boy	20	Devon	England	2
Samuel McCann	Boatswain	52	Liverpool	Ireland	2
Christopher Connor	Errand Boy	12	Liverpool	England	—
Charles Bethel	Engineer's Steward	15	Liverpool	Bahamas	2
Thomas White	Coal Trimmer	22	Liverpool	Ireland	2
William Marshall	Sailor's Boy	16	Devon	England	2
Allen Smith	Coal Passer	29	Liverpool	Ireland	2
William Campbell	Cook	27	Warren Point	Ireland	6
James Erskine	Chief Engineer	26	Wigtown	Scotland	3
David Houston	Second Engineer	23	Liverpool	Scotland	2
William Milne	Seaman	23	Dublin	Ireland	4
Henry J. Thompson	Seaman	32	Nassau	England	2
Walter McDonagh	Fireman	31	Renfrew	Scotland	4
John Byford	Seaman	24	Harwich	England	2
James McCaffrey	Fireman	28	Liverpool	Ireland	2
Owen Hughes	Fireman	39	Holyhead	Wales	2
Frederick Foley	Coal Trimmer	21	Dublin	Ireland	1
Samuel Johnson	Third Engineer	23	Liverpool	Ireland	2
John A. Power	Purser	26	Nassau	Ireland	2
Thomas Byrne	Third Mate	25	Nassau	Ireland	5
John Watson	Pilot	37	Abaco	Ireland	4
John Duff	Seaman	28	Douglas	Isle of Man	2
William Lindsay	Fireman	24	Glasgow	Scotland	2
Jerry Driscoll	Coal Passer	23	Queenstown	Ireland	2
Richard Sherrin	Fireman	36	Liverpool	Ireland	3
John McCallum	Second Cook	22	Glasgow	Scotland	2

Name	Position	Age	Place of Residence	Place of Origin	No. of Times Ran Blockade
Roger Donelley	Fireman	32	Glasgow	Scotland	7
William J. Burns	Seaman	25	Belfast	Ireland	2
Henry Rover	Seaman	40	Oldenberg	Germany	1
Thomas Sheriden	Carpenter	24	Liverpool	Ireland	3
Richard Armstrong	Chief Steward	35	Dublin	Ireland	2
Nathan Erskine	Fireman	23	Ft. William	Scotland	1
Valentine Walsh	Coal Trimmer	23	Londonderry	Ireland	2
Malcolm Wilkie	Coal Trimmer	33	Glasgow	Scotland	1
James Karnochan	Fireman	36	Liverpool	Scotland	4
Cecil Gardner	Second Mate	29	Warrenpoint	Ireland	2
George "Con" McClusky	Third Steward	20	Ireland	Ireland	2

As British subjects, most of the crew of the *Banshee* were released some ten weeks later, on 14 February 1864. Steele and Irishman Frederick Foley were not. The authorities believed that both were Americans. It took the persuasive power, and evidence presented by the British ambassador, Lord Lyons, to secure their release, on 24 February 1864. Both left the United States; and Steele returned to his wife and family, then resident at Sandstone Road, Liverpool.

It is claimed that one of the most successful of the commercial blockade-runners during the Civil War was the Middlesbrough-launched *Pet*. Depending on what source you read she ran the blockade 16, 18, 22, or even 40 times. Presumably the 40 relates to there and back. Her career was short, just under a year, and with each trip taking approximately two to three weeks there and back, perhaps a figure of 16 runs is more accurate. She was launched from Backhouse & Dixon's yard on 11 October 1862. An iron-screw steamer of 234 tons, her engines were manufactured by T. Richardson & Sons of Hartlepool. They had two 24-inch cylinders, 24-inch stroke, direct-action condensing, produced 120 horsepower, and gave a speed of 11½ knots. The *Pet* was 141 ft. 3 inches long, 20 ft. 6inches broad, and with a depth of 11 ft. 4 inches. In November she was registered in London as being owned by Charles John Purdue, but in reality was the property of Manchester based Alexander Collie & Co. The ship was taken to Liverpool where she was loaded with a mixed cargo, and under a British registered master, Captain Mason, sailed for Nassau on 10 January 1863. She arrived there on 23 March. At New Providence she acquired a new master, Ross Davis. It was he who ran the blockade in her. The U.S. consul, Samuel Whiting, was quick to notice the new arrival. In a letter to Acting Rear Admiral S.P. Lee, of the North Atlantic Blockading Squadron, he reports the arrival of 28 new blockade runners since March, including the *Pet*. The consul reckoned that each of these vessels would make at least two voyages, there and back, and worked out the profit to be made per trip:

One voyage outward cargo, say	$100,000
One voyage expense etc.	15, 000
	$115,000
She returns with 1,300 bales of cotton, weighing an average of 400 pounds per bale, equal to 45 cents per pound, or	234,000
From which deduct the cost	115,000
Leaves profit	$119,000

So each vessel would make $238,000 for two trips, and with 28 vessels at Nassau at the time, they would make a combined $6,664,000 for two months work. Multiply this by all the blockade-runners operating from Bermuda, Havana and Halifax, Nova Scotia, in comparison the $15,500,00 awarded to the United States by the Geneva Tribunal under the Alabama Claims, seems as small change.

All good things come to an end though, and on 16 February 1864, the *Pet* was caught. She had cleared Nassau late at night on the 14th, bound for Wilmington, with a mixed cargo including "provisions, fruit, vegetables, liquors and dry goods." On the following night, at 11:55 P.M., off Lockwood's Folly Inlet, she was sighted by the blockader USS *Montgomery,* under the command of Lieutenant E.H. Faucon. The *Pet* was two miles distant, in 5½ fathoms, steering for shore. Faucon ordered the *Montgomery* towards the shore, getting in before the runner. With her entry to Wilmington blocked, Captain Davis of the *Pet* changed course, southward. Faucon set off in pursuit. Closing, he signaled her by lights to heave-to. She ignored the night signal, and Faucon fired a round from his 30-pounder rifled gun at her. On she continued, getting closer to the entrance to Wilmington. At 12:45 A.M. on the morning of the 16th, Faucon fired a second shot. This concentrated Captain Davis' mind wonderfully. He heaved-to, in order to save lives. Then he lowered two boats, and got his passengers and the pilot off. There were some 13 people successfully got ashore before the Federal boarding party under Ensign W.O. Putnam could stop them. All papers except the ship's register Davis fed to the furnace so that they should not fall into the hands of the United States government. Now a prize, the *Pet* was taken, under the command of Acting Master Edmund Kemble to Boston, for adjudication. Her fruit and vegetables, "being of a perishable nature," were distributed among the officers and men of the blockading squadron. Davis and his remaining crew of 16, all being British, were eventually released.

Constructed at Middlesbrough, too, but this time at the yard of Richardson, Duck, was the iron-hulled steamship *Harriet Pinckney.* She was launched on 15 April 1862, and initially given the name of *Anonyma*. She was a 715 ton vessel, 191 ft. 3inches long, 28 ft. 9inches broad, with a depth of 17 ft. 3 inches. Her engines were by Richardson & Sons of Hartlepool, giving her a reputed speed of 18 knots. She was acquired by Lieutenant North for Fraser, Trenholm and named after Harriet Pinckney Huse, wife of Confederate purchasing agent Major Caleb Huse. The vessel was registered on 24 July under the ownership of Thomas Sterling Begbie, of 4, Mansion House Place, London. In reality she was owned by the Confederate government. The *Harriet Pinckney* was sailed down the coast and anchored in the Thames. Here she transshipped a cargo of 24,000 rifles, 18 cannon and the accoutrements appertaining from the *Sylph,* newly arrived from Hamburg. On the night of 8–9 August 1862 she sailed for Bermuda, arriving there on the 29th. Her mission had merely been to take the munitions into St. George's, rather than run the blockade herself; her deep draft of 17 feet rather militated against it. However when no ship from the Confederacy had arrived by October to transship the armaments, it was resolved that she and the blockade-runner *Minho* would run into Wilmington together. They chose the night of 9 October. That unfortunately was the night the unofficial blockade off Bermuda was particularly vigilant. The USS *Sonoma* spied them and made haste to intercept them. Discretion being the better part of valor, the two would-be blockade-runners scurried back into the safety of St. George's. On 11 December, still at Bermuda, the Confederate agent wrote to John Fraser & Co. of Charleston to remind them that the *Harriet Pinckney* was still there. Somehow the paperwork had been lost in the bureaucracy of the

Confederate government. It was mid–January before she disposed of her precious cargo, arriving back at Plymouth on 14 February 1863, with a cargo of cotton and tobacco.

In May 1863 the *Harriet Pinckney* was bought by Samuel Isaac for the firm of Isaac, Campbell & Co., and thereafter was run on a commercial basis, though agreeing to ship arms as a partial cargo as and when required. She was now based in the Thames, London, from whence she sailed on 9 May for Bermuda with a cargo of coal. She was able to service the Confederate cruiser *Florida,* though the existing records do not indicate whether this was her intended purpose. She sailed again from London on 5 November 1863, allegedly acting as a tender for the CSS *Rappahannock.* She then put in for repairs and renovation, leaving England with a mixed cargo on 2 June 1864. The *Harriet Pinckney* returned with 703 bales of cotton, 100 tons of tobacco, and £70,000 in gold for the Confederacy's English bankers, Fraser, Trenholm. Thereafter there are no further references to her in the British press or Union records.

Also from northeast was the side-wheel steamship *Peterhoff,* built at the yard of T.R. Oswald of West Hartlepool, and launched in late 1862. She left Falmouth in Cornwall on 27 January 1863, bound for Matamoras in Mexico, via the island of St. Thomas in the Danish Virgin Islands. On 20 February, just off the Danish island of St. John, and in Danish territorial waters, she was illegally fired upon by the USS *Alabama,* and forced to heave-to. A boarding party was then put aboard the British-flagged steamer, and her papers and cargo were searched, much to the protestation of her captain. Nothing was found, and the *Peterhoff* was allowed to continue on her journey to St. Thomas. As she entered the port, at anchor in the harbor were two Federal warships, under the command of Rear Admiral Charles Wilkes of *Trent* infamy. War between Great Britain and the United States was only narrowly averted following his rash action in forcibly removing the two Confederate commissioners from a registered British mail ship. Now, having apparently learned nothing from his stupidity, Wilkes potentially took both nations back to the brink of war.

As the *Peterhoff* left St. Thomas, on 25 February, Wilkes sent the USS *Vanderbilt* after her. Overtaken by the United States warship, the *Peterhoff*'s captain was ordered to heave-to and be boarded. Again her papers and cargo were searched, again with the same result: she was a neutral ship, in neutral waters, sailing from one neutral port to another neutral port. Much may have been suspected, but nothing could be proven. Then up stepped one of the *Peterhoff*'s crew, who declared that they were really sailing to Brownsville, Texas, a port just across the Rio Grande from Matamoras. Why he should have stepped up and said that is still open to question, but having said so, on his statement alone, the *Peterhoff* was seized as a prize. What differentiated the *Peterhoff* from normal trading vessels was that she was carrying the royal mail.

When her owner, Joseph Spence, heard what had happened, he called on the foreign secretary to take immediate action. In Washington Lord Lyons presented a note of formal protest at the actions of Wilkes. Denmark too registered a protest at the seizure of the *Peterhoff* in her territorial waters. While Denmark could be ignored, Great Britain could not. Amidst further veiled threats of war, the mail was returned, unopened; but in a face-saving gesture towards the American public, the *Peterhoff* was sent for adjudication before a prize court. The court, as expected, condemned the *Peterhoff,* which was then purchased by the United States Navy, and transferred to the North Atlantic Blockading Squadron. As the navy was careless with their new acquisition, she was sunk in a collision, in March 1864, with the USS *Monticello.* All her crew were fortunately saved. After the war the United States Supreme Court overturned the prize court's decision regarding the *Peterhoff*, on the grounds that the sailor's testimony in no way invalidated the ship's papers, which were in order. The owners were reimbursed for their loss.

Thanks to her exciting rediscovery in 1997, sunken in a sandbank at the entrance to Galveston Bay, the *Denbigh* is now one of the best documented of the British-built blockade-runners. She was built at Laird's Yard, Birkenhead, for the mercantile firm of Robert Gardner & Co. of Manchester at a cost of £10,150 and launched in August 1860. Fitted out, she was delivered to Gardner's on 26 September 1860. The *Denbigh* was an iron-hulled side-wheel steamer of 162 tons; 182 ft. 7 inches in length, 22 ft. 6 inches broad, and with a draft of just 7 feet. She had a wind-assisted speed of 13½ knots, on her trial trip, her feathered side-wheels turning 39 revolutions per minute. Over the next three years under Gardner, she plied between Liverpool and Rhyl, North Wales, as a packet ship. In September 1863 the *Denbigh* was purchased by the European Trading Company, an amalgam of three firms, H.O. Brewer of Mobile, Alabama, Emile Erlanger & Co. of Paris, and J.H. Shroder & Co. of Manchester.

Her sale was brought to the attention of the U.S. consul in Liverpool, Thomas Dudley, who wrote to the naval secretary, warning him of this potential blockade-runner. After further delving Dudley discovered that she was being sent to Bermuda or Havana. Her new master was one Captain McNevin, and though her crew of twenty (a captain, two mates, two engineers, six seamen, seven firemen, a cook and steward) was British, a number of Confederates are known to have had connections with the vessel, including two sailors from the *Florida*, Creaghan and Davis, and the Confederacy's coal agent at Cardiff, Abner M. Godfrey. Godfrey and his wife sailed aboard the *Denbigh* on 19 October 1863, bound for Havana, giving rise to the speculation that Godfrey later took over the running of the vessel. This, however, does not stand up to scrutiny. Before the war, in 1861, Godfrey was no more than a stevedore, a dock worker. The Captain McNevin identified by U.S. consul Thomas Dudley as the Denbigh's master was Francis McNevin, listed as Number 11250 in Lloyd's Register of Captains. He was born in St. Helier, Jersey, in 1829. Dudley's warning was passed on to the naval secretary, and by December 1863 the *Denbigh*'s details as a possible blockade-runner were passed on to the North Atlantic Blockading Squadron. She is listed as one of forty-two suspect vessels.

The *Denbigh* made her first run into Mobile from Havana, arriving there on 10 January 1864. In her run-in to the Alabama port she was discovered by the blockading force and fired upon. She made a dash for the port, but ran aground near Fort Morgan. The battery at the fort drove off the blockaders, but not before the Denbigh was hit, the shot passing through Denbigh's wheelhouse. McNevin was apparently unhurt. Over the next few days her cargo was off-loaded and the *Denbigh* was refloated. Henry Gorst, an Englishman from Worcestershire, allegedly a passenger aboard the later captured blockade-runner *Lilian*, testified that the *Denbigh* made eight successful runs into Mobile. Her trips were so regular, in fact, that she was known as the "Mobile Packet." Admiral Farragut, who reluctantly admired her captain's skill, said of McNevin "he was too smart for us and doubled us all and got in.... [He is] a bold rascal, and well he may be, for if I get him he will see the rest of his days of the war in [prison]." The *Denbigh*'s last dash into Mobile was in mid–July 1864. She was reputedly the last blockade-runner to make it out of Mobile, on 26 July, just days before the city fell to Federal forces.

Undaunted by the fall of Mobile, the *Denbigh* resumed her career by running the extra few dangerous miles into Galveston, just down the coast. Her first successful run was barely a month later, on 25 August. In all she made some six successful runs into Galveston — not all of them free from incident. At night on 19 April 1865, ten days after Lee's surrender but with the blockade still in force, she ran aground just off the harbor as she was leaving with a cargo of cotton bound for Havana. Her crew were obliged to throw 200 bales over the side before they could float her again. The *Denbigh*'s last run into Galveston was on the night of 23–24 May 1865. Again she came to grief, running aground on Bird Cay. As dawn broke she was sighted by the blockading squadron, which descended on her like vultures. Two Federal gunboats, the *Seminole* and the *Kennebec*, reportedly fired 40 rounds at her as they approached. The *Denbigh*'s crew took to the boats and got ashore safely. The gunboat crews boarded the badly damaged runner and ransacked her for anything of value before setting fire to her. Over the years her skeleton gently sank into the oozing mud of Bird Cay.

The *Lilian*, as previously mentioned, was built by J. & G. Thompson of Glasgow, and was launched in 1863. She was an iron-hulled, side-wheel steamer of 630 tons; 225 ft. 6 inches in length, and with a draft of 8 ft. 2inches. She had a top speed of 14 knots. There is a splendid engraving of her in the *Illustrated London News* (16 July 1864), showing her running the blockade into Wilmington. Her passengers display a certain British "reserve" towards the situation. As the "Special Artist," Frank Vizetelly records she was captained on this particular occasion by the redoubtable John N. Maffitt. At Wilmington the *Lilian* was handed over to the command of Maffitt's first lieutenant, who sailed her back to Bermuda, where Captain Daniel Martin, a native of Liverpool, then took command. First mate was George Gowan-Lock, a native of Glasgow, who was on $600 a trip. He had previously served aboard the blockade-runner *Venus*, captured some ten months previously. Gowan-Lock had been imprisoned at Fortress Monroe, but was released in March 1864, and returned to Liverpool. From there he signed on for work aboard the *Lilian*. The *Lilian*'s chief engineer was Francis Scuse, a Yorkshire man. He was on $800 a trip. When the *Lilian* was captured on 24 August 1864, Scuse claimed that he had never run the blockade before — but then, of course he would. Henry Gorst, from Worcestershire, nominally a passenger, had formerly been master of Scott & Co.'s Greenock-built blockade-runner *Ivanhoe*. In a run-in from Havana to Mobile, his vessel was run ashore by "an ignorant pilot," as Gorst himself described him. Subsequently the *Ivanhoe* was destroyed by Federal gunfire. Aboard the *Lilian* at the time of her capture were five Wilmington pilots who were being carried to Bermuda to ensure that other blockade-runners did not suffer the same fate. Sailing with the *Lilian*'s British crew was Charles W. Westendorff, former master of the *Bermuda*. In some ways Westendorff cuts a sad figure. He had left Charleston in November 1861 and sailed for Liverpool, there to take over command of the steamer *Bermuda* from Eugene Tessier. The vessel was captured by the USS *Mercedita*, and Westendorff, his crew and ship, were taken to Philadelphia for adjudication. Released, Westendorff sailed from New York to Bermuda aboard a British schooner. In July 1864 he ran into Wilmington aboard the Jones, Quiggins & Co.'s, Liverpool-built blockade-runner *Lynx*, owned by Fraser, Trenholm. On 22 August 1864 he boarded the *Lilian* for the run into Bermuda. When he was arrested and his belongings searched, he had $34,000 in Confederate bonds. His story was that he intended to go to England and enter into some business. When questioned further about the bonds he revealed that they belonged to one Mr. Mitchell of Wilmington, and that he, Westendorff, was taking them to Mitchell's agent in Liverpool. The probability was that they were intended for the construction, or purchase of, a blockade-runner. In his own defense,

Westendorff confessed, "I do not know anything about the blockade-running business and have had no intention of engaging in it. My physical condition unfits me for it, even if I desired to engage in it."

As the war progressed, with the use of more and more vessels the blockade did become tighter. The dangers of running it during the last days of the Confederacy increased enormously. Balanced against this was the enormous profit still to be gained from a Confederacy starved of even the basics. Captain Donald Cruikshank, master of the runner *Lady Stirling*, relates his adventure in a letter to his Liverpool employers, dated 2 November 1864. Cruikshank, an experienced blockade-runner, had earlier run into Wilmington, where he had discharged his cargo. Now laden with cotton he proceeded down river to Fort Fisher:

> The next night (28th October) at high water, being hazy we crossed the Bar at 7 P.M., keeping along the shore to the westward. In the course of quarter of an hour we sighted a vessel on our starboard bow, on which we hauled immediately to the southward and westward. He had however, noticed us, let drive and threw up a rocket, which put the whole fleet on the alert. Several of them caught sight of us shortly afterwards and opened out a heavy fire. Having cleared the first vessel we kept along the beach, steering west by north, to clear those who were bearing down on our port beam; running along we came across another on our starboard bow, in which we again hauled to the southward and westward. We were shortly afterwards saluted with a heavy fire from him, a shell striking us just before the starboard sponson guard,[11] and, exploding among the cotton over the forward bunker, immediately set us on fire. Another stove the starboard paddle-box boat, a splinter grazing my right leg (under present circumstances I wish it had taken my head off); it then knocked the valve casing off, just clearing the steam pipe. In the meantime we got the hose pumping down the hatch, trying to keep the fire under, and had kept the ship away S.S.W., endeavoring to get to sea as quickly as possible. There was, however, one fellow up with us and firing every few minutes, so we commenced throwing off the deck load, not only to lighten her, but also to clear the deck over the head of the fire, in order to cut holes sufficiently large to pass the hose down to try to extinguish it. Up to this time we had been carrying a good head of steam, but owing to the fire spreading and the increase of smoke in the forward bunker and stoke hole, the men were unable to get either a sufficient supply of fuel, or fire properly, so we commenced passing from aft forward. About 9.30 the vessel astern was about half a mile distant, plying us with shell, and cutting our rigging in various places. We had dropped all the others when, unfortunately, we came on top of another one about 2 points on the starboard bow. By now it had cleared up considerably, and we hauled up S.S.E. to avoid him, the firing of the vessel astern drawing his attention to us. He edged down to cut us off, managed to cross our bow, and poured shot and shell into us. One of the latter burst in the forehold, setting fire to the cotton there. We were thus on fire in two places. The stern vessel, who had gained some advantage by our keeping away, was now within hail; one of his shells cut the foremast nearly in halves. Up to this the crew had behaved tolerably well, but now they became perfectly panic-stricken and demoralized. It was with the greatest difficulty any of the firemen could be kept at the fires. The man left the wheel, which I was obliged to take myself. The engineer stopped the engines, his excuse being that, in the excitement of the moment, he thought someone called out to stop her. I made them start her again, notwithstanding that the vessels were one on each quarter, but the men refused to do anything further. There was nothing for it but to submit. The vessel that followed us up was the Aeolus (the same that captured the Hope about ten days ago) and the vessel that intercepted us the Calypso.[12]

Though this present work is primarily concerned with the part British sailors played in the war, one should not forget the part played by young Confederate captains who ran the blockade for purer motives. Here again, though, there is a British context, for the most successful of them employed British ships with British crews. Perhaps the most noted of these were Captain Thomas J. Lockwood, Lt. Richard H. Gayle, Lt. John Wilkinson, and of course the "Prince of the Privateers," Commander John N. Maffitt.

Tom Lockwood was born in Wilmington, North Carolina, in 1831. As a young man he worked for the Florida Steam Packet Company, a subsidiary of John Fraser & Co. He eventually became captain of the *Carolina*, a side-wheel steamer. She was a packet ship transporting mail, cargo and passengers between Jacksonville, Florida, and Charleston. Upon his marriage to Anna McDougal, in March 1860, Lockwood purchased land from Fraser & Co.'s senior partner, George Alfred Trenholm, soon to take up residence in Liverpool. With the outbreak of war Lockwood received a commission as a Confederate privateer, and took command of the *Theodora,* formerly the *Gordon.* After some success he was seconded to blockade-running, and in October of that year was entrusted with the transport of the Confederate commissioners to Great Britain and France, James M. Mason and John Slidell, along with their families and aides. He ran the blockade to Havana, Cuba, with them, returning with arms, ammunition and 200,000 cigars. Given command of the *Kate,* sister ship to his former vessel, he made a number of runs between Nassau and Wilmington. In December 1861 Lockwood transshipped arms to the value of $850,000 from the British-flagged ship *Gladiator* and ran them into Charleston. In the days before the battles fought at Shiloh, in April 1862, the *Kate* ran the blockade into Charleston with 1,000 barrels of gunpowder, and arms and ammunition for 10,000 men. In about June 1863 Lockwood was appointed master of the wooden-built steamer *Atlantic,* later renamed the *Elizabeth*. She ran a number of successful journeys between Nassau and Wilmington. On 24 September though, she came to grief when she ran aground off the entrance to Cape Fear River. Lockwood set her ablaze rather than let her fall into the hands of the Federal navy.

In the summer of 1864 Lockwood was sent to England, and appointed master of the *Colonel Lamb,* the newest of the Confederate navy's own blockade-runners. She was

The *Colonel Lamb* was captained by Wilmington-born Thomas Lockwood, C.S.N. (*Illustrated London News*)

named in honor of Colonel William Lamb, Commander of Fort Fisher, the blockade-runners' best friend. She was British built, at the yard of Jones, Quiggin & Co., Liverpool, in 1864, designated Hull No. 165. The *Lamb* was one of the new breed of blockade-runners, built especially for that task. She was constructed with four watertight bulkheads. The vessel was a two-masted, two-funneled steel, side-wheel paddle steamer of 1,780 tons. Her engines of 350 h.p. were supplied by James Jack & Co., and reached a speed of almost 17 knots on her trial trip, which took the form of a race against the steamer *Douglas,* of the Isle of Man Steam Packet Company in September 1864. She was of rakish design, 280 feet in length, 36 feet broad, with a depth of 15½ feet. The ship was originally registered in Quiggin's name, but was then quietly transferred to the ownership of the Confederate agent in Nassau, J.B. Lafitte. Her long low hull was painted "a light lead color," to make her almost impossible to see at any great distance. Ostensibly under the command of a British-registered captain, she left the Mersey, with Lockwood on board, bound for Nassau. Here Lockwood resumed his career as a blockade-runner. In his official diary, Colonel Lamb, commander of Fort Fisher, refers to his namesake on 23 November 1864: "Received a letter from J.B. Laffitte, esq., Nassau, who shipped one of my Whitworth's in Colonel Lamb; the Banshee is to bring the other."[13]

On 24 December 1864 the *Colonel Lamb,* flying the Confederate flag, ran into St. George's, Bermuda, with a cargo of 1,760 bales of cotton. From Bermuda, Lockwood sailed up to Halifax, Nova Scotia, to take aboard a cargo of ammunition and boots for Lee's bedraggled army. On 18 January 1865, the United States consul at Halifax reported that the *Colonel Lamb, Charlotte* and *Old Dominion* were preparing to run into Wilmington, not realizing that Fort Fisher had fallen to the Federals. That news overtook them, and the three ships sailed for Galveston, Texas. As the war came to an end, Lockwood sailed for Liverpool, and handed over the *Colonel Lamb* to Commander Bulloch. At the end of the war the *Colonel Lamb* was transferred to Fraser, Trenholm and renamed the *Ariel.* The company sold her to a Greek interest, and she was renamed the *Bouboulina.* A year later she was destroyed in an explosion while loading munitions in the Mersey.

Richard Haynsworth Gayle, the second of the Confederate blockade-runners, was born in 1832, the son of John Gayle, governor of Alabama, and his wife, Sarah Ann. In 1858 he was appointed United States consul at Montevideo, Uruguay. As tensions at home increased, Gayle returned to his family in Alabama, and with the outbreak of war he was appointed a captain in the Provisional Army of the Confederate States. At Christmas 1861, he transferred to the navy and was commissioned as a lieutenant. Gayle was briefly given command of the *Robert E. Lee* (formerly the *Giraffe*) in May 1863, when Lt. John Wilkinson was seconded to other duties. In June of that year he was appointed captain of the *Cornubia,* also later known as the *Lady Davis.*[14]

The *Cornubia* had been built in 1858 by Harvey & Co. of Hayle, Cornwall, for the Hayle Steam Packet Company. She worked the Hayle and St. Ives to Bristol route, as a packet ship and ferry. The *Cornubia* (the Latin name for Cornwall) was an iron-hulled, side-wheel steamer with four boilers and a 9-foot stroke engine producing 230 h.p., giving her a speed of over 19 knots. She had two funnels, mounted close together amidships. The *Cornubia* was 210 feet long, 24 ft. 6inches broad, and possessed an extremely shallow draft of just 9 ft. She began her career as a blockade-runner in December 1862, under her British captain, J.M. Burroughs. Arriving at Bermuda her color was changed from black to a light lead color, later to be known as battleship gray. On 13 December 1862, Burroughs sailed for Charleston with a cargo of munitions, and a passenger by the name of Stiles, of the late U.S. consul at Vienna, carrying secret papers for the Confederacy. Just over a month later, on 19 January 1863, the *Cornubia*, having successfully run the blockade again, returned to St. George's with a cargo of 300 bales of cotton and 80 barrels of rosin and turpentine.

On her next run out of St. George's, with ammunition and powder aboard, the *Cornubia* was sighted just beyond the marine league as dawn broke, by a Federal steamer. Burroughs ignored the initial warning shot, and with as much steam as could be raised, set off, the Federal warship in pursuit. It was eleven o'clock that morning before Burroughs succeeded in losing her. Failing to get into Charleston, Burroughs ran into Wilmington. He brought out 300 bales of cotton, and a passenger with British credit to the equivalent of $200,000 for the purchase and outfitting of a steamer for the Confederacy. Burroughs made the passage back to Bermuda, arriving on 19 February, in 71 hours. Barely a week later, on 25 February, having discharged and taken aboard a new cargo, Burroughs sailed again for Wilmington. He returned with another cargo of cotton, making the return journey in 66 hours. On 21 April the *Cornubia* made her last run into St. George's under Burroughs' command. The success of the Cornish-built steamer had attracted the attentions of the Confederate navy, which purchased her. On 8 May, Lt. Gayle was dispatched to Bermuda to take charge of the vessel. Burroughs and his crew agreed to make one last run into Wilmington. After loading the *Cornubia* with arms, Burroughs and Gayle ran the blockade into Wilmington, on the night of 9–10 June.

In the blockading fleet, Captain A Ludlow Case, of the USS *Iroquois* reported:

Sir,

I have the honor to report that at 10 P.M. yesterday a vessel was seen passing this ship, steering to the eastward. A gun was immediately fired at her and our cables slipped in pursuit. As we seemed to gain on her, she altered her course more to the northward, and finally hauled directly in for the land, and getting soon under cover of the woods, we lost sight of her, the night being dark. Several guns were fired at her to draw attention of the Shokoken, off Top-sail Inlet, and other blockading vessels.[15]

The following morning Case added to his report: "I have to report that a long, low, paddle-wheel steamer was seen at 4.15 A.M. passing over the inner rip into the river, having run the blockade inward during the night. She had two smokestacks and two light masts, and wore the new rebel flag (white, with a red union). From her length and general appearance I suppose her to be either the Cornubia or Robert E. Lee."[16] Both blockade-runners were by now well known to the blockading squadron. The flying of the Confederate flag though, was a notable change. That same day, 10 June 1863, Confederate chief of ordnance Colonel Josiah Gorgas officially appointed Gayle as captain of the *Cornubia*, to whom he wrote: "You will assume command of the Steamer Cornubia relieving Capt. J.M. Burroughs.... [He] has been requested to accompany you, giving you the benefit of his experience and advice. He will also be able to assist you very much in acquiring good officers and crew.... Take immediate steps to change your flag and register under Confederate colors.... Those who decline to reship will be discharged and furnished with free passage to Bermuda and be paid up to arrival there."[17]

In all, under his new charge, Gayle successfully ran the blockade 22 times in less than six months, bringing vital cargoes to the beleaguered Confederate armies. Crew member J.T. Gordon, a Southerner, kept a diary of his time aboard the *Cornubia*. Listed below are extracts from it[18]:

13. The Men and the Ships That Ran the Blockade

September 4, 1863, P.M.: Anchored below Fort St. Philip, opposite Fort Fisher; to leave for St. George, Bermuda, tomorrow night.

September 5, 11.25 P.M.: Got underway and proceeded slowly to the Rip; crossed without grounding. At 12.12 midnight Crossed the bar. Moon shone very brightly. Saw one blockader very near, but he did not see us, although the furnaces were so hot that flames flashed out over the tops of the funnels or smoke-Stacks. At 3.30 saw a Yankee cruiser ahead; kept off to avoid him. He did not discover us.

September 8: Made sail on starboard bow; kept off a point to avoid her. At 6.30 P.M. sighted Bermuda light, being just sixty-four and one half hours from New Inlet Bar.

September 9: Anchored in St. George 6 A.M. Found the *Venus* and *Hansa* in safely.

September 10: Discharging cargo.

September 17: Coaled the *Cornubia*..

September 18, 3.25 P.M.: Got underway, bound for Wilmington.... Machinery worked badly, very much annoying the captain.

September 21, 10 A.M.: Cleared up from northwest. At 10 P.M. made a vessel on port bow; kept up north to avoid her.

September 22: Saw a number of sail, one a three-masted steamer. Made Cape Lookout light houses in the afternoon. Made land about sunset, and were up to Bogue Inlet about that time. At 10 P.M. were up to New Topsail Inlet. At 2.30 were off Fort Fisher. At 6 A.M. Wednesday morning crossed the bar safely.

September 23: Passed over New Inlet Bar at 6 A.M. Grounded on the Rip, and remained there until the next afternoon, when we got off and went up to the quarantine station just below Wilmington.

September 24: Visiting officer came off. Went up to the wharf.

September 25: Commenced unloading.

September 30: Finished loading and anchored in the stream.

October 9: Finished coaling. Got underway and anchored off Fort Fisher. Mrs. Ex-President Tyler and two Children among the passengers.

October 11: At 6 P.M. up anchor; at 7 P.M. cross the bar; soon discovered a blockader close in to the bar, but he did not see us.

October 12: Heavy sea; saw five or six sail during the day. Our passengers are Mr. G. Alexander, Mr. Black, Captain Atkins, and Paymasters Harwood and Moses, both C.S. Navy.

October 14: Wet and squally; saw several sailing vessels. Stood off from the land from 1 until 3 at night, then stood in and made Bermuda light from the masthead at 5 A.M., eighty-two hours from New Inlet Bar. During the night saw a vessel and took her for a steamer.

October 15: At 7 A.M. island of Bermuda in full sight; at 8 A.M. took on board the pilot; at 11 A.M. anchored in St. George's harbor. Found the steamers *Alice, Ella* and *Annie* in harbor. Passengers soon went ashore.

October 24: Rained very heavily: *R.E. Lee* arrived from Halifax.

November 2: Had a dinner and dancing party on board.

November 4: Got underway at 1 o'clock for Wilmington; at 1.30 pilot left us. The steamers *A.D. Vance* and *Ella* left about 9 A.M.

November 5: Passed a full-rigged ship early in the morning.
November 7: Pleasant weather; number of sails in sight.

On the night of 7–8 November 1863, Gayle began his 23rd run into Wilmington. It was just after midnight; the *Cornubia* was eleven miles north of New Inlet as Gayle prepared his run. Over on his starboard bow a lookout aboard the blockader USS *James Adger* sighted the *Cornubia*. Its commander, T.H. Patterson, reported: "At midnight of the 7th instant, while lying in 3½ fathoms water, about 3 miles south of Masonboro Inlet, we discovered a vessel on our port bow heading to the eastward; started in chase, but in half an hour lost sight of her. I continued chasing in the direction I had last seen her until 1 A.M., when I concluded that if the chase was a vessel attempting to run the blockade, and seeing us stand to the eastward, she would steer in for the land, hug it close, and run for New Inlet."[19]

Patterson had lost her, but in the process had driven the *Cornubia* towards another vessel in the blockade, the USS *Niphon*. Her captain, J.B. Breck, takes up the story: "On the morning ... about 2 o'clock, while lying inshore near the beach in 3 fathoms water, saw a rocket thrown up from the northward; went to quarters; stood inshore to 2 fathoms water. In a few moments saw a steamer running fast toward me along the beach, the James Adger in chase. Stood in to cut him off, and when near him the steamer ran ashore, which proved to be the Cornubia."[20] Commander Patterson of the *James Adger* concludes:

> [A] few moments after came up with the strange steamer, which had been run ashore about 11 miles north of New Inlet, having been headed off by the USS Niphon, and was blowing off steam.
> I sent Lieutenant Franklin, my executive officer, and Acting Master R.O. Patterson to take possession of the prize, with an engineer and two firemen to examine into the condition of her engines.
> The officers, crew, and passengers were escaping, and all succeeded in reaching the shore except the captain, carpenter, and one seaman who remained aboard.
> As the tide was running flood, I made fast a hawser to the prize and commenced trying to haul her off, directing Acting Master Breck, commanding the Niphon, to keep to the southward, close inshore, and enfilade the beach with grape [shot] and at about 3 A.M. succeeded in hauling the Cornubia off.
> I have ordered her to Boston, in charge of Acting Master R.O. Patterson.[21]

The *Cornubia* and her captain had been captured. The vessel was taken to Boston as a prize, and purchased by the Union navy on 17 March 1864. She was assigned to the role of a blockader. Gayle was later freed in an exchange of prisoners of war. On 6 December 1864, he was appointed captain of a new blockade runner, the *Stag*. She had been built at the yard of Jones, Quiggin & Co., of Liverpool, to the order of Commander James Bulloch. The *Stag* was of 600 tons, 230 feet in length, 26 feet in breadth, and a draft of just 7½ feet. She was one of a new breed of specially designed blockade-runners known as the "Owl-class" after the prototype built by the Liverpool shipbuilders. The *Stag* ran into Wilmington on 12 December, under her British captain, Gayle's old friend Captain J.M. Burroughs. With 850 bales of cotton aboard, Gayle continued where he had left off, and ran the blockade once more. He made a couple of successful runs, but, unaware of the capture of Fort Fisher and Fort Caswell, he approached Wilmington on the night of 19–20 January 1865. The following morning Admiral D.D. Porter wrote from Smithville: "I had the blockade runners' lights lit last night, and was obliging enough to answer their signals, whether right or wrong we don't know.... *Stag* and *Charlotte,* from Bermuda, loaded with arms, blankets, shoes, etc., came in and quietly anchored ... and were taken possession of." This time there was to be no exchange of prisoners.

Lt. John Wilkinson, was small, stout, and had a receding hairline and a great bushy beard to compensate. Physically he was not the stuff of legends. Physical appearance aside, he had the heart of a lion, and was one of the most if not the most, successful of the Confederate navy's blockade-runners. John Wilkinson, the son of Jesse Wilkinson, captain of the frigate USS *United States*, was born in Amelia County, Virginia, on 6 November 1821. He was commissioned into the navy as a midshipman, and later served onboard the *Saratoga,* under Captain David G. Farragut. In 1850 he was promoted to lieutenant. He served in the coastal survey of the Florida Keys and the Bahamas during the 1850s, laying the groundwork for his later successful career as a blockade-runner. When Virginia seceded from the Union, Wilkinson tendered his resignation from the United States Navy. In the petty vindictive way that became the norm for Southern officers resigning their commissions, naval records imply that he was dishonorably discharged. Initially Wilkinson was seconded to mundane duties, but then after a summons to New Orleans, he was appointed first officer aboard the unfinished ironclad *Louisiana*. Disastrously the ironclad was seized when Farragut's fleet forced its way past the New Orleans forts, and her officers, including Wilkinson, were taken prisoner. They were imprisoned briefly in Fort Warren near Boston, but three months later Wilkinson was part of an exchange of prisoners and returned to the Confederacy. Almost immediately, in September 1862, he was sent to Britain to purchase a fast steamer, reportedly then up for sale in Glasgow.

When Wilkinson, and his party, comprising Major B.F. Ficklin, clerk John B. Tabb, and two government officials, arrived in Scotland, they discovered that the steamer *Giraffe* had already been sold. The purchasers, Alexander Collie & Co. of Manchester, were a merchant company, with a fleet of twenty blockade-running vessels. Identifying that he was acting on behalf of the Confederate government, Wilkinson persuaded Collie to sell the *Giraffe* for the same amount that he had paid for her, £32,000, with the proviso that, if the Confederate government decided to sell her, Collie would have the right of first refusal. Collie agreed.

The *Giraffe,* which had formerly run between Glasgow and Belfast, weighed 900 tons. She was a schooner-rigged, iron-hulled side paddle-steamer with two funnels; she was 260 feet long, 20 feet in breadth, with a draft of 10 feet, and had a top speed of 13 knots. Wilkinson and young Tabb proceeded south to London to see Commissioner Mason, while the remainder of the team oversaw the outfitting of the vessel. In late November the *Giraffe* was ready to sail. Her cargo consisted of arms and medicines. In addition twenty-six Scottish lithographers were recruited for the Treasury Department to assist in the design and printing of new currency. Their efforts for the Confederacy proved futile owing to the poor quality of paper and inks provided. It was claimed that the forgeries produced by the Federal government to destabilize the currency were easily identifiable by their superior quality. The *Giraffe* sailed from Glasgow under a British captain and a British crew. The U.S. consul at Liverpool, Thomas Dudley, wrote to the secretary of the navy:

November 11, 1862

> I learn from a reliable source that the steamer Giraffe will sail from Glasgow tonight or tomorrow, to be commanded by Captain J.A. Duguid, the same who took out the pirate Oreto. She is to run the blockade into Charleston; has on her a very large mail for the South and important dispatches for the rebel Government. She is said to be a fast vessel, and very likely to run in. She should be captured wherever found.. There is no doubt about her character.[22]

The *Giraffe* touched at Puerto Rico before continuing on to Nassau. Here Wilkinson took over command and recruited a partial new crew, the former having only signed articles to sail the ship to the West Indies. With the promise of good pay, some of the old crew had joined him, and with more British sailors recruited, Wilkinson embarked for Wilmington on Christmas Day 1862. On the night of 28 December he approached the mouth of the river. It was his first run through the blockade. There was a slight mishap when he briefly ran aground at the entrance to the river, but getting off he sailed on up the river past the guns of Fort Fisher to Wilmington.

The *Giraffe* was now renamed the *Robert E. Lee*. As her captain, Wilkinson made 21 successful runs through the blockade. Wilkinson later wrote, "She had run the blockade twenty-one times while under my command, and had carried

Lt. John Wilkinson, C.S.N., successfully ran the blockade over twenty times.

abroad between six thousand and seven thousand bales of cotton, worth at that time about two millions of dollars in gold, and had carried into the Confederacy equally valuable cargoes." On one occasion, during a fierce storm, with visibility down to a few yards, he ran through the blockade, but the rough seas prevented him from entering the river. He was forced to anchor off the coast, well within the firing range of the blockaders. The blockaders were too preoccupied with the storm themselves to pay Wilkinson and his ship any attention. When the weather grew calmer, Wilkinson cut his anchor chain and made a dash for the safety of Fort Fisher's guns. In his book, *Narrative of a Blockade Runner*, published in 1877, he describes the various devices he used to elude the blockade. After a few runs he noticed that, a runner having been discovered, the blockading vessel would send up a colored rocket in the direction the runner was proceeding. Wilkinson obtained a number of rockets for himself, and thereafter when he was discovered and a rocket was sent up, he would fire the same colored rocket off at a slight angle to the route he was sailing. Confusion would thus ensue among the blockaders and he could make his escape in the chaos.

In one of his runs Wilkinson had a memorable escape from the blockader USS *Iroquois*. The *Robert E. Lee* had just run the blockade out of Wilmington, en route for Bermuda. She got beyond the inner ring, but as she eased past the outer blockade she was discovered by the *Iroquois*. The Federal ship opened up on her. In the normal course of events, having superior speed, Wilkinson's ship would easily have outrun her, and escaped in the dark. Unfortunately at Bermuda, on the previous trip Wilkinson had given most of his good Welsh coal to John N. Maffitt of the *Florida*. As captain of a warship Maffitt was having difficulties in obtaining coal in a neutral port. As a consequence Wilkinson was obliged to use inferior North Carolina coal on his run out of Wilmington. His top speed was reduced to a mere 8 knots, as compared to the *Iroquois,* under steam and sail, who was approaching at more than 11 knots and firing her guns at the same time. Wilkinson changed course, taking his ship out of the wind. The *Iroquois* changed course too, taking her out of the wind. Soon her sails hung limp and useless as she followed, reducing her speed. She still had more power than the *Robert E. Lee,* and progressively gained on the blockade-runner. Wilkinson had to do something to increase pressure in his boilers. He ordered the wooden furniture to be broken up and fed to the furnace. Then it was everything else made of wood: railings, doors, planking. He succeeded in maintaining his distance, but when all the wood was consumed it was inevitable that he would be captured. Then he remembered that he had turpentine aboard as part of his cargo. There was cotton and lint, which if soaked, would burn with intensity. Wilkinson ordered the crew to prepare wads to be fed to the furnace. Within an hour the *Robert E. Lee's* speed was increased to 13½ knots, and she started to pull away. The *Iroquois* continued her barrage, but the *Robert E Lee* continued to increase the distance between them. When the pursuer could no longer be seen, Wilkinson changed course and escaped.

Wilkinson was later seconded to other duties, including an attempt to capture a Federal steamer and free Confederate prisoners, but by December 1864, he was again running the blockade. Returning from Bermuda in mid–January with a cargo of supplies aboard his new ship, the *Chameleon,* he approached Fort Fisher. As no lights were lit onshore Wilkinson decided not to proceed, but turned back to sea. The next night he made another run in; the signaling lights were lit. His signalman flashed a coded light to the shore, but the response was incorrect. Fearing a trap he notified Wilkinson, who agreed with him. Unknowingly to them, in their absence Fort Fisher had fallen to the enemy. The signaling light ruse had worked before, trapping a number of blockade-runners, but not Wilkinson and the *Chameleon.* With Wilmington closed, Wilkinson sailed for Nassau, where he met Commander Maffitt, who informed him that Fort Fisher had been captured. The two decided to try Charleston, but were chased off. Returning to Nassau they discovered that Charleston too had fallen to the enemy. They waited until 22 March, but no orders came from Richmond. The war was all but over. Wilkinson made the decision to sail to England, and place himself under the command of James Bulloch. The *Chameleon* reached Liverpool on 9 April 1865.

Following his restoration to good health, erstwhile Irishman and former captain of the *Florida* John N. Maffitt was initially given command of the iron-clad *Albermarle.* As the war began going badly for the Confederacy the emphasis of the government in relation to its navy changed. It turned more and more to blockade-running in order to supply its army. On 14 September 1864, Maffitt was seconded by Mallory to the blockade-runner *Owl.* There is a certain desperation in Mallory's letter:

> Sir,
>
> The Owl is the first of several steamers built for and on account of the Confederate Government, and which are to run under the direction of the Secretary of the Navy. Naval officers are to be placed in command, and you are selected to take charge of the Owl. All the information I have as to this vessel is derived from the enclosed copy of a letter from Colonel Bayne, which, you will perceive, says nothing as to the condition upon which the officers and crew are engaged, nor does it inform me as to the vessels [*sic*] papers. You will at once ascertain all necessary information upon these points. It is possible that, after the manner of seamen, there may be murmuring or discontent by those on board at the change of command; and, as it is difficult to find crews and engineers at pleasure, your judgment and tact are relied upon to meet such a contingency.
>
> The Owl should go to Bermuda rather than Halifax for the reason that she could bring but little cargo from the latter point in addition to the coal required for her inward and outward trips, and for the additional reason that the risks of capture and loss are far greater on the Halifax route. From Halifax the United States agents may telegraph to any naval station and city of the enemy the exact time of the departure of our ships and thus greatly increase the chances of intercepting them.

The *Owl* running the blockade under Commander Maffitt, in an engraving from the *Illustrated London News*. Notice the casual air of the crew and passengers — typical British understatement while under fire. (*Illustrated London News*, 16 July 1864)

> This Department having to defray the expenses of the vessels sailing under its direction, sterling bills will be placed in your hands to enable you to meet those of your command; and you are enjoined to see that economy and efficiency in all its departments are practiced. So soon as a naval assistant paymaster can be spared one will be sent to you.[23]

Mallory was aware of the bigger picture. The war was going badly for the South. They were short of supplies and experienced men. He was concerned about losing the British crew aboard the *Owl*, and clearly there were difficulties over finance. The blockade now had a strangle-hold over the Southern ports. Fewer and fewer vessels were getting through. Mallory added: "As commanding officer of the Owl you will please devise and adopt thorough and efficient means for saving all hands and destroying the vessel and cargo whenever these measures may become necessary to prevent capture. Upon your firmness and ability the Department relies for the execution of this important trust."

In the chaos of the closing months of the war, records relating to blockade-running are sporadic. There is an oblique reference to Maffitt in a report of Major-General Whiting to Mallory on 6 October 1864: "Last week gives us the record of the Lynx, the Night Hawk and the Condor lost with much valuable cargo, and Owl in going out compelled to throw over her cargo of cotton, if, indeed she be not caught."[24] The *Owl* was not caught, and continued to run the blockade. She arrived at Nassau with a cargo of cotton on 24 October, departing five days later with arms. In December 1864, under orders from Mallory, Maffitt collected the remaining crew from his old ship, the *Florida*, and took them into Wilmington. Lee surrendered on Sunday, 9 April 1865, and Fort Fisher fell. Maffitt transferred to Galveston. The run between there and Nassau was longer and the risks became greater. On 20 May 1865 the U.S. consul-general at Havana, William T. Minor, reported the possibility of capturing the runner:

> Sir,
>
> The blockade runner Owl, Captain Maffitt, under the rebel flag, will leave here for Galveston to-day or to-morrow. On her return from Galveston the Owl will come out by the main channel. By following the accompanying directions the Owl may be caught: Station a light-draft gunboat on the Northeast Channel (there are 7 feet of water at low tide); run in far enough to keep the Knoll buoy always in sight. If the night is very dark, cross the bar and anchor just inside. Let the Owl pass the buoy and cripple her from the start; then come in behind her. Don't trust sailors to look out.... Will you communicate it at once to the officer in command of the naval forces at New Orleans. The rebel ironclad ram Stonewall was given up on yesterday by those having charge of her to the Spanish colonial authorities of the island of Cuba.[25]

Despite their plans, Maffitt successfully ran the blockade and got out again. He ran up to Nassau to await orders. They did not come. There was nowhere to go. Wilkinson had already sailed for England. Maffitt followed him. He could not bring himself to surrender to the Yankees. On 14 July 1865 the *Owl* steamed up the river Mersey and came to anchor. For John N. Maffitt and the other blockade-runners, the great adventure was over.

14

Tales of Old Men

The Civil War was over, slavery was ended, and the Union preserved. The industrial exploitation of the North over the South was maintained, and the sense of grievance felt by the South continued. Men such as General Robert E. Lee had been brave and gallant opponents, but they could not go unpunished. In a fit of petty vindictiveness, the United States government excluded them from pardon under the post-bellum amnesty proclamations. The amnesty, which should have prepared the way for peaceful reconciliation, was carefully worded to emasculate the South, to exclude from office, or function, its most able and honest men. The act left the South without effective leadership. The offending clause nine reads as follows:

> The persons excepted from the benefits of the foregoing provisions are all who are, or shall have been, civil, or diplomatic officers or agents of the so-called Confederate government; all who have left judicial stations under the United States to aid the rebellion; all who are, or shall have been, military or naval officers of said so-called Confederate government above the rank of colonel in the army or of lieutenant in the navy; all who left seats in the United States Congress to aid the rebellion; all who resigned commissions in the army or navy of the United States and afterwards aided the rebellion....

In England there were men excluded from the general pardon, too. At the top of that list was James Murray Mason, Confederate commissioner to Great Britain. Very much aware that the war was going against them, and that the victorious United States government would not look too kindly upon him, Mason prepared for a future life in exile. He bought a private house in 1864 at 39, Clarendon Street, Leamington Spa. Curiously this Warwickshire town, just across the River Avon from Warwick, had attracted a sizeable Confederate population. The following year Mason moved to a more modest terraced house at 28, Grove Street. In April 1866 the former Confederate commissioner crossed the Atlantic and set up home in Canada. After President Johnson's second proclamation of amnesty in 1868, Mason returned to Virginia, where he discovered that his old home, "Selma," had been burned to the ground by Sheridan during the war. Mason settled at Alexandria, Virginia, where he had a new house, "Clarens," built. It was here that he died on 28 April 1871.

In the number of the excluded was James Dunwoody Bulloch and his half-brother, Irvine. During the war years, James Bulloch made a number of friends in Liverpool—not only those who shared his political ends, but also those who came to like him as a person for his intelligence, modesty and reserve. He was an accomplished gentleman, courteous and kind, a well-read man, and well versed in maritime and international law. To have returned to the United States would in all probability have led to his arrest and trial. At the urging of his friends he remained in Liverpool; he entered into a partnership as Bulloch & Barcroft, cotton brokers, at the old Fraser, Trenholm address of Borough Buildings, 7, Rumsford Place. His brother, Irvine, who later lived at 1, Sydenham Avenue, Sefton Park, joined the company. In 1871 Bulloch and his family moved from Wellington Street, Waterloo, to a larger, grander house, known as "Clifton," in Cambridge Road, Waterloo. At the instigation of his friends, Bulloch became a British citizen. He entered fully into Liverpool society and was a leading light in the Liverpool Nautical College and a benefactor to the Orphan Boys Asylum. His daughter Jessie married councilor, later alderman, Maxwell Hyslop Maxwell.

During 1881–83, Bulloch wrote his history, *The Secret Service of the Confederate States in Europe*. It sought to redress the balance, to give an alternative version of the "authorized" history. In his introduction, Bulloch writes of these earlier histories: "Some of these were written under the influence of the heat and passion aroused and fostered by the magnitude and bitterness of the contest, and cannot therefore be received with the confidence which every narrative must inspire in order to win and to maintain that worthy and lasting credit which distinguishes history from fiction.... When the future historian contemplates these results, he will naturally look for the facts relating to them, and he will look in vain among the records thus far published to the world."

This was Bulloch's justification for writing the book, to give a balanced view; it was written not in anger, but in quiet, contemplative reflection, almost twenty years after the end of the war. It is a model in its lack of egotism and its desire to praise others and their endeavors. Reputedly Bulloch was encouraged to write the account by his nephew, who was later president of the U.S.A., Teddy Roosevelt, during a visit by the family in 1879. Roosevelt, in his autobiography, fondly refers to his two uncles:

> My mother's two brothers, James Dunwoody Bulloch and Irvine Bulloch, came to visit us shortly after the war. Both came under assumed names, as they were among the Confederates who were at that time exempted from the amnesty. "Uncle Jimmy" Bulloch was a dear old retired sea captain, utterly unable to "get on" in the worldly sense of that phrase, as valiant and simple and upright a soul as ever lived, a veritable Colonel Newcome. He was an Admiral in the Confederate navy, and was the builder of the famous Confederate war vessel Alabama. My uncle Irvine Bulloch was a midshipman on the Alabama, and fired the last gun discharged from her batteries in the fight with the Kearsarge. Both of these uncles lived in Liverpool after the war.

With the children off their hands, Bulloch and his wife moved to 30, Sydenham Avenue, Toxteth Park, not far from brother Irvine, but tragically, in 1897, James' wife, Harriett, died. They had been married for almost forty years. A year later, on 14 July 1898, Irvine died while on holiday in Colwyn Bay, Wales. He had been suffering with Bright's disease, but died from a cerebral hemorrhage. He was 56 years old. Bulloch then moved in with his daughter Jessie and her husband, at their home at 76, Canning Street. Bulloch developed cancer, and died, following cardiac failure, on 7 January 1901. He was 77 at the time of his death. Bulloch was buried in Toxteth Cemetery beside the grave of his brother. In 1968 the United Daughters of the Confederacy had an inscription placed on Bulloch's headstone: "An American by birth, an Englishman by choice." In his will, proved 31 January 1901, Bulloch's very modest estate was valued at just £200. 2s. 3d. There were two witnesses to the will, his son-in-law and his old friend and confidant, John Low.

Low, whom Bulloch describes as "an able seaman, a reliable and useful officer in every situation," was likewise exempted from pardon. Upon Bulloch's recommendation he had been made master in the Confederate navy, following the successful blockade-running by the *Fingal*. Low was later given command of his own ship, the captured U.S.

barque *Conrad*, later renamed the *Tuscaloosa*. At the end of the war, the Aberdeen-born resident of Savannah set up business in Liverpool, and resided at 110, Shiel Road. He died peacefully in his sleep on 6 September 1906, and was buried at Golbourne churchyard.

John Newland Maffitt's friendship with Bulloch stretched back to the days of their service in the "old navy." Bulloch, in his letter to Maffitt regarding taking command of the *Florida*, is fulsome in his praise of his friend's capabilities: "I hope it may fall to your lot to command her, for I know of no officer whose tact and management could so well overcome the difficulties."

At the end of the war Maffitt sailed to England to confer with Bulloch. He too was exempt from pardon. In the United States his property was confiscated, and he had no choice but to become an exile. No doubt upon the advice of Bulloch and the influence of Bulloch's English friends, Maffitt found employment in the merchant navy as master of a vessel plying between Liverpool and Rio de Janeiro. In 1868, Maffitt returned home to North Carolina, and after unsuccessfully failing to have his confiscated property returned, he purchased a small farm called "Moorings," at New Hanover County. Upon the death of his first wife, Maffitt remarried in November 1870. By his second wife, Emma Martin, he had three children. Maffitt turned his hand to writing in order to make ends meet, contributing articles to newspapers and magazines. He wrote a novel entitled *Nautilus; or Cruising under Canvas*, a thinly disguised autobiography of his early years in the United States Navy. It was published in 1871. Maffitt then bought a modest home and moved his young family to Wilmington. John Newland Maffitt, who had drawn the admiration of his enemies during the war for his bravery and skills as a sailor, died, after a three month illness, on 15 May 1886 at the age of 68. He was buried in Wilmington's Oakdale Cemetery.

Charles Read, Maffitt's lieutenant aboard the *Florida* and a captain in his own right aboard the *Clarence*, sought further adventure following the end of the war. In 1867 he was second officer aboard a ship running arms to the Cuban rebels in their bid to overthrow the Spanish government. He was briefly arrested by the United States authorities for his part in the uprising, but was quickly released. Read later retired to Meridian, Mississippi, where he died on 25 January 1890.

Lieutenant John Wilkinson, who likewise had fled to England at the end of the war, turned over his ship to Bulloch, he being the surviving senior Confederate naval officer in Europe. Fearful initially of arrest and imprisonment, homesickness eventually overcame him, and he returned to North America, settling in Nova Scotia, Canada. Receiving assurances that he would not be arrested, Wilkinson traveled south, moving back to his old home in Amelia County, Virginia. Later he moved to Annapolis, Maryland, where he established a school to prepare young boys for entry to the nearby naval academy. Wilkinson wrote his wartime memoirs, *Narrative of a Blockade Runner*, which was published in 1877. He never married, and died a bachelor, on 29 December 1891, at the age of 70.

Captain James Waddell of the *Shenandoah*, after surrendering his vessel to the Royal Navy at Liverpool on 6 November 1865, also sought exile in England. Under Bulloch's patronage he also found work. In 1875, a decade after the end of the war, when it was safe to do so, Waddell returned to the United States and set up a home, like Wilkinson, in Annapolis. In 1880, at the age of 56, he was appointed by the governor of Maryland to put down a gang of "pirates," as they are described, who were poaching the oyster beds of Chesapeake Bay. It took him less than a week to complete the task. Such was the esteem felt towards Waddell that on the day of his death in 1886, the Legislature recessed its session for the day. He was buried at St. Anne's Cemetery in Annapolis; a marble monument was erected in his honor.

Raphael Semmes, after the sinking of the *Alabama,* returned home, running the blockade into the Rio Grande. From there he traveled overland to Mobile, and after spending some time with his family, he journeyed on to Richmond. There navy secretary Mallory placed him in command of the James River Fleet, with the rank of vice-admiral. As the war came to its inevitable conclusion, Semmes blew up his fleet, and gathering his men, placed them and himself under the command of General Joseph E. Johnston. Semmes rose to the rank of brigadier-general in the Confederate States Army. When Johnston surrendered to General Sherman, Semmes, along with the other officers and soldiers, was granted a parole. The United States secretary of the navy, Gideon Welles, was furious. He desperately wanted to put Semmes on trial as a pirate. Paroled, and apparently free, the former captain of the *Alabama* returned home to Mobile, where he established a law practice.

In early December 1865, at the instigation of Welles, Semmes was arrested and taken prisoner under armed guard to Washington. The initial charge was of violating the usages of war, by escaping after the sinking of the *Alabama.* He remained incarcerated in Washington for four months while incriminating evidence was sought of his cruelty to prisoners, while he was captain of the *Sumter* or *Alabama.* In truth though, Semmes had never permitted any violence to officers, crew or passengers of the vessels he had captured. Nor had he allowed any pilfering of private effects, or stealing from the cargoes. Anything taken was for the good of the vessel and its crew, and its appropriation was duly noted by the purser. No "evidence" could be gotten. While Semmes had sunk their vessels, he had never committed a single act of cruelty, nor exceeded the accepted rules of war relating to captives. With no witnesses prepared to perjure themselves, there was no case to answer. Semmes was freed, and he returned to Mobile. Semmes was then subject to a childish vindictiveness by the United State authorities. He was unanimously elected to the office of judge of the probate court, but the government prevented him from filling the post because he was an unamnestied rebel.

Saunders, Otley & Co. of London had persuaded Semmes, sometime earlier, to allow them to publish an annotated *Log of the "Sumter" and "Alabama."* Semmes was not happy with the result though, and resolved to write his own account. During 1867–8, Semmes researched and wrote his autobiography, *My Adventures Afloat.* It was published by the London firm of Richard Bentley in 1869. While it was important for him to publish his own account, to counteract his vilification in the Northern press, his actions revealed him to be an unreconstructed rebel. His stance was duly noted by the United States government. Meanwhile, friends in the South gathered around to find Semmes a position worthy of his ability. He was invited to become editor of the *Bulletin,* a daily newspaper published in Memphis, Tennessee. Semmes accepted the position, but after a few months President Andrew Johnson exerted pressure upon those with a controlling interest in the paper to have him dismissed. It was petty vindictiveness, and such actions did nothing to bind up the wounds of the Civil War. Semmes returned to his law practice, soon to be joined by his second son, John Oliver Semmes.

During these troubled years Semmes must have read with avid interest the lengthy court case known as the Alabama Claims. The United States sought recompense from Great Britain for its permitting to be built and outfitted the cruisers *Alabama, Florida* and *Shenandoah*. They had decimated its merchant fleet, all but driving American-flagged vessels from the seas' highways. The United States sought the annexation of Canada as compensation, but the proposal was risible. In the end the case went before an independent adjudication, the Geneva Arbitration of 1872. The United States was awarded the sum of $15,500,000 in gold. For Britain it was a small price to pay. Semmes alone had destroyed $6,750,000 worth of American shipping. Due to the efforts of Semmes and his fellow cruiser captains, there had been a massive reregistration of American ships seeking the protection of the British flag. At the end of the war Great Britain controlled the greatest merchant fleet the world had ever known. It was a dominance she was to hold up to the end of World War I. In addition the Arbitration led to the reform of international law, bringing the United States into the process that it had held aloof from during the Treaty of Paris. The real victor of the American Civil War was Great Britain.

In Mobile life continued. As the years passed Semmes continued in his law practice unharassed. It was as if the Geneva Arbitration had drawn a line under the past. As a mark of esteem, the people of Mobile bought Semmes a house, and there he saw out his last few years. Raphael Semmes died on 30 August 1877. He and his wife, Ann, are buried in the Catholic Cemetery in Mobile. A statue to him now stands in Government Street, Mobile. Upon its plinth is a carving of the *Alabama*.

The British naval officers who had temporarily resigned their commissions to make their fortunes as blockade-runners all returned to Britain. For Hobart-Hampden, without a war to fight — without some excitement — the Royal Navy lost its appeal. In 1867 he entered the services of the sultan of Turkey as a naval advisor, in succession to Admiral Sir Adolphus Slade. He took part in the suppression of the Cretan rebellion, ironically establishing a blockade of the island and preventing supplies arriving from Greece. As a reward he was made admiral and given the title of pasha. The British government, finding him in breach of the Foreign Enlistment Act, struck him off the British Naval List. Hobart-Hampden was not without influence at home, and in 1874, following pressure from Lord Derby, he was restored to his naval rank. England was too quiet for a man like Hobart-Hampden, though; he was a man born out of time. He would have made a flamboyant Elizabethan buccaneer. In 1877 he was again struck off the navy list when he took command of the Turkish Black Sea fleet in a war against the Russians, who were then a friendly power. The war having ended, Hobart-Hampden returned to England; and again family influence assured his forgiveness and his restoration to position. In June 1885 he was appointed to the rank of vice-admiral in the Royal Navy. The following year, suffering ill health, he went on holiday to Italy to recover, but he died at Milan on 19 June 1886.

William Nathan Wrighte Hewett, V.C. and blockade-runner, took up his commission once more and was appointed captain of HMS *Basilisk,* on the China Station, from 1865 to 1869. He became flag captain to Sir Henry Kellett aboard HMS *Ocean,* and in 1872–3, was captain of the *Devastation.* In October 1873 Hewett was appointed commodore and commander-in-chief on the west coast of Africa, in charge of naval operations during the Second Anglo-Ashanti War. On 31 March 1874 Hewett was made a Knight Commander of the Bath. The French honored him by making him a Chevalier of the Legion of Honor. Other titles followed. In 1877 Sir William was appointed to HMS *Achilles,* then stationed in the Mediterranean. He was appointed commander-in-chief in the East Indies, and during the Egyptian campaign of 1882 conducted naval operations in the Red Sea, seizing Suez and the canal. In 1884 Sir William was sent on a mission to

King John of Abyssinia, securing a favorable trading concession and a treaty of friendship. He received the Order of Mejidiye and the Abyssinian Order of Solomon as a reward. In 1884 Sir William became a vice-admiral, and from 1886 to 1888, was in command of the Channel Fleet. His increasing poor health, though, obliged him to resign his command; on 13 May 1888, Sir William Nathan Wrighte Hewett died at Haslar Hospital, Gosport, Hampshire.

Charles Murray-Aynsley, "Captain Murray" during his blockade-running days, also returned to service within the Royal Navy. In 1865 he was appointed captain of HMS *Jason*, serving the North America and West Indies Station. He eventually rose to the rank of vice-admiral, and was appointed a Companion of the Order of the Bath (C.B.). In retirement, Murray-Aynsley, great-grandson of the 3rd Duke of Atholl, became a justice of the peace. He never wrote his memoirs, which would have greatly rivaled those of Hobart-Hampden. He died on 1 April 1901, in his 80th year.

At the end of the war, French-born blockade-runner Eugene Tessier settled at Liverpool in England. To have returned to his prewar home in Charleston would have led to the same persecution that Semmes had been forced to endure. Thanks to the vigilance of U.S. consul Thomas Dudley, Tessier was well known to navy secretary Welles, who would gladly have put him on trial for piracy. Tessier found work in Liverpool, in the construction and repair of wooden vessels, but in 1867 he was invited to join the Bureau Veritas International Registry of Shipping as a surveyor. In 1872 he was appointed to the Scottish headquarters, based at Glasgow. Tessier, who had became a British citizen, died in September 1901.

Of the fate of the ordinary British seamen who worked directly or indirectly for the Confederacy little is generally known. Research has been done on the crew of the *Alabama*, and their fate is perhaps typical of the fate of the other unnamed and unknown sailors.[1] The coxswain of the *Alabama*, Michael Mars, born in Ireland but resident in Bristol at the outbreak of the American war, dived into the water to escape capture when the *Alabama* went down. He was rescued by the *Deerhound* and taken to Southampton. With the war's end Mars returned to the merchant marine. He died at Leytonstone, London, in August 1878, and was buried at St. Patrick's Cemetery. Henry William Allcot, the *Alabama*'s sailmaker, also rescued when the *Alabama* sank, made his way back to his native city of Liverpool. In October 1864 he went out on the *Laurel* to Madeira, where he signed on for service aboard the CSS *Shenandoah*. He was present when she returned to Liverpool on 6 November 1865 and surrendered to HMS *Donegal*. Allcot returned to the British merchant navy. He was living at 101, Esmond Street, Anfield, Liverpool, at the time of his death on 3 March 1891. He died at the comparatively early age of 53. Edward Burrell, a survivor of the fight with the *Kearsarge*, was paroled at Cherbourg and later rejoined the merchant navy. He died of T.B. while serving aboard the S.S. *Alfred* and was buried in Bombay, India. John Caren, also paroled at Cherbourg, returned to his adopted home of Liverpool, where he found work as a cotton porter. It was not a particularly well-paid job, and when he died in March 1914, at the age of 73, he was buried in a pauper's grave.

"Alabama" Sam, or Samuel Henry, cuts a sad figure. Returning home after the sinking of the *Alabama*, he found work as a tug man in Liverpool Docks. In old age he was to be found around the Dockland bars of Liverpool, where he would tell his story for the price of a pint. He died in Tranmere Workhouse. In August 1912 he presented himself at the offices of the *Liverpool Echo*, and they did a short feature on his life, complete with a photograph. He had got it into his head that there was an "Alabama Survivors' Relief Fund." Perhaps it was wishful thinking on his part.

It was not all gloom though. Some of the *Alabama's* former crew settled down to comfortable lives following the end of the war. Boatswain George Horwood and his wife opened a boardinghouse at 5, Kent Square, Liverpool. When he died in 1888, comfortably well off, he was buried in St. James' Cemetery, with a headstone to mark his grave. Like Horwood, others too found decent occupations at the end of the Civil War. George Yeoman, from Dover in Kent, enlisted in the British army, where he was taught the trade of barbering. Returning to Canterbury after 12 years in India, he opened a barber's shop. Among his customers, allegedly, was the Archbishop of Canterbury himself. In 1890 Yeoman moved back to Dover, where he continued his trade. He died at the age of 79, and his funeral was attended by family and friends, including members of his Masonic lodge. At the time of his death in 1924, World War I overshadowed all previous wars. Few people in Britain were aware that British men had once served in the Confederate navy—nor even cared, it might be said. It was all so long ago.

Appendix: The Sinking of the *Alabama*

1. A Unionist Account by James Magee, Seaman aboard the *Kearsage*. Reprinted from the Historical Collections of the Essex Institute, Vol. 62, 1921:

"After cruising the English Channel for some time, there was a report that the *Alabama* was expected in some part of England, and as the English press made a great deal of talk about the *Kearsarge*, the Captain proposed to go to Belgium; arriving the 27th of May 1864, ran into Flushing and went into dry dock on the following day, more for a blind than for anything else, as we were never in better repair and running order than at that time. The 29th of May the Captain gave liberty to all on board to go where they pleased, with instruction if they heard a gun and saw the colors at our foremast head, to report on board as quickly as possible, as that would be the signal for sailing orders. All went well until the 10th day of June, when the signal gun was fired. All hands made for the ship, and in less than twenty minutes all the crew was ready for duty. The Captain had all hands called to lay aft. He then told us that the *Alabama* had arrived at Cherbourg, France, for repairs, and now was the time for us to strike. Then we gave three cheers, 'spliced the main brace,' and the next tide we hauled out of dry dock and put to sea, put another 'splice in the main brace' and shaped our course for Dover, England. Arriving there the 11th at 10 o'clock A.M., took in fresh supplies, and at 12 o'clock weighed anchor and put to sea, shaping our course for Cherbourg.

"Arriving there early on the 12th, we ran into the mouth of the harbor, had a good look at our antagonist, and fired a blank shot, out of politeness, for Semmes to come out, but he did not come out that day. Here we lay off and on, running off by day and standing in by night, close enough to see all that went in and out of the harbor. We had no communication from Cherbourg up to the 16th of June; then three men pulled out from the shore in a boat, about six miles, to where we lay, came alongside, gave a note to the Captain, and then pulled back into port.

"The Captain told the boatswain to pipe all hands aft. He then produced the note, which read thus:

Captain Winslow:

Sir:—I am undergoing a few repairs here which I hope, will not take longer than the morrow. Then I will come out and fight you a fair and square fight.

Most respectfully yours,
Captain R. Semmes.

Three days after, Sunday, June 19th, the lookout at masthead espied two steamers coming out of Cherbourg harbor, one a long, black, rakish-looking craft, looking very much like the *Alabama*. The officers and men jumped into the rigging, took a good look at both vessels, and pronounced one the *Alabama;* at the same time the other tacked-ship and put back into port. The Captain gave orders to beat quarters, clear ship for action, and man the starboard battery. (We were laying off about six miles from shore.) Captain Winslow gave the chief engineer orders to go ahead slowly, at the same time putting the ship's head off shore. The *Alabama* gaining on us all the time, they thought we were afraid and were trying to get away from them, but it was not so, we only ran two miles farther out; then, the Captain calling us in neutral waters, 'put about,' and stood to receive her. When within about a mile of her, she fired her bow chaser, the shot dropping very carelessly alongside our forward pivot port within about four feet of our ship's side, and doing no damage. The next shot she fired struck us in the port bow and glanced off, doing no harm. She fired some two or three shots very wildly, that went whistling above our mastheads. During this time we did not fire one shot, but when within half a mile we hove round and gave her a broadside. Here we had it, broadside and broadside, both ships under a full head of steam, the *Alabama* firing two or three shots to our one. We engaged her at seven hundred yards, and as we fought in a circle we 'closed in' to about five hundred yards, and held this position for about half an hour. Then, finding that we were getting the best of the fight, the Captain, desiring to bring the thing to an end, closed into about two hundred and fifty yards, and discharged a full broadside.

"The men seemed to be getting demoralized; they ran the white flag up in the main rigging and the 'secesh' flag in the fore rigging. The Captain gave orders to cease firing, and on doing so we found that they thought we were off our guard, as they let fly another broadside. One of the shots went through our smoke pipe, and a sixty-eight pounder lodged in our stern post, doing no other damage as it did not explode. We then had orders to engage her; so we began to decorate her again with our eleven-inch shell. After exchanging two or three broadsides on the second part of the fight, we found that they began to show us the cold shoulder by jumping overboard, not caring to communicate with us any longer, at the same time striking their flag and firing a lee gun as a surrender. They lowered a boat and manned it with three men and pulled toward our ship. They fired one more shot, very wildly, which struck our main-top-gallant mast and checked the halyards, and the flag flew to the breeze. The flag was run up in a ball to the masthead, and orders given to one of the men that if we should go down, to pull the halyards and go down colors flying. We did not fire on them after they struck their flag. The boat from the *Alabama* came alongside, and Lieutenant Wilson delivered up his sword and surrendered the ship, and told the Captain that if he did not make haste and get out boats to save life, that there would be a good many go down in the *Alabama*.

"All our boats were disabled but two. They were lowered and manned. Just as the boats left the ship, the *Alabama* gave two surges forward and down she went. I was in one of the boats that went to pick up the prisoners. As we began to pick them up, we heard them say that they had rather drown than to be hanged on board of that ship. Some of the men we tried to save would throw up their hands and sink down, so we were obliged to take the boat-hook and reach down three or four feet and hook them up, and some were so far gone that they died in the boats. While we were picking up the men, the *Deerhound,* one of the Royal Yacht Squadron, teamed up to within hailing distance of the ship, and the Captain asked him if he would be kind enough to assist in picking up the men and deliver them up to him, as they were prisoners. He said he would, and steamed in among them and picked up quite a number, and among them was Captain Semmes. He then steamed off as fast as he could, taking advantage while a good part of our men were off in the boats; but if some of the rest on board at that time had had their way, I think one of those eleven-inch shells would have stopped his headway, and perhaps moored him alongside the *Alabama*. We spent about half an hour in picking up the prisoners, then we 'stood in' for the land, and piped for dinner, and for all hands to 'splice the main brace,' after which we sat down to grub, and feeling pretty well satisfied began to talk over the fight with the Rebs. I heard one of them say he thought if they had boarded us, the result might have been different, as they were so well drilled with small arms. As they continued to boast of what they could do at boarding, we 'turned the tables' by telling them that we still had a reserve force by which we could give them an extra dose if necessity demanded, or, in other words, that we had an appliance by which we could throw scalding water to the distance of sixty feet, and we also told them if at the same time we discharged a whole broadside from our 11-inch guns of grape and canister (as we could do), the probability is, to say the least, that they would be shaken from stem to stern.

"Here we arrived in port, and all hands called to bring ship to anchor, and not till we had arrived here did we learn how it was that the *Alabama*'s men were so willing to drown. The crew told us that Captain Semmes told them if they were taken prisoners by us that every man would hang to the yard arm; and when our boats left our ship to go and pick them up, it chanced that at the same time a man was sent aloft to reef off a whip on the main yard with which to rig the accommodation ladders, so as to enable visitors to get on board, as we were going into port. When they saw the man up there they thought that what Semmes had told them was correct, and a great many went down with that impression.

"We dropped anchor about two cable lengths astern of the French frigate *Napoleon*, and the gangway dressed to receive visitors on board. Those who came on board told us that the excitement in Cherbourg was great, that there were about forty thousand people who witnessed the fight, and that there was great betting among them as to which should be the victor — ten to five on the *Alabama,* and hard work to get anybody to take a bet at that, all odds being bet on the *Alabama*. The officers and crew of the American ship *Rockingham* also told us of the intimacy of the *Deerhound*. They said that this yacht had brought men from England here who had volunteered their services to help destroy us, and were drilled in Her Majesty's ship *Excellent* as experienced gunners. Not crediting all that these men told us, some of our officers went on shore and found from good, reliable sources, that this yacht had brought twenty-five men, twelve of whom had joined the *Alabama*. The *Rockingham* belonged in Maine. She was the last vessel the *Alabama* destroyed — twelve hours previous to her going in to Cherbourg. These men also told us that what added to the excitement of the battle was, that we were fighting in a circle and apparently got mixed; that it was impossible to tell which one had gone down, even after the fight was over, as the wind was off-shore, so that when we stood in for the land our colors trained aft, and it was impossible to tell who the victor was. We laid here for three days, in which our carpenter repaired all of our damage without any assistance from shore, with the exception of a boiler-maker, who put a patch on our smoke pipe. We got up steam at 3 o'clock P.M., weighed anchor and put to sea, escorted out by a little steam yacht chartered by a party of American gentlemen and their ladies, with a band on board and the American flag flying. The band gave us a number of national airs, and when about three miles off, outside the breakwater, steaming at about six miles an hour, they struck up the 'Star Spangled Banner' and gave us three cheers. We then gave her an extra turn ahead that sent us through the water about fifteen knots, leaving them behind us. We dipped our colors, manned the yard, gave three rousing cheers, and bade adieu and a hasty farewell to the coast of France.

"We arrived at Dover, England, early on the 24th, amidst cheer after cheer that went echoing through the lofty cliffs of Dover from a Highland Regiment and a number of others, whose acquaintance we had made while cruising in the Channel. All were anxiously waiting to learn the correct news of our loss. It had been reported that we had lost twenty-seven men and the *Alabama* had lost eight. This was the first news that the English press gave of the fight, and of course they must have known better, as the *Deerhound* brought the news and Captain Semmes, too.

"That English yacht, one belonging to the Royal Yacht Squadron and flying the white ensign, too, during the conflict, should not have assisted the Confederate prisoners to escape after they had formally surrendered themselves, according to their own statements, by firing a lee gun, striking their colors, hoisting a white flag and sending a boat to the *Kearsarge,* some of which signals must have been seen on board the yacht, is most humiliating to the national honor. The movement of the yacht early on Sunday morning was, as before shown, most suspicious, and had our captain followed the advice and reiterated request of the crew and officers, the *Deerhound* might have been lying not far distant from the *Alabama*. The captain could not believe that a gentleman who asked by himself to save life would use the opportunity to decamp with the officers and men, who, according to their own act, were prisoners of war. There is a high presumptive evidence that the *Deerhound* was at Cherbourg for the express purpose of rendering every assistance possible to the corsair, and we may be permitted to doubt whether Mr. Lancaster, the friend of Mr. Laird and a member of the Mersey Yacht Club, would have carried us to Southampton if the result of the struggle had been reversed and the *Alabama* had sent the *Kearsarge* to the bottom. The *Deerhound* reached Cherbourg on the 17th of June, and between that time and the night of the 18th a boat was observed from the shore passing frequently between her and the *Alabama*. This I got from men taken from different merchant ships by the *Alabama* and landed in Cherbourg.

"The ship was open for visitors at Dover, and at 8 bells they were shown on board. In less than ten minutes our decks were full of people. Here we lay for several days, with beautiful weather, and our ship thronged with visitors from morning till night. Boats and yachts of all descriptions and steamers from London and bands of music playing 'Yankee Doodle' and other airs for the occasion, all packed to their utmost with ladies and gentlemen, came to visit us, and everybody seemed to be having a good time. We had fiddling and dancing on board and some games of amusement, which gave the whole thing a lively appearance. The poor boatmen wished the thing would hold for three months, for they never made so much money by boating in their lives as they had since we had come. One of our visitors was the Lord Warden. In the course of conversation he said to one of the old salts, "I suppose you credit our noble Armstrong guns for the victory you have won, do you not?" The old salt said, "My good man, we had no such guns aboard here, nothing but good old Yankee guns, and between you and me they are damned headstrong guns!" We lay here till July 9th, 1864, all enjoying a good time as before stated, when the captain's gig or boat came alongside and he came on board. He then gave orders to the boatswain to pipe all hands to get anchor for the United States and all visitors to leave the ship. Why, my friend, you can just imagine our feelings. Here we were bordering on the fourth year of our cruise, and the last news we had from home was that we should not be called home till the career of the *Alabama* was ended. For some reason or other, this was the first time during the whole cruise that I ever heard anything that sounded musical in our boatswain's voice. The visitors all out of the ship, steam up, and all ready to heave away, and at 11 o'clock A.M. we ran up our long streaming pennant and cat-headed the anchor, manned the yards and gave three cheers, dipped our colors, squared away, steaming about twelve knots an hour, bidding adieu to the people of England and France, homeward bound.

"Such are the facts relating to the memorable action off Cherbourg on the nineteenth of June, eighteen hundred and sixty-four. The *Alabama* went down, riddled through and through with shot and shell, and as she sank beneath the green waves of the English Channel, not a single cheer arose from us on the *Kearsarge*. Our noble Lieutenant Commander James S. Thornton, gave the command, "Silence boys!" and in perfect silence this terror of our American commerce plunged forward twice or thrice and down she went forty fathoms deep in her own waters, amidst the hideous howls of her officers and crew."

2. A CONFEDERATE ACCOUNT from a young unnamed Englishman whose story appeared in the *Claremont (NH) National Eagle* on 9 July 1864:

"We came to Cherbourg from Cape Town to be paid off, and for the purpose of making repairs. The greater part of our copper was off the bottom. Our boilers were in a very leaky state. Our pay as able seamen was four pounds ten a moth, and we were paid off yesterday. We had received permission to go into the dock to repair, when we heard that the *Kearsarge* was outside. We came in here ship-rigged, and so disguised that had we met the *Kearsarge* outside, we intended to take her by surprise. We fully expected having a fight with her. As soon as we saw her outside, Captain Semmes ordered the after yards sent down and the vessel turned into her usual rig as a bark. This was immediately done.

"He sent ashore at the same time for permission to coal, and intended to go outside and commence the fight without delay. We commenced coaling immediately, and were occupied three or four days in this. We finished coaling on Saturday afternoon, the 18th. Capt. Semmes then prepared to go out the next day. We went to general quarters twice while in port, as a general drill, and the ship was put into fighting order. About 9 o'clock on the morning of Sunday we weighed anchor and stood outside. After getting clear of the breakwater we cast loose our starboard battery and ran out the guns loaded for action. The order then passed for all hands to lay aft.

"Capt. Semmes handed the clerk a written paper which was read to us. The substance of it was that we were going into action; that we were to fight in the English Channel, the seat of so many important naval engagements, and recalled the acts we had already performed; said the eyes of all Europe were upon us, and that he expected every man to do his duty. The men were enthusiastic and cheered considerably. The men had no idea but that they would gain the victory, and an easy one. The crew fully expected from the beginning that they would be led by Capt. Semmes close alongside the *Kearsarge,* so as to commence the action at close quarters and finish by boarding her.

"It was expected that Semmes would lead the boarders in person; for though we had as fine a crew as any ship afloat, yet we had not a single competent gunner on board, excepting the captain of the forward pivot, a hundred pound rifle gun. He was an old English man of war's man trained in the British navy. The captains of the other guns were not competent gunners, though brave men. We came in sight of the *Kearsarge,* and she steamed towards us. We closed as rapidly as possible. The men were lying down at their guns, smoking and resting, the orders having passed to make ourselves as comfortable as possible, and reserve our strength till the commencement of the action.

"When the *Kearsarge* was within about one thousand five hundred yards of us we opened fire, each gun firing as soon as it was pointed and properly elevated. We fired three broadsides before the *Kearsarge* returned a shot. The first shell she sent came through near the forward rifle port, at which I was stationed. It caused many splinters, and struck a man at our gun. He leapt away with his leg smashed, and another man at the next gun fell dead. The shell caught our slide rack, and I think the man was killed by one of our shot, which was thrown against him by the shell of the *Kearsarge.*

"The firing here became continual on both sides. We firing at least two shots to their one — we fired shells almost together. But a few solid shot were fired. At the after pivot gun, shortly after, two or three men were cut right in two, besides others being wounded. Then the crew of our after guns were ordered to fill up the vacancy at the pivot gun, which was the second gun from the stern; we were consequently then only fighting with six guns. For some time after there was very little damage done by the *Kearsarge*'s guns, their elevation being rather high, the shot passing over, and though not injuring our hull, greatly damaging our spars. About twenty minutes after the commencement of the action the spanker gaff, on which our colors was set, was shot away and the colors thus brought down nearly to the deck, the spar hanging and the colors hanging about twenty feet from the deck, the colors still remaining in sight.

"About the same time our forward pivot gun sent two well directed shells, one of which struck the chains which protected the *Kearsarge*'s boilers, penetrating the chain, but doing no such damage as was expected. We supposed then that her engines were knocked to pieces, and that the *Kearsarge* would soon go down. We gave three cheers. The shell was fired from our hundred pounder forward rifle pivot, and would certainly have penetrated the chain, and entirely disabled the *Kearsarge* had our powder been good, as this gun would have carried the shell and taken effect at five miles with dry powder. Our powder had been a long time on board, and was dampened. The night before the action we threw seven barrels of powder overboard, and had frequently thrown powder over.

"The next shell we sent struck the sternpost of the *Kearsarge* without exploding. Had this exploded the *Kearsarge* would have been blown to pieces. At this time we had received no serious damage. This was about half an hour after the fight commenced. After that the shooting on our part became worse, and that of the *Kearsarge* better. Our guns were too much elevated, and shot over the *Kearsarge.* The men fought well; but the gunners did not know how to point and elevate the guns. Capt. Semmes, during all this time, was standing just forward of the forward rigging, with an opera glass in his hands, and leaning over the rail. The gunners were left to themselves to fight the guns, and no particular orders were given to the gunners during the fight. Capt. Semmes directed the maneuvering of the ship.

"The shell man belonging to our gun was cut right in two by one of the *Kearsarge*'s shots while he was bringing a shell to our gun. His name was James Hart. He was blown all to pieces, and nothing was found of him which could be recognized except the collar of his shirt. Several men were wounded and carried below. The first serious disaster we met with was from a shell which carried away our rudder. About the same time more shell came into our coal bunkers and penetrated the boilers, putting out the fires and burying several of the firemen under the coal. Some were killed and others dug out alive. The vessel was filled with smoke and steam. All our power of movement then was over.

"The *Kearsarge* then gradually began to edge round on our port quarter. When she reached this position the order was given to lie down, as we expected to be raked fore and aft. A few minutes afterwards the sail trimmers were called away to loose the fore trysail and head sails so that she could be steered. She was then standing in to shore. We then considered ourselves done for, as the *Alabama* was rapidly settling. I do not think our screw was damaged. The *Kearsarge* kept up a continuous fire on our port side, and we shifted over our guns to that side. Our men were then very fatigued and many disabled and wounded. We still fired as well as possible from the port side, though we knew the day was lost. When the head sails were loosed the leader of our pivot gun, John Roberts, a young Welshman, while engaged in the work, had the lower part of his body cut open, which caused his entrails to protrude. With his entrails hanging out he walked towards his gun, and fell dead on deck without uttering a word. Mr. Anderson, a midshipman, stationed in the after division was knocked overboard, his leg, which was cut off, remaining on board. He was from Savannah, and was a son of Major Anderson.

"Captain Semmes, about the same time, was wounded in the hand by a splinter. He tied his handkerchief round his hand, but never left his post.

"The dead, of whom there were about eight, and the wounded, numbering perhaps twelve, instead of being carried below, were lying about the deck. The carnage was awful, some of the men being literally cut to pieces. There was much confusion on board, though nothing like a panic, excepting on the part of one or two who were not Englishmen. One young Prussian stationed at a gun, having ran below and stated to the doctor that he was wounded, was ordered on deck, he not being wounded, and was immediately shot in the back by an old man named Hicks, an English seaman, who had been long in the English navy. He shot him with his revolver. He died soon afterwards.[1]

"Our first lieutenant, Mr. Kell, seeing the battle was lost, ran to Semmes, and told him he must strike the colors, as the vessel was sinking fast. Semmes merely replied "Try to get a little more headway on her," and to the last would not order the colors to be struck. The color halyards about this time were shot away, and the colors fell to the deck. The report was circulated fore and aft that they were down, and for a moment the *Kearsarge* ceased firing. When our men saw our colors were down they were enraged and most of them turned round on their officers. Several of them ran aft to Capt. Semmes with drawn cutlasses. One of them told him that if he did not immediately hoist the colors he would cut him down. At the same time Mr. Sinclair, the fourth lieutenant, pointed a revolver at the man's head to shoot him dead in case he made an attack on the captain.

"Captain Semmes was perfectly cool, and did not even draw his sword. He said he admired the courage of the men but the colors were down, the vessel was sinking, and he did not wish any more lives should be lost. It was for their own benefit that he refused to raise the colors. As soon as the colors were shot away, by the orders of Mr. Kell, a white flag was held up as a signal of surrender. A man jumped up on the spanker boom and held it up the best way he could in his hands. This caused the officers of the *Kearsarge* to imagine that it was one of our men still persisting in holding up the Confederate Flag. They continued firing, and poured at least three broadsides into us after the white flag was held up. We had also at this time fired a lee gun in token of surrender, but seeing the *Kearsarge* still firing on us, the word was passed along the deck among us, "there's no quarter for us." Some of our guns were then fired again, particularly our foremost thirty-two, while the men were cutting away the boats.

"Capt. Semmes gave orders for the wounded to be put in the boats as quickly as possible and taken away, refusing everything in the shape of a boat himself. The men were to be taken to the yacht *Deerhound*, if possible, if not, to the *Kearsarge*. At this time the wardroom was full of water, and the ship rapidly settling.

"The chief engineer did not leave the engine room till he was up to his waist in water. While the men were cutting away the boats and putting in the wounded, Capt. Semmes walked down into his cabin without saying a word. His cabin was then partly filled with water.

"Two of our boats pulled off, carrying the wounded — the *Kearsarge* having ceased firing — the remainder of our boats (we had six) being all seriously damaged. One of these boats took the wounded on board the *Kearsarge*, on which she left them, and receiving permission to go and pick up more drowning and wounded men, instead of doing so pulled off to the yacht. This may not have been exactly right; but we were justified in anything after the *Kearsarge* had fired three broadsides at us after our colors were down. I was ordered down by the First Lieutenant to carry the wounded, and went away to the *Kearsarge*. In that boat were a few wounded men; Mr. Howell nominally occupying the rank of captain of marines (we had no marines on board); Mr. Wilson, third lieutenant; Mr. Bulloch, master, and a few others. This boat went to the *Kearsarge*.[2]

"Mr. Robinson, the carpenter, seeing that the fight was lost, drew a revolver and shot himself through the breast. He was afterwards picked up in one of the *Kearsarge's* boats, and died soon after arriving on board. This makes three officers who were lost.

"We were treated with every possible kindness on board the *Kearsarge*, for grog was given us as soon as we got on board, and we were treated much better than any prisoners had ever been treated on the *Alabama*.

"On board the *Kearsarge* the crew were very much dispirited because they had not taken either Semmes or the *Alabama*. Capt. Semmes had never told us that we would be badly treated if taken prisoners. Capt. Winslow came forward among us and gave us dry clothing, and gave orders to treat us with every possible kindness.

"When we came to anchor, we were called aft and paroled. We promised not to serve in any manner against the interests of the United States until honorably exchanged as prisoners of war. We then were sent on shore. We went to M. Bonafils, the Confederate agent, and he sent us to boarding houses. We saw Capt. Sinclair, a Confederate officer, who had come from Paris, and who is acting in place of Capt. Semmes.

"We were yesterday paid off by M. Bonafils and Surgeon Galt. Most of the men belong to the original crew. There has never been any regular payment before, and, on an average, from a hundred and fifty to two hundred dollars a piece was due them. They had liberty two or three times since the *Alabama* first went out, and on these occasions have received a little liberty money — never more than a sovereign each.

"Many of the men have been heavily fined by sentences of court martial. It has been a custom to punish the men, sometimes for the most trivial offences by taking away their pay. On one occasion a man was fined five pounds for cutting a duck's throat taken out of a prize. Whenever we took a prize the officers always made a rush for all the good eatables and drinkables, while the men were not allowed a single article, and severely punished if they touched anything. When the bread was full of maggots, and the provisions in the *Alabama* of the very description, tons of the very best of provisions, taken from prizes, have been sunk rather than give them to the men. Semmes' idea was this: — If he allowed men to take anything from a prize he supposed the men who actually went to the prize would keep it wholly themselves.

"The *Alabama* at this time was going down, and Mr. Kell passed the order for the men to save themselves if they could. The greater part of them jumped overboard. Among them was Dr. Llewellyn, our assistant surgeon. He was an Englishman, and had long been on the sick list with a sore leg, consequently, not depending upon his swimming power, he had lashed himself to a box, but the box turned, and putting him under, he was drowned.

"There were nineteen different nationalities on board the *Alabama,* principally Englishmen. There were not more than six American on board. As a rule the crew liked and respected Semmes, but detested the first lieutenant, who was a low lived bully, and a man without any principle. The ordinary seamen of the *Alabama* were shipped at the rate of four pounds a month. They were promised prize money for every vessel that was ransomed, burned or sunk. Half the value of the vessels and cargoes destroyed was to be divided among the officers and crew of the *Alabama*. When we destroyed a vessel the value of herself and cargo was obtained from the captain and recorded in the ship's log. We were to receive this at the termination of the war, and it was to be paid by the Confederate Government.

"We have never yet received a cent in prize money or in any article of value. All the money taken was kept by the captain for ship's use. All clothing, & c., taken from captured vessels, if furnished to us, were charged for. The number of officers and men on the *Alabama* was one hundred and fifty. The men, upon being paid off yesterday, were discharged from the Confederate service. I am afraid we shall never get any prize money. I do not think the majority of the men will reship in the Confederate service. Captain Sinclair has already proposed to us to go on board the *Rappahannock* and merely do duty for the present. We would gladly go out with Capt. Semmes to fight the *Kearsarge.* We generally believe that Capt. Semmes will soon have another vessel. There is no principle among the men, and little enthusiasm in the cause. They are mostly entirely mercenary. But we all think we have been swindled and will never get anything out of the promised prize money. If we get what has been promised us we shall all be rich men."

Chapter Notes

Chapter 1

1. James Dunwoody Bulloch, *The Secret Service of the Confederate States in Europe* (Bentley, 1884), vol. 1, 38.
2. Raphael Semmes, *My Adventures Afloat: A Personal Memoir of My Cruises & Services* (London: Richard Bentley, 1869), 413.
3. Bulloch, *Secret Service*, vol. 1, 23.
4. Ibid., 53.
5. Ibid., 131–2.
6. Ibid., 139.
7. Sarah Agnes Wallace and Frances Elma Gillespie, eds., *Journal of Benjamin Moran* (Chicago: University of Chicago Press, 1949), vol. 2, 952–3.
8. Papers relating to the Treaty of Washington (hereafter Treaty), vol. 1, 274.
9. Treaty, vol. 1, 276.
10. Ibid., 277–8.
11. Bulloch, *Secret Service*, vol. 1, 153.
12. Treaty, vol. 1, 281
13. Wallace and Gillespie, vol. 2, *Journal,* 964–66.
14. The CSS *Nashville* was the first ship commissioned by the Confederacy, having cost $100,000 to purchase. Initially for the Atlantic trade, she was a 1221-ton side-wheeled steamer, built at Greenpoint, New York, in 1853. The *Nashville* had a top speed of 13 knots. On 26 October 1861, with Lt. Robert Baker Pegram, CSN, as captain, she sailed with a crew of 40 officers and men for England. Her armament consisted of two 12-lb. cannons. Off the coast of Ireland the *Nashville* captured the U.S. clipper *Harvey Birch*. The crew and passengers were taken aboard and the clipper was set on fire. The passengers were later released into the custody of the U.S. consul in Southampton. Initially the attack upon the *Harvey Birch* was looked upon as an act of piracy in England, but following the Trent Affair the Confederates were looked upon in a more sympathetic light. The USS *Tuscarora* arrived at Southampton in pursuit of the *Nashville;* but under the watchful eye of the British warships *Dauntless* and *Moulton*, the *Tuscarora* was forced to abide by the rules of British neutrality. The *Nashville* left Southampton, to cheering crowds, on 26 February 1862.
15. Treaty, vol. 1, 282.

Chapter 2

1. Bulloch, *Secret Service*, vol. 1, 163–4.
2. The Journal of Lieut. J.N. Maffitt, O.R.N. Series 1, vol. 1 (hereafter Maffitt), 763–9. See also O.R.N. Series 1, vol. 3, pp. 609–23, 643–6.
3. Bulloch, *Secret Service,* vol. 1, 160.
4. Treaty, vol. 1, 284.
5. Official Records of the Union & Confederate Navies in the War of the Rebellion, Series I, Vol. I, Operations of the Cruisers, Jan. 19, 1861–Dec. 31, 1862 (hereafter O.R.N.), 399.
6. Ibid., 403–4.
7. Maffitt, 4 August 1862.
8. Having failed to stop the *Florida*, the *Adirondack* set off in pursuit, only to run aground at Elbow Cay, off the island of Abaco, one of the most dangerous reefs of the Bahamas, at about 3:30 on the morning of 23 August. Captain Gansevoort of the *Adirondack* wrote to his superior, Rear Admiral S.F. Du Pont: "The ship is, I fear, a total loss."
9. Maffitt, 17 August 1862.
10. Maffitt, 18 August 1862.
11. Bulloch, *Secret Service*, vol. 1, 169. Commander John Newland Maffitt, CSN, was born at sea on 22 February 1819, the son of Irish parents, the Rev. John Newland Maffitt and his wife, Ann Carnicke, who were emigrating to the United States. His uncle Dr. William Maffitt adopted him when he was five years old, and he was taken to Fayetteville, North Carolina. At the age of thirteen, in February 1832, he was given a commission as midshipman in the United States Navy, and served in the Mediterranean aboard the USS *Constitution,* commanded by Commodore Elliott. Later, aboard the frigate *Macedonian,* off the coast of Florida, he contracted yellow fever. His first independent command was the *Gallatin*. In 1842, then a lieutenant, he was assigned to Professor Bache's United States Coastal Survey. He spent the next fourteen years mapping and charting the coasts of the U.S.A., plotting depths, and locating shoals and sandbars. Upon the outbreak of war Maffitt resigned his commission and offered his services to the Confederacy. He was appointed to the position of first lieutenant in the Confederate States Navy and was given command of the blockade runner *Cecile*. In 1862 he was given command of the CSS *Florida*.
12. Maffitt, 4 September 1862. Commander Preble was court-martialed and dismissed from the service for permitting the *Florida* to get into Mobile. He was reinstated some five months later, though. Others were less forgiving. In London, under secretary Benjamin Moran noted the following in his journal: "Thurs. 23rd April 1863: Commander Preble has been

here this morning. This is the man who was dismissed the navy for permitting the 'Oreto' to get into Mobile, and it is a pity he was reinstated. He is a weak-minded person of some 40 years, and 5 feet 10 inches high" (1151). Curiously Commander Francis Winslow of the USS *Cuyler,* the man responsible for allowing the *Florida* to escape from Mobile, a far worse crime, escaped any real censure.

13. Maffitt, Ibid.
14. Maffitt, Journal, 1 February 1863. The ship, as Maffitt later discovered, was the USS *Sonoma* of four guns, and he bitterly regretted not having engaged her.
15. The USS *Vanderbilt* was a wooden side-wheeled steamship of 3,360 tons, built in 1856–1857 at the yard of Jeremiah Simonson, Greenpoint, Long Island, New York. She was originally a transatlantic passenger and mail steamer, but at the outbreak of the war was chartered by the U.S. Army, and eventually offered to the Army by her owner, Cornelius Vanderbilt, in 1862. The *Vanderbilt* was transferred to the Navy on 24 March 1862, and was fitted out with a heavy battery of 15 guns. While her prime aim was the capture and destruction of the CSS *Alabama,* which she failed to accomplish, she did succeed in capturing a small number of British blockade-runners.
16. Bulloch, *Secret Service,* vol. 1, 175–6.
17. Wallace and Gillespie, *Journal,* vol. 2, 1143.
18. Maffitt, 14 April 1863.
19. The narrative relating to Read is taken from Robert A. Jones' book, *Confederate Corsair: The Life of Lt. Charles W. "Savez" Read* (Mechanicsburg, Pennsylvania: Stackpole Books, 2000).
20. Subsequently, upon his release, Read was put in command of Battery Semmes and Battery Wood on the James River. He led an expedition of sailors and marines to attack Federal vessels on the James River, capturing and destroying a tug and some barges. His final command was as captain of the CSS *Webb,* a wooden side-wheeled steamer that had been converted into a ram. In an attempt to run the blockade at New Orleans, the ship was halted, and rather than let it fall into enemy hands, Read put it to the torch on 24 April 1865. After the war Read captained merchant vessels, and was later appointed president of the Board of Harbor Masters in New Orleans. He died on 25 January 1890.
21. Wallace and Gillespie, *Journal,* vol. 2, 1199.
22. Bulloch, *Secret Service,* vol. 1, 179.
23. Wallace and Gillespie, *Journal,* vol. 2, 1209.
24. Bulloch, *Secret Service,* vol. 1, 181.
25. O.R.N. Series 1, vol. 2., pp. 639–59. Report of Commander Maffitt, C.S. Navy, commanding, CSS *Florida,* of cruise and captures by that vessel from July to September, 1863.
26. Ibid., 9 Sept. 1863.
27. Ibid., Series 1, vol. 2, 661
28. Following his recovery, in 1864, Maffitt was given command of the ironclad *Albemarle.* Later he took charge of two blockade-runners, the *Lillian* and the *Owl.* With the conclusion of the war, the U.S. government, not easily forgiving those who had made fools of them, confiscated his property, forcing him into exile in England. He renewed his acquaintance with Bulloch, and, obtaining a position in the British Merchant Marine, was given command of a steamship sailing between Liverpool and Rio de Janeiro. The ship was subsequently sold to the Brazilian government and was used for army transport. Maffitt remained in command. During an outbreak of smallpox, Maffitt himself tended to the sick. He later returned home, and with money saved bought a small farm near Wilmington, North Carolina. After an illness of some three months, he died on 15 May 1886, aged 68.
29. Abstract Log of the CSS *Florida,* Lieutenant C.M. Morris, C.S. Navy, April 1 to August 13, 1864, O.R.N. Series 1, vol. 3 (hereafter Morris), 643–6.
30. Bulloch, *Secret Service,* vol. 1, 185.
31. Unattributed letter, retrieved from www.csa-dixie.com/liverpool-dixie/florida (accessed 6 July 2006).
32. Bulloch, *Secret Service,* vol. 1, 209.
33. Treaty, vol. 1, 303–4; Bulloch, *Secret Service,* vol. 1, 216–7.
34. Bulloch, *Secret Service,* vol. 1, 221.

Chapter 3

1. Biographical details relating to Semmes are taken from a short monograph written by his son, Captain S. Spencer Semmes, which appeared in *Southern Historical Society Papers* 38 (1910), 28–40.
2. Semmes, *My Adventures Afloat,* 94.
3. Pay and Muster Roll of the CSS *Sumter,* April 1–September 30, 1861. Georgia Historical Society, Collection No. 779, *Sumter,* CSS, Paper. Terry Foenander's Website, http://home.ozconnect.net/tfoen/sumter.htm (accessed 25 June 2006).
4. "The Cruise of the Confederate Ship *Sumter,*" *Cornhill* 6 (1862), 187–205.
5. Semmes, *My Adventures Afloat,* 111.
6. Ibid., 115.
7. Ibid., 120–1. This was the great comet of 1861, now designated C/1861 J1. It was discovered by sheep farmer and amateur astronomer John Tebbutt of Windsor, New South Wales, Australia, on 13 May 1861. For a while the earth was actually within the comet's tail. On 30 June, Semmes would have seen the comet sometime after 7:45 P.M. in the Great Bear star cluster when it passed closest to earth. Thereafter it withdrew from earth at a speed of 6 million miles a day. By its position in the sky, it was calculated that the comet had an elliptical orbit of 409 years. Its previous visit would have been in 1452, its next in 2270.
8. Midshipman Hudgins was later released, and made his way back to the Confederacy. In 1864, then a lieutenant, he served once more under Semmes, who was then a rear admiral, on the James River fleet. He became a captain of artillery in the later stages of the war, and was paroled at Greensboro, North Carolina, in May 1865.
9. The USS *Iroquois,* commissioned on 24 November 1859, had a displacement of 1016 tons. She was 198 ft. 11 in. long, with a width of 33 ft. 10 in. Her draft was 13 ft. 10 in. Her armament consisted of one 50-pounder gun, four 32-pounders, and one 12-pound howitzer.
10. Grog, a diluted spirit, usually rum, takes its name from Edward Vernon (1684–1757), a British admiral who in 1740 issued naval rum diluted with

water. He was known as "Old Grog," his nickname being taken from his coarse-grained cloak, the fabric of which, usually stiffened with gum, was known as grogram.

11. Myers was exchanged as a prisoner of war in August 1862. He subsequently served aboard the CSS *Georgia* and at the Charleston Station. After the war he moved to Jacksonville, Florida, where he died on 20 March 1901.

12. Treaty, vol. 1, 230.

Chapter 4

1. Bulloch, *Secret Service*, vol. 1, 226.
2. Ibid., 228.
3. Maguire, Treaty, vol. 1, 316 and 318.
4. Ibid., 18 May 1862.
5. Bulloch, *Secret Service*, vol. 1, 227.
6. Treaty, vol. 3, 82.
7. Ibid., 86.
8. Treaty, vol. 3, 315.
9. Bulloch, *Secret Service*, vol. 1, 231.
10. Wallace and Gillespie, *Journal*, vol. 2, 1023–4.
11. Bulloch, *Secret Service*, 238.
12. Ibid., 69.
13. Wallace and Gillespie, *Journal*, vol. 2, 1047–58.
14. Bulloch, *Secret Service*, vol. 1, 253.
15. Treaty, vol. 1, footnote, 151.
16. Bulloch, *Secret Service*, vol. 1, 253–4.
17. Treaty, vol. 1, 335.
18. Semmes, *My Adventures Afloat*, 404.
19. Ibid., 405.
20. Treaty, vol. 3, 151.
21. Treaty, vol. 1, 336.
22. Ibid.
23. Semmes, *My Adventures*, 413.

Chapter 5

1. Semmes, *My Adventures*, 432.
2. Ibid., 441.
3. Ibid., 443.
4. *Proceedings of the Chamber of Commerce of the State of New York on the Burning of the Ship "Brilliant" by the Rebel Pirate "Alabama,"* Tuesday, October 21, 1862 (New York: Joel W. Amerman, 1862).
5. Ibid.
6. Wallace and Gillespie, *Journal*, vol. 2, 1085.
7. Semmes, *My Adventures*, 466.
8. Ibid., 467.
9. Ibid., 479–80.
10. Ibid., 481.
11. Ibid., 489.
12. Wallace and Gillespie, *Journal*, vol. 2, 1087.
13. Retrieved from www.lib.ua.edu/libraries/hoole/digital/cssala/ander.htm (accessed 24 May 2006), William Stanley Hoole Special Collections Library, University of Alabama.
14. Semmes, *My Adventures*, 516.
15. Retrieved from www.lib.ua.edu/libraries/hoole/digital/cssala/jacinto.htm (accessed 24 May 2006).
16. Semmes, *My Adventures*, 524.
17. Retrieved from www.lib.ua.edu/libraries/hoole/digital/cssala/ariel2.htm (accessed 24 May 2006).
18. Semmes, *My Adventures*, 545–7. In *The Journal of George Townley Fullam, Boarding Officer of the Confederate Sea Raider "Alabama,"* he refers to the bogus name of the *Alabama* as "Her Majesty's Steamer *Petrel*," while Lt. Blake, USN, refers to it as "Her Britannic Majesty's ship Vixen." This apart, both accounts more or less tally.
19. Bulloch, *Secret Service*, vol. 1, 344.
20. Wallace and Gillespie, *Journal*, vol. 2, 1140–41.
21. Semmes, *My Adventures*, 568.
22. Ibid., 571–2.
23. Ibid., 595.
24. Ibid., 613.
25. Ibid., 620.
26. Ibid., 622.
27. O.R.N. Series 1, vol. 3, pp. 669–81.
28. Semmes, in his book, *My Adventures Afloat* (633), refers to the ship as HMS *Diomede*. In this he is evidently wrong. There have been three ships of this name, none in existence at the time. The three ships were (1) launched in 1781, a 4th ship of the line, broken up in 1815; (2) launched in 1919, fought during World War II, broken up in 1946; (3) launched in 1969, involved in the Icelandic "Cod War," decommissioned in 1988, and sold to the Pakistan navy.
29. In 1994, one hundred and thirty-one years later, Lt. Simeon Cummings' remains were exhumed and his body was returned to his native land. On 3 June 1994 he was reinterred at Elms Springs, Columbia, Tennessee, in a ceremony witnessed by 5,000 people. The team of people responsible for his return included Robert W. Betterton, a descendant of Raphael Semmes.
30. Semmes, *My Adventures*, 664.
31. Wallace and Gillespie, *Journal*, vol. 2, 1213.
32. The USS *Wyoming* was launched in January 1859. In size she was very similar to the *Alabama*, measuring 198 ft. 6 in. in length, 33 ft. 2 in. in breadth and with a draft of 14ft. 10 in. She had a displacement of 1457 tons. The *Wyoming* was a wooden-hulled screw sloop, with a complement of 198 officers and men. Her armament consisted of two 11-inch D.sb. (diameter small bore), one 60-pounder and three 32-pounders. Under her commander, David Stockton McDougal, she was dispatched to Far Eastern waters with the specific charge of bringing the *Alabama* to battle and defeating her. She had recently returned from Yokohama, where she had been fired upon by shore batteries; she had temporarily run aground, but had fought off two Japanese warships that had attacked her. She was a formidable vessel with a motivated crew. In his personal journal for 26 October 1863, Semmes wrote that "Wyoming is a good match for this ship.... I have resolved to give her battle. She is reported to be cruising under sail — probably with banked fires— and anchors no doubt, under Krakatoa every night, and I hope to surprise her, the moon being near its full." The outcome in Semmes' favor was by no means assured.
33. Arthur Sinclair, *Two Years on the Alabama*, Boston: Lee & Shepard, 1895.
34. *Mariners Mirror* 59 (1950), 351.
35. Wallace and Gillespie, *Journal*, vol. 2, 1268.
36. O.R.N. Series 1, vol. 3, pp. 669–81.
37. John Ancrum Winslow was born in Wilming-

ton, North Carolina, on 19 November 1811. Ironically, he was a Southerner by birth. He was a descendant of John Winslow, brother of Edward Winslow, governor of Massachusetts and a founding father of the Puritan Plymouth colony. The family was originally from Droitwich in Worcestershire. At the age of 14, John was sent north to be educated. He entered the navy as a midshipman in 1827, was promoted to the rank of lieutenant in 1839 and commander in 1855. During the Mexican War he was commended for gallantry for his activities at Tabasco. At the outbreak of the Civil War he was assigned to the Western Gunboat Flotilla and was injured while commanding the ironclad river gunboat *Benton*. Following his recovery he was promoted to captain in July 1862, and in the following year was given command of the USS *Kearsarge*. His mission was to patrol European waters in search of Confederate raiders. On 19 July 1864 his ship defeated the Confederate steamship *Alabama*. Winslow was promoted to commodore as a result of this action, and in 1870 was made a rear admiral. Winslow died, aged 62, on 29 September 1873, soon after retiring from the navy.

38. John Browne, "The Duel Between the 'Alabama' and the 'Kearsarge,' by the Surgeon of the Kearsarge," *Century Illustrated Monthly* 31 (November 1885-April 1886), 923–934.

39. O.R.N. Series 1, vol. 3, pp. 669–81.

40. Ibid.

41. Browne, "Duel," 924.

42. "Cruise & Combats of the *Alabama*," 608–9, in *Battles & Leaders of the Civil War*, vol. 4.

43. This article is printed in full on Terry Foenander's Alabama Website:
http://hub.dataline.net.au/~tfoen/cherbourg.htm.

44. Ibid.

45. The battle between the *Alabama* and the *Kearsarge* was immortalized by two French artists, Eduard Manet and J.B. Henri Durand-Brager. The Manet painting is owned by John G. Johnson (as of 2006). Durand Brager painted two versions of the battle, one of which is owned by the Union League Club of New York. The second of his paintings was auctioned at Christie's of London, on 9 November 2000.

46. O.R.N. Series 1, vol. 3, pp. 669–81.

47. Alfred Iverson Branham, "The Story of the Sinking of the *Alabama*, the Famous Confederate States Cruiser," Interview with Captain John McIntosh Kell, *Eatonton (GA) Messenger*, June 1883.

Chapter 6

1. Treaty, vol. 1, 125.
2. O.R.N. Series 1, vol. 3, pp. 74–7.
3. Ibid.
4. Treaty, vol. 1, 349–50.
5. Semmes, *My Adventures*, 786; O.R.N. series 1, vol. 3, 656.
6. Wallace and Gillespie, *Journal*, vol. 1, 1307.
7. Ibid., 1332.

Chapter 7

1. Bulloch, *Secret Service*, vol. 1, 4.
2. Treaty, vol. 4, 188.
3. Wallace and Gillespie, *Journal*, vol. 2, 1142.
4. Ibid., 1143.
5. Ibid., 1145.
6. O.R.N. Series 1, No. 2., pp. 811–18, Abstract of the Log of CSS *Georgia*.
7. Ibid., 1230.
8. Bulloch, *Secret Service*, vol. 2, 263–4.
9. Ibid., 267–8.

Chapter 8

1. Bulloch, *Secret Service*, vol. 1, 336–7.
2. Ibid., 337.
3. Treaty, 264.

Chapter 9

1. Bulloch, *Secret Service*, vol. 1, 380–1.
2. Ibid., 390.
3. Ibid., 394–5.
4. Ibid., 396.
5. The United States had begun tentative negotiations with the Russians for the purchase of Alaska. The war forestalled further moves for the present, but both nations remained on friendly terms. In September 1863 the Russian Atlantic fleet visited New York as a gesture of friendship. In October the Russian Pacific fleet entered San Francisco Bay, and remained in American waters for the next seven months.
6. Wallace and Gillespie, *Journal*, vol. 2, 1182.
7. Bulloch, *Secret Service*, vol. 1, 424.
8. Ibid., 443.
9. Ibid., 26.
10. Ibid., 31.
11. Ibid., 41.
12. Thomas J. Page, "The Career of the Confederate Cruiser *Stonewall*," *Southern Historical Society Papers*, vol. 7, No. 6, June 1879.
13. Ibid.

Chapter 10

1. William J. Morgan and Robert L. Scheina, eds., *Civil War Naval Chronology*, Washington, D.C.: Navy Department, 1971, vol. 4, 104.
2. Ibid., 107.
3. Treaty, vol. 3, 145.
4. O.R. N. Series 1, vol. 3, 339.

Chapter 11

1. Bulloch, *Secret Service*, vol. 2, 128.
2. (Dr.) F.J. McNulty, "The CSS *Shenandoah* Cruise by One of Her Officers," *Southern Historical Society Papers*, vol. 21 (1893).
3. Bulloch, *Secret Service*, vol. 2, 146
4. William C. Whittle, "The Cruise of the *Shenandoah*," *Southern Historical Society Papers*, vol. 3 (Dec. 1907), 235–258.
5. McNulty, "The CSS *Shenandoah* Cruise."
6. Log of the *Shenandoah*, O.R.N. Series 1, vol. 3, pp. 785–92.
7. Treaty, vol. 3, 117.

8. Treaty, vol. 1, 169.
9. Treaty, vol. 3, 523.
10. Treaty, vol. 2, 328.
11. Whittle, "The Cruise of the *Shenandoah*."
12. Bulloch, *Secret Service*, vol. 2, 156–7.
13. Whittle, "The Cruise of the *Shenandoah*."
14. Bulloch, *Secret Service*, vol. 2, 171.

Chapter 12

1. O.R.N. Series 1, vol. 1, pp. 234–5.
2. Ibid.
3. The British steam-ship *Kate*, not to be confused with the British schooner *Kate*, which was destroyed by the USS *Fernandina* and *Cambridge* attempting to run the blockade near Wilmington on 2 April 1862.
4. O.R.N. Series 1, vol. 1, 404.
5. Semmes, *My Adventures*, 350, 354.
6. Figures derived from David G. Surdam, *Northern Naval Superiority & the Economics of the American Civil War* (Columbia: University of South Carolina Press, 2001).
7. O.R.N. Series 1, vol. 2, 199.
8. Bulloch, *Secret Service*, vol. 2, 232.
9. O.R.N. Series 1, vol. 1, 203.
10. O.R.N. Series 1, vol. 1, 127.
11. O.R.N. Series 1, vol. 3, 320.
12. Chronology, vol. 2, 108.
13. Treaty, vol. 4. 362.
14. Information for this section is from the O.R.N. and Lloyd's Register of Shipping, 1861–65. Additional Information is derived from the University of Glasgow's Website, www.archives.gla.ac.uk/collects/lists/social/civilwar.html (accessed 10 October 2006).
15. "When Liverpool Was Dixie: The Blockade Runners," www.csa-dixie.com/liverpool-dixie/blockade.htm (accessed 11 October 2006).
16. O.R.N. Series 1, vol. 2, 613.
17. O.R.N. Series 1, vol. 9, 285–6.

Chapter 13

1. *Never Caught*, published in London by John Camden Hotten in 1867. Hobart-Hampden uses the nom de guerre Captain Roberts. The account was reprinted by William Abbatt as Extra No. 3 of the *Magazine of History*, published in New York in 1908.
2. O.R.N. Series 1, vol. 11, 745.
3. O.R.N. Series 1, vol. 10, 484.
4. O.R.N. Series 1, vol. 6, pp. 184–5.
5. O.R.N. Series 1, vol. 7, 192.
6. This story has wrongly been ascribed to Hobart-Hampden. See *Civil War Naval Chronology*, vol. 6, 214, and a number of other Civil War books and Websites (e.g., www.hazegray.org/danfs/csn/c.txt and www.civilwarhome.com/navalintro.htm). Hobart-Hampden makes no reference to this voyage in his book, *Never Caught*, which seems highly improbable if he had been involved. The entry in the *Chronology* also refers erroneously to Hobart-Hampden as being a holder of the Victoria Cross. This honor belongs to William N.W. Hewett. Consul Jackson at Halifax clearly identifies Hewett as captain of the vessel on 24 September, its last fateful voyage.
7. O.R.N. Series 1, vol. 11, 745.
8. O.R.N. Series 1, vol. 6, 171.
9. O.R.N. Series 1, vol. 9, 215.
10. O.R.N. Series 1, vol. 9, 216.
11. The sponson guard was the structural projection on the side of a paddle steamer that supported the paddle wheel.
12. Unattributed source. The story is given in Arthur C. Wardle's paper, "Mersey-built Blockade-runners of the American Civil War," *Mariner's Mirror* 28, no. 3 (July 1942).
13. O.R.N. Series 1, vol. 11, 744.
14. Lt. Richard H. Gayle is officially acknowledged as captain of three ships; the *Robert E. Lee* (May 1863), the *Cornubia* (June 1863–Nov. 1864), and the *Stag* (12 Dec. 1864–20 Jan. 1865). The official history, *Civil War Naval Chronology 1861–1865*, compiled by the Navy History Division of the Navy Department, 1971, suggests that Gayle was captured aboard the *Cornubia* on 8 November 1863 (see vol. 6, 215), and the *Robert E. Lee* on the following day, 9 November 1863 (see vol. 6, 294). It would appear that the close proximity of dates for the capture of both vessels, commanded at various times by Gayle, has led to some confusion as to which vessel Gayle was commanding at the time. Captain Louis M. Coxetter, CSN, of Charleston, was known to be master of the *Robert E. Lee* in August 1863 when he ran into St. George's, Bermuda, with a cargo of 1,030 bales of cotton. It would appear to be Coxetter, rather than Gayle, who was captured aboard the *Robert E. Lee*.
15. O.R.N. Series 1, vol. 9, 65.
16. Ibid., 67.
17. O.R.N. Series 1, vol. 9, 281.
18. O.R.N. Series 1, vol. 9, pp. 277–9.
19. O.R.N. Series 1, vol. 9, 273.
20. Ibid., 274.
21. Ibid., 273–4.
22. O.R.N. Series 1, vol. 8, 268.
23. O.R.N. Series 1, vol. 10, pp. 741–2.
24. O.R.N. Series 1, vol. 10, 775.
25. O.R.N. Series 1, vol. 22, 194.

Chapter 14

1. Much of the research in this section relating to the crew of the *Alabama* has been undertaken by the American Civil War Round Table (UK) and Roy Rawlinson, who has included it in his "When Liverpool Was Dixie" Website. The present author acknowledges his debt of gratitude.

Appendix

1. This appears to be James Higgs of Liverpool.
2. The writer is incorrect here. Sailing Master Bulloch and Lt. Becket K. Howell were rescued by the Deerhound. Lieutenant Joseph D. Wilson was taken prisoner by the Kearsarge.

Bibliography

Books

Armstrong, Warren. *Cruise of a Corsair.* London: Cassell, 1963.

Bulloch, James D. *The Secret Service of the Confederate States.* Bentley, 1884. Reprinted London: Thomas Yoseloff, 1959.

Johnson, Robert U., and Clarence C. Buel, eds. *Battles & Leaders of the Civil War.* New York: Century, 1888.

Jones, Robert A. *Confederate Corsair: The Life of Lt. Charles W. "Savez" Read.* Mechanicsburg, Pennsylvania: Stackpole Books, 2000.

Naval History Division, Navy Department. *Civil War Naval Chronology.* Washington, D.C.: Navy Department, 1971.

Papers relating to the Treaty of Washington. Washington, D.C.: Government Printing Office, 1872.

Roberts, Captain (Augustus Charles Hobart-Hampden). *Never Caught.* London: John Campden Hotten, 1867. Reprinted by William Abbatt, *Magazine of History*, Extra No. 3, New York, 1908.

Sinclair, Arthur. *Two Years on the Alabama.* Boston: Lee & Shepard, 1895.

Semmes, Raphael. *My Adventures Afloat: A Personal Memoir of My Cruises & Services.* London: Richard Bentley, 1869.

Surdam, David G. *Northern Naval Superiority & the Economics of the American Civil War.* Columbia: University of South Carolina Press, 2001.

Taylor, Thomas. *Running the Blockade.* London: John Murray, 1896.

United States Naval War Record Office. Official Records of the Union & Confederate Navies in the War of the Rebellion, 1894–1922.

Wallace, Sarah Agnes, and Frances Elma Gillespie, eds. *The Journal of Benjamin Moran, 1857–1865.* Chicago: University of Chicago Press, 1949.

Watson, William. *The Adventures of a Blockade Runner.* London: Unwin, 1892.

Periodicals and Newspapers

Cornhill 6 (1862).
Dictionary of National Biography.
Dodd's Parliamentary Year Book (1860–1865).
Economic History (1950–1953).
Hansard (1860–1865).
Harper's Weekly (1860–1865).
Illustrated London News (1860–1865).
Kelly's Directories of London, Liverpool & Warwickshire (1860–1865).
Lloyd's Register of Shipping (1858–1865).
Mariner's Mirror (1942, 1975, 1995).
Observer (1860–1865).
Statesman's Year Book (1863–1865).
London *Times* (1860–1865).

Index

A. Richards 176
A.D. Vance 243
A.J. Bird 179
Abby Bradford 65, 75
Abdallah, Sultan 134
Abeille, French warship 67
Abigail 196, 213
Abrio, Jerome 57
Acheron, French gunboat 70
Achilles, H.M.S. 254
Adams, U.S. Minister Charles F. 6, 43, 148, 202; Adams threatens war 169; letters to Russell 17, 76, 101, 127, 162, 163–164, 168
Adderley & Co. 20, 207
Adela 205
Adelaide 190, 203, 213
Adirondack, U.S.S. 23, 207
Adriatic 176
Aeolus, U.S.S. 239
Aerial, brig 47
Agrippina, supply ship 35, 78, 84, 85, 101, 102, 103, 107, 117, 123, 214, 228
Aires 215
Alabama, C.S.S. 35, 131, 253; commissioning of 86; construction of 77–78; crew 85–87; escape from Martinique 101–103; "Kappal Hantu" 130; officers 88, 92; sinks the *Hatteras* 107–109; sunk off Cherbourg 137–142; voyage 90; see also *Enrica*
Alabama, U.S.S. 236
Alabama Claims 253
Alabama Dept. of Archives 42
"Alabama" Sam (Samuel Henry) 255
Alar, supply ship 153
Albatross 213
Albermarle, ironclad 247
Albert, Prince, husband of Queen Victoria 7, 72
Albert Adams 63, 75
Albion 212
Albion Lincoln 182
Albion Trading Co. 210, 214
Aldebaran 33
Alert 93
Aleutian Islands 199
Alexander Collie & Co. 210, 234, 245

Alexandra 213
Alexandra, C.S.S. 161–162, 229
Alexandra, Danish Princess 161
Alexandria, Virginia 250
S.S. *Alfred* 255
Alfred (Old Dominion) 216
Alfred H. Partridge 36
Algeciras 74
Alice 243
Alina 189
Allcott, Henry 89, 144, 255
Alta Vela 113
Altamaha 94
Amanda 129
Amazonian 120, 121
Amelia, brig 40
Amelia (Tallahassee) 179
Amelia County, Virginia 180, 245, 252
America, yacht 163
Anderson, E.C. 16, 102
Anderson, Col. Edward 14
Anderson, Edward Maffitt 102, 141
Andrews, Midshipman William 75
Anglesey, Wales 14, 200
Anglo-Ashanti War 254
Anglo-Burmese War 225
Anglo-Confederate Trading Co. 210, 213, 231
Anglo-Saxon 42
Anglo-Saxon race 187
Anjengo, India 133
Ann 205, 214, 243
Anna F. Schmidt 122
Annapolis 38, 252
Annapolis Naval Academy 188
Annie Childs, blockade runner 16, 19
Anonyma 214, 235
Appomattox, surrender at 197
Approaching Cotton Crisis 204
Arabella 37
Arcade 71, 75
Arcas Cays 103
Archer 38, 39
Arcole 179
Areal, steamer 26
Ariel 105–106, 241
Arkansas, C.S.S. 36
Arkwright, Capt. William 168
Arman, M. 170

Armstrong, Midshipman (2nd Lt.) Richard 56, 57; letter to Barron 144
Ash, James 216
Atalanta, steam ship 175
Atkinson, Thomas 225
Atlanta, C.S.S. 48
Atlantic 176, 240
Avalanche 130
Averett, Lt. C.S.N. 27, 33, 34, 42, 48
Avon 46
Azores 32, 71, 136, 154, 155, 189
Azuma 174
Azzapadi 121

Backhouse & Dixon 214, 234
Badger I 210, 213
Badger II 213
Bahama, blockade runner 18, 22, 23, 84, 85, 86, 205, 207, 229
Bahamas 222
Bahia, Brazil 49, 119, 155
Bainbridge, U.S.S. 113
Ballarat, Australia 192
Ballarat Star 192
Ballinger, Charles 53
Bangkok 131
Banks, General, U.S.A. 103
Banshee 213, 231, 232, 241; crew list 233–234
Barclay Curle & Co. 211
Barney, Lt. Joseph, C.S.N. 27, 44
Baron de Castine 100
Barracouta, barque 199, 200
Barrett, Dr. 25, 26
Barron, Lt., C.S.N. 52
Barron, Flag Officer Samuel, C.S.N. 147, 157, 159
Basilisk, H.M.S. 226, 254
Bat 213
Batavia (Jakarta) 34, 115, 129
Bates, Edwin 158
Bay Estate 176
Bayne, Colonel, C.S.A. 247
Beagle, gun-boat 225, 226
Beaufort, Melville 57, 62, 89
Beauregard, General, C.S.A. 67
Beezee Island 129
Begbie, Thomas S. 214, 235
Behucke, F.C. 193
Belfast 83, 245

Bell, Rear Admiral, U.S.N. 108, 157
Belle, schooner 47
Belle Isle 43, 46, 171
Ben Dunning 63, 75
Ben McCree 157
Benjamin, Secretary of War Judah P. 10, 11
Benjamin F. Hoxie 41
Benjamin Tucker 94
Bentley, Richard, publisher 253
Bering Sea 196, 199
Bermuda 48, 162, 182, 205, 224, 231, 242
Bermuda, blockade runner 18, 203, 205, 207, 228, 238
Bethiah Thayer 115
Bickford, Captain R.N. 128
Bienville, mail steamer 10, 16
Bigelow, U.S. Consul General 170
Bijou 213
Billow 176
Bird Cay, Galveston 237
Birkenhead 81
Birmingham buttons 105
Blackar, Lt. John, C.S.N. 194
Blackwall Iron works 216
Blake, Commander Homer, U.S.N. 107–109; report to Gideon Welles 109, 113
Blanchard, U.S. Consul William 192
Blanquilla 103
Bocas del Drago 66
Boggs, Captain, U.S.N. 173
Bold, Thomas 152, 158
Bold Hunter 157
Bombay, H.M.S. 192
Bond, George, pilot 82, 83
Bonfils, Confederate Commercial Agent 137, 264
Bouboulina 241
Bowdler, Chaffer & Co. 213
Boynton, William 45
A Boy's Ambitions 217
Bradford, O. 22, 24
Brandywine, U.S.S. 152
Bravay & Co. 166, 169
Bray, Capt. 52
Breck, Captain J.B., U.S.N. 244
Bremontier, French ship 35
Brest 42, 43, 45, 157, 171
Brest Naval Yard 42
Brewer, H.O. 237
Brice, Friend & Co. 231
Brilliant 95
Britt, Maurice 144
Broderick, Richard 79
Brooke, Commander John, C.S.N. 186
Brooklyn, U.S.S. 27, 60, 61, 108
Brooks, William P. 57, 144
Brown, Dr., *Kearsarge* 136, 137
Brown, Engineer 27, 36, 38
Brown & Co. 211
Brownsville, Texas 236
Brunswick 197, 198
Bryan, G.D. 27

Bryan, Midshipman 22, 24, 32, 35
Bryson, Captain, U.S.N. 76
Buchanon, Admiral C.S.N. 27
Bull Dog, H.M.S. 22, 218
Bulletin 253
Bulloch & Barcroft 251
Bulloch, Hester Amarintha 9
Bulloch, Irvine 9, 141, 199, 200, 251
Bulloch, James Dunwoody 3, 6, 9, 10, 11, 14, 21, 43, 76, 79, 81, 84, 88, 100, 111, 165, 168, 169, 170, 185 241, 244, 247, 250–251, 195
Bulloch, Richard Thompson 55
Bulloch, Samuel Middleton 55
Bureau Veritas 255
Burgess, George 204
Burrell, Edward 255
Burroughs, Capt. J.M. 241–242, 244
Butcher, Captain Matthew 79, 80, 81, 82, 83, 85, 88, 228
Butler, James 48
Byzantium 38

Cadieu, Ensign Charles, U.S.N. 233
Cadiz 45, 72
Cadmus, H.M.S. 66
Caird & Co. 211
Cairngorm 100
Calais 44, 158
Caleb Cushing, U.S. Revenue ship 38
Calf of Man 83
Campbell, Lt. William, C.S.N. 158
Canada, steamer 54
Canterbury 256
Canton 162; see also *Pampero*
Canton, China 131
Cape Catoche 107
Cape Fear 227
Cape Fear River 221
Cape La Hague 136
Cape San Antonio 62
Cape Town, S. Africa 123, 125, 134, 191
Cape Town Argus 125–126
Cape Verde Islands 154, 155, 190
Cardenas, Cuba 24, 28, 181
Caren, John 255
Carnatic 168
Carolina, steamer 240
Carolina Islands 195
Carrie Estelle 176
Carroll 176
Carter, Lt. Robert, C.S.N. 17, 185, 186
Carter, Lt. William, C.S.N. 158
Case, Captain A. Ludlow 242
Caskie, Elizabeth Euphemia 10
Castor, supply ship 119, 155
Catherine 197
Cayman Islands 64
Ceylon (Sri Lanka) 117, 133
Challenger, H.M.S. 110, 113
Chameleon, C.S.S., (*Olustee*) 179, 247

Chapman, George 161
Chapman, Lt. R.T., C.S.N. 56, 57, 63, 64, 120
Charles Hill 116
Charleston 163, 179, 189, 203, 205, 207, 224, 240, 245, 247, 255
Charlotte 209, 241, 244
Charter Oak 189, 190
Chastelaine 113
Chatham 213
Chattahoochee, C.S.S. 189
Cheek, Lt., R.N. 202
Cherbourg 136, 157, 171, 255, 261
Cherokee, U.S.S. 183
Chesapeake, ocean liner 38, 39
Chesapeake Bay 36, 252
Chew, Lt., C.S.N. 190
Chickahominy, battle 13, 207
Chickamauga, C.S.S. 180; list of crew 181, 184
Chicora Exporting Co. 210, 213
Chippewa, U.S.S. 76
Christabel 156
Christine 182
Cienfuegos, Cuba 62, 63
City of Bath 155
City of Richmond, blockade runner 171
Clara, barque 40
Clare, Allen 81
Claremont (NH) *National Eagle* 139, 261
Clarence, C.S.S. 36, 37, 38, 252
Clary, Commander A., U.S.N. 208
Clematis, U.S.S. 183
Clyde, river 211
Clyde Bank Iron Shipyard 13, 162
Clydesdale 205
Clydeside-built blockade runners 211
Cockburn, Lord Chief Justice 154
Codrington, Governor Sir William 74
Colletis 13
Collie & Co. 210, 234, 245
Collins, Commander Napoleon, U.S.N. 49–50, 51, 53
Colonel Lamb 213, 240–241
Columbia 205
Columbus, U.S.S. 11
Commerce, U.S.S. 203
Commonwealth 35
Comore Archipelago 134
Condor 224, 226, 227
Congress 198
Connecticut, U.S.S. 173
Conrad 121, 134
Considine, ___, C.S.S. *Florida* 53
Constitution 155
Contest 130
Conway, ___, C.S.S. *Florida* 53
Coquette, blockade runner 185
Corbett, Captain G.H. 185, 186
Cornubia (*Lady Davis*) 210, 215, 216, 241, 242; diary of voyage 243–244
Corris Ann 29
Corsets 221

Cory, Captain 223, 224
Couronne, French frigate 138
Courser 94
Court of Exchequer 162
Covel, William 45
Covington 198
Coxeter, Captain 17
Craig's Royal Hotel 192
Craven, Captain (Comm.) Thos. A., U.S.N. 75, 82, 83–84, 158, 172
Creaghan, ___ 237
Crenshaw 99
Crenshaw & Co. 210, 213
Crest of the Wave, clipper 231
Crimean War 81, 225
Cross, Brigadier General Osborne 10
"crossing the line," naval tradition 190–191
Crown Point 40
Cruikshank, Captain Donald 239
Crusader, U.S.S. 64
Cuba 62, 67, 75
Cuddy, Thomas, gunner 89
Cummings, Lt. Simeon, C.S.N. 57; death of 124
Curaçao 64
Curlew 213
Curlew, H.M.S. 49
Cuyler, U.S.S. 23, 28
Czar 214

D.G. Godfrey 190
Da Costa, John 161
Daffen Island 123
Dakar, Senegal 189
Daniel Trowbridge 68, 75
Danish government 166
Danville, Virginia 197
Darling, Governor Sir Charles 192, 193
Darling, Lt. George, U.S.A. 233
Dartmouth Naval College 217
Da Silva Gomes, President Antonio 50
Davenport, Lt. Dudley U.S.N. 38, 39
Davidson, Captain A.B. 163
Davidson, Lt. Hunter, C.S.N. 171
Davidson, James "Charley" 193
Davies, James Edwards (pseud. Clarence R. Yonge) 112
Davis, Lt. Comm. J.L., U.S.N. 163
Davis, President Jefferson, C.S.A. 3, 4, 27, 86, 175, 197, 224, 227
Davis, Ross 235
Dayton, U.S. Ambassador William 43, 136, 158
De Costa, John 81
Deer 213
Deerhound, steam yacht 138, 142, 146, 255, 258, 259, 260
De Gueyton, Vice Admiral Count 43
De l'Huys, Drouyn 43
De Long, U.S. Consul James W. 75

Delphine 191
Demerara, British Guiana 217
Denbigh 213, 237–238
Denny & Bros. 152, 211
Derby, Lord 254
Desertas Islands 187
Devastation, H.M.S. 254
De Videky, L. 50, 52
Diamond 155
Dictator 154, 155
Diomede, H.M.S. 122–123
"Dixie" 113
Dolan, R.J., Collector of Customs 153
Dolphin, H.M.S. 218
Don 215, 219
Donegal, H.M.S. 200, 255
Donna Januaria, corvette 50, 51
Dorcas Prince 118
Dorris, ___, C.S.S. *Florida* 53
Douglas, blockade runner 185, 241
Dover 136, 256
Dream 213
Drewry's Bluff, Virginia 189
Drinkwater, Capt. & Mrs. 182
Driver, H.M.S. 218
Druid 212
Dublin 83
Duchatel, Captain 70
Dudgeon, Messers. J.& W. 175, 180, 215, 219
Dudley, U.S. Consul Thos. Haines 17, 19, 43, 79, 81, 82, 101, 153, 154, 158, 161, 162, 168, 179, 202, 237, 245, 255
Duguid, Capt. James Alexander 18, 19, 20, 245
Dunkirk 96
Dunlap, Commodore, R.N. 110–111
Du Pont, Flag Officer Samuel 15, 215
Dupont Munitions Works 32
Dwyer, James 52
Dyke, Midshipman 27, 34, 52

Eastman, U.S. Consul 42
Eben Dodge 71, 75
Economist 205, 207
Edith (Chickamauga) 180, 181
Edward 191
Edward Carey 195
Edward Lawrence & Co. 213
E.F. Lewis 179
Eggleston, U.S. Consul 72
Egyptian government 166, 168, 169
El Mounassur, ram 166
El Tousson, ram 166
Electric Spark 49
Elisha Dunbar 95
Eliza Bonsall 203
Ella 243
Emily Farnum 95
Emily St. Pierre 203, 228, 231
Emma Jane 133
Emma L. Hall 181
Empress, mail-ship 175

Empress Theresa 179
Endymion, H.M.S. 55
English Channel 136
Englishman, brig 47
Enrica (C.S.S. *Alabama*) 78, 79 81, 82
Ericson, U.S.S. 41
Erie, U.S.S. 172
Erlanger & Co. 237
Eskimos 196
Estelle 28
Etta Caroline 177
Euphrates 196
European Trading Co. 210, 237
Euston Square, London 76
Evans, James 17
Evans, Lt. William E, C.S.N. 56, 57, 63, 98, 120, 157
Excellent, H.M.S. 218
Excelsior, brig 47
Express 123

Factory Girl 155
Fairchild, U.S. Consul George H. 100–101
Fairy, steamer 205
Falcon, blockade runner 211
Falcon, brig 69
Falcon Fisher, steamer 224
Falmouth, Cornwall 236
Farragut, Admiral David 36, 139, 180, 237, 245
"Fate of the Alabama," song 145
Faucon, Lt. E.H., U.S.N. 235
Fauntleroy, Lt. C.M., C.S.N. 158, 159, 207
Favorite 197, 198
Fawcett, Preston & Co. 13, 17, 84, 161, 162
Fayal, Azores 16
Fernando de Norohna, Brazil 35, 117
Ferrol, port 171
Ficklin, Major B.F., C.S.A. 245
Fingal, blockade runner 13, 14, 15, 16, 80, 251
Flambeau, U.S.S. 75
Fleming, Jock, pilot 178
Fleur de Bois, brig 69
Flora, blockade runner 175
Floral Wreath 177
Florida, C.S.S. 24, 25, 27, 28, 38, 40, 43–44, 48, 49, 120, 171, 228, 236, 248; sunk 54; see also *Oreto*
Florida, U.S.S. 229
Florida Steam Packet Co. 240
Florrie 212
Floyd, Acting Master 27, 30, 35, 41
Foley, Frederick 234
Foreign Enlistment Act 11, 22, 81, 128, 159, 193, 254
Formby Lighthouse 79
Forrest, George 96
Forrest City, cruise ship 39
Forster, William, M.P. 6
Forsyth, Captain R.N. 126
Fort Caswell 175, 244

Index

Fort Fisher 179, 183, 184, 220, 227, 24, 243, 244, 247
Fort Lafayette 233
Fort Monroe 48, 238
Fort Morgan 25
Fort Pulaski 15, 223
Fort St. Philip 243
Fort Sumter 10, 15, 203
Fort Warren 39, 54, 245
Foster, Charles 14
Foster, Harriott Cross 10
Fox 123
Foxhound, gunship 218
Francis Milly, brig 47
Frank Leslie's Illustrated Newspaper 105
Fraser & Co., Charleston 15, 193, 203, 240
Fraser, Trenholm & Co. 11, 14, 15, 17, 18, 76, 79, 80, 88, 161, 165, 168, 179, 185, 203, 207, 210, 228, 229, 23, 236, 238, 241
Freeman, Engineer Miles, C.S.N. 57, 60, 61, 100, 142
Freemantle, George 15
French government 168
Fullam, Lt. George Townley, C.S.N. 80, 105, 132, 142
Fulton, U.S. troopship 232
Funchal, Madeira 46, 186, 211
Fyffe, Mr. 111

G. & J. Thompson 13, 162, 165, 211, 238
Gale, Col. John, Governor of Alabama 239
Gale, Richard H., C.S.N. 239, 242, 244
Galt, Surgeon Francis 22, 56, 57, 76, 97, 123, 129, 142, 147, 207
Galveston 103, 107, 237–238, 249
Gansevoort, Commander G., U.S.N. 23, 205, 207
Gardner & Co. 237
Garretson, Asst. Surgeon, C.S.N. 27, 30
Gaspar Strait 129
Gayle, Lt. Richard H., C.S.N. 241
General Berry 48
General Pike 197
General Williams 197
Geneva Arbitration 133, 204, 235, 254
George Griswold 155
George Latimer 48
Georgia, C.S.S. 45, 119, 152, 158
Georgia Belle 213
Georgiana, screw steamer 163
Germantown, U.S.S. 11
Gettysburg, Battle of 7
Ghifinsi Bay 196
Giant's Causeway 83
Gibbs, Master W.P. 49
Gibraltar 73, 74, 75
Gibraltar 76
Gildersleeve 120
Gilliard, Dr. 25
Gipsy 197

Gipsy Queen 214
Giraffe 168, 180, 205, 210, 241, 245
Gladiator 214, 240
Gladstone, Miss 151
Gladstone, Prime Minister William 6, 151
Glasgow 238, 245, 255
Glenavon 176
Godfrey, Abner 237
Godspeed 38, 182
Godwin, Charles 144
Golconda 48
Golden Eagle 114
Golden Rocket 62, 75
Golden Rule 113
Goldsborough, Flag Officer, U.S.N. 227
Gondar 203
Good Hope 155
Gordon 240
Gordon, Rear Admiral, U.S.N. 199
Gordon, Robert 31, 41
Gordon Coleman & Co. 158
Gorgas, [Major] Col. Josiah, C.S.A. 204, 242
Gorst, Henry 237, 238
Goshawk, gun-boat 200
Gowan-Lock, George 238
Grafton, Asst. Surgeon C.S.N. 27, 34, 35; drowned 40
Graham, U.S. Consul Walter 126, 127
Grampus Island 196
Grand Gulf, U.S.S. 176, 232
Grant, General U.S., U.S.A. 197
Grapeshot 215
Green Cay 23, 24, 29
Green Turtle Cay 222
Greenhithe 171
Greenhow, Mrs. Rose O'Neal 227, 229
Greenland 48
Greyhound 212
Greyhound, H.M.S. 110, 113
Grier, Mr. Justice 5
Grover, ___, C.S.S. *Florida* 53
Guadalquiver, Spanish gunboat 25

Habana, steamer 56; see also C.S.S. *Sumter*
Hagar, Captain, description of the *Alabama* 95
Halifax, Nova Scotia 178, 181, 205, 209–210, 241, 247
Hamburg 204, 20, 235
Hamilton, Lt. J.R., C.S.N. 80
Hammer, Captain 16
Hampton Roads 36, 54, 176
Hansa 215, 225, 228, 243
Harding, Sir John 83
Harper's Weekly 99–100, 106, 230
Harriet Pinkney, C.S.S. 31, 214, 235, 236
Harriett Stevens 48
Harris, Lt. Commander, U.S.N. 209
Harrocke, Thomas, pilot 195
Harvest 195

Harvey & Co. 210, 241
Harvey Birch 72
Harwood, George 187
Hatteras, U.S.S. 107–109
Havana 25, 173, 209, 234
Hawley, U.S. Consul Seth 208
Hawthorn, James 45
Haya Maro (*Tallahassee*) 179
Hayle Steam Packet Co. 241
Hector 195
Helm, Major Charles, C.S.A. 24, 25, 28, 209
Henrietta 35
Henry, Samuel ("Alabama" Sam) 255
Herald 17, 205
Herbert, Lord 88
Hercules, tug 65, 82, 85
Hewett, Captain William N.W., R.N. 224, 225–226, 228, 254–255
Heyle, D.B. 42
Heyleger, Louis 21, 207
Hickley, Commander R.N. 22
Hicks, Midshipman Wm. A. 56, 57, 65
Higgs, James 141
Highlander 132
Hillman 198
Hillyar, Captain, R.N. 66
Hindoo, barque 40
Hobart-Hampden, Augustus Charles, R.N. 217, 218–219, 254
Hogan, John 45
Holden, Midshipman John F. 56, 57, 59
Hong Kong 154
Hoole, 2nd Lt., C.S.N. 27, 30, 32
Hope 213, 239
Hope, Admiral Sir James, R.N. 178
Hopkins, Lt. Col. James, U.S.A. 49
Hore, Capt., R.N. 169
Horner, Captain 175
Hornet 213, 226
Hornet, U.S.S. 180
Horsman, Edward, M.P. 5
Horwood, George 256
Howard 48, 177
Howell, Lt. Marines Beckett 22, 59, 264
Hudgins, Midshipman Albert G. 56, 57, 63
Hughes, Peter 88
Hunter, Master's Mate 50, 51
Huse, Harriet Pinkney 235
Huse, Major Caleb, C.S.A. 13, 204, 207
Huth & Co. 41

Illustrated London News 163, 175, 179, 225, 229, 238
Inglefield, Captain, R.N. 231
Ino, U.S.S. 75
Investigator 73, 75
Iona 205
Iroquois, U.S.S. 70, 71, 104, 191, 242, 246–247

Index

Isaac, Campbell & Co. 200, 214, 236
Isaac Howland 198
Isaac Webb 38
Isabel 213
Isabella 197
Ish-y-Paw, King 195
Isle of Man Steam Packet Co. 241
Ivanhoe 238

J. & G. Thompson 13, 162, 165, 211, 238
J.W. Seaver 155
Jabez Snow 120
Jack & Co. 241
Jackson, Engineer 27
Jackson, U.S. Consul 162
Jackson, U.S. Consul Mortimer 178, 226, 227
Jackson, "Stonewall" 31
Jacksonville 240
Jacob Bell 30
Jacop Cappe 182
James Adger, U.S.S. 229, 231, 232, 244
James Funk 176
James Jack & Co. 241
James Littlefield 177
James Murray 198
James River Fleet 253
Japan (C.S.S. *Georgia*) 152, 153, 154
Jason, H.M.S. 110, 113, 255
Jeff Davis, blockade runner 17
Jerah Swift 197
Jewett, Jebediah 39
Johanna, Port of 134
John, King of Abyssinia 255
John A. Parks 115
John Adams, U.S.S. 189
John Fraser & Co., Charleston 15, 193, 203, 240
John Fraser, blockade runner 193, 203
John Watts 157
Johnson, U.S. President Andrew 199, 250
Johnson, John 40
Johnson, General Joseph, C.S.A. 207, 253
Jones, Captain, of the *Ariel* 106
Jones, Charles 175
Jones, Evan Parry 142
Jones, John D. 176
Jones & Co. 153, 154
Jones, Quiggin & Co. 213, 231, 238, 241, 244
Joseph Maxwell 65, 66, 75
Joseph Parke 68, 75
Josiah Achom 178
Julia, blockade runner 205
Julia Usher 168
Justitia 214

Kaiten 174
Kamtchatka 196
Kansas, U.S.S. 183
Karnack, steamship 80
Kate, steam-ship 207, 240
Kate Cory 118
Kate Dyer 35
Kate Prince 190
Kate Stewart 37
Kearsarge, U.S.S. 42–43, 45, 46, 75, 101, 136, 157, 251, 262; sinks the *Alabama* 137–142
Kehoe, Thomas 36, 45
Kell, Lt. John McIntosh C.S.N. 22, 56, 57, 74, 76, 84, 123, 130, 139, 207, 263
Kellett, Sir Henry, R.N. 254
Kelley, Thomas 158
Kemble, Acting Master Edmund, U.S.N. 235
Kennebec, U.S. gunboat 238
Kent 155
Keystone State, U.S.S. 67, 69
King, Commander, R.N. 192
King, Master's Mate 52, 53
King Edward VII 151
King John of Abyssinia 255
Kingfisher 116
Klingender, Melcher George 76, 80, 210, 214
Kliprug Farm, S. Africa 124
Kotetsu 174
Kuril Islands 196

Ladrone Islands 196
Lady Davis blockade runner 111, 216, 241
Lady Stirling 239
Lafayette 98–99
Lafayette, whaler 118
Lafitte, J.B. 241
Lafone, Henry 162, 213
Laing, James 215
Laird & Sons 13, 43, 76, 77, 79, 81, 163, 166, 213, 237
Lake Erie 181
Lamb, Colonel William, C.S.A. 225, 228, 241
Lamont Du Pont 177
Lamplighter 97
Lamson, Lt. R.H., U.S.N. 225
Lancaster, John 142, 146–150
Lane, schooner 49
Lapwing (*Oreto II*) 34, 40
Lara Mara, brig 33
Lark 213
La Rocas, Portugal 158
Latham, John 85, 86–87
Laurel, packet ship 185, 186, 255
Lauretta 99
Lawrence & Co. 213
Lawrie's Shipyard 163
Leamington Spa 36, 195, 250
Lee, General Robert E., C.S.A. 7, 31, 179, 197, 249, 250
Lee, Rear Admiral S.P., U.S.N. 231, 234
Lelia 213
Lemprieu, Charles 204
Leonard 205
Leonce Lacoste, French brig 30
Leopard 178
Leopoldina 213
Let Her Be 213
Levi Starbuck 100
Lewis, Mr., of Alderney 153
Leytonstone, London 255
Lighthouse Bureau 55
Lilian 237, 238
Lincoln, President Abraham 4, 199
Linda, bark 52
Little Ada 212
Liverpool 84, 186, 199, 203, 217, 237, 25, 255
Liverpool Echo 255
Liverpool Mercury 200, 202
Liverpool Nautical College 251
Lizzie M. Stacey 190
Llewellyn, Surgeon David H. 80, 88, 144, 265
Lloyds, screw steamer 214
Lockwood, Captain Thomas, J., C.S.N. 208, 239, 240, 241
Lockwood's Folly Inlet 235
Londona 205
Los Frailes 66
Los Jardnes 196
Louisa Hatch 117
Louisa Kilham 63, 75
Louisiana, ironclad, C.S.N. 180, 189, 245
Low, John 14, 16, 80, 94, 98, 121, 251–252; letter to Bulloch 20
Lucy 213
Ludlow St. County Jail, N.Y. 233
Lynch, Asst. Paymaster 27
Lynx 213, 238
Lynx, H.M.S. 225
Lyons, Lord 7, 69, 227, 236

M.A. Schindler 37
M.J. Colcord 34
Macebo, Commander Gervasio 51
Machios 62, 75
Macomber 38
Madeira 46, 166, 186
Maffei, Count 17
Maffitt, Eugene 16
Maffitt, Commander John N. 19, 20–21, 23, 42, 76, 207, 238, 239, 246, 247, 252; appointed Commander 39; letter from Mallory 247; letter to Bulloch 24; runs into Mobile 26, 27; succumbs to yellow fever 24–25
Magee, James 257
Magnolia 178
Magruder, General, C.S.A. 107
Maguire, Matthew 17, 79, 80, 82
Mahon, John 154
Majestic, H.M.S. 231
Makin, John 14
Malacca 132
Malgar & Cie 215
Malita, blockade runner 205
Mallory, Naval Secretary Stephen 10, 11, 12, 15, 27, 80, 131, 157, 175, 253; letter to Semmes 56; letters from Bulloch 16, 84, 168,

170; letters to Bulloch 165, 166, 170; letters to Maffitt 40, 247–248
Manassas, Battle of 67, 68
Manassas, C.S.S. 18
Manchester 97
Mandamis 49
Mann, Commissioner Dudley 11
Marcus Island 196
Margaret and Jessie (*Douglas*), blockade runner 185
Margaret Island 196
Margaret Y. Davis, schooner 48
Margarita, Spanish ship 47
Margarita Island 66
Maria Frederica, bark 48
Mark L. Potter 181
Marmelstein, Adolphe 121
Mars, Michael 88, 144, 255
Martaban (*Texas Star*) 132, 133, 175
Martha 198
Martha Wenzell 126
Martin, Captain Daniel 238
Martin, Emma 252
Martinique 32, 69, 100
Mary, brig 47
Mary A. Howes 177
Mary Alvina 37
Mary Celestina 213
Mary Kendall 122
Maryland, Governor of 252
Mason, Captain 214, 234
Mason, Confederate Commissioner James M. 6–7, 75, 76, 165–166, 240, 245, 250; letter to Bulloch 195; letter to Lancaster 150
Masonboro Inlet 183
Matamoras, Mexico 236
Matheson's Clyde Service 163
Maury, Commander Matthew, C.S.N. 44, 152, 154, 186, 209
Maury, Commander William, C.S.N. 154, 155, 157
Maussion de Conde, Rear Admiral 69
Maxwell, Liverpool Councilor M.H. 251
McAndrews of Preston 213
McAskill Island 195
McCabe, ___, C.S.S. *Florida* 53
McCartney, Thomas M. 115
McCaskey, Benjamin 89, 142
McCauley, Commodore 11
McClellan, General, U.S.A. 209
McDonald, James 45
McDonnell, Governor Richard 178
McDougal, Commander Charles, U.S.N. 199
McDouglas, Anna 240
McDowell, General, U.S.A. 67
McGrath, Master's Mate 53
McKillop, Captain, R.N. 22
McMillan, Thomas 88
McNair, J., Engineer 15, 80
McNevin, ___, C.S.N. 53

McNevin, Captain Francis 237
McNulty, Dr. F.J. 186, 189, 191
McQueen, Alexander 78, 84, 117
McRae, C.S.S. 36
Meio River 67
Melbourne, Australia 191, 193
Melita, blockade runner 22, 76, 207
Memphis 205
Mercantile Trading Co. 204, 210
Mercedita, U.S.S. 206, 238
Meridian, Mississippi 252
Merrimac 11
Mersey, river 200, 241, 249
Mersey-built blockade runners 213
Mexican War 9, 55
Michigan, U.S.S. 181
Middleton, Arthur 55
Middleton, Catherine Hooe 55
Milan 254
Miller, Lewis 116
Miller & Sons 12, 43, 77, 161, 213, 229
Milo 197
Minho 20, 235
Minnesota, U.S.S. 227
Minor, U.S. Consul General, William 249
Mississippi, C.S.S. 189
Mobile 25, 237, 253
"Mobile Packet" (*Denbigh*) 237
Modern Greece 214
Moelfra Bay, Anglesey 82, 111
Mohican, U.S.S. 117
Mona Passage 103
Montauk Point, Long Island 182
Montevideo 241
Montgomery, U.S.S. 235
Monticello, U.S.S. 236
Montmorency 71, 75
Moran, Benjamin, Asst. Sec. 6, 17, 18, 33, 41, 42, 43, 81, 83, 97, 111, 127, 135, 150, 153, 154, 157, 169
Morgan, Edward, Surveyor 18, 82
Morning Star 31, 116
Morris, Captain Charles M. 44
Morris, Lt. (Captain) Charles Manigault, C.S.N. 45, 46
Morro Castle, Spanish gunboat 28
Morse, U.S. Consul Samuel 153; letter to Adams 210; letter to Seward 180
La Mouche Noire, brig 68
Moukouruski Island 196
Murdaugh, Lt. William, C.S.N. 159
Murray, Captain 225
Murray, Joseph 158
Murray, Sir John, Duke of Atholl 225
Murray-Aynsly, Charles, Vice-Admiral, R.N. 225–226, 255
My Adventures Afloat 115, 253
Myers, Paymaster Henry, C.S.N. 56, 57, 65, 74, 75, 91

Naiad 63, 75
Nansemond, U.S.S. 225

Nantes 170
Napoleon, ship of war 144, 259
Napoleon III 5, 169, 170
Narcissus, H.M.S. 126, 128
Narrative of a Blockade Runner 246, 252
Nashville, C.S.S. 14, 18, 67, 72, 189, 207
Nassau 22, 23, 24, 84, 162, 179, 207, 208, 223, 228, 234, 240
Nassau 198
National Eagle see *Claremont* (NH) *National Eagle*
Nautilus, a novel 252
Neapolitan 73, 75
Ned, former slave 67
Neutrality Act 31, 203
Neva 178
Never Caught 217
New Inlet 183, 243
New York 176, 238
New York Herald 97
Newcastle, Duke of 134
Niagara, U.S.S. 64, 158, 172
Night Hawk 213, 227
Nile 198
Nimrod 197
Niphon, U.S.S. 244
Nora 116
Norfolk Navy Yard 11
North, Captain, C.S.A. 152, 165, 21, 235
North America 178
North Carolina 219
North Carolina, U.S.S. 55
Nova Scotia 252
Nye 118
Nye, Ebenezer 196

Oakdale Cemetery, Wilmington 252
Obiano, Frederic P. 215
O'Brien, Matthew, engineer 57
Ocean, H.M.S. 254
Ocean Rover 91, 93
Ocmulgee 90, 91, 100
Ogden, Henry W. 9
Ogilvie, Mr. 119
Ohkotsk Sea 196
Old Dominion 209, 216, 241
Olive Jane 115
Olustee, C.S.S. (*Tallahassee*) 179
Oneida 35
Oneida, U.S.S. 25
Onward, U.S.S. 117, 229
Oreto 12–13, 17, 19, 22, 245; see also C.S.S. *Florida*
Oreto II (formerly *Lapwing*) 33, 34, 35, 36, 41, 42
Orphan Boys' Asylum, Liverpool 251
Orr, John 65
Osaaca, corvette 169
Oswald, T.R. 236
Otter Rock 182
Ottone 133
Overman, barque 93
Owl 213, 247–248, 249

Index

P.C. Alexander 178
Page, Capt. Thomas J. 171
Palmer, Captain J., U.S.N. 70
Palmer Shipbuilding & Iron Co. 214
Palmetto 114
Pampero, C.S.S. 162, 163
Paraense, sailing ship 51
Paramaribo 66
Parker Cooke 104
Parry Jones, Evan 142
Passmore, William 81, 82
Patros 214
Patten, William 45
Patterson, Commander T.H., U.S.N. 231, 244
Pauvre Orphelin, brigantine 69
Paynter, Captain, R.N. 200
Pearce, Lockwood & Co. 214, 228
Pearl 178, 195
Pearson, Rear Admiral George, U.S.N 199
Pearson, Zachariah 214
Peck, Captain Penn 203
Pegram, Captain R.B. 14, 18
Penguin 213
Pennsylvania, U.S.S. 11
Percival, Captain F. 116
Pernambuco (Recife) 47, 118, 120
Perquot, U.S.S. 224
Perry, U.S. Minister Horatio 73
Pet 234–235
Peterhoff 236
Petrel, H.M.S. 23, 108
Petro Beys 214
Phantom 213, 229
Philadelphia 238
Philippines 131
Phoebe 205
Physical Geography of the Seas 152, 186
Pickering, Captain Charles, U.S.N. 75
Pike, Captain 132
Pile, Spence & Co. 214
Pim, Bedford 151
Plover 48, 69, 213
Plymouth, U.S.S. 11
Pollock, Lord Chief Baron 161
Ponape Island 195
Pontusuc, U.S.S. 178
Port Royal, Jamaica 110, 113
Porter, Admiral David, U.S.N. 9, 39, 184, 244
Porter, 1st Lt., C.S.N. 50, 51, 54
Porter, Lt., U.S.N. 69
Porter, Naval Constructor 165
Porter, S.G. 208
Portland, Maine 38
Portrush, N. Ireland 83
Potter & Co. 213
Powhatan, U.S.S. 36, 60, 69
Praya Bay, Azores 14, 85, 228
Preble, Commander, U.S.N. 25, 46, 211
Price Edwards, J., collector 81
Prince Albert (*Mary*) 213
Prince Albert, husband of Queen Victoria 7, 72

Prince Alfred, blockade runner 23
Prince of Wales 155
Prince of Wales, Edward VII 151
Prince Petropoliski 196
Princess Alexandra 161
Prioleau, Charles K. 11, 13, 79, 16, 185, 203
Prussia 30, 170
Puerto Rico 246
Puggard, Rudolph 171
Pulo Condore 130
Pundt, Asst. Engineer 142
Purdue, John Charles 214, 234
Putnam, U.S. Consul James 157
Putnam, Ensign W.O., U.S.N. 235

Quackenbush, Lt. Stephen, U.S.N. 224
Quang Tung 135
Queen of Beauty 121
Queen Victoria 5, 203
Queenstown, Cork 16, 42, 82, 231
Quinn, Engineer 22, 24, 27

Rachel Seaman, U.S.S. 25
Racoon 213
Ramsay, Lt. J.F., C.S.N. 186
Randle, James 225
Ranger 215
Ransom, Commander, U.S.N. 233
Rappahannock, C.S.S. 157, 158, 159, 171, 236
Rariton, U.S.S. 11
Rathlin Island 83
Rattler, H.M.S. 218
Ray 213
Read, Lt. Charles W., C.S.N. 22, 24, 27, 34, 36–39, 252
Read, J. Laurens, C.S.N. 22, 25
Read & Co. 210
Recollections of a Naval Life 120
Red Gauntlet 41
Reliance 182
Restless 177
Rhode Island Cavalry, U.S.A. 233
Rhyl, North Wales 237
Richardson, Duck 214, 235
Richardson & Sons 214, 234, 235
Richardson Brothers 214
Richibucto, brig 72
Richmond, Virginia 224, 253
Ridge, Samuel S. 225; see also Hewett, Captain William
Ridgely, Captain Daniel, U.S.N. 209
Rienzi 41
Rinaldo, H.M.S. 226
Rio De Centes, yacht 52
Rivers, ___, C.S.S. *Florida* 53
Roach, David 88
Roan 178
Robert Downs 196
Robert E. Lee (*Giraffe*) blockade runner 180, 210, 241, 242, 243, 246
Robert E. Packer 176
Robert Gardner & Co. 237

Roberts, Captain 217, 224
Roberts, John 140
Robinson, Messers. 185
Robinson, William, carpenter 5, 89
Rocas Island 36
Rocas Shoals 40
Rockingham 135, 259
Rogers, Commander John 15
Ronckendorff, Commander, U.S.N. 101
Roosevelt, President Theodore 9, 251
Rose 212
Rose, H.M.S. 218
Rosine 213
Ross, John 45
Rothsay, brigantine 69
Rouher, French Minister 170
Rover, H.M.S. 218
Ruby III 213
Ruhl, Quartermaster Eugene 57
Rumble, Govt. Inspector 158, 159
Runnymede, brig 33
Russell, Lord John 6, 17, 43, 80, 83, 127, 164, 165, 168, 179, 195, 200; letter to Adams 148; letter to Confederate commissioners 146
Russia 168
Sabine River 209
Sacramento, U.S.S. 172
Saginaw, U.S.S. 188, 199
St. Catharina, Brazil 121–122
St. Domingo 113, 114
St. George, Bermuda 14, 48, 182, 208, 219, 235, 241, 242, 243
St. George's Channel 83, 200
St. George's Museum, Bermuda 231
St. Helena Island 135
St. John, Virgin Islands 236
St. Lawrence Island 196, 198
St. Lawrence Seaway 178
St. Louis, U.S.S. 46, 211
St. Malo 153, 154
St. Paul Island 128
St. Peter Island 128
St. Peter's, Belsize, London 151
St. Pierre, Martinique 48, 69, 101, 102
St. Thomas, Virgin Islands 31, 71, 236
Saldana Bay, S. Africa 123, 125
San Francisco 196, 199
San Jacinto, U.S.S 29, 31, 32, 101, 102–103
Santee 125
Santiago de Cuba, U.S.S. 29, 184, 209
Sarah B. Harris 177
Sarah Louise 178
Sarah Nickels 31
Sarah Sands, brig 47, 115
Saranac, U.S.S. 200
Saratoga, U.S.S. 180, 245
Sartori, Commander, U.S.N 106

Saunders, Otley & Co. 253
Savannah 203, 223, 228
Savannah, C.S.S. 17
Schah Gehaad, steamer 101
Scorpion, H.M.S. 169
Scotia 205
Scott, Engineer 22
Scott & Co. 211, 238
Scuse, Francis, engineer 238
Scylla, H.M.S. 74
Sea Bride 125, 126, 127
Sea King 185, 186, 200; see also *Shenandoah*
Sea Lark 119
Sea Queen 214
Secret 213
Secret Service of the Confederate States in Europe 79, 152, 251
Seeley, Engineer 22
Seminole, U.S. gunboat 238
Semmes, John Oliver 253
Semmes, Commander Raphael 11, 22, 55, 56, 57, 59, 207; appointed captain of the *Alabama* 80, 85; description of Nassau 208, 228; letter to Bonfils 137; letters to Barron 136, 137; letters to Mallory 60, 76, 131; rescued from the sea 142
Semmes, Richard Thompson 55
Semmes, Samuel Middleton 55
Seven Pines, battle 13, 207
Seward, U.S. Secretary of State, William Henry 7, 53, 146, 162, 169, 180
Seymour, Charles 88
Shanghai 131, 231
Sharkey, William 45
Shatemuc 38
Shefeldt (Shufeldt), U.S. Consul 64
Sheffield 216
Sheldrake 214
Shenandoah, C.S.S. 187, 189, 199, 200–20, 252, 254, 255; crew enlisted at Melbourne by nationality 194; crew list by nationality 188; officers and crew 187
Sherman, General, U.S.A. 253
Shilo, battle of 207, 240
ships captured: *A. Richards* 176; *Abby Bradford* 65, 75; *Abigail* 196; *Adelaide* 190; *Adriatic* 176; *A.J. Bird* 179; *Albert Adams* 63, 75; *Albion Lincoln* 182; *Aldebaran* 33; *Alert* 93; *Alfred H. Partridge* 36; *Alina* 189; *Altamaha* 94; *Amanda* 129; *Amazonian* 120, 121; *Anglo-Saxon* 42; *Anna F. Schmidt* 122; *Arabella* 37; *Arcade* 71, 75; *Archer* 38, 39; *Arcole* 179; *Ariel* 105–106; *Atlantic* 176; *Avon* 46; *Baron de Castine* 100; *Bay Estate* 176; *Ben Dunning* 63, 75; *Benjamin F. Hoxie* 41; *Benjamin Tucker* 94; *Bethiah Thayer* 115; *Billow* 176; *Bold Hunter* 157; *Brilliant* 95; *Brunswick* 197, 198; *Byzantium* 38; *Carrie Estelle* 176; *Carroll* 176; *Catherine* 197; *Charles Hill* 116; *Charter Oak* 189, 190; *Chastelaine* 113; *City of Bath* 155; *Clarence* 36, 37; *Commonwealth* 35; *Congress* 198; *Conrad* 121, 134; *Constitution* 155; *Contest* 130; *Corris Ann* 29; *Courser* 94; *Covington* 198; *Crenshaw* 99; *Crown Point* 40; *Cuba* 62, 67, 75; *Daniel Trowbridge* 68, 75; *Delphine* 191; *D.G. Godfrey* 190; *Dictator* 154, 155; *Dorcas Prince* 118; *Dunkirk* 96; *Eben Dodge* 71, 75; *Edward* 191; *Edward Carey* 195; *E.F. Lewis* 179; *Electric Spark* 49; *Elisha Dunbar* 95; *Emily Farnum* 95; *Emma Jane* 133; *Emma L. Hall* 181; *Empress Theresa* 179; *Estelle* 28; *Etta Caroline* 177; *Euphrates* 196; *Express* 123; *Favorite* 197, 198; *Floral Wreath* 177; *General Berry* 48; *General Pike* 197; *General Williams* 197; *George Griswold* 155; *George Latimer* 48; *Gildersleive* 120; *Gipsy* 197; *Glenavon* 176; *Godspeed* 38, 182 ; *Golconda* 48; *Golden Eagle* 114; *Golden Rocket* 62, 75; *Golden Rule* 113; *Good Hope* 155; *Greenland* 48; *Harriett Stevens* 48; *Harvest* 195; *Harvey Birch* 72; *Hector* 195; *Henrietta* 35; *Highlander* 132; *Hillman* 198; *Howard* 48, 177; *Investigator* 73, 75; *Isaac Howland* 198; *Isaac Webb* 38; *Isabella* 197; *Jabez Snow* 120; *Jacob Bell* 30; *James Funk* 176; *James Littlefield* 177; *James Murray* 198; *Jerah Swift* 197; *John A. Parks* 115; *John Watts* 157; *Joseph Maxwell* 65, 66, 75; *Joseph Parke* 68, 75; *Josiah Achom* 178; *J.W. Seaver* 155; *Kate Cory* 118; *Kate Dyer* 35; *Kate Prince* 190; *Kate Stewart* 37; *Kingfisher* 116; *Lafayette* 98–99; *Lafayette* (whaler) 118; *Lamont Du Pont* 177; *Lamplighter* 97; *Lapwing* 34; *Lauretta* 99; *Leopard* 178; *Levi Starbuck* 100; *Lizzie M. Stacey* 190; *Louisa Hatch* 117; *Louisa Kilham* 63, 75; *M.A. Schindler* 37; *Machios* 62, 75; *Macomber* 38; *Magnolia* 178; *Manchester* 97; *Mandamis* 49; *Margaret Y. Davis* 48; *Mark L. Potter* 181; *Martaban* 132; *Martha Wenzell* 126; *Martaban (Texas Star)* 132, 133, 175; *Martha* 198; *Mary A. Howes* 177; *Mary Alvina* 37; *Milo* 197; *M.J. Colcord* 34; *Montmorency* 71, 75; *Morning Star* 31, 116; *Naiad* 63, 75; *Nassau* 198; *Neapolitan* 73, 75; *Neva* 178; *Nile* 198; *Nimrod* 197; *Nora* 116; *North America* 178; *Nye* 118; *Ocean Rover* 91, 93; *Ocmulgee* 90, 91, 100; *Olive Jane* 115; *Oneida* 35; *Otter Rock* 182; *Palmetto* 114; *Parker Cooke* 104; *P.C. Alexander* 178; *Pearl* 178, 195; *Prince of Wales* 155; *Punjaub* 115–116; *Red Gauntlet* 41; *Restless* 177; *Rienzi* 41; *Roan* 178; *Robert E. Packer* 176; *Rockingham* 135, 259; *Santee* 125; *Sarah B. Harris* 177; *Sarah Louise* 178; *Sarah Nickels* 31; *Sea Bride* 125, 126, 127; *Sea Lark* 119; *Shatemuc* 38; *Shooting Star* 182; *Sonora* 132; *Sophia Thornton* 197; *Southern Cross* 41; *Southern Rights* 49; *Speedwell* 182; *Spokane* 176; *Star of Peace* 32; *Starlight* 91; *Suliote* 176; *Surprise* 41; *Susan* 190; *Susan Abigail* 197, 199; *Talisman* 120; *T.D. Wagner* 179; *Texan Star* 132, 175; *Thomas B. Wales* 100–101; *Tonawanda* 96, 97; *Tycoon* 118, 135; *Umpire* 38; *Union* 104; *Union Jack* 119; *Vapor* 179; *V.H. Hill* 41; *Vigilant* 71, 75; *Virginia* 94; *Washington* 115; *Wave Crest* 96, 97; *Waverley* 198; *W.B. Nash* 41; *Weather Gauge* 93, 94; *West Wind* 63, 75; *Whistling Wind* 36; *William Bell* 176; *William C. Nye* 197; *William Thompson* 196; *Windward* 29; *Winged Racer* 129; *Zelinda* 48
Shoeburyness 166
Shooting Star 182
Shroder & Co. 237
Shryock, Lt. G.S., C.S.N. 170, 171
Shufeldt, U.S. Consul 64
Sicardi 14
Simons & Co. 211
Simonstown, S. Africa 125, 127, 156
Sinclair, Midshipman Arthur 22, 24, 26, 27, 4, 98, 121, 130, 263
Sinclair, (Lt.) Commander G.T., C.S.N. 76, 162, 163, 164
Singapore 130, 131
Sir Colin Campbell (Rechid) 49, 214
Sir Isaac Newton, schooner 195
Slade, Admiral Sir Adolphus, R.N. 254
Sliddel, C.S.A. Commissioner John 6–7, 42, 136, 147, 168, 169, 240
Smith, John, photographer 65
Smith, Captain Leon, C.S.N. 107
Smith, William Breedlove 57, 89
Smithville 181, 244
Snipe 213
Sonoma, U.S.S. 2, 235
Sonora 132
Sophia 205
Sophia Thornton 197
Soubooko 129

Index

Southern Confederacy newspaper 46
Southern Cross 41
Southern Historical Society Papers 172
Southern Rights 49
Southerner, blockade runner 188
Southwick 205
Spartan 68
Speedwell 182
Spence, Joseph 236
Spencer, Anne Elizabeth 55
Spencer, Colonel Oliver 55
Sphinx, corvette 170
Spidell, Engineer 22, 24, 27
Spokane 176
Sprague, U.S. Consul Horatio 74
Stag 213, 244
Staniforth, Mr., agent 153
Stanley 205
Star of Peace 32
Star of the West, tender 59
Starlight 91
Steamship Pet Co. 210
Steele, John Walkden 231–232, 234
Stephen & Sons 185, 211
Stephenson, Marine Sergeant George 75
Stettin, blockade runner 21
Stewart, John 216
Stone, Lt. Josiah, U.S.N. 229
Stone, 2nd Lt., C.S.N. 27, 48
Stonewall, C.S.S. 171, 172, 173
Straits of Magellan 199
Straits Times 131, 132
Stribling, Lt. John, C.S.N. 22, 24, 26, 56, 57
Stringham, Flag Officer Silas, U.S.N. 226
Styles, U.S. Consul 242
Suliote 176
Sullivan, Barry, actor 191
Sullivan, Dennis, C.S.S. *Florida* 53
Sumter, C.S.S. 57, 59, 61, 69, 70, 80, 207, 253
Sumter, U.S.S. 229
Sumter, Fort *see* Fort Sumter
Sunda Straits of 128
Surinam 66
Surprise 41
Susan 190
Susan Abigail 197, 199
Susan G. Owens 203
Sveaborg (Helsingfors), Finland 218
Swan 213
Sylph 205, 235
Symonds, Capt. T.E., R.N. 175, 179

T.D. Wagner 179
Tabb, John B. 245
Table Bay, S. Africa 135
Tacony 37, 38
Tait, Thomas 91
Talisman 120
Tallahassee, C.S.S. 175

Tausk Bay 196
Taylor, Paymaster 52
Tees-built blockade runners 214
Tenerife, Canary Islands 46, 49, 163, 172, 188
Terceira 84, 111, 168
Terrible, H.M.S. 81, 225
Tessier, Captain Eugene 18, 85, 203, 207, 228, 238, 255
Texan Star 132, 175
Texas see *Pampero*
Theodora 240
Thetis, bark 47
Thomas B. Wales 100–101
Thomas, John Henry 13, 17–18
Thompson, ___, C.S.S. *Florida* 53
Thompson, Edward 154
Thompson, George 13, 162, 165, 211, 238
Thompson, James 13, 162, 165, 211, 238
Thornton, Lt. Com. James, U.S.N. 142
Tierra del Fuego 157
Tilton, Captain 94
Tioga, U.S.S. 208
Todd & McGregor 211
Tonawanda 96, 97
Toxteth, Liverpool 251
Tremlett, Rev. F.W. 151
Trenholm, George Alfred 240
Trent, R.M.S 7
Trent Incident 6–7, 69, 72, 149
Trinidad 65, 66, 155
Tristan da Cunha 191
Tubal Cain 205
Tunstall, Thomas T. 75
Turkish Black Sea Fleet 254
Tuscaloosa, C.S.S. (*Conrad*) 121, 125, 127, 134, 252; crew 121, 134
Tuscarora, U.S.S. 17, 75, 82, 83, 101
Tuskar Rock 83, 200
Two Years on the Alabama 98
Tybee Island 15
Tycoon 118, 135
Tynan, John, engineer 175

Umpire 38
Una, brig 55, 69
Underwood, U.S. Consul 33, 153, 163
Union 104
Union Jack 119
United Services Club 151
United States, U.S.S. 9, 180, 245
Universal Trading Co. 210
Ushant, Brittany 153
Usher, blockade runner 205

V.H. Hill 41
Valorous, H.M.S. 126
Vanderbilt, U.S.S. 30, 128, 182, 236
Vapor 179
Venezuela, Ex-President 52, 65
Venus 225, 238, 243
Vesterling, Paymaster A. 24
Victor, H.M.S. 158

Victoria, Queen 5, 203
Victoria Cross 225
Vigilant 71, 75
Viper, H.M.S. 226
Virginia 94, 152
Vizitelly, Frank, artist 238
Vogel, Paymaster Lionel 22, 24, 27, 46
Voruz of Nantes 170
Vulture, French convict ship 66

W.B. Nash 41
Wachusetts, U.S.S. 29, 42, 49, 50–51, 53
Waddell, Captain James, C.S.N. 187, 188–189, 252
Walker, Rear Admiral Sir Baldwin, R.N. 126, 135
Walker, Captain, U.S.N. 200
Walker, Major Norman, C.S.A. 208, 209
Wallace, Jefferson 175
Walmsley, Thomas, stationer 114
Ward, Lt. (Capt.) William, C.S.N. 175, 17, 184
Warden, Captain Frederic R.N. 74
Washington 115
Wasp 213
Wassaw Sound 15
Waterman, Lt., U.S.A. 49
Wave Crest 96, 97
Waverley 198
Weather Gauge 93, 94
Webb, General Watson, U.S.A. 53
Welles, Navy Secretary Gideon, Welsh, James 22, 23, 32, 38, 41, 45 176, 205, 209, 253; called an imbecile by Moran 157
West Hartlepool 203, 228
West Hartlepool Steam Navigation Co. 214
West India Regiment 29
West Wind 63, 75
Westendorff, Captain Charles, C.S.N. 206, 238
Weymouth, schooner 69
W.H. Potter & Co. 213
Whisper[s] 181, 214
Whistling Wind 36
White, David, former slave 97, 144
White, Seaman Isaac 32
White, Joseph G. 115
Whiting, Major General, C.S.A. 248
Whiting, U.S. Consul Samuel 21, 22, 234
Whittle, Captain William C., C.S.N. 186, 189, 193
Wiblin, Dr. J.S. 150
Wicke, Herman 193
Widgeon 213
Wier, Benjamin 209
Wild Dayrell 213
Wilderness, U.S.S. 183
Wilding, Consul Henry 17, 228
Wilkes, Captain (Rear Admiral) Charles, U.S.N. 6–7, 29, 31, 32, 236

Wilkinson, Capt. Jesse, U.S.N. 245
Wilkinson, Capt. John, C.S.N. 179, 180–182, 245, 214, 239, 241, 245, 252
William Bell 176
William C. Miller & Sons 12, 43, 77, 161, 213, 229
William C. Nye 197
William Denny & Bros. 152, 211
William L. Hughes 208
William Simons & Co. 211
William Thompson 196
Williams, John 193
Williamson, Chief Engineer 165
Wilmington 16, 175, 176, 179, 183, 205, 219, 223, 231, 232, 238, 240, 242, 246, 252
Wilson, Midshipman Joseph D. 56, 57, 142, 258
Wilson, Thomas, U.S. Consul 50, 52
Wilson, Captain William 229–230
Wind & Current Charts of the North Atlantic 152
Windward 29
Winfield Scott, General, U.S.A. 67
Winged Racer 129
Winona, U.S.S. 25
Winslow, Commander Francis, U.S.N. 23
Winslow, Captain John, A. 45, 136, 137, 157; letter to Gideon Welles 146
Wiseman, Commodore, R.N. 192
Wiseman, S.J., photographer 150
Wissahickon, U.S.S. 163
Wivern, H.M.S. 169
Wood, John Taylor, C.S.N. 175, 177
Woods, Matthew 45
Worrel, C., wardroom steward 24
Worth, Captain (*Edward*) 191
Wren 213
Wright, Governor of Indiana 119
Wright, Rev. Franklin 119
Wright, Richard 185
Wyman, Marine Officer 22
Wynn, William 159
Wyoming, U.S.S. 128, 130

Yancey, Confederate Commissioner William 11, 74
"Yankee Doodle" 113
Yantic, U.S.S. 209
Yeddo, corvette 169
Yeoman, George 3, 256
Yokohama 179
Yonge, Clarence R. 16, 80, 111–112, 161

Zelinda 48